LAW AND POLITICS ON EXPORT RESTRICTIONS

Delving into export restrictive measures this book links the key areas of WTO law, public international law, investment and competition law to expose how and why WTO rules on export dimension are insufficient due to export bias; how public international law helps to justify their adoption or maintenance; and how investment and competition laws contribute to their regulation. Built on works on accession protocols and national security exceptions, this book goes beyond international trade law and looks into international political economy, competition and investment law. It contributes to debates in conceptualising public and private forms of export restrictions, appreciating the complementary nature of trade and competition law in disciplining them; capturing the dynamic between trade and investment policies for their effectuation and circumvention; and bridging trade law and public international law to better understand their impositions for political and diplomatic purposes with the invocation of the national security justification.

CHIEN-HUEI WU earned his doctoral degree in EUI in 2009 and was awarded Ta-You Wu Memorial Award in 2014. He published *WTO and the Greater China: Economic Integration and Dispute Resolution* (2012) and co-edited *Law and Diplomacy in the Management of EU–Asia Trade and Investment Relations* (2019).

CAMBRIDGE INTERNATIONAL TRADE AND ECONOMIC LAW

Series editors

Processes of economic regionalisation and globalisation have intensified over the last decades, accompanied by increases in the regulation of international trade and economics at the levels of international, regional and national laws. At the same time, significant challenges have arisen with respect to economic liberalisation, rule-based systems of trade and investment, and their political and social impacts. The subject matter of this series is international economic law, in this contemporary context. Its core is the regulation of international trade, investment, finance and cognate areas such as intellectual property and competition policy. The series publishes books on related regulatory areas, in particular human rights, labour, environment and culture, as well as sustainable development. These areas are horizontally interconnected and vertically linked at the international, regional and national levels. The series also includes works on governance, dealing with the structure and operation of international organisations related to the field of international economic law, and the way they interact with other subjects of international and national law. The series aims to include excellent legal doctrinal treatises, as well as cutting-edge interdisciplinary works that engage law and the social sciences and humanities.

Books in the series

Energy in International Trade Law: Concepts, Regulation and Changing Markets
Anna-Alexandra Marhold

Essential Interoperability Standards: Interfacing Intellectual Property and Competition in International Economic Law
Simon Brinsmead

Shareholders' Claims for Reflective Loss in International Investment Law
Lukas Vanhonnaeker

Transparency in the WTO SPS and TBT Agreements: The Real Jewel in the Crown
Marianna B. Karttunen

Emerging Powers in International Economic Law: Cooperation, Competition and Transformation
Sonia E. Rolland and David M. Trubek

Commitments and Flexibilities in the WTO Agreement on Subsidies and Countervailing Measures
José Guilherme Moreno Caiado

The Return of the Home State to Investor-State Disputes: Bringing Back Diplomatic Protection?
Rodrigo Polanco

The Public International Law of Trade in Legal Services
David Collins

Industrial Policy and the World Trade Organization: Between Legal Constraints and Flexibilities
Sherzod Shadikhodjaev

The Prudential Carve-Out for Financial Services: Rationale and Practice in the GATS and Preferential Trade Agreements
Carlo Maria Cantore

Preferential Services Liberalization: The Case of the European Union and Federal States
Johanna Jacobsson

Judicial Acts and Investment Treaty Arbitration
Berk Demirkol

Distributive Justice and World Trade Law: A Political Theory of International Trade Regulation
Oisin Suttle

Freedom of Transit and Access to Gas Pipeline Networks under WTO Law
Vitalily Pogoretskyy

Reclaiming Development in the World Trading System, 2nd edition
Yong-Shik Lee

Developing Countries and Preferential Services Trade
Charlotte Sieber-Gasser

WTO Dispute Settlement and the TRIPS Agreement: Applying Intellectual Property Standards in a Trade Law Framework
Matthew Kennedy

Establishing Judicial Authority in International Economic Law
Edited by Joanna Jemielniak, Laura Nielsen and Henrik Palmer Olsen

Trade, Investment, Innovation and their Impact on Access to Medicines: An Asian Perspective
Locknie Hsu

The Law, Economics and Politics of International Standardisation
Edited by Panagiotis Delimatsis,

The WTO and International Investment Law: Converging Systems
Jürgen Kurtz

Export Restrictions on Critical Minerals and Metals: Testing the Adequacy of WTO Disciplines
Ilaria Espa

Optimal Regulation and the Law of International Trade: The Interface between the Right to Regulate and WTO Law
Boris Rigod

The Social Foundations of World Trade: Norms, Community, and Constitution
Sungjoon Cho

Public Participation and Legitimacy in the WTO
Yves Bonzon

The Challenge of Safeguards in the WTO
Fernando Piérola

General Interests of Host States in International Investment Law
Edited by Giorgio Sacerdoti, with Pia Acconci, Mara Valenti and Anna De Luca

The Law of Development Cooperation: A Comparative Analysis of the World Bank, the EU and Germany
Philipp Dann

WTO Disciplines on Subsidies and Countervailing Measures: Balancing Policy Space and Legal Constraints
Dominic Coppens

Domestic Judicial Review of Trade Remedies: Experiences of the Most Active WTO Members
Edited by Müslüm Yilmaz

The Relevant Market in International Economic Law: A Comparative Antitrust and GATT Analysis
Christian A. Melischek

International Organizations in WTO Dispute Settlement: How Much Institutional Sensitivity?
Marina Foltea

Public Services and International Trade Liberalization: Human Rights and Gender Implications
Barnali Choudhury

The Law and Politics of WTO Waivers: Stability and Flexibility in Public International Law
Isabel Feichtner

African Regional Trade Agreements as Legal Regimes
James Thuo Gathii

Liberalizing International Trade after Doha: Multilateral, Plurilateral, Regional, and Unilateral Initiatives
David A. Gantz

Processes and Production Methods (PPMs) in WTO Law: Interfacing Trade and Social Goals
Christiane R. Conrad

Non-Discrimination in International Trade in Services: 'Likeness' in WTO/GATS
Nicolas F. Diebold

The Law, Economics and Politics of Retaliation in WTO Dispute Settlement
Edited by Chad P. Bown and Joost Pauwelyn

The Multilateralization of International Investment Law
Stephan W. Schill

Trade Policy Flexibility and Enforcement in the WTO: A Law and Economics Analysis
Simon A. B. Schropp

Law and Politics on Export Restrictions: WTO and beyond
Chien-Huei Wu

LAW AND POLITICS ON EXPORT RESTRICTIONS

WTO and Beyond

CHIEN-HUEI WU

Academia Sinica, Taipei, Taiwan

CAMBRIDGE
UNIVERSITY PRESS

CAMBRIDGE
UNIVERSITY PRESS

University Printing House, Cambridge CB2 8BS, United Kingdom

One Liberty Plaza, 20th Floor, New York, NY 10006, USA

477 Williamstown Road, Port Melbourne, VIC 3207, Australia

314–321, 3rd Floor, Plot 3, Splendor Forum, Jasola District Centre, New Delhi – 110025, India

103 Penang Road, #05–06/07, Visioncrest Commercial, Singapore 238467

Cambridge University Press is part of the University of Cambridge.

It furthers the University's mission by disseminating knowledge in the pursuit of education, learning, and research at the highest international levels of excellence.

www.cambridge.org
Information on this title: www.cambridge.org/9781108844789
DOI: 10.1017/9781108953566

First published 2021

A catalogue record for this publication is available from the British Library.

Library of Congress Cataloging-in-Publication Data
Names: Wu, Chien-Huei, author.
Title: Law and politics on export restrictions : WTO and beyond / Chien-Huei Wu, Academia Sinica, Taipei, Taiwan.
Description: Cambridge, United Kingdom ; New York, NY : Cambridge University Press, 2021. | Series: Cambridge international trade and economic law | Includes bibliographical references and index.
Identifiers: LCCN 2021019432 (print) | LCCN 2021019433 (ebook) | ISBN 9781108844789 (hardback) | ISBN 9781108948869 (paperback) | ISBN 9781108953566 (epub)
Subjects: LCSH: Export controls. | World Trade Organization.
Classification: LCC K3950 .W83 2021 (print) | LCC K3950 (ebook) | DDC 343.08/78–dc23
LC record available at https://lccn.loc.gov/2021019432
LC ebook record available at https://lccn.loc.gov/2021019433

ISBN 978-1-108-84478-9 Hardback

To *Chia-Hua*,
for her warm companionship in the past three decades

CONTENTS

PREFACE

The genesis of this work dates back to 2012 and the publication of my first book based on my doctoral dissertation and the Panel Report on *China – Raw Materials*. Intrigued by the complexities surrounding the accession protocols, general exception and the limited regulation of export restrictions in the GATT/WTO system, I wished to explore the rationale responsible for the lack of disciplines under international trade law, which had resulted in only limited scholarly work and a general lack of attention to the subject matter. Eight years later, export restrictions proliferate – often, in the name of national security. Importantly, the Trump Administration has relied on export restrictions and controls in its trade war and technological race with China. The subsequent Clean Network Initiative and Economic Prosperity Network remind us of the East–West divide of the Cold War era when the Coordinating Committee for Multilateral Export Control played a critical role in governing trade flows.

The international economic relations we now face differ in important ways from those of the Cold War era. Crucially, international economic relations in the past few years have seen a process of securitisation – a reaction against the means employed by architects of the post-war economic order, de-politicisation and constitutionalisation, to prevent another catastrophe. Today, both China and Russia are members of the WTO, and GATT/WTO rules, originally designed for market economies, have been extended to these (formerly) communist countries. Besides, given economic globalisation, the economic interdependence between the United States and China is far closer than that between the United States and the Soviet Union. Moreover, due to technological advances, the line between civilian trade and controlled trade on strategic and military items is blurred. Thus, it is not entirely clear whether decoupling between the US and Chinese economies may be realised, and if so, in what way.

This work spans a good deal of time, both in terms of its production and what is covered. It was finalised on 10 October 2020 and all information and websites and links were up to date then. I have benefited from funding from the Ministry of Science and Technology in Taiwan, and research visits to the World Trade Institute in Bern, the Law School of Georgetown University in Washington, DC, and the Max Planck Institute for Comparative Public Law and International Law in Heidelberg. I am also grateful to Ms Esther Liao for her research assistance, Jeffrey Cuvilier for proofreading the manuscript, and Joe Ng and Gemma Smith from Cambridge University Press for editorial help and bringing this book into being.

In my first book, I cited the words of Lord Alfred Tennyson in *Ulysses*. I would like to repeat in this book and hope my academic career will continue

To strive, to seek, to find, and not to yield

TABLE OF LEGISLATION

TABLE OF CASES

ACRONYMS AND ABBREVIATIONS

1956 FCN	1956 Treaty of Friendship, Commerce and Navigation between the US and Nicaragua
ADA	Anti-Dumping Agreement
AoA	Agreement on Agriculture
ASCM	Agreement on Subsidies and Countervailing Duties
ASG	Agreement on Safeguards
ATT	Arm Trade Treaty
BIS	Bureau of Industrial Security
CCL	Commerce Control List
CFI	Court of First Instance
CFIUS	Committee on Foreign Investment in the United States
CHINCOM	China Committee
CJEU	Court of Justice of European Union
CNOOC	China National Offshore Oil Corporation
CNPC	China National Petroleum Corporation
COCOM	Coordinating Committee for Multilateral Export Controls
CPTPP	Comprehensive and Progressive Agreement for Trans-Pacific Partnership
DDA	Doha Development Agenda
DDTC	Directorate of Defence Trade Control
DoS	Department of State
DPA	Defense Production Act
DSU	Dispute Settlement Understanding
EAA	Export Administration Act
EAR	Export Administration Regulation
ECA	Export Control Act
ECJ	European Court of Justice
ECRA	Export Control Reform Act of 2018
ECT	Energy Charter Treaty
ECtHR	European Court of Human Rights
EEC	European Economic Community
FDA	Food and Drug Administration

FDI	Foreign Direct Investment
FINSA	Foreign Investment and National Security Act
FIRRMA	Foreign Investment Risk Review Modernization Act of 2018
FOCAC	Forum on China-Africa Cooperation
FTA	Free Trade Agreement
FTC	Federal Trade Commission
GATT	General Agreement on Tariffs and Trade
GCC	Gulf Cooperation Council
ICJ	International Court of Justice
ICT	Information and Communication Technologies
IEEPA	International Emergency Economic Powers Act
ILC	International Law Commission
IMF	International Monetary Fund
ISIL	Islamic State of Iraq and the Levant
ISIS	Islamic State of Iraq and Syria
ITAR	International Traffic in Arms Regulation
KEXIM	Export-Import Bank of Korea
LDC	Least Developed Countries
LIBERTAD	Cuban Liberty and Democratic Solidarity
MAI	Multilateral Agreement on Investments
MNC	Multinational Corporation
MTCR	Missile Technology Control Regime
NAAEC	North American Agreement on Environmental Co-operation
NAFTA	North American Free Trade Area
NAMA	Non-Agriculture Market Access
NATO	North Atlantic Treaty Organization
NFIDC	Net Food Importing Developing Country
NPT	Treaty on the Non-Proliferation of Nuclear Weapons
NSG	Nuclear Supplier's Group
NZDB	New Zealand Dairy Board
OECD	Organisation for Economic Cooperation and Development
OFAC	Department of Treasury's Office of Foreign Assets Control
OMA	Orderly Marketing Arrangement
OPEC	Organization of the Petroleum Exporting Countries
RTA	Regional Trade Agreement
SCRM	Supply Chain Risk Management
SFRY	Socialist Federal Republic of Yugoslavia
Sinopec	China Petroleum and Chemical Corporation
SLA	Softwood Lumber Agreement
TFEU	Treaty on the Functioning of the European Union
THAAD	Terminal High Altitude Area Defence
TPP	Trans-Pacific Partnership Agreement

TRIMs	Trade-Related Investment Measures
TRIPS	Agreement on Trade-Related Aspects of Intellectual Property Rights
TSCA	Toxic Controlled Substances Act
TSMC	Taiwan Semiconductor Manufacturing Company
Unocol	Union Oil Company of California
UNSC	United Nations Security Council
URAA	Uruguay Round Agreements Act
USDOC	Department of Commerce of the US
USDOD	Department of Defence
USEPA	US Environment Protection Agency
USITA	US International Trade Administration
USMCA	United States-Mexico-Canada Agreement
USML	Munition List
USSR	Union of Soviet Socialist Republics
VAT	Value Added Tax
VCLT	Vienna Convention on Law of Treaties
VERs	Voluntary Export Restraints
VRA	Voluntary Restraint Arrangement
WFP	World Food Program
WGTCP	Working Group on Trade and Competition Policy
WTO	World Trade Organization
WTO	Agreement Agreement Establishing the World Trade Organization
ZTE	Zhongxing Telecommunications Equiment Corporation

1

Introduction

1.1 The Underlying Logic of the GATT/WTO System

The Punta del Este Declaration that launched the Uruguay Round in 1986 resulted in the Final Act Embodying the Results of the Uruguay Round of Multilateral Trade Negotiations, the most important achievement of which was the signing of the Agreement Establishing the World Trade Organization (the WTO Agreement). Compared with its predecessor, the General Agreement on Tariffs and Trade (the GATT), the WTO not only has wider scope because it includes trade in services and trade-related intellectual property rights but also deeper disciplines of positive integration on sanitary and phytosanitary measures, and on technical barriers to trade. The Uruguay Round negotiations resulted in the adoption of a comprehensive and ambitious trade liberalisation package; the resultant WTO rules were most concerned with access to foreign markets and the establishment of disciplines that would ensure regulatory measures were not merely protectionist measures in disguise.

The emphasis on the liberalisation of import barriers can be attributed to the built-in mercantilist tendencies of the GATT/WTO system – an arm of the post–World War II international economic order – and viewed as a direct response to the earlier erection of insurmountable import tariffs, which led to the Great Depression and the accompanying political turmoil. As Douglas Irwin, Petros Mavrodis and Alan Sykes point out, 'to understand the origins of the GATT, one must appreciate the traumatic events of the 1920s and 1930s',[1] a period of political and economic disasters. During this period, 'beggar-thy-neighbour' commercial policies were prevalent, as many countries raised trade barriers with a view to protecting national economies from economic downturn. The 1929 passage of the Hawley-Smoot Act by the United States pushed

[1] Douglas A. Irwin, Petros C. Mavroidis and Alan O. Sykes, *The Genesis of the GATT* (Cambridge University Press 2008) 5.

already high protective tariffs much higher; in response, Canada, Spain, Italy and Switzerland retaliated directly, leading to spiralling tariffs, a contraction of world trade and a severe breakdown of the multilateral trade and payments system.[2] Therefore, in negotiating the GATT system the objectives included establishing a legal framework for commercial policy and reducing import tariffs through bilateral negotiations – benefits to be extended to all contracting parties via the Most-Favoured-Nation principle.[3] In this way, the GATT aims to limit trade restrictions to customs tariffs: taxes imposed by importing countries 'as a condition of importation of goods into its territory'.[4]

The GATT/WTO system, with its built-in export bias, touches only slightly on the export dimension of the international trading system, which stands in stark contrast to voluminous market access commitments and heavy disciplines on domestic regulatory measures. Whether export tariffs fall within the scope of the schedule of concessions as contained in Article II:1(a) of the GATT and are thus subject to the fundamental principle of Most-Favoured-Nation treatment is subject to dispute.

Article II:1(a) of the GATT instructs each Contracting Party to 'accord to the *commerce* of the other contracting parties treatment no less favourable than provided for in the appropriate Part of the appropriate Schedule'.[5] Depending on one's interpretation of 'commerce', views diverge as to whether this Most-Favoured-Nation treatment obligation applies to schedules of concessions and export tariffs. As the late renowned international economic lawyer John Jackson observed, no concession relating to export taxes was made during the GATT negotiations. He further maintained that export taxes do not fall within the scope of the 'commerce' of the other contracting parties. Even if there were such a concession, it would have been treated like any independent bilateral agreement, and Article I of the GATT, rather than Article II, would apply. His arguments rely mainly on the legal text of the GATT, which, in the subsequent paragraphs of Article II, is concerned only with

[2] Ibid. 6–7.

[3] Ibid. 1. See also Frieder Roessler, 'GATT and Access to Supplies' (1975) 9 *Journal of World Trade Law* 25 [noting that 'the principal purpose of the GATT was to provide a legal framework for the removal of these import restrictions of multilateral negotiations and rules to prevent a new breakdown of international trade'].

[4] Andreas F. Lowenfeld, *International Economic Law* (Oxford University Press 2008) 31.

[5] The GATT, Art. II:1(a).

importation.[6] Jackson's reading of Article II is bolstered by textual interpretation, as Article II explicitly limits the effects of the Schedule to imports into the territories of contracting parties.

By contrast, Frieder Roessler argues that 'commerce' is not limited to importation but also includes exportation. Whereas the following paragraphs of Article II speak only of importation, the wider scope of the introductory paragraph to Article II:1(a) remains unaffected. This broad interpretation is shared by Mitsuo Matsuhita, who argues that the textual interpretation of 'commerce' can include imports and exports. The exclusion of export tariff concessions from the scope of Article II merely because Article II:1(b) and subsequent provisions do not mention exports is too restrictive an interpretation.[7] According to Roessler, during negotiations, the drafters intended that export taxes be included – a view supported by reference to Article XXVIII *bis*, which instructs contracting parties to enter into negotiations on a reciprocal and mutually advantageous basis with a view to 'substantial reduction of the general level of tariffs and other charges on imports and exports'.[8] The same wording can be found in the *Note* to Article XVII on trading by state enterprises, which aims for 'the reduction of duties and other charges on imports and exports'.[9] Roessler also refers to the schedules of Malaysia and Singapore on export duties on tin ore and tin concentrates as evidence that the Schedules as set out in Article II of the GATT cover export taxes.[10] While one may have different interpretations of the meaning of 'commerce', and make conflicting observations on whether the schedules of concessions of the GATT contracting parties cover export tariffs, it is crystal

[6] John H. Jackson, *World Trade and the Law of GATT* (The Michie Company Law Publishers 1969) 499.

[7] Mitsuo Matsushita, 'Export Controls of Natural Resources and the WTO/GATT Disciplines' (2011) 6 *Asian Journal of WTO and International Health Law and Policy* 281, 291.

[8] The GATT, Art. XXVIII *bis*: 1.

[9] The GATT, *Ad* Art. XVII:3.

[10] Roessler, 'GATT and Access to Supplies' (n. 3) 35. Roessler notes that at first glance there is no difference between GATT concessions and commitments contained in an independent bilateral agreement in the context of the GATT where the Most-Favoured-Nation Treatment applies as set out in Article I. Differences arise in case of the withdrawal of such commitments on export taxes. If the commitment on export taxes is part of the concessions of the Schedules, the withdrawal of such commitments can be made only with appropriate compensation to affected third countries. By contrast, a commitment under an independent bilateral agreement can be withdrawn subject only to agreement between parties.

clear that within the world trading system, trade restrictions on exports have received much less attention than those on imports.

Then how shall we define export restrictions? Like import restrictions, export restrictions cover tariffs and non-tariff measures and may take the form of bans, taxes, quotas, licensing, minimum prices and reductions of value added tax (VAT) rebates.[11] The deciding element of export restrictions is the *limiting* effect on exportation or the *potential to limit*. The most important provision pertaining to such export restrictive measures in the existent WTO framework is the general elimination of quantitative restrictions. This general obligation to eliminate quantitative restrictions applies both to the importation and exportation of goods.[12] Besides, the Agreement on Agriculture (AoA), in response to concerns that the reform programme may threaten food security in net food importing countries and least developed countries, also addresses export restrictions on agricultural products. Additionally, when export restrictions are imposed with a view to ensuring a sufficient supply of inputs to domestic processors, they may constitute subsidies as regulated by the Agreement on Subsidies and Countervailing Duties (ASCM), as export restrictions lead to a comparative advantage for domestic processors due to price differentials.[13] Furthermore, the WTO Agreement has brought so-called grey area measures, such as voluntary export restraints (the VERs), within the purview of the Agreement on Safeguards (the ASG).

Since the signing of the WTO Agreement, export restrictions have gradually caught the attention of WTO members, as is reflected in subsequent accession negotiations and on-going Doha Round negotiations. A large number of newly acceded or acceding countries, in particular natural-resource-rich countries, have been subject to requests to undertake commitments or obligations relating to export restrictions. Under the auspices of Doha Round negotiations, various proposals aiming to discipline export restrictions have been advanced during agriculture negotiations and under non-agricultural market access (NAMA)

[11] Jeonghoi Kim, Recent Trends in Export Restrictions on Raw Materials, in OECD (ed), *The Economic Impact of Export Restrictions on Raw Materials* (OECD Paris 2010) 14.

[12] Export ban, export quota and minimum export price may be thus held WTO-incompatible in terms of Article XI:1. By contrast, export taxes fall outside the realm of the Uruguay Round Agreements. Ibid. 23.

[13] On this point, see e.g., Merit E. Janow and Robert W. Staiger, 'The Treatment of Export Restraints as Subsidies under the Subsidies Agreement of the WTO' in Henrik Horn and Petros C. Mavroidis (eds), *The WTO Case Law of 2001* (Cambridge University Press 2004) 201–235.

negotiations. Export restrictions are also an important element during negotiations on free trade agreements.

Due to the slow progress of the Doha Development Agenda (the DDA), and in view of a series of export restrictions on agricultural products introduced between 2007 and 2009, some WTO members have advanced proposals addressing export restrictions outside the framework of the DDA. With the aim of extending application of the commitment in accordance with paragraph 40 of the *Action Plan on Food Price Volatility and Agriculture*, under the auspice of the World Food Program to all WTO members, the EU, along with other members, submitted a draft declaration for consideration and acceptance at the 2011 Ministerial Conference.[14] This Ministerial declaration would transcribe the pertinent paragraph of the Action Plan

> We recognize that the first responsibility of each WTO Member is to ensure the food security of its own population. We also recognize that food export barriers restricting humanitarian aid penalize the most needy. We agree to remove food export restrictions or extraordinary taxes for food purchased for non-commercial humanitarian purposes by the World Food Programme (WFP) and we agree not to impose them in the future.[15]

While recognising the utmost responsibility of members to secure food supplies for their own population, the draft declaration also cautions against the danger of penalising the most needy by imposing food export barriers restricting humanitarian aid. Therefore, the draft declaration urges WTO members to eliminate food export restrictions or extraordinary taxes from food purchases for non-commercial purposes by the WFP.

Similarly, for developing countries that are net food importers, African and Arab groups proposed a draft declaration entitled *WTO Work Programme to Mitigate the Impact of the Food Market Prices and Volatility on WTO Least-Developed and Net-Food Importing Developing Members*.[16] This Work Programme has two arms: trade and finance. The trade arm of the Work Programme aims to develop rules to exempt purchases of least developed countries (LDCs) and net food importing

[14] Food Export Barriers and Humanitarian Food Aid by the WFP (World Food Programme), Communication from the European Union (18 November 2011) WT/GC/138, 2.

[15] Ibid. 3.

[16] The WTO Response to the Impact of the Food Crisis on LDCs and NFIDCs, Communication from NFIDCS, African and Arab Groups (25 November 2011) WT/GC/140/Rev.1.

developing countries (NFIDCs) from export restrictions adopted by foodstuff-exporting members based on Article XI:2(a) of the GATT 1994. In other words, while food-exporting members may invoke Article XI:2(a) of the GATT 1994 as a justification for the imposition of export quantitative restrictions, LDCs and NFIDCs may seek exemptions from these export restrictions and thus secure their food supplies. These exemptions would shield food-exporting members imposing export quantitative restrictions from discipline due to this breach of their MFN obligations.

Unfortunately, neither the EU's proposal to extend the commitment under paragraph 40 the *Action Plan on Food Price Volatility and Agriculture* to all WTO members nor the African and Arab groups' draft declaration on *WTO Work Programme to Mitigate the Impact of the Food Market Prices and Volatility on WTO Least-Developed and Net-Food Importing Developing Members* was adopted at the 2011 Geneva Ministerial Conference. Export restrictions by food exporting countries may continue to adversely impact LDCs and NFIDCs in the years to come. Whereas the Bali Package adopts a decision on Public Stockholding for Food Security Purposes, it seems that most WTO members are not ready to accept WTO rules on export restrictions beyond the present weak rules, even though 'export prohibitions as well as export taxes and quotas [are] a major cause of the food crisis and of price volatility'[17] and twice victimize NFIDCs.

In parallel with food insecurity exacerbated by export restrictions on agricultural products, the race to secure access to rare earths has been heating up since 2010. Due to a dispute over the Diayu (Senkoku) Islands, China reportedly imposed an export embargo on rare earths to Japan. Although this export embargo was soon lifted, the incident aroused concern in Japan and other major trading powers.[18] Eventually, the United States, Japan and the European Union (EU), brought the dispute before the WTO dispute settlement mechanism.[19] Before that, in *China – Measures Related to the Exportation of Various*

[17] Christian Häberli, 'After Bali: WTO Rules Applying to Public Food Reserves' (2014) FAO Commodity and Trade Policy Research Working Paper No 46, 12.

[18] Yuko Inoue, 'China Lifts Rare Earth Export Ban to Japan: Trader', *Reuters*, 29 September 2010, available at www.reuters.com/article/us-japan-china-export-idUSTRE68S0BT2010 0929.

[19] Appellate Body Reports on *China – Measures Related to the Exportation of Rare Earths, Tungsten, and Molybdenum*, WT/DS431/AB/R / WT/DS432/AB/R / WT/DS433/AB/R, adopted 29 August 2014, DSR 2014:III, p. 805.

Raw Materials (*China – Raw Materials*), a complaint brought by the United States, EU and Mexico, China was found to have violated its WTO obligations and accession commitments by imposing export restrictions on various raw materials.[20] Although *China – Raw Materials* was not the first dispute wherein the WTO Panel/Appellate Body was called on to examine the WTO-consistency of a member's export restrictive measures,[21] it has attracted the most attention and debate, by far, among both academics and practitioners.

China – Raw Materials involves several thorny issues. First, the Panel and Appellate Body had to adjudicate whether the pertinent raw materials fell within the scope of 'other products essential to the exporting contracting party' as set forth in Article XI:(a) of the GATT 1994. If so, what is the relationship between the specific exceptions put forward in Article XI:(a) and the general exception of Article XX? The Panel and Appellate Body had to clarify the relationship between obligations contained in the accession protocols and the WTO Agreement – more specifically, the applicability of the general exception of Article XX of the GATT 1994. If the general exception is applicable, then the Panel and Appellate Body have to ascertain whether it justifies China's export restrictions. As commitments and obligations relating to export restrictions are largely assumed by newly acceded members during accession negotiations, the ruling of the Panel and Appellate Body in *China – Raw Materials* has had a great impact on the interpretation of these 'WTO-plus' commitments or obligations, in particular with regards to the applicability of general exception.

In the wake of the Ukraine Crisis in 2013, the EU, the United States and other Western countries adopted a number of sanction measures, taking mostly the form of import and export restrictions, against Russia. In response, Russia during the 10th Ministerial Conference held in

[20] Appellate Body Reports on *China – Measures Related to the Exportation of Various Raw Materials* (*China – Raw Materials*), WT/DS394/AB/R / WT/DS395/AB/R / WT/DS398/AB/R, adopted 22 February 2012.

[21] For example, in a complaint against Argentina, the EU argued that Argentinean export procedures which allowed the presence of representatives of the ADICMA constituted a *de facto* export prohibition. The EU asserted that given the ADICMA's access to confidential information and its concentrated market power, the participation of the representatives of the ADICMA in export procedures effectively prevented exporters from exporting bovine hides. Panel Report on *Argentina – Measures Affecting the Export of Bovine Hides and Import of Finished Leather* (*Argentina – Hides and Leather*), WT/DS155/R and Corr.1, adopted 16 February 2001, DSR 2001:V, 1779, para. 11.8.

Nairobi, proposed an agenda focusing on the interpretation of security exception to be adopted. It reads as follows

> With reference to the "Decision Concerning Article XXI of the General Agreement" adopted by the CONTRACTING PARTIES on November 30, 1982 and with the view to ensure clarity and predictability of implementation of Security Exceptions Provisions of the WTO Agreements Members shall develop a General Council decision on joint understanding on the interpretation of the scope of the rights and obligations of the WTO Members under these Provisions. With this in mind the Members shall engage in negotiations and the General Council shall take the decision on interpretation of the said Provisions pursuant to Article IX:2 of the Marrakesh Agreement by 1 June 2016. To this end, the negotiations shall focus on identification of circumstances when application of the measures pursuant to Security Exceptions is justified, as well as provision of specific transparency requirements and possible retaliatory measures.[22]

This proposal was an attempt to clarify the meaning of security exception through legislative approach,[23] either by authoritative interpretation or 'subsequent agreement between the parties'. However, Russia's proposal did not obtain sufficient support to be adopted at the 10th Ministerial Conference and thus died away.

Nonetheless, export restrictions with potential invocation of national security for justification do not fade away but rather turn out to be a preferred instrument for trade nations to wield in the pursuit of geopolitical and geostrategic purpose. In the wake of the US–China trade war since the start of the Trump presidency in 2017, export restrictions have been adopted by the Trump Administration, first against Zhongxing Telecommunications Equipment Corporation (ZTE)[24] and subsequently

[22] WTO, Proposal on the MC10 Ministerial Declaration – Part III, para. 1.5, WT/MIN(15)/W/14, dated 11 November 2015.

[23] On the legislative approach in clarifying the meaning of WTO agreements and resolving disputes, see Chien-Huei Wu, 'From Fragmentation to Coherence: A Constitutionalist Take on the Trade and Public Health Debates' in Andrzej Jakubowski and Karolina Wierczyńska (eds), *Constitutionalisation of International Law Re-Visited: Between Pluralism and Unity* (Routledge 2016) 232–236.

[24] Bureau of Industry and Security, Commerce. In the Matter of: Zhongxing Telecommunications Equipment Corporation ZTE Plaza, Keji Road South Hi-Tech Industrial Park Nanshan District, Shenzhen China; ZTE Kangxun Telecommunications Ltd. 2/3 Floor, Suite A, Zte Communication Mansion Keji (S) Road Hi-New Shenzhen, 518057 China Respondent; Order Activating Suspended Denial Order Relating to Zhongxing Telecommunications Equipment Corporation and Zte Kangxun Telecommunications Ltd., 15 April 2018, 83 Federal Register 17644.

against Huawei and its affiliates.[25] In the midst of the Japan–Korea dispute over wartime labour compensation, Japan removed South Korea from its whitelist of preferred trading partners on 2 August 2019,[26] which may cause significant delay to the export of critical components of semiconductors to South Korea. In response, South Korea did the same against Japan and launched a WTO complaint. It is reported that Japan would invoke Article XXI of the GATT 1994 as a justification.[27] Similar geopolitics-induced trade measures are apparent in Gulf countries. In the context of Qatar's diplomatic crisis, Saudi Arabia, in conjunction with other Gulf countries, imposed a scheme of diplomatic, political and economic measures against Qatar. Qatar referred these measures to the WTO dispute settlement mechanism and Saudi Arabia invokes the national security exception as a justification.[28] The link between export restrictions under the trade regime and sanctions (or export control) under the public international law context poses a thorny issue of the justifiability of national security exception. Does the WTO adjudicator have the jurisdiction to hear a case relating to national security? Is national security self-judging?

In the midst of the Coronavirus (COVID-19) pandemic, sovereign nations imposed export restrictions on a number of goods to secure domestic supply, ranging from medical devices to food. This led to a joint statement by the WTO and IMF, expressing their concerns about the pervasive use of export restrictions threatening disruption of global supply. Whereas the IMF and WTO recognise that WTO rules allow for export restrictions 'applied to prevent or relieve critical shortages', they urge sovereign nations to refer to these measures cautiously.

[25] Bureau of Industry and Security, Commerce. Addition of Entities to the Entity List, 16 May 2019, 84 Federal Register 22961.

[26] Junichi Sugihara, Japan Officially Ousts South Korea from Export Whitelist, *Nikkei Asian Review*, 28 August 2019, available at https://asia.nikkei.com/Spotlight/Japan-South-Korea-rift/Japan-officially-ousts-South-Korea-from-export-whitelist.

[27] Edward White, Robin Harding and Kang Buseong, 'South Korea Files WTO Complaint over Japan Trade Restrictions', *Financial Times*, 11 September 2019, available at www.ft.com/content/ea993216-d42d-11e9-8367-807ebd53ab77.

[28] *Saudi Arabia – Measures Relating to Trade in Goods and Services, and Trade-Related Aspects of Intellectual Property Rights*, WT/DS528 (consultation requested, panel not yet established); *Saudi Arabia – Measures Concerning the Protection of Intellectual Property Rights* (panel established, panel report not yet released), WT/DS567.

> [Export restrictions being] Taken collectively, export restrictions can be dangerously counterproductive. What makes sense in an isolated emergency can be severely damaging in a global crisis. Such measures disrupt supply chains, depress production, and misdirect scarce, critical products and workers away from where they are most needed. Other governments counter with their own restrictions. The result is to prolong and exacerbate the health and economic crisis – with the most serious effects likely on the poorer and more vulnerable countries.[29]

Beyond the trading system, there are some legal instruments which may have a bearing on export restrictions: international investment law and competition law. First, investment policies may be used as instruments to circumvent export trade restrictions and secure access to raw materials. Prior to the entry phase, export restrictions might enhance incentives for foreign investors to invest in local industries and lead to investment diversion. An export restriction, when imposed after an investment is made, may constitute indirect expropriation, and thus should result in compensation. Therefore, to assess the impact of export restrictions, it is essential to further explore the linkages and boundaries between trade and investment regimes.

Another vehicle outside of WTO law for tackling export restrictions is competition law. Here, two issues are most pertinent. The first is so-called grey-area measures, such as voluntary export restraints. Whereas the ASG lays down some regulations on grey-area measures, it does not guarantee the absence of such measures. Further, whether all grey-area measures are incompatible with WTO law is still subject to debate. Private export agreements taking the form of export cartels may be subject to the scrutiny of domestic competition law. The second issue relates to the practices of the Organization of the Petroleum Exporting Countries (OPEC). Is domestic competition law sufficient to tackle the practices of OPEC, or is new international competition law necessary? If the latter, what would be the relationship between trade rules and competition law?

Finally, such trade, investment and competition law and policy linkage has to be appreciated in the context of the global supply chain, where production processes have been distributed to different parts of the world and the imposition of export restrictions, regardless of economic or

[29] WTO and IMF Heads Call for Lifting Trade Restrictions on Medical Supplies and Food, 24 May 2020, available at www.imf.org/en/News/Articles/2020/04/24/pr20187-wto-and-imf-joint-statement-on-trade-and-the-covid-19-response.

political motivations, will seriously disrupt its good functioning. How to manage supply chain security is a critical issue facing multinational enterprises.

1.2 Aim, Purpose and Contribution of the Book

To date, export restrictions under WTO law have remained largely unexplored. Most of the relevant literature relates to export embargoes and sanctions under public international law; few researchers have systemically studied export restrictions from the perspective of international economic law. Ilaria Espa's study of export restrictions on critical minerals and metals is one of the forerunners of such study. However, her work focuses on two sectors where export restrictions are frequently imposed and the focus of her analysis remains the WTO regime.[30] At the peak of surging commodity prices in 2007 and 2009, the OECD published a study examining the economic impact of export restrictions on raw materials.[31] This study was conducted in the wake of *China – Raw Materials* and its focus is the economic impact of export restrictions. Recently, Gabriella Marceau wrote about WTO rules on export restrictions and pointed to their insufficiency.[32] Similarly, Mark Wu commented on the constraints of the WTO rules on export restrictions and their inability to discipline China's use of such restrictions.[33] With the release of *China – Raw Materials* and *China – Rare Earths*, several authors also commented on the jurisprudence of the WTO adjudicator.[34] These analyses are useful starting points for understanding WTO rules in the context of the proliferation of export restrictions but have not taken into account the trade and geopolitics complexities as manifested by the heavy reliance on the national security exception.

[30] Ilaria Espa, *Export Restrictions on Critical Minerals and Metals: Testing the Adequacy of WTO Disciplines* (Cambridge University Press 2015).

[31] OECD (ed), *The Economic Impact of Export Restrictions on Raw Materials* (OECD Paris 2010).

[32] Gabrielle Marceau, 'WTO and Export Restrictions' (2016) 50 *Journal of World Trade* 563.

[33] Mark Wu, 'China's Export Restrictions and the Limits of WTO law' (2017) 16 *World Trade Review* 673.

[34] Baris Karapinar, 'Defining the Boundaries of Export Restrictions: A Case Law Analysis' (2012) 15 *Journal of International Economic Law* 443; Han-Wei Liu and John Maughan, 'China's Rare Earths Export Quotas: Out of the China-Raw Materials Gate, but Past the WTO's Finish Line?' (2012) 15 *Journal of International Economic Law* 971; Eric W. Bond and Joel Trachtman, 'China–Rare Earths: Export Restrictions and the Limits of Textual Interpretation' (2016) 15 *World Trade Review* 189.

This book serves as a modest attempt to examine systematically the role of export restrictions in the world trade system, link it to public international law and expand to investment and competition law and policy in the context of the global supply chain. From the outset, the book examines all of the relevant WTO provisions on the export restrictions, commitments and obligations that new members assumed during accession negotiation processes. Additionally, as export restrictions are employed as an instrument to achieve different policy goals, including food and energy security; environment and development objectives; and even national security purposes, this book investigates the policy implications of export restrictions. The question is then asked: can export restrictions be justified by the exceptions provided under the WTO Agreement, or, alternatively, does the WTO Agreement provide sufficient policy space for trading nations to pursue their policy goals? An intriguing question relevant to this inquiry concerns the relationship between the general exception, as set out in Article XX of the GATT, and specific exceptions such as that in Article XI:2. Further, one has also to determine whether the general exception as set out in Article XX of the GATT 1994 is applicable to the obligations and commitments contained in accession protocols or working party reports. An even more controversial issue relates to the interpretation and application of national security exceptions as set out for in Article XXI of the GATT 1994, if the respondent member decides to invoke it. Would this national security exception turn out to be a self-interpreting clause? What would be the role that international political economy plays in this inquiry? Moving beyond the realm of WTO law, it is essential to explore the boundaries and linkages between trade and investment regulatory regimes, assess how competition law and policy impact export restrictions and reflect how to manage supply chain security once the chain is disrupted by export restrictions. In so doing, we may have a broad and comprehensive understanding of law and politics on export restrictions in international economic relations.

The core thesis of this book is that the GATT/WTO regime is built on an export bias, with trading nations aiming to export goods and services while keeping foreign producers from their domestic market so as to protect domestic producers from competition. Due to this export bias, the vast majority of WTO rules are concerned with regulation of the liberalisation of import restrictions, tariffs and non-tariff barriers, but touch only lightly on export restrictions. This book thus first examines the limited number of WTO rules impacting export restrictions, notably, Article XI of the GATT 1994, Article 12 of the AoA and Article 11 of the

ASG. Nonetheless, one-sided regulation focusing on import restrictions proves insufficient in a globalised economy – considering that countries may impose export restrictions on critical components or raw materials of strategic importance and that enterprises between upstream and downstream producers, buyers and suppliers may also enter into private agreements limiting exports. In recognition of such insufficiency, trading nations aim to discipline export restrictions using three approaches: WTO accession negotiations, multilateral Doha negotiations and regional trade agreements. When countries/territories seek WTO accession, it has become common to compel these applicants to commit to disciplines on export restrictions. This bilateral rule-making through accession negotiations nonetheless introduces the thorny issue of the applicability of Article XX of the GATT 1994 (general exception) to obligations and commitments in accession protocols and working party reports. While countries have aimed, through the Doha negotiations, to introduce multilateral disciplines on export restrictions, there has been no measurable progress; therefore, export restrictions are only patchily disciplined in the regional trade agreements context.

Second, export restrictions are measures that represent the changing international political economy of the dissolution of the Coordinating Committee for Multilateral Export Controls (COCOM), the collapse of the Soviet Union and the expansion of WTO membership, as well as technological progress blurring the line between civilian and dual-use goods, which in turn gives rise to frequent references to the national security exception. In the post-war era, free trade was conducted mainly in the Western camp within the GATT context and controlled trade mainly targeted the former Soviet Union and China through the COCOM. However, the logic of free trade and controlled trade, and the division of the GATT/WTO regime on the one hand and the COCOM and Wassenaar Arrangement on Export Controls for Conventional Arms and Dual-Use Goods and Technologies (Wassenaar Arrangement) on the other ceased to be feasible as the line among civilian, military/strategic and dual-use goods grew increasingly blurred, and former Soviet countries and China joined the WTO. The technological complexities of goods and services, and expansion of WTO membership, have created a new challenge for the WTO: reliance on trade measures for political and diplomatic aims seeking justification based on the national security exception. These developments point to the links between WTO law and public international law on different fronts. Obviously, countries may adopt export restrictions to comply with their UN obligations if a

UN resolution is passed, for instance, imposing an export embargo. Even in the absence of such an explicit resolution, relevant decisions in the UN may constitute evidence to determine the existence of war, or some other emergency in international relations. As for the Wassenaar Arrangement, it plays a key role in defining the scope of XXI:(b)(ii), in particular goods and materials directly or indirectly for the purpose of suppling a military establishment. Finally, a country may use trade measures as countermeasures against infringements of obligations other than WTO law, as demonstrated by *Germany – Icelandic Fishery Dispute.*[35]

Export restrictions are closely intertwined with investment and competition; so investment law and policy complement and sometimes conflict with international trade law, while competition law complements international trade law in regulating private forms of export restrictions. When a country imposes export restrictions, enterprises in foreign countries may wish to circumvent these export restrictions by investments in that country, which may also try to prevent this by an investment screening mechanism, such as the Committee on Foreign Investment in the United States (CFIUS). At the same time, export restrictions, as far as existent investors and investment are concerned, may infringe international investment laws. Competition law complements international trade law in regulating private forms of export restrictions maintained by private enterprises, vertically or horizontally. Demands for regulation of private forms of export restrictions are surging in view of global supply chains. Among these private forms of export restrictions, export cartels, shared with similar export bias, are mostly permitted on condition that they do not affect the domestic market.

By looking into the specific measure of export restrictions, this book links four key areas of WTO law, public international law, investment and competition law to expose how and why WTO rules on export dimension are insufficient due to export bias, how public international law helps to justify their adoption or maintenance, and how investment and competition law contribute to their regulation. Built on such research and the growing volume of literature on accession protocols and national security exceptions, this book endeavours to go beyond international trade law and look into international political economy, competition and investment law. By using export restrictions as subject

[35] *Germany – Icelandic Fishery Dispute – Ban on Icelandic Fish Landings*, C/M/103, 18 February 1975, Minutes of Meeting, held in the Palais des Nations, Geneva, on 3 and 17 February 1975, p. 13.

matter to link the aforementioned two growing strands of scholarly works, this book contributes to academic debates in conceptualising public and private forms of export restrictions; appreciating the complementary nature of trade and competition law in disciplining them; capturing the dynamic between trade and investment policies for their effectuation and circumvention; and bridging trade law and public international law to better understand their imposition for political and diplomatic purposes with the invocation of the national security justification. In addition, this book is of great policy relevance, as it also offers practical guidance for practitioners by covering trade remedies for export restrictions, export control regimes in the EU and United States, and investment screening mechanisms.

1.3 Scope, Approach and Structure of the Book

This book takes as its departure point the underlying logic of the world trading system in which nations vie for access to foreign markets, and explores the rationale for a trading nation to impose export restrictions. After surveying the relevant WTO provisions on export restrictions, obligations and commitments as contained in the accession protocols and working party reports, the book further investigates the policy implications of export restrictions imposed by trading nations and asks whether there is sufficient policy space available. In addition, the political economy surrounding export restrictions, in particular when the national security exception is invoked, will also be appreciated. The investigation reaches farther from the realm of international trade law into international investment law and competition law and policy, and reflects on how these different regimes impact on determinations of the legality of export restrictions.

The introductory chapter clarifies some of the terminology employed. This book largely uses the term 'export restriction' instead of 'export control' or 'export restraint', as 'export control' is in widespread use and may apply to unrelated areas, the most pertinent being in the context of public international law.[36] Nonetheless, when referring to domestic law,

[36] See e.g., A. L. C. de Mestral and T. Gruchalla-Wesierski, *Extraterritorial Application of Export Control Legislation:Canada and the U. S. A.* (Kluwer Academic Publishers 1990); Michael Mineiro, *Space Technology Export Controls and International Cooperation in Outer Space* (Springer 2012); Cedric Ryngaert, 'Extraterritorial Export Controls (Secondary Boycotts)' (2008) 6 *Chinese Journal of International Law* 625; Daniel H. Joyner, 'Restructuring the Multilateral Export Control Regime System' (2004) 9 *Journal of Conflict Security Law* 181.

in particular, US law, and under some public international law regimes, such as the COCOM and the Wassenaar Arrangement, the term 'export control' will also be used. In fact, the boundaries between trade regime and public international regimes may overlap and complicate with each other.

According to the Dictionary of Trade Policy Terms, export controls refer to 'measures instituted by exporting countries to supervise export flows. Reasons for these include compliance with United Nations economic sanctions, adherence to voluntary restraint arrangements, observance of export quotas under international commodity arrangements, management of strategic exports and administration of rules concerning dual purpose exports, as well as a policy of preserving some raw materials and other articles for domestic production or consumption.'[37] According to this definition, export controls mostly cover measures taken under public international law but also relate to policies implemented with a view to securing sufficiency for domestic production or consumption.

Some scholars offer alternative definitions of 'export control'. As Yann Aubin and Arnaud Idiart explain, 'for security reasons mainly, but also for other reasons such as technology protection, nations control the hardware, software or the technology/data from leaving their territory'.[38] Typical examples of export controls on arms or strategic materials are sanctions imposed by resolutions of the United Nations General Assembly or relevant international conventions, such as the Convention on the Prohibition of the Development, Production and Stockpiling of Bacteriological (Biological) and Toxin Weapons and on their Destruction (Biological Weapon Convention); the Convention on the Prohibition of the Development, Production, Stockpiling and Use of Chemical Weapons and on their Destruction (Chemical Weapons Convention); the Treaty on the Non-Proliferation of Nuclear Weapons (NPT) and the Arms Trade Treaty (ATT). This definition resembles that set forth in the *Dictionary of Trade Policy Terms*, which suggests that export controls have more public international law implications. Given that this book approaches the subject matter from the perspective of international economic law, the term 'export control' does not seem to be a good option.

[37] Walter Goode (ed), *Dictionary of Trade Policy Terms* (3rd ed., Cambridge University Press 2003) 139 (emphasis omitted).

[38] Yann Aubin and Arnaud Idiart, *Export Control Law and Regulations Handbook: A Practical Guide to Military and Dual-Use Goods Trade Restrictions and Compliance* (3rd ed., Kluwer Law International 2016) 5.

The term 'export restraint' is used in *US – Export Restraints*, wherein Canada challenged the WTO-consistency of US legislation by treating export restraints as subsidies. For the purpose of resolving the dispute before it, the Panel in *US – Export Restraints* defined an export restraint as 'a border measure that takes the form of a government law or regulation which expressly limits the quantity of exports or places explicit conditions on the circumstances under which exports are permitted, or that takes the form of a government-imposed fee or tax on exports of the product calculated to limit the quantity of exports'.[39] So defined, an export restraint is a measure, tariff or non-tariff, imposed by a government through law or regulation, with a view to limiting the quantity of exports. However, as the United States pointed out in that dispute, the term 'export restraint' does not appear in the legal text of the WTO agreements, and thus it is neither practicable nor desirable for the Panel to define it in the abstract. The definition of an export restraint, as noted previously, is offered mainly for the purpose of resolving the dispute before the Panel.

By contrast, the term 'restriction', sometimes in conjunction with 'prohibition', is widely used throughout the WTO agreements; it is thus appropriate to use a term that appears in the legal text of WTO agreements. From the outset, it is clear that a restriction does not necessarily entail prohibition, as many legal provisions expressly cover 'prohibition or restriction'. Further, the Panel in *China – Raw Materials*, in referring to previous Panel reports, addresses the definition of a 'restriction'. The Panel first points to the dictionary definition of a 'restriction' as 'a thing which restricts someone or something, a limitation on action, a limiting condition or regulation'.[40] The Panel refers to the approach set forth in *EEC – Minimum Import Prices* (taken in the case of importation), and followed in *Japan – Semi-Conductors*, and holds that the very potential to limit trade is sufficient to constitute a restriction on the exportation, or sale for export, of any product.[41] Therefore, an export restriction is a measure with a limiting effect on exportation, or sale for export, of any

[39] *US – Export Restraints*, para. 8.17. See also Kent Albert Jones, *Export Restraint and the New Protectionism: The Political Economy of Discriminatory Trade Restrictions* (University of Michigan Press 1994) 3–4. Jones notes that export restraint may take other forms of a less formal nature. The examples he refers to are export forecasts, import surveillance, price monitoring, bilateral consultations, industry-to-industry arrangements and import licensing requirements, which have the potential to monitor import deliveries from a specific exporter.

[40] Panel Report on *China – Raw Materials*, para. 1079.

[41] Panel Report on *China – Raw Materials*, para. 1081.

product. At the same time, it should also be noted that the limiting effects also extend to 'measures that create uncertainties and affect investment plans, restrict market access for imports or make importation prohibitively costly'.[42] The potential to adversely affect exportation, or sale for export, of a given product is the decisive element for the definition of an 'export restriction'. Therefore, an export restriction is to be interpreted, in a broad sense, as a capacity to capture all measures directly or indirectly limiting exports.

A similar definition is embraced by the Appellate Body in *China – Raw Materials*, which, based on the dictionary definition, defines a restriction as 'a thing which restricts someone or something, a limitation on action, a limiting condition or regulation', which refers generally to something that has a limiting effect.[43] The Appellate Body further notes, 'the use of the word "quantitative" in the title of the provision informs the interpretation of the words "restriction" and "prohibition" in Article XI:1 and XI:2. It suggests that Article XI of the GATT 1994 covers those prohibitions and restrictions that have a limiting effect on the quantity or amount of a product being imported or exported.'[44]

With regards to the practices of the WTO, the WTO Trade Policy Review reports normally include a section under the heading of measures (directly) affecting exports: taxes and levies, prohibitions, quotas, licensing and minimum prices. In view of these measures, it is clear that export restrictions, like import restrictions, take the form of tariff and non-tariff measures.[45] In addition to the aforementioned measures, the reduction of VAT rebates is usually regarded as tantamount to an export restriction given that it has similar effects.[46]

It should also be noted that this book takes a measure-specific approach instead of a sector-specific approach, and avoids focusing solely on natural resource sectors, even though export restrictions are frequently employed in these sectors. This book looks at various forms of

[42] Panel Report on *China – Raw Materials*, para. 1078.

[43] Appellate Body Report on *China – Raw Materials*, para. 319.

[44] Appellate Body Report on *China – Raw Materials*, para. 320.

[45] It should, however, be noted that export taxes are considered as non-tariff barriers in the Indicative List of Notifiable Measures annexed to the Ministerial Decision on Notification Procedures adopted by the Trade Negotiating Committee on 15 December 1993. Export taxes are placed in the category of other non-tariff measures.

[46] Jeonghoi Kim, 'Recent Trends in Export Restrictions on Raw Materials' in OECD (ed), *The Economic Impact of Export Restrictions on Raw Materials* (OECD Publishing 2010) 14.

export restrictions, the rationales for trading nations that adopt them, their legality under WTO law and their complexities surrounding international political economy and national security. The reasons for this choice are, first, that such an approach is in line with the practices of the WTO dispute settlement process, under which a dispute may be filed when a member 'considers that any benefits accruing to it directly or indirectly under the covered agreements are being impaired by measures taken by another Member'.[47] In filing a complaint, the complaining member is required to 'identify the specific measures at issue'.[48] Thus, readers should be quite familiar with a measure-specific approach. Second, there are abundant sector-oriented works examining the agriculture sector in relation to food security, or the energy sector in relation to energy security.[49] A measure-specific approach would bring a new element to the debates.

Finally, I provide a roadmap for readers. This book comprises five chapters. After this introduction, Chapter 2 offers an analysis of WTO provisions relating to export restrictions, notably, Article XI of the GATT 1994, Article 12 of the AoA and Article 11 of the ASG. It also offers analysis of 'WTO-plus' obligations as contained in the accession protocols and working party reports, and of trends in regional trade agreements aimed at regulating export restrictions. Chapter 3 explores governance issues arising from the imposition of export restrictions, ascertains whether the exceptions set out for in the WTO agreements can justify export restrictions imposed by a trading nation and reflects on whether sufficient policy space is provided. Chapter 4 extends the discussion from WTO law to investment, and competition law and policy, and examines how these different regulatory regimes impact states' and enterprises' decisions on the imposition and formation of export restrictions/cartels in the context of the global supply chain. Chapter 5 concludes the book.

47 DSU, Art. 3.3.

48 DSU, Art. 6.2.

49 See, e.g., Melaku Geboye Desta, 'The Organization of Petroleum Exporting Countries, the World Trade Organization, and Regional Trade Agreements' (2003) 37 *Journal of World Trade* 523; Yulia Selivanova (ed), *Regulation of Energy in International Trade Law – WTO, NAFTA and Energy Charter* (Wolters Kluwer 2012); Yulia Selivanova, 'World Trade Organization Rules and Energy Pricing: Russia's Case' (204) 38 *Journal of World Trade* 559; Gabrielle Marceau, 'The WTO in the Emerging Energy Governance Debate' (2010) 5 *Global Trade and Customs Journal* 83.

2

WTO Rules on Export Restrictions

2.1 Introduction

As noted in the introductory chapter, the underlying logic of the GATT/WTO system is the liberalisation of import barriers with a view to obtaining access to foreign markets. The first step is to transform all import barriers into tariffs, then bind and reduce them. Therefore, as early as the GATT era, there was already a general obligation to eliminate quantitative restrictions based on the logic that quantitative restrictions are normally more trade-distortive than tariffs. The tariffication of quantitative restrictions also enhances the transparency of the customs regulatory regime of an importing country. However, this general obligation to eliminate quantitative restrictions does not limit its scope to the import dimension; therefore, it has the capacity to impact the export dimension of the global trading regime.

This general obligation to eliminate (export) quantitative restrictions is nonetheless subject to two exceptions: to prevent or relieve critical shortage of foodstuffs or essential products of the exporting countries; and to implement standards or regulations necessary for the classification, grading or marketing of commodities in international trade. The need to maintain sufficient foodstuffs to safeguard the food security of national populations is widely shared and recognised in the Uruguay Round negotiations. The Agreement on Agriculture (the AoA), in Article 12, reinstates this spirit but also puts forward some procedural requirements and limited substantive requirements with which a member must comply when imposing new export prohibitions or restrictions on foodstuffs in accordance with Article XI:2(a) of GATT 1994.

On the other hand, with the evolution of the trading system and the emergence of Japan as a trading power in the 1970s and 1980s, Japanese exports brought great competitive pressure to bear on the domestic industries of the United States. This led political leaders of the United States to engage with Japan to reach voluntary export restraints (VERs, also known as grey-area measures), under which Japan agreed to maintain a ceiling on exports to the United States.[1] These VERs nonetheless had trade diversionary effects.[2] Therefore, finding means to bring these grey-area measures into discipline became a major objective of the Uruguay Round negotiations and led to an explicit provision in the Agreement on Safeguards (the ASG).

Further, export restrictions may be challenged under the Agreement on Subsidies and Countervailing Duties (the ASCM), as they may add comparative advantage to domestic downstream producers once the added advantage is qualified as a financial contribution and a benefit is conferred. In fact, in *US – Export Restraints*,[3] the treatment of export restrictions as countervailable subsidies under US trade law has been subject to the scrutiny of the WTO dispute settlement mechanism. In that dispute, Canada alleged that under the US trade regulatory regime, an 'export restraint' is considered to meet the criteria of 'financial contribution' if the 'export restraint' has the effect of increasing the supply of the restricted good.[4] While the Panel found in favour of the United States, it is nonetheless clear that the ASCM has a role to play in WTO law on export restrictions.

With the establishment of the WTO, the trade-distorting effects of export restrictions have been widely recognised, as has the need to bring them into discipline. Existent WTO members thus take advantage of

[1] On this issue, see, e.g., Michael William Lochmann, 'The Japanese Voluntary Restraint on Automobile Exports: an Abandonment of the Free Trade Principles of the GATT and the Free Market Principles of United States Antitrust Laws' (1986) 27 *Harvard International Law Journal* 99, 99–157; Mitsuo Matsushita, 'A Japanese View of United States Trade Laws' (1987) 8 *Northwestern Journal of International Law and Business* 29, 43–56; Thomas J. Schoenbaum, 'The International Trade Laws and the New Protectionism: The Need for a Synthesis with Antitrust' (1994) 19 *North Carolina Journal of International Law and Commercial Regulation* 393, 409–415. For a critique of the capacity of WTO law to inhibit the VERs, see further, Dennis Kitt, 'Note: What's Wrong with Volunteering? The Futility of the WTO's Ban on Voluntary Export Restraints' (2009) 47 *Columbia Journal of Transnational Law* 359, 359–386.

[2] See, e.g., Richard Pomfret, 'The Economics of Voluntary Export Restraint Agreements' (1989) 3 *Journal of Economic Surveys* 199; Jaime de Melo and L. Alan Winters, 'Do Exporters Gain from VERs?' (1993) 37 *European Economic Review* 1331; Michael O. Moore, 'VERs and Price Undertakings under the WTO' (2005) 13 *Review of International Economics* 298.

[3] Panel Report on *United States – Measures Treating Exports Restraints as Subsidies*, WT/DS194/R and Corr.2, adopted 23 August 2001, DSR 2001:XI, 5767.

[4] Panel Report on *US – Exports Restraints*, para. 3.1.

accession negotiations to force acceding members to undertake obligations or commitments relating to export restrictions: the most illustrative examples being China and Russia. This bilateral rule-making approach nonetheless has its pitfalls. Demanding during accession negotiation processes that a natural–resource-rich country undertake obligations and commitments on export restrictions helps to lessen the adverse effects of potential export-restrictive measures imposed by the acceding country; these obligations and commitments are nonetheless asymmetric, meaning that these obligations and commitments are binding only on the acceding member, not existent members. Therefore, existent WTO members are still free to impose export restrictions. Further, these 'WTO-plus' obligations pose great challenges to their relationship with the WTO agreements, as can be clearly seen in the *China – Raw Material* dispute.

Finally, in the context of the Agriculture and Non-Agriculture Market Access (NAMA) negotiations under the auspices of the Doha Development Agenda (the DDA), various proposals have been advanced with a view to disciplining export restrictions. Some proposals aim to strengthen the procedural transparency of domestic export restrictions; others aim to impose substantive obligations by tariffing, binding and reducing export restrictions. Outside the multilateral framework, trading nations have attempted to regulate export restrictions under regional or bilateral free trade agreements, the North American Free Trade Area (NAFTA, now replaced by United States-Mexico-Canada Agreement, USMCA) and the European Union being the prime examples. In contrast to these two prototypes, it may be worth exploring whether South–South FTAs display different characteristics.

This chapter thus aims, first, to examine relevant WTO rules in WTO agreements relating to export restrictions, covering Article XI of the GATT 1994, Article 12 of the AoA, Article 11 of the ASG and relevant provisions of the ASCM. It will then take China's accession protocol and Russia's Working Party Report as examples that illustrate how existent WTO members use accession negotiations as leverage to legislate WTO-plus rules relating to export restrictions. The chapter then introduces proposals advanced by WTO members in the DDA negotiations and explores how these proposals would contribute to the discipline of the export dimension of the world trading system. Moving beyond the multilateral framework, it will then examine the regulation of export restrictions under NAFTA, the EU and some major South–South FTAs. A short conclusion will be provided at the end of this chapter.

2.2 Limited Regulation in the WTO Agreement

2.2.1 General Elimination of Quantitative Restrictions

The most important provision impacting the export dimension of the world trading system is Article XI of the GATT 1994, which sets out an obligation to pursue the general elimination of quantitative restrictions. It is an effort to transform non-tariff barriers into tariffs, namely, to 'tariffy' trade barriers and then to bind and reduce them. In recognition of the ambition to discipline non-tariff measures, and in tribute to this ambition, Rüdiger Wolfrum, citing Christian Tietje, argues that the prohibition of non-tariff trade barriers in respect of exports indicates that 'GATT not only deals with measures affecting other states, which would be in keeping with traditional international law dealing with economic relations among states, but it also has an effect on the internal normative order of states'.[5]

This comment illustrates the significance of Article XI of the GATT 1994 in regulating both imports and exports of states, which prevents conflicts between trade liberalisation in importation and restrictions in exportation. In regulating exportation and importation with the same rule, the GATT thus rationalises the economic legal order of states. Nonetheless, Wolfrum may read too much into the GATT system from Article XI, as such provisions as Article XI covering both imports and exports are rather exceptional. Such an approach stands in stark contrast to the Treaty Establishing the European Economic Community (the EEC Agreement, now the Treaty on the Functioning of the European Union, the TFEU), which provides for a general elimination of export restrictions.[6] Further, as Wolfrum notes, notwithstanding the potential of Article XI to have the same legal significance for the WTO system as Articles 34 and 35 of the TFEU do for the EU economic legal order, the WTO Panel/Appellate Body has not developed as refined and sophisticated jurisprudence as the Court of Justice of the European

[5] Rüdiger Wolfrum, 'Article XI GATT' in Rüdiger Wolfrum, Peter-Tobias Stoll and Holger P. Hestermeyer (eds), *WTO-Trade in Goods* (Martinus Nijhoff Publishers 2010) 285.

[6] Roessler, 'GATT and Access to Supplies', 28. With a view to establishing a customs union or free trade area, EU (then EEC) Member States and EFTA countries are directed to abolish, and refrain from imposing, between themselves any new customs duties on imports or exports or any charge having equivalence. Admittedly, the EU and EFTA aim to pursue closer economic integration under Article XXIV of the GATT and thus impose more stringent obligations on export duties. Nonetheless, it is clear that such stringency is dictated by the GATT rules.

Union (the CJEU).[7] Articles 34 and 35 of the TFEU provide that quantitative restrictions on imports, exports and all measures having equivalent effect shall be prohibited between Member States. The main difference between Article XI of the GATT 1994 and Articles 34 and 35 of the TFEU is whether 'other measures' may have the same wide scope as 'all measures having equivalent effects' and whether they are subject to the same degree of scrutiny in the GATT as in the EU.[8]

As Article XI:1 of the GATT 1994 states, 'no prohibitions or restrictions other than duties, taxes, or other charges, whether made effective through quotas, import or export licenses or other measures shall be instituted or maintained'.[9] This Article is under the heading of 'General Elimination of Quantitative Restrictions', which applies both to the importation and exportation of goods. The legal text first provides the example of 'export quota, import or export licenses' and then includes a catch-all clause of 'other measures'. Therefore, there would be little doubt that export bans, export quotas, export licenses and minimum export price fall squarely within the scope of Article XI:1, but would be subject to dispute as to how far 'other measures' can stretch. Do these 'other measures' have to share the same characteristics of export quotas or export licenses, or do these 'other measures', being restrictions, suffice? So far, the WTO panel/Appellate Body has laid down some jurisprudence regarding this matter. The following observations can be made. Article XI:1 is broad in scope and comprehensive in coverage, and is not limited to restrictions in quantitative nature. Competition in the marketplace may play a role in determining the limiting effect of a restriction, but adverse trade effect is not a necessary condition. These observations will be further elaborated in what follows.

At the outset, the Panel in *India – Quantitative Restrictions* declares the broad scope of Article XI:1 with the following observation: Article XI:1 provides for a general ban on import or export restrictions or prohibitions 'other than duties, taxes or other charges'. In referring to the GATT Panel decision in *Japan – Trade in Semi-conductors*, the Panel recognises the comprehensive coverage of Article XI:1: it applies 'to all measures instituted or maintained by a [Member] prohibiting or restricting the

7 Wolfrum, 'Article XI GATT' (n. 5), at 295.

8 See further, Section 2.5.2. Regarding the jurisprudence of export restrictions in CJEU, see Marek Szydlo, 'Export Restrictions within the Structure of Free Movement of Goods. Reconsideration of an Old Paragigm' (2010) 47 *Common Market Law Review* 753, 753–789.

9 Article XI:1 of the GATT 1994.

importation, exportation, or sale for export of products other than measures that take the form of duties, taxes or other charges'.[10] In supporting its observation, the Panel in *India – Quantitative Restrictions* also refers to the dictionary meaning of a 'restriction', meaning 'a limitation on action, a limiting condition or regulation'.[11]

The broad scope and comprehensive coverage of Article XI:1 is also supported by the Panel in *India – Autos*, which throws light on the nature of a restriction and clarifies the scope of these 'other measures'. According to the Panel,

> Although the title of Article XI refers to the elimination of 'quantitative restrictions', the text of the provision makes no distinction between different types of restrictions on [exportation]. On the contrary, the words 'No prohibitions or restrictions ... whether made effective through quotas, import or export licenses or other measures' ... suggest an intention to cover any type of measures restricting the entry of goods [out of] the territory of a Member, other than those specifically excluded, namely, duties, taxes or other charges.[12]

As the Panel in *India – Autos* makes clear, Article XI:1 is not limited to quantitative restrictions but covers all types of restrictions that limit the exportation of a good taking a form other than a duty, tax or other charge. Therefore, a restriction under the purview of Article XI:1 is not necessarily quantitative in nature, but extends to all restrictions having limiting effects.

The Panel in *Columbia – Port of Entry*, after reviewing previous case-law, addressed the objective of Article XI:1: protecting market access. In the words of the Panel,

> a number of GATT and WTO panels have recognized the applicability of Article XI:1 to measures which create uncertainties and affect investment plans, restrict market access for imports or make importation prohibitively costly, all of which have implications on the competitive situation of an importer. Moreover, it appears that findings in each of these cases were based on the design of the measure and its potential to adversely affect importation, as opposed to a standalone analysis of the actual impact of the measure on trade flows.[13]

In the context of importation, the Panel in *Columbia – Port of Entry* clarifies that the measures set forth in Article XI:1 are able to alter the

[10] *India – Quantitative Restrictions*, para. 5.128.
[11] Ibid.
[12] *India – Autos*, para. 7.264.
[13] *Columbia – Port of Entry*, para. 7.240.

competitive situation given that a restriction creates uncertainties and affects investment plans, restricts market access for imports or makes importation prohibitively costly. The Panel further emphasises that a restriction does not have to lead to an actual impact on trade flows; it is nonetheless the design of that restriction and its potential to adversely affect importation that changes the condition of competition and thus constitutes a restriction. The decisive point here is the modification of the condition of competition, which does not necessarily lead to actual adverse trade flows. This point is further clarified in *US – COOL*. According to the Panel, in determining whether a measure makes effective a restriction in the context of Article XI:1 of the GATT 1994, 'the focus is on the competitive opportunities of imported products, not the trade effects.'[14] Therefore, a complaining party claiming the existence of a restriction need not prove actual trade effects.

Translating this holding into the exportation context, the same logic holds. Wherever an export measure modifies the condition of competition, that measure may be qualified as a restriction subject to the scrutiny of Article XI:1. The pertinent measure does not have to prevent the actual exportation of a given product; a measure having a deterring effect for exportation may suffice. Such interpretation is confirmed by the Panel in *China – Raw Materials*. As the Panel holds, 'any measure that creates uncertainty as to the ability to import/export, and otherwise "compete" in the marketplace, violates Article XI:1'.[15] Therefore, the key point in determining whether a measure falls under the purview of Article XI:1 lies in the modification of market competition.

After laying down a general obligation to eliminate quantitative restrictions, Article XI in the second paragraph provides three exceptions. As Article XI:2(c) concerns import restrictions on agricultural or fisheries products, it does not relate to the main interests of this book. Thus only Articles XI:2(a) and XI:2(b) are relevant here.

2.2.1.1 Export Prohibitions or Restrictions Temporarily Applied to Prevent or Relieve Critical Shortage of Foodstuffs or Other Products Essential to the Exporting Contracting Party

Article XI:2(a) provides that export prohibitions or restrictions may be temporarily applied to 'prevent or relieve critical shortage of foodstuffs or

[14] *US – COOL*, para. 7.571.
[15] *China – Raw Materials*, para. 7.1801.

other products essential to the exporting contracting party'.[16] According to this provision, export prohibitions and restrictions can be imposed to prevent or relieve critical shortages of two categories of products: foodstuffs and other products essential to exporting members.

Regarding foodstuffs, a quick question would be whether the foodstuffs subject to export quantitative prohibitions or restrictions need be essential to the exporting members or not. Namely, does the phrase 'essential to export Contracting Parties' only apply to other products or foodstuffs as well? In *China – Raw Materials*, the Panel first separated the products identified in Article XI:(a) into two categories: foodstuffs and 'other products'. The Panel then noted that the term 'other products' is qualified by the term 'essential to the exporting member'.[17] the Panel seemed to suggest that the criterion of being essential to the exporting member applies only to 'other products', not to foodstuffs. This provision has been frequently relied on by agriculture-exporting countries to impose export restrictions on agricultural products, with a view to securing food supplies for their national populations, which nonetheless exacerbates food insecurity in least developing countries (LDCs) or net food importing developing countries (NFIDCs).

With respect to other essential products, Wolfrum, referring to *Canada – Ice Cream and Yoghurt*, argues that this exception is designed for agricultural production as such, but not for the industrial processing of agricultural products. However, the Panel in *China – Raw Materials* did not embrace such a narrow interpretation. According to the Panel, 'a product may be "essential" within the meaning of Article XI:2(a) when it is "important" or "necessary" or "indispensable" to a particular member. This may include a product that is an "input" to an important product or industry'.[18] In determining whether a product is essential to a member, due account has to be taken of the particular circumstance faced by that member when imposing the export restrictions.[19] Based on these criteria, the Panel concluded that in view of the role of the raw material in question, namely, refractory-grade bauxite in the production of steel and the role of steel in the manufacturing and construction industries and the contribution of the steel industry to Chinese employment,

[16] The GATT 1994, Article XI:2(a).

[17] Panel Report on *China – Raw Materials*, para. 7.273.

[18] Panel Report on *China – Raw Materials*, para. 7.282.

[19] Panel Report on *China – Raw Materials*, para. 7.282.

refractory-grade bauxite is a product essential to China.[20] This position is supported by the Appellate Body, which saw essential products as 'absolutely indispensable or necessary products'.[21]

In hearing the appeal, the Appellate Body also took the opportunity to clarify the meaning of 'temporarily applied' and 'critical shortage' and the relationship between XI:2(a) and Article XX. In investigating the ordinary meaning of 'temporarily' and understanding 'temporarily' connected with 'applied', the Appellate Body saw the definitional element of 'temporarily', which is to supply a passing need, as implying the interim nature of export-restrictive measures. According to the Appellate Body, 'a measure applied "temporarily" in the sense of Article XI:2(a) is a measure applied in the interim, to provide relief in extraordinary conditions in order to bridge a passing need. It must be finite, that is, applied for a limited time.'[22] However, the Appellate Body, in reversing the Panel's holding, ruled that the term 'temporarily' does not necessarily dictate a pre-fixed time limit.[23]

Regarding 'critical shortage', the Appellate Body first looked into the ordinary meaning of shortage and saw the term 'shortage' to be qualified by the adjective 'critical'. The Appellate Body thus reached the conclusion that 'critical shortage' refers to 'those deficiencies in quantity that are crucial, that amount to a situation of decisive importance, or that reach a vitally important or decisive stage, or a turning point'.[24] The Appellate Body found the term 'general or local short supply' in Article XX:(j) can provide relevant context for the interpretation of 'critical shortage'. While the term 'in short supply' has the same meaning as 'shortage', Article XX:(j) does not include the term 'critical'. The difference in the wording of these provisions, according to the Appellate Body, must be given meaning. Therefore, the Appellate Body concluded that the kinds of shortage envisaged by Article XI:2(a) must be more narrowly circumscribed than those falling within the ambit of XX:(j).[25]

In addressing the mutual impact of different concepts contained in XI:2(a), the Appellate Body first prescribed that meaning should be given to these different concepts and opined that they may impact one another,

[20] Panel Report on *China – Raw Materials*, para. 7.340.

[21] Appellate Body Report on *China – Raw Materials*, para. 326.

[22] Appellate Body Report on *China – Raw Materials*, para. 330.

[23] Appellate Body Report on *China – Raw Materials*, para. 324.

[24] Appellate Body Report on *China – Raw Materials*, para. 331.

[25] Appellate Body Report on *China – Raw Materials*, para. 325.

which in turn would define the scope of the XI:2(a). The Appellate Body further elaborates, 'whether a shortage is "critical" may be informed by how "essential" a particular product is.[26] In addition, the characteristics of the product as well as factors pertaining to a critical situation, may inform the duration for which a measure can be maintained in order to bridge a passing need in conformity with Article XI:2(a).'[27] Accordingly, the different terms of 'critical', 'essential' and 'temporarily' may influence one another. Therefore, whether a member's measure may be satisfied with the criteria of XI:2(a) should be assessed on a case-by-case basis.

Finally, the Appellate Body clarified the relationship between XI:2(a) and Article XX(g) of the GATT 1994. One the one hand, the obligation of the general elimination of quantitative restrictions does not extend to the items listed in lits. (a)–(c) of Article XI:2. Article XI:2 thus sets out a limit for the application of Article XI:1. Therefore, whenever the requirements of Article XI:2 are met, there is no room for the application of Article XX since the obligation to eliminate quantitative restrictions does not exist.[28] On the other hand, an Article XI:2(a) measure may operate simultaneously with a conservation measure complying with the requirements of Article XX(g). As the Appellate Body explains, the reach of XI:2(a) and XX(g) is not identical and should be interpreted as containing different legal obligations and having different functions. Nonetheless, 'a measure falling within the ambit of Article XI:2(a) could relate to the same product as a measure relating to the conservation of an exhaustible natural resource'.[29] The Appellate Body then used a critical shortage, resulting from natural disaster, of an exhaustible natural resource, being at the same time a foodstuff or other essential product, as an example to illustrate that in addition to a measure taken under Article XI:2(a) to relieve the critical shortage of this exhaustible natural resource, a member may also take measures in accordance with XX(g) to conserve it.[30] In other words, to the extent that a measure meets with the criteria of Article XI:2(a), Article XX has no role to play since there is no obligation to eliminate quantitative restrictions. By contrast, in addition to the measure taken under XI:2(a) to address the critical shortage of foodstuffs or other essential products, which are at the same time exhaustible

[26] Appellate Body Report on *China – Raw Materials*, para. 328.
[27] Appellate Body Report on *China – Raw Materials*, para. 328.
[28] Appellate Body Report on *China – Raw Materials*, para. 334.
[29] Appellate Body Report on *China – Raw Materials*, para. 337.
[30] Appellate Body Report on *China – Raw Materials*, para. 337.

natural resources, a member may also refer to XX(g) for the conservation of these exhaustible natural resources when such measure does not pass the scrutiny of Article XI:(a). Given the wider scope of Article XX(g), the Appellate Body, in confirming the reasoning of the Panel, thus concluded that Article XX:(g) includes additional elements in the chapeau to ensure that the measures in question would not result in arbitrary and unjustifiable discrimination or constitute disguised restriction on international trade.

2.2.1.2 Necessity for the Application of Standards or Regulations for the Classification, Grading or Marketing of Commodities in International Trade

Article XI:2(b) then provides that export prohibitions or restrictions may be imposed to the extent 'necessary to the application of standards or regulations for the classification, grading or marketing of commodities in international trade'.[31] In the GATT era, a panel was established to examine the legality of Canada's export prohibitions on unprocessed sockeye salmon, pink salmon and herring.[32] Whereas Canada admitted that the export prohibitions were subject to the purview of Article XI of the GATT 1947, it nevertheless invoked Article XI:2(b) as a justification. Canada contended that it applied strict quality and marketing regulations to these three products, which were necessary to maintain Canada's reputation for safe and high-quality fish products. Therefore, its export prohibitions could be justified by Article XI:2(b) of the GATT 1947.[33] However, this argument failed to persuade the Panel.

The Panel first noted that some unprocessed herring and salmon meeting the quality standards set by Canadian authorities were nonetheless prevented from exportation. The export restrictions in question could not be considered 'necessary' for the application of standards within the meaning of Article XI:2(b).[34] More importantly, the Panel held that the 'export prohibitions on certain *unprocessed* salmon and *unprocessed* herring were not "regulations for the marketing" of *processed* salmon and herring in international trade within the meaning of

[31] The GATT 1994, Article XI:2(b).

[32] Panel Report on *Canada – Measure Affecting Exports of Unprocessed Herring and Salmon*, adopted on 22 March 1988, L 6268, 35S/98.

[33] Panel Report on *Canada – Herring and Salmon*, para. 3.3.

[34] Panel Report on *Canada – Herring and Salmon*, para. 4.2.

Article XI:2(b)'.[35] As Canada noted, the prohibition of exports of certain unprocessed herring and salmon was necessary for the international marketing of processed herring and salmon. Without these measures, Canada would not have been able to maintain a high quality of fish products for marketing abroad. This contention was nonetheless rejected by the Panel. According to the Panel, the word 'regulations' in Article XI:2(b) does not extend to 'all regulations that facilitate foreign sales but only those that apply to the marketing as such'.[36] In referring to the drafting history, the Panel held that, whereas export restrictions may be imposed with a view to promoting sales of a restricted product by spreading its supply over a longer period of time, these restrictions cannot be imposed for the purpose of promoting the sales of another product. A broad interpretation of marketing regulations would lead to the protection of domestic industry at the expense of foreign industry, which is against the purpose of this provision.[37]

In view of this holding, it is clear that the exception envisaged by Article XI:2(b) is limited to export prohibitions or restrictions necessary to the application of the standards or regulations for the classification, grading or marketing of the product subject to export restrictions but does not cover those prohibitions or restrictions imposed against a specific product with a view to promoting the marketing of another. Otherwise, these export prohibitions or restrictions would afford protection to domestic downstream producers at the expense of foreign producers.[38]

2.2.2 *Discipline on Export Prohibitions and Restrictions of Foodstuffs in Agreement on Agriculture*

In opening the Uruguay Round negotiations, the GATT contracting parties agreed that 'there is an urgent need to bring more discipline and predictability to world agricultural trade by correcting and preventing restrictions and distortions including those related to structural

[35] Panel Report on *Canada – Herring and Salmon*, para. 4.2 (emphasis added).

[36] Panel Report on *Canada – Herring and Salmon*, para. 4.2.

[37] Panel Report on *Canada – Herring and Salmon*, para. 4.2.

[38] In addition of Article XI:2, the obligation to eliminate quantitative (export) restrictions may also be subject to general exception as set out in Article XX of the GATT, of which lit. (g), (i) and (j) are most relevant. However, given the constraint of time and space, this book will not deal with these issues. Further, Article 12 of the AoA also touches on export restrictions but it will not be dealt with in this book.

surpluses so as to reduce the uncertainty, imbalances and instability in world agricultural markets'.[39] The negotiators were directed to 'achieve greater liberalisation of trade in agriculture and bring all measures affecting import access and export competition under strengthened and more operationally effective GATT rules and disciplines'.[40] Specifically, the negotiators were instructed to improve market access through, *inter alia*, the reduction of import barriers and to improve the competitive environment with stricter discipline on the use of direct or indirect subsidies or other measures affecting agricultural trade.[41]

As observed by Ramesh Sharma and Panos Konandreas, while agricultural trade was never officially outside the GATT, sufficient policy space was made possible for some major players in agricultural trade through exceptions to GATT rules, which provided legal cover for import restrictions and subsidised production, leading to structural surplus. In order to channel this structural surplus, export subsidies and food aid were two main legal instruments.[42] This was an era of cheap food policy when the GATT contracting parties were preoccupied with the structural surplus in agricultural products and thus aimed to bring more discipline and predictability to world agricultural trade. Greater liberalisation was considered an antidote to the uncertainty, imbalances and instability in world agricultural markets; the reduction of import barriers and greater discipline on the use of subsidies are two important concrete measures to achieve this liberalisation objective.

Similarly, the AoA speaks of its long-term objective to 'establish a fair and market-oriented agricultural trading system'[43] through 'substantial progressive reductions in agricultural support and protection'[44] with a view to 'correcting and preventing restrictions and distortions in world agricultural markets'.[45] With this aim, the drafters of the AoA laid down a three-pillar regime to regulate world agricultural trade: market access, domestic support and export competition. Therefore, the AoA and its

[39] Punta del Este Declaration launching the Uruguay Round in 1986.
[40] Ibid.
[41] Ibid.
[42] Ramesh Sharma and Panos Konandreas, 'WTO Provisions in the Context of Responding Soaring Food Prices' FAO Commodity and Trade Policy Research Working Paper No. 25, 1.
[43] AoA, 2nd preambular.
[44] AoA, 3rd preambular.
[45] AoA, 3rd preambular.

built-in agenda for the continuation of the reform programme are to address over-production in developed countries.

This overarching aim may nonetheless have the potential to constrain developing countries that suffer from underproduction due to their inadequate support to agriculture and heavy taxation burden. Besides, the reduction of production in developed countries and the strengthening of suppressed prices of agricultural products may impact developing countries unevenly. While some advanced developing countries may have the capacity to exploit this opportunity, some developing countries may not benefit from the reduction of production in developed countries but suffer as a result of higher food prices arising thereof.[46] Indeed, the drafters of the AoA have recognised this danger by speaking of food security and other non-trade concerns in its preamble. Unfortunately, recognition of this has only limited effects. For example, whereas food aid is included as an element of the Marrakesh Decision to address the potential food insecurity that LDCs and NFIDCs may be faced with, it is nonetheless also, perhaps predominantly, regulated under the export competition pillar. The underlying rationale of the AoA lies in addressing the structural surplus by reducing over-production and liberalising import restrictions with a view to accessing foreign markets, with the notable exception of Article 12 of the AoA regulating export prohibitions and restrictions.

Article 12 of the AoA is situated in the export competition pillar. From the outset, Article 12(1) recognises a member's right to institute a new export prohibition or restriction on foodstuffs in accordance with Article XI:2(a) of the GATT 1994, which provides that the obligation of a general elimination of quantitative restrictions shall not extend to 'export prohibitions or restrictions temporarily applied to prevent or relieve critical shortages of foodstuffs or other products essential to the exporting contracting party'.[47] Therefore, an export prohibition or restriction may be temporarily applied to prevent or relieve a critical shortage of foodstuffs or other essential products. In order to be consistent with Article XI:2(a) of the GATT 1994, such export prohibition or restriction has to be *temporarily* applied; it has also to be aimed at preventing or relieving *critical shortages* of foodstuffs or other essential products.

[46] Sharma and Konandreas, 'WTO Provisions in the Context of Responding Soaring Food Prices', n. 42, at 1.

[47] Article XI:2(a) of the GATT 1994.

In addition to the requirement of Article XI:2(a) of the GATT 1994, Article 12(1) of the AoA puts forward two additional procedural requirements. The legal text reads as follows,

> Where any Member institutes any new export prohibition or restriction on foodstuffs in accordance with paragraph 2(a) of Article XI of GATT 1994, the Member shall observe the following provisions:
>
> (a) the Member instituting the export prohibition or restriction shall give due consideration to the effects of such prohibition or restriction on importing Members' food security;
> (b) before any Member institutes an export prohibition or restriction, it shall give notice in writing, as far in advance as practicable, to the Committee on Agriculture comprising such information as the nature and the duration of such measure, and shall consult, upon request, with any other Member having a substantial interest as an importer with respect to any matter related to the measure in question. The Member instituting such export prohibition or restriction shall provide, upon request, such a Member with necessary information.

First, the member instituting a foodstuff export prohibition or restriction has to 'give due consideration' to the effects of such prohibition or restriction on the food security of importing members. Second, the member instituting such prohibition or restriction should give notice in writing to the Committee on Agriculture as far in advance as practicable. Information as to the nature and duration of such prohibition or restriction should be provided. Further, the instituting member, on request, should consult with any other member having a substantial interest as an importer. The instituting member is also obliged to provide necessary information, if requested.

In a word, Article 12(1) of the AoA put forward two requirements to be satisfied when a WTO member institutes a new export prohibition or restriction on foodstuffs. The first relates to its obligation to take account of the impact of such export prohibition or restriction on the food security of other importing members. The second concerns the notification requirement and consultation obligation. While Article 12(1) of the AoA obliges the instituting member to notify the Committee on Agriculture, it does not provide any sanction mechanism in case of non-compliance. The consultation obligation arises only on request of an interested importing member, made to the instituting member. Again, this provision does not offer any detail about the nature of the consultation requirement. As it is silent concerning the legal effect of the export prohibition or restriction on foodstuffs when the consultation fails, it seems that the export prohibition or restriction remains unaffected even when the exporting and importing members do not reach a satisfactory result.

Article 12(2) of the AoA then excludes developing country members from the scope of application of Article 12(1), unless the developing country member concerned is a net food exporter of a given foodstuff. Therefore, unless a developing country member is a net exporter of a specific foodstuff, it is not subject to the discipline of Article 12(1) of the AoA. Nowadays, there are a number of developing countries exporting the lion's share of basic foodstuffs. It follows that these developing countries will have to abide by the requirements laid down in Article 12(1) of the AoA.

Nonetheless, in practical terms, this provision suffers from some weaknesses. First, there is no clear definition of net food exporters. Determining the base year by which a country is to be categorised as a net food exporter is also a matter of dispute. While there is a list of NFIDCs based on self-designation, this list was compiled mainly for the purposes of the Marrakesh Decision. Further, a country's omission from such a list of NFIDCs does not necessarily suggest that the country does not rely on other countries for food imports.[48] Therefore, in view of the increasing role of some developing countries as major food exporters, Article 12(2) of the AoA provides additional leeway for such developing countries to escape the discipline as set out in Article 12(1), which is very lenient in the first place. The resultant consequence is thus: in imposing export prohibitions or restrictions on foodstuffs, these food-exporting developing countries further exacerbate the food insecurity of LDCs and NFIDCs.

The last point to note with regards to the export dimension of the AoA regulatory regime is that the AoA has not touched on export taxes. While import liberalisation through tariff reduction in agricultural trade was one of the main issues of the Uruguay Round negotiations, export taxes of agricultural products remained outside the realm of those negotiations. As noted in Chapter 1, it is subject to dispute whether Article II of the GATT 1994 (Schedules of Concessions) extends to export taxes. This controversy then extends to the AoA and leaves export tariffs in the agricultural sector unregulated. In the current Doha negotiations, there are some proposals advanced by WTO members with a view to disciplining export tariffs on agricultural products. However, like the fate of the Doha round, such proposals are in peril. Greater detail will be provided in Section 2.4 when various proposals in the DDA are examined.

[48] Sharma and Konandreas, 'WTO Provisions in the Context of Responding Soaring Food Prices', n. 42, at 5.

2.2.3 *Export Restrictions as Subsidies to Downstream Processors*

The treatment of export restrictions as subsidies has a long history running through the GATT era to the WTO age. In the late 1980s, when the Uruguay Round negotiations were underway, the European Economic Community (the EEC, now the EU) initiated an anti-subsidy investigation against Argentinian and Brazilian oil processors on the grounds that with the imposition of differential export tax regimes on exports of soybeans, these two countries were subsidising their oil processors. Similarly, in the early 1990s, the United States initiated two countervailing investigations against leather products from Argentina and softwood lumber products from Canada on the grounds that the export restraints maintained by these two countries constituted 'bounty or grant' within the meaning of the US countervailing duty law. Given that the Tokyo Round Subsidies Code did not provide any definition for a 'subsidy', it was thus left to contracting parties to decide the scope of a countervailable subsidy. Due to differing interpretations of subsidy, the EEC and the United States reached different decisions. Nonetheless, the scenario has greatly changed in the WTO context given that the ASCM clearly defines a subsidy to exist only when a financial contribution by the government or public body exists and a benefit is conferred. Therefore, whether the United States' practice of treating export restrictions as subsidies is WTO-compatible became the subject matter in *US – Export Restraints*, where the Panel held that export restraints cannot constitute a financial contribution and thus do not satisfy the definitional criteria of a subsidy.

This section will thus examine the controversy arising from whether a WTO member may treat export restrictions maintained by another member as a countervailable subsidy. I will thus examine countervailing investigations in the domestic context, namely *Fediol* v. *Commission* (*FEDIOL*)[49]

[49] Case 187/85, *Fediol* v. *Commission* [1988] ECR 4155; Case 188/85, *Fediol* v. *Commission* [1988] ECR 4193. Given that these two cases concern similar issues, I will examine only Case 187/85 and will refer to this case as FEDIOL. Also, *FEDIOL* has a very long litigation history before the ECJ and has greatly impacted GATT/WTO in the EU legal order. FEDIOL and Nakajima are generally referred to as FEDIOL/Nakajima exceptions. See e.g., Fernando Castillo de la Torre, 'The EEC New Instrument of Trade Policy: Some Comments in the Light of the Latest Developments' (1993) 30 *Common Market Law Review* 687; Antonis Antoniadis, 'The European Union and WTO Law: A Nexus of Reactive, Coactive, and Proactive Approaches' (2007) 6 *World Trade Review* 45; Ilona Cheyne, 'International Agreements and the European Community Legal System' (1994) 19 *European Law Review* 581.

in the EEC context and *Argentina – Leather*[50] and *US – Softwood Lumber*[51] in the US context. In addition, challenges of US countervailing decisions in the US–Canada Binational Panel will also be examined. After these, I will examine the *US – Export Restraints* dispute in the WTO dispute settlement mechanism. When referring to these domestic investigations and the *US – Export Restraints* dispute, the original terms 'export embargo' or 'export restraint' as used in the US International Trade Administration (USITA) reports and the WTO Panel report will be followed, with a view to correctly reflecting the letter and spirit of these reports.[52]

2.2.3.1 EEC and US Practices in the GATT Era and Decisions of US–Canada Binational Panel

In the GATT era, the EEC's regulation on subsidy was governed by Council Regulation (EEC) No 2176/84.[53] Article 3(1) of Council Regulation No 2176/84 provides that '[a] countervailing duty may be imposed for the purpose of offsetting any subsidy bestowed, directly or indirectly, in the country of origin or export, upon the manufacture, production, export or transport of any product whose release for free circulation in the Community causes injury'.[54] While Council Regulation (EEC) No 2176/84 included an illustrative list on export subsidy, it did not provide a definition of the term 'subsidy'. This arrangement mirrored the GATT 1947 and the Tokyo Round Subsidies Code.

As a result, in *FEDIOL*, the European Court of Justice (the ECJ, now the Court of Justice of the European Union, the CJEU) was called on to decide whether 'a charge on the public account' was an essential element in its countervailing duty law.[55] In *FEDIOL*, two measures were contested

[50] Final Affirmative Countervailing Duty Determination and Countervailing Duty Order; Leather from Argentina (*Argentina – Leather*), 55 FR 40212, 2 October 1990.

[51] Final Affirmative Countervailing Duty Determination: Certain Softwood Lumber Products from Canada (*Canada – Softwood Lumber*), 57 FR 22570, 28 May 1992.

[52] In *Canada – Softwood Lumber*, the USITA used export restrictions and export restraints interchangeably.

[53] Council Regulation (EEC) No 2176/84 of 23 July 1984 on protection against dumped or subsidized imports from countries not members of the European Economic Community, OJ L 201/1, 30/07/1984. On EEC/EU anti-subsidy law, see generally, Ivo Van Bael, *EU Anti-Duming and Other Trade Defence Instruments* (5th ed., Wolters Kluwer Law & Business 2011), part II; Kostantinos Adamantopoulos and Maria Pereyra-Friedrichsen, *EU Anti-Subsidy Law and Practice* (2nd ed., Sweet & Maxwell 2007).

[54] Council Regulation No 2176/84, Art. 3(1).

[55] Luca Rubini, *The Definition of Subsidy and State Aid: WTO and EC Law in Comparative Perspective* (Oxford University Press 2009) 138; Marc Benitah, *The Law of Subsidies under the GATT/WTO System* (Kluwer Law International 2001) 138.

before the ECJ: differential tax regimes and export barriers. The differential tax regime imposed by Argentina levied a 25 per cent tariff on soybeans and 10 per cent for products intended to be crushed, including soy meal. With this differential tax regime, the Argentinian domestic oil seed crushing industry was guaranteed a supply of raw materials at a low price. When exported to the EEC market, Argentinian soy meal thus had a price advantage obtained from the lower rate of taxation.[56] At the same time, the applicant claimed that the Argentinian government maintained a licensing and registration system that had an effect convergent with, or similar to, that of a differential tax regime.[57]

The ECJ focused on the first measure and ruled that a subsidy must be related to a charge from the public account. In applying the same reasoning to the measures, the ECJ dismissed the applicant's request to strike down the European Commission's decision in terminating the anti-subsidy investigation. The ECJ reasoned by looking at the legal text of Council Regulation (EEC) No 2176/84 and observed that there was no express legislative definition of the term 'subsidy'. However, the ECJ noted that there was an illustrative list of export subsidies annexed to that Regulation. The final paragraph of that illustrative list read as follows: any other charge on the public account constituting an export subsidy in the sense of Article XVI of GATT. From this paragraph, the ECJ thus inferred that 'in the mind of the Community legislature the concept of export subsidy necessarily implied a financial burden borne directly or indirectly by public bodies'.[58] This conclusion was also compatible with the EEC's international obligations since neither the GATT 1947 nor the Tokyo Round Subsidies Code provided any definition of a subsidy. It was thus left open to the contracting parties to define its meaning.

The applicant further argued that if the differential tax regime did not constitute an export subsidy, it fell into the scope of domestic subsidy since it reduced the production costs of Argentinian soy meal producers. As the differential export tax regime had the same damaging effect on competition by favouring a specific (group of) undertaking and satisfied the criteria set out in Article 3 of Council Regulation (EEC) No 2176/84, in this case a subsidy bestowed on manufacture, it thus constituted a domestic subsidy. In contrast, the European Commission and the

[56] *FEDIOL*, para. 7.
[57] *FEDIOL*, para. 19.
[58] *FEDIOL*, para. 11.

intervening Argentinian government argued that the financial contribution element was missing, and further that the criteria of specificity was not met. The ECJ found in favour of the European Commission and the intervener by stating that 'the applicant has not shown that in order specifically to favour soya meal the Argentinian State deprived itself of revenue which it would normally have collected under the general system'.[59]

The gravity of the ECJ's reasoning on export subsidy relies on the legal text of the illustrative list, which requires 'a charge from public account' to be an export subsidy. Regarding the applicant argument on domestic subsidy, the ECJ's reasoning seems unsatisfactory. It is not entirely clear whether the ECJ rejected the applicant's request on the grounds of the absence of specificity or the absence of revenue forgone. Whether the criterion of 'a charge from public account' extends to domestic subsidy is also not clarified. In *FEDIOL*, the criterion of financial contribution surfaced, which was also contested in the context of US domestic countervailing proceedings (and the WTO dispute settlement mechanism as well). However, the USITA reached a different decision from that of the European Commission, which will be examined next.

Before the adoption of the Uruguay Round Agreement Act in implementing the WTO Agreement, the Tariff Act of 1930, as amended, in Section 771(5)(A) defined a subsidy as follows,

> (A) In general. – The term 'subsidy' has the same meaning as the term 'bounty or grant' as that term is used in section 303, and includes, but is not limited to, the following:
>
> (ii) The following domestic subsidies, if provided or required by government action to a specific enterprise or industry, or group of enterprises or industries, whether publicly or privately owned and whether paid or bestowed directly or indirectly on the manufacture, production, or export of any class or kind of merchandise:
>
> (I) The provision of capital, loans or loan guarantees on terms inconsistent with commercial considerations.
>
> (II) The provision of goods or services at preferential rates.
>
> (III) The grant of funds or forgiveness of debt to cover operating losses sustained by a specific industry.
>
> (IV) The assumption of any costs or expenses of manufacture, production or distribution.[60]

[59] *FEDIOL*, para. 16.

[60] 19 U.S.C. 1677(5)(A) (1991), citing from *Canada – Softwood Lumber*, F57 FR 22570, at 22607.

This provision was legislated by the Trade Agreements Act of 1979 with the aim of implementing the Tokyo Round Subsidies Code.[61] Before the enactment of the Trade Agreements Act of 1979, Section 303 of the Tariff Act of 1930 was the sole legal instrument governing US countervailing duty investigations, which continued to apply to imports originating from countries that were not contracting parties to the Tokyo Round Subsidies Code. Section 303 of the Tariff Act of 1930 regulated 'bounty or grant' by providing

> Whenever any country . . . shall pay or bestow, directly or indirectly, any bounty or grant upon the manufacture or production or export of any article or merchandise produced in such country, then upon the importation of such article or merchandise into the United States, there shall be levied and paid, in all such cases, in addition to any duties otherwise imposed, a duty equal to the net amount of such bounty or grant.[62]

With regards to administrative practices, the USITA had maintained a long-standing position of declining to treat border measures as countervailable subsidies. This position was changed in *Argentina – Leather* and reaffirmed with rigorous reasoning in *Canada – Softwood Lumber*. I will address these two cases here.

In *Argentina – Leather*, the USITA was called on to determine whether the export embargo on cattle hides adopted by Argentina through Resolution 321 constituted a bounty or grant as set out in Section 303 of the Tariff Act of 1930. The aim of Resolution 321 was 'to maintain the volume of supply of raw materials adequate to the needs of the domestic market of the leather tanning and manufacturing sector, facilitating a smooth flow of supplies while avoiding any undue increase in prices'.[63] Two issues were disputed before the USITA: whether the export embargo had a direct and discernible effect on hide prices in Argentina, and, if so, whether the benefit arising from the price suppression was specific to a certain group of entities. The USITA compared the historical price differential between hides in Argentina and those in the United States and found that whenever there was an export embargo in place, the

[61] On the implementation of Tokyo Round agreements, see generally, John H. Jackson, Jean-Victor Louis and Mitsuo Matsushita (eds), *Implementing the Tokyo Round: National Constitutions and International Economic Rules* (University of Michigan Press 1984); on the evolution of subsidy rules from the GATT to the WTO, see, Andrew L. Stoler, 'The Evolution of Subsidies Disciplines in GATT and the WTO' (2010) 44 *Journal of World Trade* 797, 797–808.

[62] 19 U.S.C. 1303 (1991), citing from *Canada – Softwood Lumber*, F57 FR 22570, at 22607.

[63] *Argentina – Leather*, 55 FR 40212, at 40213.

price of Argentinian hides fell consistently below that of the US hides. When the export embargo was lifted, the two prices were in parity, and sometimes the price of Argentinian hides exceeded that of the US hides. The USITA thus concluded that the export embargo imposed by Argentina had a direct and discernible effect on the price of Argentinian hides. Given that the export embargo applied only to cattle hides, which were mainly, if not exclusively, used for leather tanning industries, the price suppression arising from the export embargo brought about a benefit specific to leather tanning industries.[64] Since the criteria of benefit and specificity were satisfied, the USITA thus concluded that the export embargo on cattle hides maintained by Argentina constituted a countervailable bounty or grant under the US countervailing duty law.

This position was reaffirmed in *Canada – Softwood Lumber*, where the USITA spent much effort in justifying its decision to deviate from past practices in not imposing countervailing duty against border measures but instead following *Argentina – Leather*. The overarching argument of the USITA decision was as follows: none of the legislative history, prior judicial and administrative precedents or the GATT 1947 and the Tokyo Round Subsidies Code ruled out the possibility of treating border measures, in this case, export restraints, as subsidies. According to the USITA, the statutory language, legislative history and past administrative and judicial precedents had not prevented the US investigation authority from treating border measures as a subsidy. This practice would also conform to the GATT 1947 and the Tokyo Round Subsidies Code given that these two international agreements did not clearly define the term 'subsidy' and did not explicitly prohibit the contracting parties from doing so. Throughout its analysis, the USITA had first to establish that log export restrictions imposed by Canada resulted in a direct and discernible effect on the price of lumber and constituted a benefit to lumber industries. The log export restrictions had then to pass the specificity test to be treated as a countervailable subsidy.

The USITA first clarified that, regardless of the long-standing practice of not treating border measures as countervailable subsidies, the administration was not precluded from deviating from its practices provided that it offered a reasonable and rational explanation for doing so and demonstrated that the new practice was not inconsistent with the applicable statute.[65] This principle was of greater relevance when there was no

[64] Ibid.

[65] *Canada – Softwood Lumber*, F57 FR 22570, at 22606.

statutory definition of a given term. The administration thus enjoyed wide latitude in defining such term if its construction was reasonable and supported by substantial evidence. A careful examination of the statutory language, legislative history, judicial decisions and the objective and purpose of the statute would lead to the following conclusion: had Congress had a chance to decide whether export restrictions fall within the scope of the US countervailing duty law, Congress would have answered it in the affirmative. Further, such determination would also be in line with the GATT 1947.[66]

The USITA referred to the decision *Hammond Lead Products, Inc.* v. *United States* delivered by the Customs Court,[67] where the Court rejected the Treasury's determination that the disputed Mexican export tax regime, regardless of its capacity in reducing the price of the major input to the finished products under investigation, did not constitute a countervailable subsidy. While this decision was repealed in the appellate proceedings on jurisdictional grounds, such reversal did not undermine the force of the merit of *Hammond Lead*. Further, whereas Congress amended the relevant statute by offering remedies to challenge the decisions of the Treasury, it, fully aware of *Hammond Lead*, chose not to define the scope of a countervailable subsidy and left the question open. Given that the legislature had not expressly addressed whether export restrictions might be subject to countervailing duties, the task before the USITA was to discern dispositive legislative intent by projecting 'how the legislature would have dealt with the concrete situation if it had spoken'.[68] In fulfilling this task, the USITA had to determine whether the log export restrictions maintained by Canada conferred countervailable benefit or subsidy to Canadian lumber producers within the meaning of the US countervailing duty law. Again, this involved a two-tier inquiry: '(1)[w]hether these export restrictions provide a benefit to such manufacturers; and, if so, (2) whether the [British Columbia] Government provides the benefit to a "specific" group of industries.'[69]

In this two-tier inquiry, the starting point is the statutory language. While the Trade Agreements Act of 1979 did not define the term

[66] Ibid.

[67] *Hammond Lead Products, Inc.* v. *United States*, 306, F. Supp. 460 (Cust. Ct. 1969), reversed on procedural grounds, 440 F.2d 1024 (C.C.P.A. 1971), cert. denied. 404 U.S. 1005 (1971) (*Hammond Lead*).

[68] *Canada – Softwood Lumber*, F57 FR 22570, at 22607.

[69] Ibid.

'subsidy', it was nonetheless clear that Congress intended to incorporate the definitional elements of 'a bounty or grant' and related practices into this new act. Also when Congress passed the Trade Agreements Act of 1979, the Customs Court had struck down the Treasury's decision not to impose a countervailing export tax in *Hammond Lead*. The same court also maintained a lenient attitude towards the definition of 'a bounty or grant' by ruling that the reduction of production costs via indirect foreign government funding constituted a countervailing subsidy. These developments may be read to infer that Congress intended the term 'subsidy' to be read in a broad and comprehensive sense. In setting out the illustrative examples, Congress by no means aimed to restrict the scope of a countervailable subsidy. This interpretation finds additional support in the statutory language 'includes, but is not limited' employed in Section 771(5)(A) of the Trade Agreements Act of 1979. Accordingly, when a foreign government conferred benefits on its domestic producers in such a way that is not enumerated in the illustrative list, whether it might be subject to US countervailing duties depended mainly on whether such a measure shared the same characteristics as those appearing on the illustrative list. This is what the maxim of *ejusdem generis* dictates. Based on this reasoning, the USITA further rejected the arguments of Canadian producers that export restrictions did not constitute a countervailable subsidy in that there was no financial contribution by the government of British Columbia or any government revenue forgone. According to the USITA, such interpretation would run counter to the maxim of *ejusdem generis* and read out of 'indirectly' and 'but not limited' from the statute.[70]

With a closer look at the examples in the illustrative list, the USITA found that they shared the following common characteristics,

> The direct transfer of tangible resources with a tangible value from a foreign government to a particular beneficiary or recipient (e.g., direct provision of capital); (2) the indirect bestowal of tangible resources with a measurable value from a foreign government to a recipient (e.g., indirect provision of goods or services at preferential rates), and (3) the indirect bestowal of intangible but, nonetheless, measurable benefits from a government to a specified class of recipients (e.g., indirect assumption of any production costs).[71]

[70] *Canada – Softwood Lumber*, F57 FR 22570, at 22609.
[71] *Canada – Softwood Lumber*, F57 FR 22570, at 22609.

The USITA stated that Congress intended to cover other government indirect schemes that had the same substantial effects of indirect provision of goods or services at preferential rates or indirect assumption of any production costs. Given that export restrictions maintained by British Columbia effectively lowered the production costs of lumber producers, these restrictions constituted a countervailable subsidy, as the net effect was in no way different from what it would be if the government gave refunds directly to the producers on sale. Since the benefit was not given directly to lumber producers and was contingent on export performance, the USITA thus concluded that export restrictions were an indirect domestic subsidy.

After reaching such conclusion, the next task for the USITA was to determine the existence of 'direct and discernible effect' as set out in *Argentina – Leather*. The export restrictions arbitrarily reduced the demand for the logs and led to price suppression of logs in domestic markets of British Columbia. Given that logs were the major input to the softwood lumber industry, softwood lumber producers enjoyed a benefit from lower input or the reduction of production costs. Therefore, export restrictions maintained by British Columbia had a direct and discernible effect on the domestic price of logs in British Columbia.[72]

After establishing a direct and discernible effect, the USITA continued to determine whether the export restrictions in question satisfy the requirement of specificity to be countervailable, namely, whether the benefit was provided 'to a specific enterprise or industry, or group of enterprises or industries' within the meaning of Section 771(5)(A) of the Trade Agreements Act of 1979. The USITA found it in the affirmative, as the benefit was *de jure* given to primary timber processing industries.

In passing the two tests of direct and discernible effect and specificity, the USITA thus concluded that the export restrictions maintained by British Columbia constituted countervailable subsidies.[73] In reaching such a determination, the USITA nonetheless did not stop its analysis. It went further to examine whether its determination was consistent with GATT 1947 and the Tokyo Round Subsidies Code. In its analysis, one of the key elements was the criterion of financial contribution, which surfaced during the Uruguay Round negotiations and in the subsequent *US – Restraints* dispute.

[72] *Canada – Softwood Lumber*, F57 FR 22570, at 22609–22610.
[73] *Canada – Softwood Lumber*, F57 FR 22570, at 22610.

Two points were made with regards to GATT-consistency when export restrictions were treated as countervailable subsidies: the definition of subsidies and the mutual exclusivity between countervailing duties and other GATT provisions on border measures. The USITA first pointed to the absence of any definition of the term 'subsidy' either in the GATT 1947 or the Tokyo Round Subsidies Code. Importantly, the Tokyo Round Subsidies Code also provided an illustrative list of examples, where the maxim of *ejusdem generis* equally applied. This illustrative list covered, *inter alia*, fiscal incentives. As export restraints maintained by the Canadian government involved a complex fiscal tax regime that taxed log exports but exempted those for domestic usage; the net result of this fiscal tax regime was the reduction of production costs of softwood lumber producers. Therefore, such export restraints based on the fiscal tax regime were similar in nature or analogous to those examples identified in the illustrative list of internationally recognised domestic subsidies.[74] With regards to the mutual exclusivity of countervailing duty and other border measures, the USITA referred to Article VI:5 of the GATT 1947[75] and stated that, if the drafters of the GATT 1947 intended to exclude border measures from the scope of countervailing duties, similar arrangements would have been provided. However, this was not the case. Therefore, the GATT 1947 did not rule out the possibility of treating border measures, in this case export restrictions, as countervailable subsidies.[76]

Finally, the USITA addressed the criterion of financial contribution advanced by Canadian producers. The USITA stated that there was no mention in the GATT 1947 or the Tokyo Round Subsidies Code of such a term as financial contribution. The USITA also rejected Canadian producers' attempt to rely on the Dunkel Text[77] as evidence demonstrating that a financial contribution is one of the definitional elements of a countervailable subsidy. As the USITA noted, if financial contribution

[74] *Canada – Softwood Lumber*, F57 FR 22570, at 22611.

[75] Article VI:5 of the GATT 1947 reads, '[n]o product of the territory of any contracting party imported into the territory of another contracting party shall be subject to both anti-dumping and countervailing duties to compensate for the same situation of dumping or export subsidization'.

[76] *Canada – Softwood Lumber*, F57 FR 22570, at 22611.

[77] The Dunkel Text referred to the legal text presented by the Director-General of the GATT, Arthur Dunkel, at the late stage of the Uruguay Round negotiations. On the analysis of subsidies rules in the Dunkel Text, see, Andrew D. M. Anderson, 'An Analysis of the Proposed Subsidies Code Procedures in the "Dunkel Text" of the GATT Uruguay Round – The Canadian Exporters' Case' (1993) 27 *Journal of World Trade* 71, 71–100.

was *per se* a definitional element of a countervailable subsidy, the Dunkel Text need not perform a redundant exercise in creating an existent criterion.[78] The USITA thus held that for a measure to be subject to countervailing duties, the existence of a financial contribution was not necessary.

Before entering into the dispute in the WTO age, I will record some further developments in the GATT era. After the USITA determined that export restrictions constituted a countervailable subsidy, this determination was challenged by the Canadian government and softwood lumber producers before the US–Canada Binational Panel pursuant to Article 1904.2 of the Canada–United States Free Trade Agreement. While the Binational Panel agreed that export restrictions might constitute a countervailing subsidy, it held that the USITA failed to provide a clear explanation of the 'direct and discernible effect'. Whether this test equals 'a proximate causal relationship or correlation (i.e., regression analysis) between the [British Columbia] export restrictions and the domestic price of [British Columbia]'[79] was not entirely clear to the Panel. Further, the USITA determined that Canadian export restrictions were *de jure* limited to a specific group of industries and thus satisfied the requirement of specificity. Nonetheless, the Panel found the language of the relevant Canadian statute provided no benefit to a specific group of industries; rather, it was aimed at equally applying to all actors in the relevant industries.[80] The Panel thus remanded this case to the USITA. When the determination on remand came back to the Panel again in December, the Panel was still not persuaded by the reasoning of the USITA.[81] Finally a US–Canada agreement on softwood lumber lasting five years was signed in 1996 and consequently put a halt to this dispute. Nonetheless, with the envisaged expiry of this agreement in 31 March 2001,[82] Canada resorted

[78] *Canada – Softwood Lumber*, F57 FR 22570, at 22611.

[79] United States–Canada Free Trade Agreement Article 1904 Binational Panel Review, U.S.A.-92-1904-01, Decision of the Panel (6 May 1993), p. 110.

[80] Ibid., at 71.

[81] United States–Canada Free Trade Agreement Article 1904 Binational Panel Review, U.S.A.-92-1904-01, Decision of the Panel (17 December 1993).

[82] Benitah, *The Law of Subsidies under the GATT/WTO System* (n. 55) 219; Merit E. Janow and Robert W. Staiger, 'US – Export Restraints United States – Measures Treating Export Restraints as Subsidies' in Henrik Horn and Petros C. Mavroidis (eds), *The WTO Case Law of 2001* (Cambridge University Press 2011) 226; see also, Leonila Gugiya, 'The Interplay of International Dispute Resolution Mechanisms: The Softwood Lumber Controversy' (2011) 2 *Journal of International Dispute Settlement* 175, 175–207, for the complex softwood lumber dispute.

to the WTO dispute settlement mechanism, resulting in the *US – Export Restraints* complaint. The definitional element of financial contribution of a countervailable subsidy lingers.

2.2.3.2 US – Export Restraints

With the coming into force of the WTO agreements, legal rules governing subsidies and countervailing duties have been substantially reshaped – the most important being the adoption of the ASCM with a clear definition of a subsidy. On 19 May 2000, in view of the expected expiry of the US–Canada agreement on softwood lumber, Canada requested consultation with the United States, but no concrete result was achieved. At the request of Canada, a panel was established to examine the treatment of export restraints as a countervailable subsidy under the US countervailing duty law. The specific measures identified by Canada included Section 771(5) of the Tariff Act of 1930, as amended by the Uruguay Round Agreements Act (the URAA), as interpreted by the Statement of Administrative Action (the SAA) accompanying the URAA and the Explanation of the Final Rules (the Preamble), the Final Rule of the US Department of Commerce, Countervailing Duties (63 Federal Register 65348, at 65349-51 (25 Nov. 1998)), and US practice thereunder. The subject matter before the Panel was two-fold. On the one hand, the Panel had to determine whether export restraints may be treated as a countervailable subsidy under the WTO agreements, in particular, the ASCM; on the other hand, the Panel had to adjudicate the mandatory/discretionary nature of the alleged measures in order to ascertain whether the US administration was obliged to treat export restraints as a countervailable subsidy. The issue of relevance to this book relates to the first inquiry, which I will address next.

From the outset, the Panel defined the scope of issues before it with care. Given that the term 'export restraints' is not found in any WTO agreements, the Panel agreed with the United States that it was not in a position to define such term. Nonetheless, for the purpose of resolving the dispute before it, the Panel had to clarify the subject matter falling into its terms of reference. Given that the scope of claims was determined by the complaining member, the Panel thus defined the term 'export restraints' as suggested by Canada for the purpose of resolving this present dispute. According to the Panel, an export restraint refers to 'a border measure that takes the form of a government law or regulation which expressly limits the quantity of exports or places explicit conditions on the circumstances under which exports are permitted, or that takes the form of a government-imposed fee or tax on exports of the product calculated to limit the quantity of exports'.[83] Based on this definition, the Panel went on to examine substantive aspects of the dispute.

The contention of the disputing parties centred on the definition of a subsidy, specifically, whether export restraints may be considered a financial contribution within the meaning of Article 1.1(a)(1) of the ASCM.[84] The pertinent provision relates to Article 1.1(a)(1)(iv), which provides that there is a financial contribution by a government or any public body within the territory of a member, where

> a government makes payments to a funding mechanism, or entrusts or directs a private body to carry out one or more of the type of functions illustrated in (i) to (iii) above which would normally be vested in the government and the practice, in no real sense, differs from practices normally followed by governments; a government makes payments to a funding mechanism, or entrusts or directs a private body to carry out one or more of the type of functions illustrated in (i) to (iii) above which would normally be vested in the government and the practice, in no real sense, differs from practices normally followed by governments.[85]

With a careful reading of the legal text, the Panel thus found five requirements put forward by this provision, (i) a government 'entrusts or directs' (ii) 'a private body' (iii) 'to carry out one or more of the type of functions illustrated in' subparagraphs (i)–(iii) of Article 1.1(a)(1) (iv), 'which would normally be vested in the government' and (v) 'the practice, in no real sense, differs from practices normally followed by governments'.[86] The most debated criterion in this case is related to the term 'entrusts or directs'. According to Canada, the plain meaning of the words 'entrust' and 'direct' entails an explicit and affirmative instruction by the government to the private entity to provide goods.[87] Such explicit and affirmative instruction did not exist in the case of export restraints, where the domestic log producers subject to these restraints were not instructed to sell to domestic producers. By contrast, the United States argued that a limitation or an outright prohibition on exports was only

83 *US – Export Restraints*, para. 8.17.

84 The definitional elements of a subsidy include both financial contribution and benefits conferred. As both parties agreed that benefits conferred in case of export restraints exist, the contention was thus mostly related to the criterion of financial contribution.

85 ASCM, Art. 1.1(a)(1)(iv).

86 *US – Export Restraints*, para. 8.25.

87 *US – Export Restraints*, para. 8.23.

semantically different from a direct instruction to a private entity to provide goods to domestic softwood lumber producers. 'An export restraint is "functionally equivalent" to an entrustment of or direction to a private body to provide goods domestically.'[88]

The Panel found in favour of Canada. In the first place, the Panel declared that the purpose of this provision is to regulate the situation where the government of a member executes its policy via a private entity. This provision is in effect an anti-circumvention arrangement precluding a member from escaping its WTO obligation by acting behind a private entity.[89] The Panel then referred to the ordinary meaning of 'entrust' and 'direct' and stated that these two terms contained a notion of delegation or command. To satisfy the requirement of entrustment or direction, three criteria must be met, '(i) an explicit and affirmative action, be it delegation or command; (ii) addressed to a particular party and (iii) the object of which action is a particular task or duty'.[90] In other words, entrustment or direction necessarily involves an affirmative and explicit delegation or command to someone to do something. Entrustment and direction should be distinguished from a government's intervention in the market in a certain way, which may or may not have a particular result depending on the given circumstances and the responses of actors in the market to this intervention. While two different governmental actions may have the same result, it does not transform the nature of these actions. In other words, these two different actions cannot be one and effectively the same simply because they bring about the same result.[91]

In view of this reasoning, the debate circling the *US – Export Restraints* relates to the nature or effects approach in ascertaining the existence of a financial contribution and thus of a subsidy. According to the United States, an export restraint can be caught by Article 1.1(a)(1)(iv) of the ASCM if its effect is to induce domestic producers to sell its products in greater quantity or exclusively to domestic users. In other words, if the domestic log producers have no alternative, economically or practically, but to sell their products to domestic users, then an export restraint should be considered functionally equivalent to entrusting or directing a private entity to provide goods. In contrast, the Panel focused on the

[88] *US – Export Restraints*, para. 8.22.

[89] *US – Export Restraints*, paras. 8.28 and 8.53.

[90] *US – Export Restraints*, para. 8.29.

[91] *US – Export Restraints*, para. 8.31.

nature of the action. Given that different governmental actions may lead to the same effect, amounting to a financial contribution, the effect approach advanced by the United States would read the criterion of financial contribution out of Article 1 of the ASCM. Therefore, the appreciation of the criterion of financial contribution should focus on the government's action, instead of the response by other actors to it, even if the response is certain and can be expected.[92]

However, the Panel's strict interpretation of the terms 'entrust' and 'direct' has been modified by the Appellate Body in subsequent disputes. Specifically, the Appellate Body does not limit entrustment and direction to delegation and command. According to the Appellate Body in *US – DRAMS*, the objective of Article 1.1(a)(1)(iv) of the ASCM is to prevent a member from escaping its obligations by 'tak[ing] actions that would otherwise fall within Article 1.1(a)(1), were they to be taken by the government itself'.[93] The decisive point is whether the government of a member gives responsibility to a private body or exercises its authority over a private body with a view to granting a financial contribution to its domestic producers. In this interpretive exercise, limiting entrustment and direction to delegation and command is of no help.

The Appellate Body in *US – DRAMs* pointed to a tension between the objective of anti-circumvention and the limiting effect of the definitional element of financial contribution. In fact, the Panel in *US – Export Restraints* was also fully aware of this tension when it mentioned that '[t]he phrase "entrusts or directs" in Article 1.1(a)(1)(iv) is immediately preceded by the phrase "a government makes payments to a funding mechanism or"',[94] and concluded that Article 1.1(a)(1)(iv) of the ASCM aims to capture equivalent governmental actions. Clearly, not all actions are subject to the control of Article 1.1(a)(1)(iv) of the ASCM. However, the objective and purpose of this provision is to prevent anti-circumvention. A strict reading of Article 1.1(a)(1)(iv) would undermine its effectiveness. In light of this tension and turning back to the context of export restraints as a countervailable subsidy, it is doubtful whether

[92] Rubini, *The Definition of Subsidy and State Aid: WTO and EC Law in Comparative Perspective* (n. 55) 109–110; Janow and Staiger, 'US – Export Restraints United States – Measures Treating Export Restraints as Subsidies' (n. 82) 218–219.

[93] Appellate Body Report on *United States – Countervailing Duty Investigation on Dynamic Random Access Memory Semiconductors (DRAMS) from Korea*, WT/DS296/AB/R, adopted 20 July 2005, DSR 2005: XVI, 8131, para. 113.

[94] *US – Export Restraints*, para. 8.32.

export restraints may fulfil the requirement of entrustment or direction even though the Appellate Body relaxed the threshold.

2.2.3.3 Analysis and Comments

The question of whether export restrictions may be treated as countervailable subsidies involves different domestic practices in the EU and the United States and legislative evolution from the GATT to the WTO. In the GATT era, given the silence of the GATT 1947 and the Tokyo Round Subsidies Code regarding the definition of a subsidy, contracting parties enjoyed a great margin of appreciation in defining the scope of countervailing subsidies.[95] In this context, the EEC and the United States opted for different positions. The EEC adhered to the criteria of 'a charge from public account' and thus dismissed the petition to countervail differential tax regimes favouring domestic soybean processors. On the contrary, the United States decided to impose countervailing duties against Argentinian leather products and Canadian softwood lumber on the grounds that export restrictions reduced the production cost of Argentinian and Canadian domestic downstream producers. The underlying rationale for their different positions lies in the nature or effect approach in finding the existence of a subsidy. The EEC maintained that governmental action, namely, a charge from the public account, was an essential element for a subsidy; by contrast, the United States emphasised the question of whether the production costs of domestic downstream producers were effectively reduced.

These different approaches resulted from the absence of an explicit definition of a subsidy in the GATT 1947 and the Tokyo Round Subsidies Code. Therefore, whether financial contribution constituted a definitional element of a subsidy was subject to debate. The EEC (and Canada) believed so, while the United States held otherwise. These different attitudes towards the definition of a subsidy were duly reflected in the course of the Uruguay Round negotiations. In the end, the EEC and Canada succeeded in including financial contribution as a criterion for the subsidy. This, however, has not brought the controversy to an end. With the threat of countervailing duties being imposed on it, Canada, which maintained export restraints on logs, initiated the WTO dispute settlement proceeding. In *US – Export Restraints*, the legal regime has changed. Article 1 of the ASCM provides a clear definition of a

[95] Cheyne, 'International Agreements and the European Community Legal System' (n. 49) 582.

subsidy by setting out two criteria: financial contribution and a benefit conferred. In this context, the United States had to argue with painful efforts to justify its position that export restrictions, in some particular circumstances, may be treated as a countervailable subsidy.

The Panel in *US – Export Restraint* took a strict position in interpreting entrustment and direction as delegation and command. The Panel stressed that such delegation and command must take place in an affirmative and explicit way. Otherwise, the criterion of financial contribution through entrustment or direction via a private entity cannot be satisfied. In that connection, the Panel emphasised the difference between entrustment and direction to a private entity to carry out functions normally vested in the government, and the government's intervention in the market leading to a particular result. This strict interpretation was nonetheless relaxed by the Appellate Body in *US – DRAMS*, holding that entrustment and direction are not necessarily limited to delegation and command. Entrustment and direction can be affirmative and explicit, or made in a subtler manner. In view of the holding of the Appellate Body, whether or not export restrictions may be treated as a countervailable subsidy under the WTO agreements, in particular the ASCM, depends on whether the investigation authority establishes the fact that a foreign government, by imposing export restrictions, in fact entrusts or directs domestic producers to provide the restricted goods to domestic downstream producers. This would largely rely on the weighing of factual evidence and can only be decided on a case-by-case basis.

Even if export restrictions may be considered entrustment or direction within the meaning of Article 1.1(a)(1)(iv) of the ASCM and constitute a financial contribution, some challenges exist for the United States to continue its practice of treating export restrictions as a countervailable subsidy. Before the US–Canada Binational Panel, Canadian governments and softwood lumber producers challenged the criterion of benefit in addition to the financial contribution element. This challenge was accepted by the Binational Panel. According to the Binational Panel, it is confusing that the USITA treated export restrictions as an indirect subsidy but nevertheless found that the export restrictions in question had a direct and discernible effect. Whether this direct and discernible effect means proximate causal relationship or correlation remained unclear to the Binational Panel. Further, the Panel in *US – Export Restraints* explicitly rejected this causal relationship approach. The US contention that, for a financial contribution to exist, there would have to be the requisite causal connection between the government measure and the behaviour of private actors would effectively lead to the following conclusion, 'any government measure that caused an increase in the domestic supply of a good would, for that reason alone, constitute government-entrusted or government-directed provision of goods and hence a financial contribution'.[96] The major flaw of this causal relationship approach is that it would merge the criteria of a financial contribution and a benefit conferral into one: only the benefit criterion remains. Further, as the USITA admitted in *Canada – Softwood Lumber*, given the absence of a competitive benchmark price, in the case of log export restrictions, 'the effects on the firm's marginal costs can only be shown through a market distortion analysis'.[97] Notwithstanding the vagueness of such market distortion analysis, it is also doubtful whether such analysis, in appreciating the benefits conferral, is in line with the existent WTO jurisprudence.[98]

Finally, Merit Janow and Robert Staiger advance an interesting argument related to the specificity of export restrictions. According to Janow and Staiger, an export restriction is 'conceptually equivalent to an alternative program in which a production subsidy of the same magnitude is placed on *every other good* in the economy and a consumption tax of the same magnitude is placed on *every other good* in the economy'.[99] The Panel might accept the effects approach advanced by the United States for the sake of argument and agree that export restrictions did constitute a financial contribution, but nonetheless ruled that the specificity requirement was not satisfied. As they explain, while the idea that the production subsidy conferred by an export restriction extends to every other good in the economy is counter-intuitive, the equivalence result 'says nothing about the expected effects of these (equivalent) policies on trade volumes relative to an alternative of no intervention'.[100] In particular, this equivalence does not exclude the possibility that an export restriction on logs would result in a large expansion of lumber exports. In this connection, the specificity requirement of a countervailing duty has not been met. In fact, the specificity requirement was also challenged

[96] *US – Export Restraints*, para. 8.36.
[97] *Canada – Softwood Lumber*, F57 FR 22570, at 22605.
[98] Benitah, *The Law of Subsidies under the GATT/WTO System* (n. 55) 221.
[99] Janow and Staiger, 'US – Export Restraints United States – Measures Treating Export Restraints as Subsidies' (n. 82) 230 (emphasis added).
[100] Ibid. 232.

by the Canadian government and producers in the US–Canada Binational Panel, which in the end agreed with the Canadian government and producers.

2.2.4 Anti-Dumping Measures as Response to Export Restrictions

As noted previously, export restrictions arguably constitute subsidies and may result in anti-subsidy investigations. Moreover, in conjunction with, or independent of, anti-subsidy investigations, trade nations may initiate anti-dumping investigations against downstream producers of a given product subject to export restrictions. The critical issue here is whether the investigating country is entitled to construct the normal value based on information and price in third countries relying on, in particular, Article VI:1(b)(ii) and *Ad* Article VI of the GATT 1994, as the market price in the exporting country is regulated or distorted. Such controversies have surfaced before the General Court of the EU and in the WTO dispute settlement mechanism.

In *Acron*,[101] the General Court of the EU was asked to rule on the legality of anti-dumping measures against Russian ammonium nitrate, a product made mainly from natural gas. As natural gas is heavily regulated in Russia, notably through dual pricing and export taxes, the Council found that the cost of production was artificially low and, relying on Article 2(5) of the Council Regulation (EC) 384/96 (now, 1225/2009, Basic Regulation), it decided to adjust the price after considering prices in representative markets.[102] While the applicants did not dispute the fact that natural gas constituted a significant proportion of the production cost and its price was regulated in Russia, they contended that Article 2(5) of the Council Regulation was inconsistent with the Anti-Dumping Agreement (the ADA), and the construction of normal value based on information or price in third countries is only applicable to a list of enumerated non-market economies. The General Court found in favour of the Council, ruling that the price adjustment for constructing the normal value was based on Article 2(5) of the Basic Regulation instead of Article 2(7), which regulates normal value from non-market economies.[103] Moreover, given that the ADA does not address the

[101] Case T-235/08, *Acron OAO and Dorogobuzh OAO* v. *Council of the European Union* Judgment of the General Court (Eighth Chamber), 7 February 2013, EU:T:2013:65.
[102] *Acron*, para. 36.
[103] *Acron*, paras. 43–51.

unreliability or unrepresentativeness of domestic prices as Article 2(5) of the Basic Regulation does, the General Court found no support from WTO law to support the applicants' argument.[104]

In *Unitec Bio SA*,[105] the General Court of the EU was again called on to address a similar issue, namely, the legality of an Implementing Regulation imposing first provisional and finally definite anti-dumping duties against Argentinian (and Indonesian) biodiesel producers,[106] which also resulted in *EU–Biodiesel (Argentina)*[107] in the WTO forum. *Unitec Bio SA* resulted from parallel anti-dumping and anti-subsidy (subsequently terminated) investigations against Argentinian biodiesel, with the root cause being Argentina's Differential Export Tax (DET) system on two main raw materials for producing biodiesel, soya and soybean. In the Implementing Regulation, the Council, citing *Acron*, maintained that the domestic prices of raw materials used for biodiesel were artificially lower than international prices due to DET, and therefore the records kept by the producers under investigation did not reasonably reflect the cost of production.[108] Interestingly, these arguments failed to persuade the General Court. According to the General Court, Article 2(5) of the Basic Regulation permits factoring costs of production other than the exporting country due to market distortion in that country and such market distortion is not limited to direct regulation. However, it does not mean 'any measure of the public authorities of the exporting State which could have an influence on the prices of the main raw materials and, as a result, on the price of the product in question, may be the source of a distortion that permits, in the context of the calculation of the normal value of the like product, the prices included in the records of the party under investigation to be disregarded'.[109] Only when the measure causes *appreciable* distortion of the prices of those raw materials can the investigating authorities disregard the records of the producers under

[104] *Acron*, paras. 67–70.

[105] Case T-111/14, *Unitec Bio SA* v. *Council of the European Union*, Judgment of the General Court (Ninth Chamber) of 15 September 2016, ECLI:EU:T:2016:505.

[106] Council Implementing Regulation (EU) No 1194/2013 of 19 November 2013 imposing a definitive anti-dumping duty and collecting definitively the provisional duty imposed on imports of biodiesel originating in Argentina and Indonesia, OJ L 315/2, 26 December 2013.

[107] Panel Report, *European Union – Anti-Dumping Measures on Biodiesel from Argentina*, WT/DS473/R and Add.1, adopted 26 October 2016, as modified by Appellate Body Report WT/DS473/AB/R, DSR 2016:VI, p. 3077.

[108] Council Implementing Regulation (EU) No 1194/2013, recital 38.

[109] *Unitec Bio SA*, para. 55.

investigation. Otherwise, it would *disproportionately* impair the principle that those records are the prime source of information for constructing normal value.[110]

The EU's practice was also criticised by the WTO panel, as Argentina also launched a complaint in the WTO forum. In *EU–Biodiesel (Argentina)*, Argentina contended that export taxes on raw materials are not costs associated with production of biodiesel, and the EU's derogation from principles of calculating normal value by failing to consider records kept by the producers under investigation was inconsistent with Article 2.2.1.1 of the ADA.[111] As the Panel ruled, the clause 'reasonably reflect the costs associated with the production and sale of the product under consideration' under Article 2.2.1.1 of the ADA is to establish costs reported in the producers/exporters' records that reasonably reflect costs *actually* incurred, rather than 'some hypothetical costs that might have been incurred under a different set of conditions or circumstances and which the investigating authority considers more 'reasonable' than the costs actually incurred'.[112]

Therefore, the critical issue in referring to anti-dumping measures to address price distortion arising from export restrictions lies in the method for calculating or constructing the normal value. Whereas it is undisputed that restrictions may suppress domestic prices that give advantage to downstream producers, such an advantage does not necessarily enable the investigating authority to reject the costs of production in the records of producers under investigation, as the EU did in the aforementioned cases. Whereas the EU tried to argue before the Panel that dumping arose not only from producers'/exporters' voluntary pricing behaviour but also from governments measures,[113] such an argument eventually failed given the limited exception for the investigating authorities to disregard domestic costs and prices for determining the normal value, namely the second *Ad* Article to Article VI of the GATT 1994 and some accession protocol provisions.[114] In brief, as long as the records of producers reasonably reflect costs associated with the production and sale of the product, they must be relied on for the calculation or construction of normal value. As a consequence, referring

[110] *Unitec Bio SA*, para. 56.
[111] Panel Report on *EU–Biodiesel (Argentina)*, paras. 7.183–184.
[112] Panel Report on *EU–Biodiesel (Argentina)*, paras. 7.242.
[113] Panel Report on *EU–Biodiesel (Argentina)*, para. 7.239.
[114] Panel Report on *EU–Biodiesel (Argentina)*, para. 7.241.

anti-dumping measures to address export restriction is of limited help since the price advantage arising from export restrictions may not be captured under this method.

2.2.5 Voluntary Export Restraints, Orderly Marketing Arrangements or Any Other Similar Measures

In the later years of the GATT era, the widespread use of VERs and orderly marketing arrangements (the OMAs), generally referred to altogether as grey-area measures due to their ambiguous legal status in the GATT, was one of the most contested phenomena. Grey-area measures are restrictive measures affording protection to domestic industry against international competition by limiting the quantity of imports through the implicit or explicit consent of the countries with which the trade is primarily affected.[115] The pervasion of grey-area measures was institutional in that the GATT rules prohibit a contracting party only from unilaterally raising tariffs or imposing quantitative restrictions.[116] Given that grey-area measures escaped the discipline of the GATT rules, they turned out to be a preferable instrument to limit the quantity of imports in response to the protectionist pressure of domestic industry. The major reason why the exporting country is willing to 'voluntarily' restrain its exports to the importing countries stems from the fear of suffering from more severe penalties, most likely, trade defence measures or other congressional legislation from the importing country. However, the exporting country may also benefit from grey-area measures resulting from the segmentation of the market of importing countries by import or export cartels and from the shift of the quota-rent from the government of the importing country to the government of the exporting country or the exporting industries themselves.[117]

As Richard Pomfret, using both perfect competition and imperfect competition models, explains, exporting industries and domestic industries may reap the benefits arising from VERs. In the perfect competition model with no uncertainty, a VER has the same effect as a tariff on

[115] Frank Wolfram, 'Agreeement on Safeguard, Article 11 SA' in Rüdiger Wolfrum, Peter-Tobias Stoll and Michael Koebele (eds), *WTO-Trade Remedies* (Martinus Nijhoff Publishers 2008) 378.

[116] Pomfret, 'The Economics of Voluntary Export Restraint Agreements' (n. 2) 199.

[117] Alan Sykes, *The WTO Agreement on Safeguards: A Commentary* (Oxford University Press 2006) 23.

domestic price and output. Nonetheless, the revenue of a tariff accrues to the importing countries while the quota rent arising from the VER goes to the government of the reporting country or exporting industries. The transfer of quota rent helps to explain the popularity of VERs. Under the imperfect competition model, export industries prefer a VER not only to trade barriers but also to free trade, as the pre-commitments of suppliers may be able to reap monopoly benefit in the importing country. In other words, exporting industries prefer a VER to free trade because they can have their share of monopoly rent in the importing country at the expense of consumers in that country.[118]

Although the exporting country and exporting industries may voluntarily restrict their exports into importing countries, such grey-area measures are not without cost. The most noticeable cost is the erosion of consumer plus. Further, the cost per job saved through grey-area measures may be significantly higher than the average wages earned by typical workers in those industries. In broader terms, grey-area measures protect economically inefficient industries, which would be otherwise uncompetitive without such restrictive measures. Through an arbitrary lessening of the competition level, grey-area measures lead to inefficient international division of labour and allocation of resources.[119] Legally, grey-area measures may also seriously impede the domestic discipline of competition law, in particular under the scenario of imperfect competition; from the perspective of international trade law, such grey-area measures also undermine the multilateral nature of the GATT system since they run afoul of the fundamental non-discrimination principle due to their selective nature.[120] The complexity circling grey-area measures finally prompted negotiators in the Uruguay Round, mostly from developing countries, to bring them into the purview of the WTO agreements, or precisely, Article 11 of the ASG, which dictates that WTO members eliminate these measures and refrain from imposing new ones.[121]

118 Pomfret, 'The Economics of Voluntary Export Restraint Agreements' (n. 2) 200–204.

119 Wolfram, 'Agreeement on Safeguard, Article 11 SA' (n. 115) 378.

120 Sykes, *The WTO Agreement on Safeguards: A Commentary* (n. 117) 22; Wolfram, 'Agreeement on Safeguard, Article 11 SA' (n. 115) 378–379; R. Pomfret, 'The Economics of Voluntary Export Restraint Agreements' (1989) 3 *Journal of Economic Surveys* 199(n. 2) 204–207; Lochmann, 'The Japanese Voluntary Restraint on Automobile Exports: An Abandonment of the Free Trade Principles of the GATT and the Free Market Principles of United States Antitrust Laws'(n. 1) 211.

121 Sykes, *The WTO Agreement on Safeguards: A Commentary* (n. 117) 25–26.

The ASG does not employ the term 'grey-area measures'; rather, it chooses to use the general term 'certain measures'. The ASG, in Article 11, regulates these certain (grey-area) measures in three steps. First, it clarifies the scope of certain measures to be prohibited or eliminated. Second, it sets out a schedule for WTO members to phase out existing grey-area measures. Third, it addresses the role of the government of a member in encouraging or supporting the adoption or maintenance of grey-area measures by non-governmental entities. From the outset, the ASG in Article 11(1)(a) prohibits a WTO member from taking or seeking any emergency action under Article XIX of the GATT 1994 unless the action complies with the requirement of that article and is applied in accordance with the ASG. The objective of this provision is to reiterate the determination of the negotiators to discipline all emergency actions and bring them into the scrutiny of Article XIX of the GATT 1994 and the ASG. The ASG in Article 11(1)(b) then dictates that a WTO member does not 'seek, take or maintain any voluntary export restraints, orderly marketing arrangements or any other similar measures on the export or the import side'.[122] Three elements are put forward in this provision: VERs, OMAs and any other similar measures.

According to the Dictionary of Trade Policy Terms, a VER (or voluntary restraint arrangement, VRA) refers to '[a] bilateral arrangement whereby an exporting country (government or industry) agrees to reduce or restrict exports so that the importing country does not have to use quotas, raise tariffs or impose other import controls'.[123] An OMA means 'a bilateral arrangement whereby an exporting country (government or industry) agrees to reduce or restrict exports without the importing country having to make use of quotas, tariffs or other import controls'.[124] These two definitions seem not to reveal a great difference between a VER and an OMA. Both measures share the same feature that an exporting country (government or industry) agrees to restrict exports so that the importing country will not resort to import control measures.

By contrast, Frank Wolfram distinguishes between VERs and OMVs by drawing the line at the participation of the importing country. Specifically, VERs refer to measures which are imposed by the exporting country itself, restricting exports and affording protection to a domestic industry in the importing country against foreign competition. By

[122] ASG, Art. 11(1)(b).
[123] Goode (ed), *Dictionary of Trade Policy Terms* 397.
[124] Ibid. 275.

contrast, OMAs refer to international arrangements between two or more countries in which those countries concerned agree to limit the quantity of imports or exports to offer protection to domestic industries from international competition.[125] This distinction may find support in the second sentence of Article 11(1)(b), which states that 'these [measures] include actions taken by a single Member as well as actions under agreements, arrangements and understandings entered into by two or more Members'. It is thus clear that all unilateral or bilateral (or even plurilateral) actions limiting the quantity of imports equally fall into the scope of this provision.

It nonetheless deserves further clarification of the blanket clause of 'any other similar measures on the export or the import side'. This clause refers to other measures having the same trade-limiting effects analogous to those of VERs and OMAs, namely, being able to 'restrict export or imports and to afford protection to a domestic industry in an importing country against foreign competition'.[126] This interpretation may also find support from the illustrative and non-exclusive list in footnote 4, which reads in part, '"any of which afford protection'. As footnote 4 provides, '[e]xamples of similar measures include export moderation, export-price or import-price monitoring systems, export or import surveillance, compulsory import cartels and discretionary export or import licensing schemes, any of which afford protection'.[127] These similar measures cover the import and export sides; price measures; and other monitoring, surveillance and licensing procedures. From the perspective of the importing country, it even covers compulsory import cartels. Thus, the key element here is to afford protection in a similar manner to VERs and OMAs, namely, control of export quantity.

Article 11(2) then sets out the schedule for phasing out all those grey-area measures. Within 180 days of the entry into force of the WTO Agreement, any WTO member still maintaining grey-area measures is required to present a schedule for phasing out these measures. All outstanding grey-area measures have to be phased out before 31 December 1998. Exceptions to this deadline can only be sought when the specific criteria are met. First, the members concerned have to mutually agree on the maintenance of grey-area measures after 31 December 1998. Second, the intended maintenance has to be notified

[125] Wolfram, 'Agreeement on Safeguard, Article 11 SA' (n. 115) 381.
[126] Ibid (n. 115) 382.
[127] Footnote 4 to Article 11 of the ASG.

to the Committee on Safeguards. Third, it has to be reviewed and accepted by the Committee on Safeguards.[128]

Finally, Article 11(3) extends coverage to regulate the activities of non-governmental entities. This is actually an area subject to international competition law rather than traditional international trade law. Since the WTO agreements only binds national governments, only measures of governments or public bodies are subject to WTO control. An industry-to-industry agreement aiming to limit the quantity of imports and exports does not fall under the purview of Article 11 of the ASG. However, Article 11(3) obligates a WTO member not to encourage or support the adoption or maintenance by public and private enterprises of non-governmental measures equivalent to those referred to in Article 11 (1). Therefore, while unilateral actions or agreements between non-governmental entities are outside the realm of the ASG, it does prohibit the participation of governments by encouragement or support.

With the explicit prohibition of VERs under Article 11 of the ASG, VERs faded in importance for about two decades but again caught the attention of academics and policy makers after US President Donald Trump was sworn into office in 2017. One of the most controversial trade measures adopted by the Trump Administration has been the launch of Section 232 investigations against steel and aluminium products and automobile parts on the grounds of national security concerns. As President Trump declared, 'steel articles [and automobiles and certain automobile parts] are being imported into the United States in such quantities and under such circumstances as to threaten to impair the national security of the United States'.[129] President Trump, referring to the opinion of the Secretary of Commerce, declared that imports of steel (and automobiles and certain automobile parts) and global excess production capacity of steel are weakening the US economy and resulting in the closure of domestic production facilities, thus shrinking the ability of the United States to meet national security production requirements in times of national emergency.[130] In view of the close relationship between economic welfare and national security, and the risk that the United

[128] Wolfram, 'Agreeement on Safeguard, Article 11 SA' (n. 115) 384.

[129] Executive Office of the President. Proclamation 9705 of March 8, 2018, Adjusting Imports of Steel into the United States, 28 August 2020, 83 Federal Register 11625, para. 2; see also Executive Office of the President. Proclamation 9888 of 17 May, 2019, Adjusting Imports of Automobiles and Automobile Parts into the United States, 17 May 2019, 84 Federal Register 23433, para. 8.

[130] Ibid.

States may not be able to meet demands for national defence and critical industry in a national emergency, 'the present quantities and circumstances of steel articles imports threaten to impair the national security as defined in section 232 of the Trade Expansion Act of 1962, as amended'.[131] President Donald Trump thus decided that 'under current circumstances, this tariff is necessary and appropriate to address the threat that imports of steel articles pose to the national security'.[132]

With the potential threat of punitive tariffs, third countries were forced to enter into negotiations with the United States. Interestingly, one of the responses to the tariffs and end products of the negotiations is the outdated and WTO-incompatible VERs. South Korea,[133] Argentina[134] and Brazil[135] are reported to have agreed to limit steel exports to the United States with a view to avoiding tariffs arising from Section 232 investigations. Such moves negate the efforts of the Uruguay Round negotiations in disciplining grey-area measures and bring VERs into the realm of WTO agreements.

[131] Ibid. see also Executive Office of the President. Proclamation 9888 of May 17, 2019 Adjusting Imports of Automobiles and Automobile Parts into the United States, 17 May 2019, 84 Federal Register 23433, para. 8 [The Secretary found that these imports are 'weakening our internal economy' and that '[t]he contraction of the American-owned automotive industry, if continued, will significantly impede the United States' ability to develop technologically advanced products that are essential to our ability to maintain technological superiority to meet defense requirements and cost effective global power projection'.]

[132] Executive Office of the President. Proclamation 9705 of March 8, 2018, Adjusting Imports of Steel into the United States, 28 August 2020, 83 Federal Register 11625, para. 8; see also Executive Office of the President. Proclamation 9888 of May 17, 2019 Adjusting Imports of Automobiles and Automobile Parts into the United States, 17 May 2019, 84 Federal Register 23433, para. 15(1) [(1) The Trade Representative, in consultation with the Secretary, the Secretary of the Treasury and any other senior executive branch officials the Trade Representative deems appropriate, shall pursue negotiation of agreements contemplated in 19 U.S.C. 1862(c)(3)(A)(i) to address the threatened impairment of national security with respect to imported automobiles and certain automobile parts from the European Union, Japan and any other country the Trade Representative deems appropriate.]

[133] Hyunjoo Jin and Joyce Lee, 'U.S., South Korea revise trade deal, Korea steel faces quotas', *Reuters*, 26 March 2018, available at www.reuters.com/article/us-southkorea-trade-usa/u-s-south-korea-revise-trade-deal-korean-steel-faces-quota-idUSKBN1H206V.

[134] Fastmarkets, 'Argentina agrees to steel export quota following US' Section 232 investigation', 2 May 2018, available at www.metalbulletin.com/Article/3804455/Argentina-agrees-to-steel-export-quota-following-US-Section-232-investigation.html.

[135] Bruno Federowski and Albert Alerigi, 'U.S. cuts off Brazil tariff talks, adopts steel import quotas', *Reuters*, 2 May 2018, available at www.reuters.com/article/us-usa-trade-brazil/us-cuts-off-brazil-tariff-talks-adopts-steel-import-quotas-idUSKBN1I31ZD.

2.3 Bilateral Rule-Making through Accession Negotiations and Its Consequences

Rule-making with a view to filling the legal vacuum in WTO law with regards to export restrictions has been carried out mainly through accession negotiations. This is particularly true when the acceding country is rich in natural resources, China and Russia being the prime examples. Therefore, bilateral rule-making constitutes a major feature of the regulation of export restrictions. With a view to capturing the characteristics of such a bilateral rule-making approach and its impact on the existing multilateral trading regime, this section will start with a brief introduction to accession negotiation processes and take China and Russia as examples to illustrate the consequences arising from this process.

During the GATT era, the application of the Anti-Dumping Code to a limited number of contracting parties has been termed 'fragmentation' of rights and obligations of the GATT contracting parties.[136] In contrast, the Single Undertaking approach embraced in the Uruguay Round negotiations that led to the adoption of the WTO Agreement is seen as a cure. The virtue of the Single Undertaking approach is that members, through a give-and-take mechanism, make concessions during negotiation processes to reach a good balance of rights and obligations. More importantly, it establishes a set of multilateral trading rules binding on all WTO members, which contributes to security and predictability in the multilateral trading system. The WTO system is thus widely regarded as a rule-based regime.

Nonetheless, such give-and-take bargaining and collective rule-making is not present during accession processes. While the WTO agreements puts forward a set of detailed trade rules, WTO law governing accession procedures remains largely the same as its predecessor. The criterion of 'terms to be agreed' remains the key element for a new member to accede to this organisation; nonetheless, this criterion is still left undefined in the WTO Agreement. As a result, the GATT practices on accession negotiations have great influence in shaping those in the WTO.[137] As the late

[136] Alexander Polouektov, 'Non-Market Economy Issues in the WTO Anti-Dumping Law and Accession Negotiations: Revival of a Two-tier Membership' (2002) 36 *Journal of World Trade* 1, 2.

[137] John H. Jackson, William J. Davey and Alan O. Sykes Jr., *Legal Problems of International Economic Relation: Case, Materials and Texts on the National and International Regulation of Transnational Economic Regulations* (4th ed., West Group 2002) 234.

John Jackson wrote in the GATT context, the willingness to negotiate tariff concessions with the existing contracting parties, known as 'negotiating the ticket of admission', was essential to obtain enough votes to accede to the Agreement.[138] Thus, an acceding country would have to conduct bilateral negotiations with interested WTO members on market access with a view to obtaining its ticket of admission to the club. Negotiation processes are seen as being dominated by power politics rather than rule-based; legalisation of international trade relations has not been seen in these regards.[139] In addition to bilateral negotiations, multilateral negotiations would be conducted under the auspices of the Working Party established on receipt of an application for accession. The objective of multilateral negotiations is to examine the trading regulatory regimes of the acceding countries and ensure their compatibility with WTO law.[140] The Working Party is also mandated to draft an accession protocol, which is to be adopted by the Ministerial Conference.

During accession negotiations, the obligation to make market access concessions is incumbent only on the acceding country in exchange for its ticket of admission. The acceding country cannot demand reciprocal concessions from interested WTO members. Moreover, a new acceding country is often requested to commit more than the average level of market access that existent WTO members assume.[141] This raises concerns about inequality of rights and obligations of WTO members, and poses challenges to the ambition of the WTO to universally integrate all trading nations into this regime.[142] In addition to market access commitments, a new acceding country may be obliged to assume legal obligations which are specially designed for and applied only to it. These particular legal obligations go beyond the coverage of the WTO agreements and are generally referred to as WTO-plus obligations. These WTO-plus obligations pose great challenges to the interpretative exercise

[138] John H. Jackson, *The World Trading System: Law and Policy of International Economic Relations* (The MIT Press 1994) 45.

[139] Hardeep Basra, 'Increased Legalization or Politicalization? A Comparison of Accession under the GATT and WTO' (2012) 46 *Journal of World Trade* 937, 937–938.

[140] Ibid. 952. See also Anna Lanoszka, 'The World Trade Organization Accession Process: Negotiating Participation in a Globalizing Economy' (2001) 35 *Journal of World Trade* 575.

[141] Basra, 'Increased Legalization or Politicalization? A Comparison of Accession under the GATT and WTO', n. 139, at 938.

[142] Roman Grynberg and Roy Mickey Joy, 'The Accession of Vanuatu to the WTO: Lessons for the Multilateral Trading System' (2000) 34 *Journal of World Trade* 159, 159–174.

of the WTO panel and Appellate Body and may undermine the coherence of WTO law.[143]

WTO-plus obligations resulting from bilateral rule-making during accession negotiations may be written into the Working Party Report, which will then be incorporated into the Accession Protocol. They may also be put into black letter explicitly in the Accession Protocol itself, as in the case of China's Accession Protocol. These two legal drafting techniques yield different results in interpreting the relationship between WTO-plus obligations and existent WTO agreements. Among WTO-plus obligations, export restrictions are one of the highlights. Such examples can be seen in the cases of China, Saudi Arabia, Vietnam, Ukraine and Russia. Next, I will focus on China's Accession Protocol and Russia's Working Party Report, as they are the most important newly acceded members since the establishment of the WTO. In addition, their accession documents cover the most comprehensive commitments and obligations relating to export restrictions and represent two different approaches in rule-making on export restrictions. Furthermore, China is the respondent country of two important cases: *China – Raw Materials* and *China – Rare Earths*, and Russia tried to avoid the same mistake China made during the negotiation process and thus incorporated all the commitments into the Working Party Report. Finally, they all belong to the camp of socialist countries with which the Coordinating Committee for Multilateral Export Controls (COCOM) aimed to govern trade relations.

2.3.1 *Legal Obligations on Export Restrictions in Accession Protocols*

Unlike other accession protocols, including that of Russia, China's Accession Protocol is not a standardised form of instrument but puts

143 See, e.g., Julia Yin Qin, '"WTO-plus" Obligations and Their Implications for the World Trade Organization Legal System – An Appraisal of the China Accession Protocol' (2003) 37 *Journal of World Trade* 483, 483–522; Julia Yin Qin, 'The Challenge of Interpreting WTO-Plus Provisions' (2010) 44 *Journal of World Trade* 127, 127–172. An even more difficult interpretative issue relates to paragraph 242 of China's Working Party Report, which regulates the special safeguard mechanism against Chinese textile products. See, Dongli Huang, 'Legal Interpretation of Paragraph 242 of the Report of the Working Party on the Accession of China under the World Trade Organization Legal Framework' (2006) 40 *Journal of World Trade* 137, 137–152. Thomas Weishing Huang, 'The Gathering Storm of Antidumping Enforcement in China' (2002) 36 *Journal of World Trade* 255, 255–283.

forward a set of detailed rules governing China's rights and obligations under the WTO.[144] Among these rules are WTO-plus obligations regulating export restrictions with a view to providing a general obligation to meet the compelling regulatory demand in view of the vast number of natural resources vested in China. Therefore, China's Accession Protocol is the best, and perhaps the only, example to illustrate bilateral rule-making through explicit prescription in an accession protocol in the WTO age. Specifically, it touches on export taxes and export licensing.

2.3.1.1 Export Duties

China's Accession Protocol, at Paragraph 11, regulates taxes and charges levied on imports and exports. Specifically, Paragraph 11.3 addresses export taxes, providing that 'China shall eliminate all taxes and charges applied to exports unless specifically provided for in Annex 6 of this Protocol or applied in conformity with the provisions of Article VIII of the GATT 1994'.[145] In accordance with this provision, China is obligated to eliminate all export duties except as provided in Annex 6 of the accession protocol or in accordance with Article VIII of the GATT 1994.[146] This provision has become one of the most debated issues in *China – Raw Materials*.

2.3.1.2 Export Licensing

China's Accession Protocol, at Paragraph 8, regulates import and export licensing, giving it wider scope than the WTO agreements, which focus mainly on import licensing. China's Accession Protocol puts forward two obligations, transparency and Most-Favoured-Nation Treatment. The transparency obligation relates to publication and notification requirements. China is obliged to publish in the official journal the names of the organisations in charge of imports or exports authorisation; procedures

[144] Qin, '"WTO-plus" Obligations and Their Implications for the World Trade Organization Legal System – An Appraisal of the China Accession Protocol', 483; see also Steve Charnovitz, 'Mapping the Law of WTO Accession' in Merit E. Janow, Victoria Donaldson and Alan Yanovich (eds), *The WTO: Governance, Dispute Settlement & Developing Countries* (Juris Publishing 2008) 855–920.

[145] China's Accession Protocol, Article 11.3.

[146] Comparing to China's Accession Protocol, Russia's commitment to eliminate or reduce export taxes is through binding its export taxes in its Schedule of Concessions and Commitments on Goods, which then constitutes part of the Schedule of Concessions and Commitments annexed to GATT 1994. This difference in legislative techniques gives rise to different interpretation approaches. The pertinent point is the applicability of Article XX of the GATT 1994.

and criteria for authorisation; a list of products subject to tendering procedures; and a list of products subject to export restrictions and prohibitions. Copies of these submissions should also be posted to the WTO.[147] Regarding Most-Favoured-Nation Treatment, China's Accession Protocol provides concrete and specific regulation on the application of Most-Favoured-Nation Treatment to the distribution of export licenses and quotas. Foreign individuals and enterprises and foreign-funded enterprises are to be provided 'treatment no less favourable than that accorded to other individuals and enterprises'.[148]

2.3.1.3 Legal Status of Obligations in Accession Protocol

These obligations on export restrictions, according to Paragraph 1.2 of China's Accession Protocol, constitute an integral part of the WTO Agreement. Therefore, through this 'integration clause' the accession protocol would become an integral part of the WTO Agreement. Nonetheless, this thesis is not without controversy. The thorny issue is how an accession protocol constitutes an integral part of the WTO Agreement. Has the 'integration clause' deprived the accession protocol of its bilateral nature?

As Julia Ya Qin writes, the accession protocol is technically a bilateral agreement between the WTO and the acceding country. The WTO, through its internal decision-making procedure, approves the protocol at the Ministerial Conference. This bilateral agreement will then bind both the WTO and the acceding country.[149] By virtue of this 'integration clause', the accession protocol constitutes an integral part of the WTO Agreement, a multilateral agreement among WTO members. Doubts thus arise as to how a bilateral agreement between the WTO and the acceding country becomes a multilateral agreement among all WTO members. According to Qin, the 'integration clause' adds a multilateral character to the accession protocol but does not diminish its bilateral nature.[150] However, this claim does not explain how it happens. The fact that all WTO members are bound by the accession protocol, as a result of approval at the Ministerial Conference or Council Meeting, does not mean that the accession protocol is a multilateral agreement. A multilateral agreement comes into being as a result of a number of

147 China's Accession Protocol, Art. 8.1(a).
148 China's Accession Protocol, Art. 8.2.
149 Qin, 'The Challenge of Interpreting WTO-Plus' Provisions', n. 143, at 132.
150 Ibid. 133.

states or international organisations agreeing to be bound by it. Such collective consent to a single legal instrument is absent in the conclusion of the accession protocol.

In contrast, Claus-Dieter Ehlermann and Lothar Ehring see the accession protocol as an amendment to the WTO Agreement, as the Agreement is modified to include additional subjects of international law. According to them, the accession protocol amends the WTO Agreement by becoming an integral part of it.[151] Admittedly, the accession protocol does modify the WTO Agreement in a sense that it adds new subjects of international law to the Agreement. However, as they acknowledge, the accession protocol is an agreement between the new member and the WTO, but not an agreement between the new member and old members. Thus, this amendment approach does not offer a convincing answer as to how the accession protocol becomes an integral part of the WTO Agreement. A contrast can be drawn between the accession protocol and the Protocol Amending the TRIPS Agreement, which has to go through domestic ratification procedures and then deposit an 'instrument of acceptance' with the Director General. The accession protocol does not share the same characteristics.

Based on Ehlermann and Ehring's analysis, Steve Charnovitz further argues that an accession protocol is a 'legal instrument that modifies the WTO Agreement without being an actual amendment to it'.[152] Nonetheless, this answer is not satisfactory either since it also fails to explain what the accession protocol is. With regards to the 'integration clause', Charnovitz doubts whether an accession protocol can transform itself into an integral part of the WTO Agreement with the inclusion of such an 'integration clause'. He refers to this claim as *petito principi* fallacy. Using a hypothetical example of an agreement concluded by the WTO and the International Labour Organization with the same 'integration clause', he questions the legality of such an agreement being an integral part of the WTO Agreement.[153] In referring to Article XV:6 of the GATT 1994, which provides that 'any special exchange agreement entered into by a contracting party under this paragraph shall thereupon

[151] Claus-Dieter Ehlermann and Lothar Ehrin, 'Decision-Making in the World Trade Organization: Is the Consensus Practice of the World Trade Organization Adequate for Making, Revising and Implementing Rules on International Trade?' (2005) 8 *Journal of International Economic Law* 51, 57.

[152] Charnovitz, 'Mapping the Law of WTO Accession', n. 144, at 50.

[153] Ibid., n. 144, at 42–43.

become part of its obligations under this Agreement',[154] he argues that a similar provision should be included in Article XII of the WTO Agreement. In doing so, the WTO Agreement provides a legal basis for the accession protocol to be integrated into it.[155]

Another interesting attempt made by Mitali Tyagi is to characterise the accession protocol, insofar as it deviates from existent WTO rules, as impermissible reservation 'because they are "unilateral" and have the legal effect of modifying or excluding the operation of provisions of the WTO Agreement'.[156] What Tyagi aims to pursue is an argument that the provisions in the accession protocol, which impose additional obligations but limit the rights of the acceding country, are impermissible but severable reservations. Given that these impermissible reservations are separable from other obligations in the accession protocol, judiciary may have to invalidate these WTO-plus obligations with a view to preserving the coherence of WTO law, while keeping the accession protocol intact.[157] This argument echoes what Antonio Parenti wrote in 2000. He first notes that any alteration to the WTO obligations of a member can be made only through the conditions explicitly set out in the WTO Agreement, which comprise two possible means: specific and general. The specific ways for a member to deviate from its WTO obligations include raising its tariff level in case of balance of payments difficulties, as foreseen in Articles XII and XVIII of the GATT 1994. If the alteration of a member's WTO obligations is of a general nature, it amounts to amendment of the WTO agreements, which has to be governed by Article X of the WTO Agreement. Based on this reasoning, he maintains

> An alteration occurring in case of an accession would therefore not be consistent with the WTO rules. This could not be rectified by even the eventual unanimous voting on the terms of accession, because such an alteration would have occurred without the respect of the rules of the WTO.

However, this passage was written in 2000, prior to the 2002 Doha Ministerial Conference when China acceded to the WTO. The subsequent developments prove that more and more alterations of WTO rules are to be included in the accession protocols (and/or Working Party Reports).

[154] GATT 1994, Art. XV:6.

[155] Charnovitz, 'Mapping the Law of WTO Accession', n. 144, at 46.

[156] Mitali Tyagi, 'Flesh on a Legal Fiction: Early Practice in the WTO on Accesion Protocols' (2012) 15 *Journal of International Economic Law* 391, 436.

[157] Ibid. 416–418.

While scholars have divergent views on the nature of accession protocols, the WTO judiciary seems to have little difficulty in exercising its jurisdiction over disputes relating to WTO-plus obligations and in confirming their enforceability. From *China – Auto Parts*,[158] when the WTO judiciary was first called on to rule on China's compliance with its commitments made in the Working Party Report, the Panel/Appellate Body assumed their enforceability since neither party to the dispute contested it.[159] The same reasoning is followed in *China – Raw Materials*, where the Panel notes

> In this dispute, as with previous disputes concerned with China's Accession Protocol, all parties agree that China's Accession Protocol forms an integral part of the WTO Agreement. Moreover, all parties agree that WTO Members can initiate WTO dispute settlement proceedings on the basis of a claim of violation of China's Accession Protocol. Finally, all parties agree that commitments included in the related Working Party Report, and incorporated into the Accession Protocol by cross-reference, are binding and enforceable through WTO dispute settlement proceedings.[160]

The WTO judiciary seems satisfied with the consent of parties and feels comfortable in exercising its jurisdiction on this foundation regardless of the fact that Appendix 1 to the DSU does not mention accession protocols. The WTO judiciary thus makes no further inquiry into the legal basis of its jurisdiction over WTO-plus obligations in accession protocols and Working Party Reports and their enforceability in the WTO dispute settlement mechanism. The WTO judiciary also fails to provide a clear explanation on the nature of the 'integration clause' and how it functions. While the jurisprudence of the WTO Panel/Appellate Body seems to be settled with regard to the enforceability of obligations under the accession protocols, the lack of a convincing explanation as to how the 'integration clause' functions prevents the accession protocol from being smoothly integrated into WTO law. What is embedded in the debate about the 'integration clause' is a fundamental issue of the relationship between the WTO Agreement and accession protocols, which

[158] Panel Reports on *China – Measures Affecting Imports of Automobile Parts (China – Auto Parts)*, WT/DS339/R / WT/DS340/R / WT/DS342/R / and Add.1 and Add.2, adopted 12 January 2009, upheld (WT/DS339/R) and as modified (WT/DS340/R / WT/DS342/R) by Appellate Body Reports WT/DS339/AB/R / WT/DS340/AB/R / WT/DS342/AB/R, DSR 2009:I, 119-DSR 2009:II, 625.

[159] *China – Auto Parts*, para. 7.740–741.

[160] Panel Report on *China – Raw Materials*, para. 7.114.

would in turn impact on the Panel/Appellate Body's reasoning on the applicability of the general exception to acceding members' obligations in accession protocols.

In *China – Rare Earths*, the Panel/Appellate Body had a chance to elaborate the relationship between the accession protocol and the WTO Agreement further. In *China – Rare Earths*, China argued that the general exception, as contained in Article XX of the GATT 1994, should be made available to its obligation to eliminate export duties as set out in Paragraph 11.3. One of the major arguments advanced by China is that 'Paragraph 11.3 of China's Accession Protocol has to be treated as an integral part of the GATT 1994.'[161] According to China, '[t]he legal effect of Paragraph 1.2 of China's Accession Protocol and Article XII:1 of the Marrakesh Agreement is to make China's Accession Protocol an integral part of the Marrakesh Agreement, and *also to make each of the Accession Protocol-specific provisions an integral part of one of the Multilateral Trade Agreements (e.g. GATT 1994) annexed to the Marrakesh Agreement*'.[162] Based on this argument, China then maintained that in order to determine which Multilateral Trade Agreements specific provisions of China's Accession Protocol are integral parts of, the Panel had to ascertain to which agreements such provisions are intrinsically related. However, these two arguments failed to impress the Panel.

The Panel first looked at the legal text of China's Accession Protocol, which in Paragraph 1.2 provides that '[t]his Protocol, which shall include the commitments referred to in paragraph 342 of the Working Party Report, shall be an integral part of the WTO Agreement'.[163] The Panel then pointed to the Preamble of China's Accession Protocol, where the term 'WTO Agreement' is used as an abbreviation for Marrakesh Agreement Establishing the World Trade Organization.[164] The Panel opined that the ordinary meaning of the words used in Paragraph 1.2 of China's Accession Protocol is that the Accession Protocol, in its entirety rather than individual provisions, constitutes an integral part of the Marrakesh Agreement. Individual provisions could have been made integral parts of specific Multilateral Trade Agreements; in fact, the drafters of the Accession Protocol, in Paragraph 1 of Part II, did so by making the schedules annexed to the Accession Protocol become 'the

[161] Panel Report on *China – Rare Earths*, para. 7.62.
[162] Panel Report on *China – Rare Earths*, para. 7.76 (emphasis added).
[163] Paragraph 1.2 of China's Accession Protocol.
[164] Panel Report on *China – Rare Earths*, para. 7.79.

Schedule of Concessions and Commitments annexed to the GATT 1994 and the Schedule of Specific Commitments annexed to the GATS relating to China'.[165] Moreover, whereas China strived to argue that export duties are intrinsically related to Article II and XI of the GATT 1994, such argument finds no solid basis in the legal text. Had the negotiators been aware of this intrinsic relationship and had they intended to make export duties an integral part of the subject matter falling into the purview of Article II of the GATT 1994, the drafters could have incorporated export duties into the Schedule of Concessions and Commitments. This is not what the drafters chose to do.[166]

Furthermore, prior Panel and Appellate Body reports do not support China's interpretation that the term 'the WTO Agreement' as used in Paragraph 1.2 of China's Accession Protocol refers to something other than the Marrakesh Agreement. Although this is the first occasion on which a panel or the Appellate Body has been called on to interpret the meaning of the terms 'the WTO Agreement' as used in Paragraph 1.2 of China's Accession Protocol, the Panel referred to prior cases relating to the interpretation and application of China's Accession Protocol and observed that, in these cases, 'panels and the Appellate Body have proceeded on the assumption that Paragraph 1.2 has the following functions: (i) to make the obligations of China's Accession Protocol (and specified provisions of the Working Party Report) enforceable under the DSU and (ii) to ensure that those obligations are interpreted in accordance with the "customary rules of interpretation of public international law" pursuant to Article 3.2 of the DSU'.[167] The Panel then opined that '[t]hese two functions are fully achieved in interpreting "the WTO Agreement" as a reference to the Marrakesh Agreement'.[168] As the Panel elaborated,

> This is because the Marrakesh Agreement is listed in Appendix 1 to the DSU as an agreement covered by the DSU, and hence that agreement, and any instrument that is an "integral part" of it, is enforceable under the DSU. For the same reason, the Marrakesh Agreement and any instrument that is an integral part thereof must be interpreted in accordance with the "customary rules of interpretation of public international law", pursuant to Article 3.2 of the DSU. The interpretation of Paragraph 1.2 advocated

165 Paragraph 1, Part II of China's Accession Protocol.

166 Panel Report on *China – Rare Earths*, paras. 7.84–88.

167 Panel Report on *China – Rare Earths*, para. 7.85.

168 Panel Report on *China – Rare Earths*, para. 7.85.

> by China in this dispute appears to depart significantly from the understanding of the legal effect of this provision, as reflected in prior panel and Appellate Body reports.

In response to China's argument that 'there is an intrinsic link between the provisions contained in post-1994 accession protocols on the one side and those enshrined in the WTO Agreement and the Multilateral Trade Agreements annexed thereto on the other',[169] the Panel held that Article XII:1 of the Marrakesh Agreement does not entail such interpretation of an intrinsic relationship. Besides, while China contended that 'its Accession Protocol merely serves to specify, including by means of "WTO-plus" commitments, China's obligations under the WTO Agreement and the multilateral trade agreements annexed thereto',[170] it is difficult to accept that a WTO-plus obligation, which by definition goes beyond the obligations contained in Multilateral Trade Agreements, merely serves to specify a member's obligations under Multilateral Trade Agreements.[171] Moreover, as the Panel noted, Article XI of the GATT 1994 relates to export restrictions other than duties, taxes or charges, which cannot be said to intrinsically relate to export duties as regulated by Paragraph 11.3 of China's Accession Protocol.[172]

In rejecting China's appeal that the Panel erred in concluding that 'the legal effect of the second sentence of Paragraph 1.2 is to make China's Accession Protocol, in its entirety, an "integral part" of the Marrakesh Agreement, and not that, in addition, the individual provisions thereof are also integral parts of Multilateral Trade Agreements annexed to the Marrakesh Agreement',[173] the Appellate Body held,

> In our view, Paragraph 1.2 of China's Accession Protocol serves to build a bridge between the package of Protocol provisions and the package of existing rights and obligations under the WTO legal framework. Nonetheless, neither obligations nor rights may be automatically transposed from one part of this legal framework into another. The fact that Paragraph 1.2 builds such a bridge is only the starting point, and does not in itself answer the questions of whether there is an objective link between an individual provision in China's Accession Protocol and existing obligations under the Marrakesh Agreements and the Multilateral Trade Agreements, and whether China may rely on an exception provided for

[169] Panel Report on *China – Rare Earths*, para. 7.90.
[170] Panel Report on *China – Rare Earths*, para. 7.90.
[171] Panel Report on *China – Rare Earths*, paras. 7.84–88.
[172] Panel Report on *China – Rare Earths*, para. 7.91.
[173] Appellate Body Report on *China – Rare Earths*, para. 5.12.

> in those agreements to justify a breach of such Protocol provision. Such questions must be answered through a thorough analysis of the relevant provisions on the basis of the customary rules of treaty interpretation and the circumstances of the dispute. The analysis must start with the text of the relevant provision in China's Accession Protocol and take into account its context, including that provided by the Protocol itself and by relevant provisions of the Accession Working Party Report, and by the agreements in the WTO legal framework. The analysis must also take into account the overall architecture of the WTO system as a single package of rights and obligations and any other relevant interpretative elements, and must be applied to the circumstances of each dispute, including the measure at issue and the nature of the alleged violation.[174]

In this passage, the Appellate Body provides further guidance on the relationship between the accession protocol on the one hand, and the Marrakesh Agreement and Multilateral Trade Agreements on the other. The role of the accession protocol is to bridge the rights and obligations in the accession protocol and those in the WTO legal framework. However, the Appellate Body was not persuaded by China's argument that its WTO-plus obligation is to be examined in conjunction with a WTO provision which a pertinent obligation is intrinsically related to, and held that there is no objective link between a provision of China's accession protocol and the provisions of the WTO agreements. Therefore, in appreciating the relationship between the obligations in accession protocols and provisions under the WTO legal framework, a thorough analysis must be conducted in accordance with the customary rules of interpretation of public international law.

2.3.2 Commitments on Export Restrictions in Working Party Reports

In contrast to a general obligation set out by accession protocols with a view to meeting a comprehensive regulatory demand on export restrictions, commitments may be sought to satisfy selective needs to ensure access to supplies of raw materials. As Baris Karapinar observes, in cases where commitments on export restrictions are present in the Working Party Report, they are provided under the title of export regulation, which normally comprises three pillars: export duties, quantitative restrictions and export licensing.[175] In these cases, the acceding country commits in the Working Parties Report to eliminate or reduce

[174] Appellate Body Report on *China – Rare Earths*, para. 5.74.
[175] Karapinar, 'Defining the Boundaries of Export Restrictions: A Case Law Analysis' 458.

export taxes; to lift export bans on specific products, such as rice and ferrous and non-ferrous scraps and metals; or to improve the transparency of their export licensing procedures. In practice, the commitments to eliminate or reduce export taxes or to lift export bans apply to limited products that are of interest to existent WTO members. Rare is a fully fledged obligation to eliminate export taxes or lift export bans with wide-ranging coverage. This piecemeal approach suggests that rule-making on export restrictions through requesting commitments in the Working Party Report by an acceding country serves the purpose of satisfying the selective strategic needs of existent WTO members to access to natural resources and raw materials in that acceding country.

So far, Russia's Working Party Report provides the most comprehensive commitments on export restrictions. In addition to the three pillars mentioned in the previous paragraph, namely, export duties, quantitative restrictions and export licensing, Russia's Working Party Report also addresses the administration of law on exports. What Russia committed in its Working Party Report may simply reaffirm that it would bring its regulatory regime on export restrictions in conformity with WTO law; it may also commit to imposing more stringent disciplines on export restrictions than existent WTO rules. The affected products relate mostly to gas, crude oil, precious metals and stones, and other raw materials such as timber. These commitments will be examined in greater detail next.

2.3.2.1 Export Duties

According to Russia, export duties are largely imposed on raw materials mainly for three purposes. In most cases, export duties are levied mainly for fiscal purposes; in very few cases, such as oil seeds, raw hides and skins, export duties are imposed with a view to maintaining greater availability of raw materials for domestic industry. Export taxes may also be used as an instrument to address environmental concerns, in the cases of ferrous and non-ferrous metal waste and scraps.[176] Finally, export duties imposed on raw timber are used as an industrial policy instrument to accelerate the restructuring of the Russian wood and paper industry and to pursue environmental goals.[177]

By contrast, some of the Working Party members were of the view that export duties serve as indirect subsidies to domestic downstream uses

[176] WT/ACC/RUS/70 (17 November 2011), para. 626.
[177] Ibid. para. 633.

and can distort international trade. Export duties may also divert investment and give producers located in Russia a cost-advantage.[178] Russian representatives and Working Party members disputed the legality and status of export duties. According to Russia, export duties are permitted under WTO rules and the request to establish a timetable for phasing out export duties is too excessive.[179] In fact, some Working Party members are also of the view that export duties are a legitimate tool for trade policy.[180]

In the end, four categories of commitments were made by Russia with regards to export duties: tariff concessions, measures having an equivalent effect to export duties, Most-Favoured-Nation Treatment in export duties and the allocation of export tariff rate quotas. To be more precise, Russia first confirmed that it would implement its tariff concessions and commitments on the date of its accession. Thus, subject to the terms, conditions or qualifications of its Schedule of Concessions and Commitments on Goods, products specified in part V of that Schedule will be exempted from export duties. Russia then went on to assure that these products would also not be subject to measures having an equivalent effect to export duties. Russia further committed that 'with respect to export duties and charges of any kind imposed on, or in connection with exportation, any advantage, favour, privilege or immunity granted by the Russian Federation to any product destined for any other country shall be accorded immediately and unconditionally to the like product destined for the territories of all other WTO Members'.[181] Finally, Russia committed that it would administer export tariff rate quotas in a manner consistent with the WTO agreements, in particular the GATT 1994 and the Import Licensing Agreement.[182]

The first and second commitments can be read in the context of Article II:1(a) and II:1(b) of the GATT. The inclusion of export taxes in Russia's Schedule of Concessions and Commitments on Goods further supports Roessler's argument that Article II applies to export duties.[183]

[178] Ibid. para. 629.
[179] Ibid. para. 635.
[180] Ibid. para. 630.
[181] Ibid. para. 638.
[182] Ibid.
[183] In fact, Roessler points out that already in the GATT era, Malaysia and Singapore had made commitments on export duties on tin ore and tin concentrates. Roessler, 'GATT and Access to Supplies', 35. Therefore, it may be subject to debate whether the commitment on export taxes is a WTO-plus commitment. On the one hand, such commitment

In recognition that Article II extends to export duties, the commitment not to impose measures having an equivalent effect to export duties can be read as a paraphrase of Article II:2(b) of the GATT 1994. Given that Article II:2(b) relates only to importation, this commitment complements Article II:2(b) in the exportation dimension.

The third commitment concerns the application of Most-Favoured-Nation Treatment, as enshrined in Article I of the GATT 1994. At first glance, Russia merely repeats its obligation under the WTO Agreement. However, it should be noted that Russia has concluded a Customs Union with Belarus, Kazakhstan, Tajikistan and the Kyrgyz Republic and a Free Trade Agreement with Ukraine; the commitment that any advantage or privilege accorded to products destined to *any other country* should be granted immediately and unconditionally to the like product destined for the territories of all other WTO members may lead to the following conclusion: even in the case of benefits accruing from a customs union or free trade agreement, the same benefits on or in connection with exportation should be granted to all WTO members.

The fourth commitment relating to the administration of law on exportation poses a tricky question. While the GATT 1994, notably, Article X, may relate to the administration of law on exportation, it is doubtful whether the Import Licensing Agreement directly addresses export tariff quotas. Therefore, the Import Licensing Agreement should provide context for interpreting this commitment, and the spirit of that agreement should be translated into the administration of the law on exportation.

2.3.2.2 Export Quantitative Restrictions

According to the Russian Representative, the competence of imposing non-tariff barriers on exports has been transferred to the Customs Union Commission. So far, quantitative restrictions on exports, including export bans, are imposed on wheat, precious metals and stones, and other mineral raw materials with a justification similar to those provided in Articles XII, XX and XXI of the GATT 1994, namely, for balance of

had already surfaced in the GATT era and therefore export tax is not WTO-plus; on the other hand, such commitment is placed in the category of non-tariff barriers according to the Indicative List of Notifiable Measures annexed to the Ministerial Decision on Notification Procedures adopted by the Trade Negotiating Committee on 15 December 1993. Thus, export tax is not part of the normal tariff binding and reduction negotiation process and can be viewed as WTO-plus.

payments purposes and general exception and security exception.[184] However, some Working Party members questioned this rationale and its legality under WTO law. In response, Russia committed that it would 'apply such quantitative export restrictions, in accordance with Article XI of the GATT 1994 and Article 12 of the WTO Agreement on Agriculture'.[185] This passage merely reinstates Russia's obligations under the WTO agreements on quantitative restrictions. It may be argued that, as Article XI of the GATT 1994 (and Article 12 of the AoA) is broad enough to cover the export dimension of quantitative restrictions, 'regulatory deficiency'[186] under the WTO agreements does not exist. A reference to existent WTO rules would secure WTO members' interests.

2.3.2.3 Export Licensing

As regards export licensing, some Working Party members expressed concerns on the non-automatic nature of the Russian export licensing regime. With a view to addressing these concerns, Russia first committed that, on its accession, quantitative restrictions on exports or restrictions on the sale for export of goods, including permits, prior authorisation requirements, licensing requirements, domestic market supply requirements or measures having an equivalent effect which are unjustifiable under the WTO agreements, would be eliminated. This commitment applies to measures carried out by Russia or the competent bodies of the Customs Union. Second, Russia committed that the discretionary authority to temporarily ban exports or restrict exports, both by the Russian Federation and by the Customs Union Commission, would be exercised in a manner consistent with the provisions of the WTO agreements. Third, in the case of seeking resort to Article XX(i) to restrict exports of domestic materials necessary to ensure essential quantities of such materials to a domestic or Customs Union processing industry, 'such measures would not operate to increase the exports of or the protection of such industry'.[187] Finally, in view of the improvement of Russia's exchange position, Russia committed to ensuring the WTO-consistency of the export licensing regime for precious stones and metals and semi-precious stones.[188]

[184] Russia's Working Party Report, paras. 641 and 644.
[185] Russia's Working Party Report, para. 647.
[186] Karapinar, 'Defining the Boundaries of Export Restrictions: A Case Law Analysis' n. 175, at 443.
[187] Russia's Working Party Report, para. 668.
[188] Russia's Working Party Report, para. 669.

A closer look at these commitments would find that these commitments largely reaffirm Russia's obligations under the WTO Agreement. Admittedly, the first commitment may have wider coverage, dealing with both quantitative restrictions on exports and restrictions on the sale for export of goods. Nonetheless, given that existent WTO rules have limited regulation on the sale for exports and that Russia is only obliged to eliminate measures unjustified by WTO rules, this commitment may not really bite. Similarly, the remaining three commitments merely dictate that the exercise of discretion be consistent with WTO rules or recap the wording of Article XX(i) of GATT 1994. Therefore, these three commitments, in fact, do little to further burden Russia in terms of its export licensing procedures. Finally, it is worth noting that these commitments apply both to the Russian Federation and the competent bodies of the Customs Union. This is because relevant competence may have already been transferred to the Customs Union Commission. Therefore, measures imposed by the Customs Commission should also be subject to the scrutiny of the WTO law.

2.3.2.4 Administration of Law on Exportation

With regards to the administration of law on exportation, Russia and some Working Party members have divergent views on the designation of specific customs checkpoints for the exportation of specific types of goods. Russia considers this designation a mechanism to ensure the effectiveness of law enforcement on customs control.[189] By contrast, some Working Party members were concerned with its potential trade-distorting effects.[190] In view of these, Russia first confirmed that products subject to these specific designated checkpoints are limited to those explicitly referred to in Tables 13 and 14 of the Working Party Report. Based on this, Russia then committed that if the designation of specific checkpoints for exportation is incompatible with the WTO agreements, they would be eliminated on Russia's accession to the WTO. Only WTO-consistent measures would remain in place.[191] The troubling point here is that the legality of such designations would not be resolved until a ruling by the WTO Panel/Appellate Body was issued. Therefore, such checkpoints for specific types of export products would remain intact pending an adverse ruling from the WTO judiciary. In addition to these

[189] Russia's Working Party Report, para. 672.
[190] Russia's Working Party Report, para. 670.
[191] Russia's Working Party Report, para. 677.

commitments on specific checkpoints, Russia also made commitments with regards general administration of laws and regulations on exports, which are close to Article X:1 and X:3(a) of the GATT 1994. The particular point is that these laws and regulations should be published promptly in the official website of the responsible governments. This obligation extends to those laws and regulations adopted by the competent bodies of the Customs Union.

2.3.2.5 Legal Status of Commitments in Working Party Reports

After reviewing Russia's commitments on export restrictions, one may easily find that some are beyond the scope of WTO law, while others are merely a reaffirmation of Russia's obligations under the WTO Agreement. Regarding the legal status of these commitments made in the Working Party Report, they are first listed in paragraph 1450 of Russia's Working Party Report and then referred to in Russia's Accession Protocol, which states, 'This Protocol, which shall include the commitments referred to in paragraph 1450 of the Working Party Report, shall be an integral part of the WTO Agreement.'[192] As a consequence, in paraphrasing the Panel's reasoning in *China – Auto Parts*, one can reach the following conclusion

> As Russia's Accession Protocol is an integral part of the WTO Agreement pursuant to Part I, Article 2 of the Accession Protocol, and in turn, paragraph 1450 of Russia's Working Party Report incorporates Russia's commitments under its Working Party Report into the Accession Protocol, Russia's commitments in the Working Party Report are thus also an integral part of the WTO Agreement.

Nonetheless, this conclusion suffers from the same weaknesses of legal indeterminacy with regard to the effects of an 'integration clause'. The same *petito principi* fallacy argued by Charnovitz applies to those commitments contained in Russia's Working Party Report.

However, differences in legislative techniques in setting out obligations in the accession protocols and commitments in Working Party Reports may lead to different interpretation results. First of all, one may be curious about the applicability of Article XX of the GATT 1994 to those commitments in Working Party Reports. In *China – Raw Materials*, the Panel and Appellate Body rely on the textual difference between

[192] Protocol for the Accession of Russian Federation to the Marrakesh Agreement Establishing the World Trade Organization, WT/L/839 (17 December 2011), Art. 2.

Paragraphs 5.1 and 11.4 of China's Accession Protocol and rule that given the absence of the same language of 'without prejudice to China's right to regulate trade in a manner consistent with the WTO Agreement' in Paragraph 11.4, Article XX is not applicable in China's obligation on export taxes. One may wonder whether the same interpretative approach applies to Russia's commitments in the Working Party Report given that Russia's Accession Protocol is a standardised form without any hint on Russia's right to regulate trade.[193] With regards to the specific case of export taxes, Russia commits to bind export duties on those products identified in Russia's Schedule, which in turn becomes part of the Schedule of Concessions and Commitments annexed to GATT 1994.[194] It is safe to say that Article II will then govern the implementation of the commitment on export tariff reduction.

The legal status of the commitment of Russia's Working Party Report was addressed in *Russia – Pigs*, where the Panel appreciated the legal relevance of paragraph 893. Specifically, the Panel was called on to answer whether Russia can, based on paragraph 893, shield itself from the scrutiny of the DSU and SPS Agreement.[195] The Panel answered this question in the negative. The Panel first referred to the Appellate Body's ruling in *China – Rare Earths* and held that the relationship between a commitment in the Working Party Report and the provisions under the WTO framework 'should be appreciated through a thorough analysis of the relevant provisions on the basis of customary rules of treaty interpretation and the circumstances of the dispute'.[196] In conclusion, the Panel found that paragraph 893 of the Working Party Report does not contain clear and unambiguous language to shield Russia's contested measure from the challenge of WTO-inconsistency.[197]

Subsequently, the Panel on *Russia – Traffic in Transit*[198] had an opportunity to examine whether the national security exception as set out in Article XXI is applicable to Russia's commitments made in the Working Party Report. The Panel first recalled the jurisprudence of the

193 Qin, 'The Challenge of Interpreting WTO-Plus' Provisions', n. 143, at 154.

194 Russia's Accession Protocol, Art. 5

195 Panel Report on *Russian Federation – Measures on the Importation of Live Pigs, Pork and Other Pig Products from the European Union*, WT/DS475/R and Add.1, circulated to WTO Members 19 August 2016, para. 7.98.

196 Panel Report on *Russia – Pigs*, para. 7.105.

197 Panel Report on *Russia – Pigs*, para. 7.110.

198 Panel Report on *Russia – Measures concerning Traffic in Transit (Traffic in Transit)*, WT/DS512/R, adopted on 26 April 2019.

Appellate Body delivered in *China – Rare Earths* and reaffirmed that 'the specific relationship between individual provisions in accession protocols and provisions of the GATT 1994 (and other WTO agreements)' must be ascertained 'through scrutiny of the provisions concerned, read in light of their context and object and purpose, with due account being taken of the overall architecture of the WTO system as a single package of rights and obligations, and any specific provisions that govern or shed light on the relationship between the provisions of different instruments'.[199] In line with this interpretive approach, the Panel on *Russia – Traffic in Transit* looked closely at the legal text of paragraphs 1161, 1426, 1427 and 1428 of Russia's Working Party Report. The Panel found that these paragraphs contain such language as 'conformity with the provisions of Article V of the GATT 1994 and other relevant provisions of the WTO Agreement',[200] 'applicable requirements of the WTO Agreement, including those of Article X of the GATT 1994',[201] and 'as provided for in the applicable provisions of the WTO Agreement, including the GATT 1994'.[202] Relying on the legal text and in accordance with textual interpretation of 'relevant' 'applicable provisions' of the WTO Agreement, the Panel thus arrived at the conclusion that Article XXI is applicable to Russia's commitments under the Working Party Report.

2.4 Various Proposals Advanced in the Doha Round Negotiations

In addition to the bilateral rule-making approach during accession negotiations, under the framework of the Doha Round negotiations, various attempts have been made with a view to disciplining export restrictions. These efforts can be seen both in the Agriculture and Non-Agriculture Market Access (NAMA) negotiation groups. Next, I will discuss various proposals advanced by WTO members and evaluate the progress made thus far.

2.4.1 Agriculture

In view of the loophole in export prohibitions or restrictions and in response to spiralling food prices, policy-makers and commentators are

199 Appellate Body Report on *China – Rare Earths*, para. 5.55, cited from *Russia – Traffic in Transit*, para. 7.231.
200 Russia's Working Party Report, para. 1161.
201 Russia's Working Party Report, para. 1426.
202 Russia's Working Party Report, para. 1428.

proposing to discipline export prohibitions or restrictions. Two different approaches have been suggested. The first is a procedural attempt to strengthen the discipline on notification and other transparency requirements; the second is a substantive one which aims to tariffy export prohibitions or restrictions or to bind and reduce export taxes. In the early stage of agriculture negotiations within the WTO, some proposals have also been advanced by WTO members with regard to export prohibitions, restrictions or taxes.

First, in the context of food security, the United States claimed that non–trade-distorting domestic support measures and further liberalisation of trade in agricultural products and legitimate assistance are important elements in strengthening food security. In accordance with this principle, the United States proposed to 'strengthen substantially WTO disciplines on export restrictions to increase the reliability of global food supply'.[203] However, the United States did not specify how to substantially strengthen WTO disciplines on export restrictions.

The Cairns Group, which is famous for its role as a catalyst for the liberalisation of trade in agricultural products, also tabled its proposal on export restrictions and export taxes. The Cairns Group advocated the idea that 'an effective multilateral trading system contributes to food security through improved resource allocation, the removal of barriers to production for domestic and export markets, increased numbers of potential suppliers, higher income levels and improved stability of price and supply'.[204] Therefore, the imposition of export restrictions may undermine the confidence of LDCs and NFIDCs in the international market for agricultural products to meet essential food and feed needs. LDCs and NFIDCs may be tempted to refer to self-sufficiency to safeguard food security. The Cairns Group thus held that stricter disciplines on export restrictions and taxes are essential to assure WTO members' access to food and feedstuffs in world markets.[205] The Cairns Group also pointed to the relationship between tariff escalation and export restrictions. In addition to its capacity to hinder exporting countries from developing the processing industry and adding value to their exports, tariff escalation may prompt exporting countries to refer to

[203] Proposal for Comprehensive Long-Term Agricultural Trade Reform Submission from the United States, WT/AG/NG/W/15 (23 June 2000), p. 6.

[204] WTO Negotiations on Agriculture – CAIRNS Group Negotiating Proposal, WT/AG/NG/W/93 (21 December 2000), p. 2.

[205] Ibid. 1.

export restrictions or export taxes as a response. Therefore, the Cairns Group maintained that further liberalisation in agricultural trade, including the elimination of tariff escalation, will contribute to the formulation of effective discipline on export restrictions and export taxes. This is also in line with the aim of the AoA to establish 'a fair and market-oriented agricultural trading system' but at the same time contributes to economic development in developing country WTO members.[206]

With regards to concrete measures to be taken, the Cairns Group proposed to

> develop both improved disciplines on export restrictions and taxes and eliminate tariff escalation; and preserve Article 12.2 of the Agreement on Agriculture and provide additional special and differential treatment provisions to address the legitimate needs of developing countries, including least developed and net food-importing developing countries.[207]

This proposal has two major elements: more liberalisation of trade in agricultural products; and more special and differential treatment for developing countries. On the one hand, the Cairns Group aimed to legislate stricter disciplines on export restrictions and export taxes and eliminate tariff escalation. These measures are meant to pursue further liberalisation in trade in agricultural products. On the other hand, the Cairns Group aimed to preserve Article 12(2) of the AoA but at the same time aimed to provide further special and differential treatment for developing countries to address their legitimate needs. The end result of this proposal would thus be mixed. The additional special and differential treatment is an instrument to lessen the concerns of developing countries in disciplining export restrictions and export taxes. Nonetheless, this special and differential treatment may have the potential to erode the fruit of liberalisation obtained by stricter discipline on export restrictions and taxes, especially in view of the fact that some developing countries have become major food exporters. It is thus essential to ensure that Article 12(2) of the AoA and additional special and differential treatment really are used to address legitimate needs of developing countries and not for other purposes, such as biofuel.

Switzerland, a member of Friends of Multifunctionality, which seeks to pursue agricultural policies while taking due account of non-trade concerns, including food security, went farther and proposed a simple but

[206] Ibid. 1–2.
[207] Ibid. 2.

ambitious proposal that aims to eliminate all export restrictions on agricultural products and bind export tariffs at zero while providing some flexibility for LDCs.[208] This proposal is clear, concrete and comprehensive, but it is doubtful whether it will find support from developing countries. While this proposal promises to provide some flexibility for LDCs, it is not entirely clear whether such flexibility is sufficient to meet all the needs of developing countries, especially in light of their reliance on export taxes on agricultural products for revenue purposes.

Finally, Japan, also a member of Friends of Multifunctionality, advanced a sophisticated proposal. As Japan observed, during the Uruguay Round negotiations, one of the major achievements was to replace non-tariff barriers with tariffs and bind and reduce them. Nonetheless, this success is limited to the import dimension and does not extend to exports; export restrictions are largely not subject to the discipline of WTO rules. Therefore, an imbalance exists between the rules and disciplines on imports and exports. If the continued reform programme strengthens rules and disciplines on imports but does not address exports, the imbalance will be further aggravated. In strengthening rules and disciplines on exports, it is important to take account of food security of food-importing countries. As agricultural products are now dominated by a small number of exporting countries, stricter rules and disciplines with a view to increasing the stability and predictability of world trade on agricultural products are indispensable to ensure that measures taken by food-exporting countries will not undermine the food security of importing countries.[209] With regards to food security, Japan underlined the government's responsibility to its population. Although in some cases, food-exporting countries consider it legitimate or necessary to impose export restrictions on agricultural products, and such measures are applied only on a temporary basis, they may severely affect the food security of importing countries.[210]

In view of these factors, Japan thus proposed three steps to discipline export restrictions. The first step is to tariffy export restrictions, namely, to replace export prohibitions or restrictions with export taxes. The second step is to bind export taxes and then reduce them. When export

[208] WTO: Negotiations on Agriculture Proposal by Switzerland, WT/AG/NG/W/94 (21 December 2000), para. 6.4.

[209] Negotiating Proposal by Japan on WTO Agricultural Negotiations, G/AG/NG/W/91 (21 December 2000), p. 16.

[210] Ibid. 17.

taxes are imposed on a certain product, a given number of quotas exempt from such export taxes should be provided. The third step is to provide an exception for a country not levying export taxes to impose export restrictions in case of emergency events, the criteria of which should be further defined.[211] In clarifying such criteria, the following elements should be taken into account

(i) To establish strict requirements for the application of such emergency measures;
(ii) To introduce consultations with other Members as a prerequisite for imposing emergency measures, and to clarify the measures to be taken when the consultations do not result in a satisfactory solution;
(iii) To obligate Members, when introducing emergency measures, to maintain the proportion of exports to domestic production at the level of the preceding x years, in order to allow importing countries to secure the necessary level of imports;
(iv) To limit the duration of such emergency measures.[212]

According to Japan's proposal, the negotiators have first to lay down strict conditions for a member to impose emergency measures. Second, before such emergency measures are introduced, the imposing member has to consult with other members. The negotiators also clarify the legal consequences if the consultations fail to reach a satisfactory result. This procedural requirement will remedy some defects as contained in Article 12(1) of the current AoA, since it sets out the consultation as a prerequisite for the imposition of emergency measures. It will also ameliorate the current provision by defining the legal effects of failed consultations. In Japan's proposal, such emergency measures should also be subject to a clearly set expiry deadline, which is also missing in the current AoA. An innovative initiative in Japan's proposal is that when a member imposes such emergency measures, a proportion of domestic production at the level of the preceding years should be made possible for exports so that importing countries can maintain the necessary level of imports. This designation is similar to when the EU proposed to extend paragraph 40 of the *Action Plan on Food Price Volatility and Agriculture* under the auspices of the World Food Program to all WTO members and what African and Arab groups proposed in their draft declaration *WTO Work Programme to Mitigate the Impact of the Food Market Prices and*

[211] Ibid. 17.
[212] Ibid. 15–16.

Volatility on WTO Least-Developed and Net-Food Importing Developing Members. These two initiatives also aim to exempt LDCs and NFIDCs from export restrictions when food-exporting countries impose such restrictions.

2.4.2 *Non-Agriculture Market Access*

In filling in the gaps in WTO disciplines on export restrictions, Japan, under the negotiation group NAMA, proposed a WTO Agreement on Export Licensing Procedures, aiming to enhance the transparency of export licensing.[213] In contrast, the EU proposed a WTO Agreement on Export Taxes.[214] While Japan's proposal was revised and transformed into a protocol to the GATT 1994, and has gradually gained some limited support from other WTO members, no other member joined the EU in sponsoring the proposed WTO Agreement on Export Taxes.

2.4.2.1 Proposed WTO Agreement on Export Licensing Procedures and Protocol on Transparency in Export Licensing to the General Agreement on Tariffs and Trade 1994

Japan's proposal on a WTO Agreement on Export Licensing Procedures is adapted from the WTO Agreement on Import Licensing Procedures. Therefore, the legal text of the draft Agreement on Export Licensing Procedures mirrors that of the Agreement on Import Licensing Procedures by substituting the term 'import' with 'export'. The proposed Agreement on Export Licensing Procedures aims to address three issues: publication of the rules and administration of export restrictions; notification to the WTO; and publication of domestic statistics.[215] In its proposal, Japan emphasises that the proposed agreement aims mainly to enhance procedural transparency. Thus, it does not curtail a member's legitimate rights under the WTO Agreement to impose export restrictions or to introduce new substantive rules.[216] A revised version of this proposed agreement in the form of a protocol to the GATT 1994 was

213 Text-based Proposal for Negotiation on Enhanced Transparency on Export Restrictions, *Communication from Japan*, TN/MA/W/15/Add.4 (18 April 2006).

214 Negotiating Proposal on Export Taxes, *Communication from the European Communities*, TN/MA/W/11/Add.6 (27 April 2006).

215 TN/MA/W/15/Add.4, para. 2.

216 TN/MA/W/15/Add.4, para. 3.

presented by Japan and the United States in 2008.[217] The draft protocol has only five articles addressing the definition of export licensing; notification; request for information; confidential information; and review.

Article 1 of the proposed protocol defines export licensing as 'any administrative procedures involving the submission of an application or other documentation (i.e., other than customs purposes) to the relevant administrative boy or bodies as a prior condition for exportation from the customs territory of the exporting Member'.[218] Whereas this definition excludes the procedures for customs purposes from the scope of export licensing, it may bring about ambiguity since ultimately an export license would be required by customs for shipping activities. Separating customs purposes from non-customs purposes may thus be subject to dispute.[219]

Article 2 of the proposed protocol regulates the notification of export licensing. Members are obliged to notify the Committee on Market Access within sixty days of the entry into force of this protocol. A member imposing new measures on export licensing should also notify the Committee on Market Access within sixty days of the entry into force of the new measures.[220] In view of the fact that many members do not spontaneously notify the WTO under current practices, the proposed protocol introduces a novel practice. According to Article 3.4 of the proposed protocol, an interested member considering that another member has failed to notify new or existent export licensing measures may bring this matter to the attention of another such member. If another such member still fails to promptly notify the Committee, the interested member may itself notify the pertinent new or existent export licensing measures. This counter-notification mechanism offers a possibility for other members to bring the pertinent measures to the attention of the Committee on Market Access and may thus contribute to the transparency of export licensing measures.

[217] Protocol on Transparency in Export Licensing to the General Agreement on Tariffs and Trade 1994 (hereinafter the Proposed Protocol on Transparency on Export Licensing), *Communication from Japan and the United States*, TN/MA/W/15/Add.4/Rev.1 (18 April 2006).

[218] Proposed Protocol on Transparency on Export Licensing, Art. 1.

[219] Enhanced Transparency on Export Licensing, *Communication from the Separate Customs Territory of Taiwan, Penghu, Kinmen and Matsu; Japan; Republic of Korea and the United States*, TN/MA/W/130 (11 December 2009), p. 3.

[220] Proposed Protocol on Transparency on Export Licensing, Art. 2.1.

Article 3 of the proposed protocol identifies export-licensing information to be offered on request of a member. However, a member is not obliged to provide such information the disclosure of which would impede law enforcement, be contrary to public interest or essential security interests, or prejudice legitimate commercial interests of particular enterprises.[221] The proposed protocol in Article 5 instructs the Committee on Market Access to review the implementation and operation of this protocol at least once every two years.[222]

2.4.2.2 Proposed WTO Agreement on Export Taxes

In contrast to the procedural approach of Japan and the United States, the EU aimed to address the legal vacuum around export taxes. According to the EU, export taxes remain a policy instrument not subject to disciplines due to the GATT's traditional focus on import policies.[223] With a view to redressing their distortive effect on international trade, the EU thus proposed to regulate export taxes having the effects of transferring gains of trade between WTO members; creating unfair advantage to domestic industries at the expense of producers of other WTO members; and evading existent WTO rules on export restrictions by shifting to prohibitive export taxes on the exportation of goods.[224]

Article 1 of the proposed Agreement on Export Taxes regulates two kinds of levies imposed on the exportation of non-agricultural goods. The first relates to the duties, taxes or other charges collected on, or in connection with, their exportation from the territory of one member to another. The second deals with internal taxes and other charges imposed on exporting products that are in excess of those imposed on like products for internal sale. The former is normally collected by customs while the latter is generally imposed by other administrative agencies such as the Ministry of Finance.

Article 2 of the proposed Agreement on Export Taxes provides special and differential treatment for developing country members and least developed country (LDC) members, in particular. Article 3 then prescribes two conditions for developing country members to maintain low-level export taxes on a limited number of products listed in their

221 Proposed Protocol on Transparency on Export Licensing, Art. 4.
222 Proposed Protocol on Transparency on Export Licensing, Art. 5.1.
223 Non-Tariff Barriers, *Communication from European Communities*, TN/MA/W/11/Add.3 (1 April 2003), para. 13.
224 TN/MA/W/11/Add.6, p. 1.

schedules. First, the export taxes are necessary 'to maintain financial stability to satisfy fiscal needs, or to facilitate economic diversification and avoid excessive dependence on the export of primary products'.[225] In order to achieve these objectives, the developing country member concerned should adopt relevant domestic measures in conjunction with export taxes. Second, the maintenance of export taxes should not adversely affect international trade either by limiting the availability of the goods subject to export taxes to WTO members or by raising the world price of such goods. The maintenance of export taxes should not seriously prejudice the interests of other developing country members.[226] When imposing export duties, the rules on customs valuation as set out in Article VII of the GATT 1994 should be followed.[227]

Article 3.2 of the proposed Agreement on Export Taxes then makes it clear that the obligation of Most-Favoured-Nation Treatment applies wherever export taxes are maintained by a developing country member. Besides, the proposed agreement also reaffirms members' rights to collect fees and charges in accordance with Article VIII of the GATT 1994 and their rights to impose export taxes based on general exception and security exception as set out in Article XX and XXI thereof.[228] The rights of developing country members relating to balance of payments, exchange arrangements and governmental assistance to economic development remain unaffected.[229] Further, Article XXII and XXIII of the GATT 1994, as elaborated in the Dispute Settlement Understanding, should be applicable to this Agreement on Export Taxes.[230]

The proposed Agreement on Export Taxes reiterates members' obligation on transparency and notification as set out in Article X of the GATT 1994 and in the Ministerial Decision on Notification Procedures. A member imposing a new export tax or increasing existing export taxes is obliged to notify the WTO Secretariat sixty days before the entry into force of such measures. On request, the member concerned should provide relevant information and offer adequate and prompt opportunities for consultation.[231]

[225] Proposed Agreement on Export Taxes, Art. 3.1(a).
[226] Proposed Agreement on Export Taxes, Art. 3.1(b).
[227] Proposed Agreement on Export Taxes, Art. 6.
[228] Proposed Agreement on Export Taxes, Art. 5(a) and (b).
[229] Proposed Agreement on Export Taxes, Art. 5(c).
[230] Proposed Agreement on Export Taxes, Art. 8.
[231] Proposed Agreement on Export Taxes, Art. 7.

2.4.2.3 Comparison

The Proposed Protocol on Transparency on Export Licensing and the proposed Agreement on Export Taxes address two important issues of export restrictions which are largely left untouched in the WTO Agreement: export licensing and export taxes. Japan and the United States chose to focus on procedural transparency of export licensing and include no substantial obligation in their proposal. The only obligation incumbent on members under this proposed protocol is to notify the WTO of their export licensing measures with a possibility of counter-notification by other interested members.

In contrast, the EU's proposed Agreement on Export Taxes is much more ambitious and aggressive. It aims to eliminate all export taxes maintained by developed country members. While developing country members are entitled to maintain or institute export taxes, their maintenance or institution is subject to stringent criteria. Further, the proposed Agreement is wide in scope. It covers not only export duties, taxes and other charges imposed on or in connection with exportation but also excessive internal taxes and other charges on exported products. The proposed Agreement also situates itself in the framework of the WTO Agreement and thus affirms the applicability of relevant provisions of the GATT 1994, such as general exception and special and differential treatment and the dispute settlement mechanism.

Although the ambition of the EU to lay down disciplines on export taxes should be applauded, this aggressive proposal makes it difficult to generate support from other members. Even though both the EU's and Japan and the United States' proposals enjoy only limited support, the Proposed Protocol on Transparency on Export Licensing has won some support from other members, while the EU remains the only sponsor for its proposed Agreement on Export Taxes. Notwithstanding its aiming high, the EU's proposal may lose relevance at the negotiation table in the end. As the Chairman of the NAMA negotiation group commented on the Draft Modalities for Non-Agricultural Market Access, members do not have sufficient incentives to engage in the discussion of export taxes, as this issue is not in the right balance of concessions agreed in Doha.[232] The inclusion of export taxes in the NAMA negotiation may first go beyond the mandate of the NAMA on non-tariff barriers since export

[232] Draft Modalities for Non-Agricultural Market Access, TN/MA/W/103 (8 February 2008), p. 16.

taxes constitute a tariff. It also runs counter to the objectives of the DDA, which puts development at the heart of this round of negotiations. The imposition of disciplines on export taxes leading to their reduction or elimination may adversely impact the economic development of developing country members.

Such concerns can be seen in the Dar Es Salaam Declaration made at the sixth LDC trade ministers' meeting in Dar Es Salaam, Tanzania, in 2009. The LDC Members called on WTO members to agree not to 'impose any disciplines on export taxes, as these are legitimate tools for development'.[233] Whereas the EU sees export taxes as a distortion to international trade, developing country members view them as legitimate tools for development. The differences in characterising export taxes between the EU and developing country members effectively prevent any agreement on this subject matter. While the proposed Agreement on Export Taxes provides a special and differential treatment for developing country members, the conditions are all too strict. The imposition of export taxes, in conjunction with domestic measures of developing country members, may be permitted for only limited purposes; these should not adversely affect international trade. These over-strict requirements cannot be said to sufficiently address the development needs of developing country members. In light of the development aim of the DDA, it would be difficult for the EU to justify its proposal on export taxes under the NAMA negotiation group and to find sufficient support.

2.5 Disciplining Export Restrictions in RTAs

2.5.1 General Overview

Given the deficiency of multilateral rules in the WTO framework governing export restrictions, trading nations may refer to regional trade agreements in disciplining export restrictions, if there is a strong regulatory demand. However, as with the negotiations in the multilateral context, not all trading nations are enthusiastic about strong disciplines on export restrictions. Therefore, chances may be that RTAs contain even weaker rules on export restrictions and provide greater policy space for parties to the RTAs. In a recent report conducted by the Organisation for Economic Co-operation and Development (OECD), Jane Korinek

[233] WT/MIN(09)/2 (21 October 2009), para. 26.

and Jessica Bartos, after surveying ninety-three RTAs, conclude that disciplines on export restrictions contained in these RTAs may be stronger than, equal to or weaker than those in the WTO Agreement. Korinek and Bartos refer to these three categories as 'WTO-plus', 'WTO-equal' and 'WTO-minus' export restriction disciplines. Given that there is no discipline on export taxes under the WTO Agreement and that there is nonetheless an obligation to eliminate export quantitative restrictions, the benchmark of 'WTO-plus', 'WTO-equal' and 'WTO-minus' may vary. Regarding export taxes, an RTA carrying no obligation on export taxes is regarded as 'WTO-equal', whereas an RTA regulating export taxes in one way or another is considered 'WTO-plus'. A WTO-plus RTA may impose a general obligation to eliminate export taxes; it may also prevent the contracting parties to the pertinent RTA from increasing existing export taxes. With respect to export quantitative restrictions, a WTO-plus RTA may impose more stringent conditions for exceptions to the general obligation to eliminate quantitative restrictions or permit fewer exceptions. A WTO-equal RTA may just import the provisions of the GATT 1994. A WTO-minus may simply provide nothing about export quantitative restrictions or provide a multi-sectoral exception or a list of exceptions on specific products, such as fuel-related goods and precious stones.[234] Of the RTAs surveyed by the OECD report, around 70 per cent contain disciplines on export taxes. With regards to quantitative restrictions, fifteen agreements contain stronger language than the WTO Agreement and are thus WTO-plus, while thirty-eight are equal and twenty-two are weaker (WTO-minus).[235] In this section, two prototypes of regional integration arrangements/organisations, namely, the EU and USMCA (United States–Mexico–Canada Agreement, formerly, North American Free Trade Area, NAFTA), will be examined to see whether and how these age-old RTAs go beyond GATT/WTO disciplines. Moreover, three types of FTAs, US-FTAs, EU-FTAs and some South–South RTAs, will be examined to view regulation of export restrictions in greater detail.

[234] Jane Korinek and Jessica Bartos, 'Multilateralising Regionalism: Disciplines on Export Restrictions in Regional Trade Agreements' (2012) OECD Trade Policy Papers, No. 139, 17–30.

[235] Korinek and Bartos further note that some WTO-minus agreements that do not include disciplines on quantitative restrictions are earlier agreements predating the WTO. Ibid. at 4. However, the fact that they are prior-WTO RTAs does not help to explain the absence of such regulation given that the GATT 1947 had already provided disciplines on export restrictions.

2.5.2 European Union

Founded in 1957 through the Treaty Establishing the European Economic Community, the EU has undergone a number of treaty changes and evolved into its current form.[236] Regardless of treaty revision, the main legal provisions regulating export restrictions, including export taxes and quantitative restrictions, remain unaffected. Export taxes and export quantitative restrictions are now regulated in Articles 30 and 35 of the TFEU, respectively. Article 30 of the TFEU provides that '[c]ustoms duties on imports and exports and charges having equivalent effect shall be prohibited between Member States'.[237] Article 35 of the TFEU then provides that '[q]uantitative restrictions on exports, and all measures having equivalent effect, shall be prohibited between Member States', which is in parallel to Article 34 of the TFEU that regulates quantitative restriction on imports.[238] The key point here is how to interpret 'charges having equivalent effect' in the context of export taxes and 'all measures having equivalent effect' in the context of export quantitative restrictions. The CJEU has delivered a very rich jurisprudence, and academics have also expended tremendous efforts interpreting these terms, particularly in the context of import restrictions. The rationale as set out by the CJEU and interpretation by academic work in the import restrictions dimension, subject to some limitation, may apply *mutatis mutandis* to export restrictions.[239] However, whether the disciplines in export restrictions should exactly mirror import restrictions is nonetheless subject to dispute. Some argue that in interpreting all 'measure/charges having equivalent effect' in import and export restrictions, there must be a conceptual unity. Nonetheless, the prevailing view seems to suggest that the interpretation in export restrictions should be narrower than that in import restrictions.[240]

[236] See generally, Koen Lenaerts and Piet Van Nuffel, *European Union Law* (3rd ed., Sweet & Maxwell 2011); Alan Dashwood and others, *Wyatt and Dashwood's European Union Law* (6th ed., Hart Publishing 2011).

[237] Moreover, this prohibition extends to customs duties of a fiscal nature.

[238] The prohibition on quantitative restrictions on exports is nonetheless subject to exceptions provided in Article 36 on such grounds as public morality, public policy or public security; and the protection of health and life of humans, animals or plants.

[239] Peter Oliver, *Free Movement of Goods in the European Community under Articles 30 to 36 of the Rome Treaty* (3rd ed., Sweet & Maxwell 1996) 173; Laurance W. Cormley, *EU Law of Free Movement of Goods and Customs Union* (Oxford University Press 2009) 449.

[240] Oliver, *Free Movement of Goods in the European Community under Articles 30 to 36 of the Rome Treaty*, ibid. at 121.

Before entering the field of export restrictions, it is feasible to recall one of the most famous cases in import restrictions concerning the meaning of having an effect equivalent to quantitative restrictions: *Dassonville*.[241] In that case, the ECJ (now, the CJEU) was called on to examine Belgian legislation requiring an official document issued by the government of the exporting country for products bearing a designation of origin. This requirement placed a heavy burden on importers wishing to import, from other Member States, products already placed into free circulation of the Community. In that case, the ECJ set out comprehensive coverage for 'all measures having equivalent effect'. According to the ECJ, '[a]ll trading rules enacted by Member States which are capable of hindering, directly or indirectly, actually or potentially, intra-Community trade are to be considered as measures having an effect equivalent to quantitative restrictions'.[242] Therefore, once a trading rule may directly or indirectly, actually or potentially hinder intra-Community trade, it is caught by the phrase 'all measures having equivalent effect'. As noted previously, this holding, subject to some limitation, may apply *mutatis mutandis* to export restrictions. Given the vast number of cases delivered by the CJEU and voluminous academic work, a detailed examination of these decisions falls outside the scope of this book. In the following, I will examine three leading cases handed down by the ECJ in the earlier days of European integration: *Groenveld*[243] and *Oebel*[244] and *Delhaize* v. *Promalvin*.[245]

In *Groenveld*, the ECJ was called on to examine whether a Dutch regulation prohibiting any sausage manufacturers, subject to express exceptions, from having in stock or processing horse meat was compatible with the EEC Treaty. According to the ECJ, Article 34 of the EEC Treaty (now, Article 35 of the TFEU) was aimed at preventing

> national measures which have as their specific object or effect the restriction of patterns of exports and thereby the establishment of a difference in treatment between the domestic trade of a Member State and its export trade in such a way as to provide a particular advantage for national production or for the domestic market of the State in question at the expense of the production or of the trade of other Member States.[246]

241 Case 8-74, *Procureur du Roi* v. *Benoît and Gustave Dassonville*, [1974] ECR 00837.

242 *Dassonville*, para. 5.

243 Case 15/79, P. B. *Groenveld BV, Haarlem,* v. *Produktschap voor Vee en Vlees, Rijswijk* (*Groenveld*), [1979] ECR 03409.

244 Case 155/80, Summary proceedings against Sergius Oebel (*Oebel*), [1981] ECR 01993.

245 Case C-47/90, *Établissements Delhaize frères and Compagnie Le Lion SA* v. *Promalvin SA and AGE Bodegas Unidas SA* (*Delhaize* v. *Promalvin*), [1992] ECR I-03669.

246 *Groenveld*, para. 7.

Three points should be noted. First, this provision relates to a discriminatory measure between domestic trade of a Member State and its export trade. Second, such discrimination may lie in its object or its effect; either will be caught by Article 35 of the TFEU. Third, discrimination as referred to here means a particular advantage for national production or for domestic markets at the expense of production or trade of other Member States.

As the ECJ explained, the purpose of the contested regulation was to safeguard the reputation of Dutch meat products, especially as there were psychological or legal obstacles in other Member States or non-Member States with the consumption of horse meat. Further, the same prohibition was applicable to products in the Dutch domestic market. Therefore, no discrimination existed between the domestic market and export trade; at the same time, the object and effect of the contested regulation was not aimed at favouring the domestic market at the expense of trade with other Member States.[247] Based on this reasoning, the ECJ upheld the legality of the contested regulation.

The same holding was reiterated by the ECJ in *Oebel* with the final phrase 'at the expense of the production or of the trade of other Member States' being dropped.[248] *Oebel* related to a piece of German legislation prohibiting bakery workers from working from 10 pm to 4 am with the objective of preventing family bakery workers from damaging their health by engaging in permanent night work. With a view to effectively implementing this rule, no person was allowed to work in ordinary and fine bakeries delivering to consumers or retail outlets. The applicants argued that such restrictions prevented them exporting abroad, especially in view of the fact that the products concerned had to be delivered fresh in time for breakfast, and consequently demanded night work. The ECJ declared that the contested legislation served mainly economic and social policy and was applicable to a specific industry within the territory of a Member State without distinguishing between domestic consumption or export trade. The disputed legislation did not thus provide any advantage for national production or the domestic market.[249]

Similarly, the ECJ in *Delhaize* v. *Promalvin* reinstated the same holding. The subject matter before the ECJ concerned a Spanish regulation requiring Spanish wine to be locally bottled before exportation.

[247] *Groenveld*, para. 8.
[248] *Oebel*, para. 15.
[249] *Oebel*, para. 16.

According to the ECJ, the contested regulation had 'the specific effect of restricting exports of wine in bulk and in particular, of procuring a special advantage for bottling undertakings situated in the region of production'.[250] Namely, the requirement for Spanish wine to be locally bottled in effect added a special advantage for national production. Such favourable effect on national production was caught by Article 34 of the EEC Treaty within the meaning of 'all measures having equivalent effect'. The ECJ nonetheless further investigated whether such a bottling requirement was necessary for designation of origin with quality (*denominación de origen calificada*) by ensuring that designated products came from a specified geographic region and displayed particular characteristics, which might be justified under Article 36 of the EEC Treaty aiming to protect industrial and commercial property. The ECJ found in the negative. According to the ECJ, such bottling operation was not a practice essential to endow restricted Spanish wine with specific characteristics or to maintain such characteristics.[251] Based on this reasoning, the ECJ thus ruled that the local bottling requirement had the equivalent effect to quantitative restrictions and could not be justified by Article 36 of the EEC Treaty.

2.5.3 United States–Mexico–Canada Agreement

After President Trump was sworn in as US president, one of the key objectives of his administration was to renegotiate the NAFTA and this led to the USMCA, which entered into force on 1 July 2020. The USMCA largely resembles NAFTA. Therefore, I will first recap the regulations of NAFTA and then examine new rules.

In NAFTA, export taxes and export quantitative restrictions are regulated in Chapter 3 under the heading of non-tariff measures. According to the criteria advanced by Korinek and Bartos, NAFTA contains WTO-plus obligations both on export taxes and export quantitative restrictions. In terms of export taxes, NAFTA imposes Most-Favoured-Nation treatment and National Treatment obligations. Regarding export quantitative restrictions, NAFTA first incorporates the disciplines as set out in the WTO Agreement, notably, Article XI of the GATT 1994, and then further defines the effect of an export quantitative restriction against a non-party on parties to NAFTA. In addition, NAFTA also sets out more

[250] *Delhaize* v. *Promalvin*, para. 14.
[251] *Delhaize* v. *Promalvin*, para. 19.

stringent rules for a contracting party to impose export restrictions on the basis of Articles XI:2(a) or XX(g), (i) or (j) of the GATT 1994. These elements will be addressed below in order.

With regards to export taxes, Article 314 reads as follows,

> Except as set out in Annex 314, no Party may adopt or maintain any duty, tax or other charge on the export of any good to the territory of another Party, unless such duty, tax or charge is adopted or maintained on:
>
> a) exports of any such good to the territory of all other Parties; and
> b) any such good when destined for domestic consumption.

Instead of imposing an obligation to eliminate export duties, NAFTA dictates that contracting parties abide by Most-Favoured-Nation treatment and National Treatment when adopting or maintaining export taxes. In accordance with this obligation, a specific export tax, when imposed against a particular product exported to the territory of a contracting party, should be equally applied to products exported to the territory of other contracting parties. Similarly, whenever an export tax of a given product is imposed, the same tax should be levied on the product for domestic consumption.

With respect to export quantitative restrictions, Article 309.1 of NAFTA provides that, except as otherwise provided in the agreement, no party may adopt or maintain any prohibition or restriction on 'the exportation or sale for export of any good destined for the territory of another party, except in accordance with Article XI of the GATT, including its interpretative notes'.[252] In effect, NAFTA incorporates Article XI of the GATT and its interpretative notes into the agreement. Therefore, this provision basically maintains the same disciplines on export quantitative restrictions as the GATT 1994 does. However, Article 309 of NAFTA in the following paragraphs adds some new elements in the regulation of export quantitative restrictions. In the first place, the parties to NAFTA put forward a legislative interpretation of the implementation of Article XI in the NAFTA context. To be more precise, NAFTA, in Article 309.2, clarifies the parties' understanding of the incorporated Article XI to prohibit export price requirements in any circumstances and in any form.[253]

NAFTA then continues to define the relationship between contracting parties and non-parties in case an export restriction is imposed against a

[252] NAFTA, Art. 309.1.
[253] NAFTA, Art. 309.2.

good exported to a non-party. According to Article 309.3, even if an export restriction is imposed against a non-party, NAFTA does not entail an obligation for contracting parties to ensure that such good is meant for domestic consumption of contracting parties only and will not be directly or indirectly re-exported to that non-party.[254] In other words, while contracting parties are free to impose export quantitative restrictions against a non-party, this restriction does not prevent other contracting parties from re-exporting the good subject to export restriction, once it is exported to other contracting parties from the territory of the imposing contracting parties. The practical effect of this provision is that the non-party against which an export quantitative restriction is imposed may circumvent this restriction by importing from other contracting parties to NAFTA. Therefore, the effectiveness of an export restriction may be undermined. However, it should be borne in mind that quantitative restrictions, whether on imports or exports, are prohibited by Article XI of the GATT. Such restrictions may thus only be imposed against a non-WTO member. Second, in light of the potential distortion effects that might arise and the objective of NAFTA to foster free trade, exempting contracting parties from any obligation to refrain from re-exporting to the non-party seems harmless.

Finally, NAFTA provides a set of clearer rules for contracting parties to follow when the contracting parties refer to Articles XI:2(a) or XX(g), (i) or (j) of the GATT in imposing export restrictions. First, the export restriction cannot reduce the proportion of the total export of the specific good made available to other contracting parties compared to the proportion prevailing in the most recent 36 months.[255] Second, if a contracting party imposes a higher price for exports of a given good through licenses, fees, taxation or minimum price requirements, the same price should be charged against such good for domestic consumption. Nonetheless, such obligation does not apply to cases where the increase in the price of the exported good results from restriction of the volume of exports.[256] Finally, the imposition of export restrictions should not lead to disruption of normal channels of supply to other contracting parties or a normal proportion of a given good supplied to these contracting parties.[257] With a view to effectively controlling exports to any non-

[254] NAFTA, Art. 309.3.
[255] NAFTA, Art. 315.1(a).
[256] NAFTA, Art. 315.1(b).
[257] NAFTA, Art. 315.1(c).

party, NAFTA then instructs the contracting parties to cooperate in implementing these obligations.[258]

Based on the rules of NAFTA, the USMCA regulates three aspects of export restrictions: export taxes, export quantitative restrictions and transparency in export licensing. The USMCA regulates export taxes in Article 2.15, which reads

> No Party shall adopt or maintain any duty, tax, or other charge on the export of any good to the territory of another Party, unless the duty, tax, or charge is also applied to the good if destined for domestic consumption.

A close look at this provision will reveal that it drops the clause 'exports of any such good to the territory of all other Parties', originally contained in Article 314 of NAFTA. A quick question thus surfaces: whether such textual difference leads to the conclusion that export taxes may be imposed against one party of the USMCA but not another. Again, this question reflects the old debates on the applicability of the principle of Most-Favoured-Nation treatment.

Regarding export quantitative restrictions, following NAFTA, the USMCA, in Article 2.11.1, imports Article XI of the GATT 1994 and interpretative notes. Based on the rights and obligations of the GATT 1994, the contracting parties to the USMCA add an understanding that export price requirements, in any form and in any circumstance, are prohibited.[259] Moreover, the USMCA explicitly prohibits the imposition of voluntary export restraints 'inconsistent with Article VI of the GATT 1994, as implemented under Article 18 of the SCM Agreement and Article 8.1 of the AD Agreement'.[260] Articles 2.11.3 and 2.11.4 basically follow NAFTA in regulating the imposition of export restrictions against products from non-parties and subsequent consultation between parties.

The USMCA, in Article 2.14, goes beyond NAFTA and adds new discipline on export licensing through transparency requirements, including publication of licensing procedures, contact point and the administrative body. Relevant information, such as the aggregate number of licenses and 'measures, if any, that the Party has adopted in conjunction with the licensing procedure to restrict domestic production or consumption or to stabilize production, supply, or prices for the relevant good'[261] are to be provided on request.

[258] NAFTA, Art. 315.2.

[259] USMCA, Art. 2.11.2(a).

[260] USMCA, Art. 2.11.2(c).

[261] USMCA, Art. 2.11.3.

However, such transparency requirements do not lead to the granting of an export licence. More importantly, the USMCA, in Article 2.14.4, clarifies its relationship with contracting parties' obligations or commitments under United Nations Security Council Resolutions and other multilateral non-proliferation regimes[262] and thus links (or more precisely, disconnects) trade law and public international law obligations. The linkage or disconnection between export restrictions in international trade law and export control in public international law is a thorny issue circling measures invoking the national security exception. The regulation of the USMCA is reflective of the current trend of sovereign states' reliance on the national security exception in adopting trade measures for political or strategic purposes.[263]

2.5.4 EU FTAs

The EU's desire to discipline export restrictions through FTAs has gradually intensified, and significantly strengthened after the adoption of the Raw Material Initiative.[264] The EU's FTA policies can be separated into two phases: before and after the adoption of the Global Europe strategy.[265] Before the Global Europe strategy, the EU–South Africa Trade, Development and Cooperation Agreement (EU–South Africa TDCA), the EU–Mexico Cooperation Agreement and the EU–Chile Association Agreement were some of the most representative trade agreements. These three agreements put forward obligations to progressive, reciprocal liberalisation of 'customs duties on imports and exports and charges having an equivalent effect'.[266]

[262] USMCA, Article 2.14.4. Such non-proliferation regimes include Wassenaar Arrangement on Export Controls for Conventional Arms and Dual-Use Goods and Technologies; Nuclear Suppliers Group; the Australia Group; Convention on the Prohibition of the Development, Production, Stockpiling and Use of Chemical Weapons and on Their Destruction, completed in Geneva, 3 September 1992, and signed in Paris, 13 January 1993; Convention on the Prohibition of the Development, Production and Stockpiling of Bacteriological (Biological) and Toxin Weapons and on Their Destruction, completed in Washington, London and Moscow, 10 April 1972; Treaty on the Non-Proliferation of Nuclear Weapons, completed in Washington, London and Moscow, 1 July 1968; and the Missile Technology Control Regime.

[263] See Chapter 3.

[264] COM(2008) 699 final, 4 November 2008.

[265] COM(2006) 567 final, 10 October 2006.

[266] EU-Mexico Cooperation Agreement, Art. 5(b); see also EU-South Africa TDCA, Art. 19.3; EU-Chile Association Agreement, Arts. 57 and 58.

After the launch of the Global Europe strategy, the EU has concluded several important bilateral agreements with its trading partners, including South Korea, Singapore and Vietnam. Export taxes and export quantitative restrictions are two major elements relating to export restrictions with new disciplines on export licensing.

Regarding export duties, the EU–Korea FTA first instructs the parties not to maintain or institute 'any duties, taxes or other fees and charges imposed on, or in connection with, the exportation of goods to the other Party, or any internal taxes, fees and charges on goods exported to the other Party that are in excess of those imposed on like goods destined for internal sale'.[267] The key element here is not to exceed those 'imposed on like goods destined for internal sale', which otherwise provides domestic downstream producers competitive advantage and may constitute subsidies. This obligation mirrors the language of the EU's proposed Agreement on Export Taxes. The EU effectively wrote into the EU–Korea FTA what it aimed to achieve in the multilateral framework but did not succeed. Regarding export restrictions, the EU–Korea FTA incorporates Article XI of the GATT 1994 and its interpretative notes, which *mutatis mutandis* constitute part of the EU–Korea FTA.[268] The EU–Singapore FTA follows this practice but the EU–Vietnam FTA adds some new elements by expressly prohibiting voluntary export restraints.[269]

Finally, some EU FTAs touch on export licensing. The EU–Singapore FTA and the EU–Vietnam FTA represent two types of regulation with similar effects. The former groups import and export licensing into one provision and applies *mutatis mutandis* the rules of import licensing to exportation.[270] It further instructs the party to ensure all export licensing procedures are 'neutral in application'[271] and 'administered in a fair, equitable, non-discriminatory and transparent manner'.[272] The EU–Vietnam FTA regulates export licensing with one single provision but combines it with a transparency requirement. The EU–Vietnam FTA, in Article 2.17, instructs the parties to notify each other on export licensing, including the legal text, products, contact point and administrative

[267] EU–Korea FTA, Art. 2.11; see aslo EU-Singapore FTA, Art. 2.7; EU-Vietnam FTA, Art. 2.12.

[268] EU–Korea FTA, Art. 2.9; see also EU–Singapore FTA, Art. 2.9; EU–Vietnam FTA, Art. 2.14.1.

[269] EU–Vietnam FTA, Art. 2.14.2(b).

[270] EU–Singapore FTA, Art. 2.11.2.

[271] EU–Singapore FTA, Art. 2.11.3.

[272] EU–Singapore FTA, Art. 2.11.3.

bodies, and obliges the party to provide information on request. The EU–Vietnam FTA dictates the design of export licensing procedures. It first incorporates relevant provisions of the WTO Import Licensing Agreement, which constitutes part of the FTA, *mutatis mutandis*[273] and obligates the party to ensure all export licensing procedures are 'neutral in application and administered in a fair, equitable, non-discriminatory and transparent manner'.[274] A party may only apply automatic licensing procedures to 'fulfil legitimate objectives after having conducted an appropriate impact assessment',[275] while non-automatic licensing procedures may only be used for implementing a measure not inconsistent with the EU–Vietnam FTA.[276] When an application for an export license is denied, a written explanation must be provided and a right to appeal offered.[277] In short, the EU–Vietnam FTA has the most comprehensive regulation on export licensing, ranging from transparency, provision of information on request, substantial rules of the licensing procedures and right to appeal in case of denial of an application.

Before turning to the practices of US FTAs, it is worth noting that the EU filed a complaint against Ukraine on the latter's export ban on woods under the EU–Ukraine Association Agreement signed in 2014. This dispute relates to an export ban adopted in 2005 prohibiting the export of timber and sawn wood of ten wood species and an export ban adopted in 2015 prohibiting all exports of unprocessed wood temporarily for ten years. The EU alleges that such export bans violate Article 35 of the Association Agreement, which incorporates relevant rules of the GATT 1994, in particular Article XI thereof. In its written submission to the Arbitral Panel, the EU contends that such export bans cannot be justified under Article XI:2(a) and XX(g) of the GATT 1994 for the prevention or relief of a critical shortage of essential products or the conservation of exhaustible natural resources. The legal issues surrounding this dispute mirror those in *China – Raw Materials* and the EU, in fact, relies heavily on this case in its first written submission.[278] As Article 320 of the

[273] EU–Singapore FTA, Art. 2.17.6.
[274] EU–Singapore FTA, Art. 2.17.7.
[275] EU–Singapore FTA, Art. 2.17.10.
[276] EU–Singapore FTA, Art. 2.17.11.
[277] EU–Singapore FTA, Art. 2.17.9.
[278] *Ukraine – Export Prohibitions on Wood Products*, Arbitration Panel established pursuant to Article 206 of the Association Agreement between the European Union and the European Atomic Energy and their Member States and Ukraine, Written Submission by the European Union, Brussels, 17 February 2020.

Association Agreement dictates that, when interpreting those provisions identical to WTO agreements, the interpretation of such provisions should be consistent with the WTO jurisprudence, it is reasonable to expect that the ruling of this dispute will follow the jurisprudence of the WTO.

2.5.5 US FTAs

The United States has woven a dense web of FTA networks, despite the Trump Administration's withdrawal from the Trans-Pacific Partnership Agreement (TPP), subsequently transformed into the Comprehensive and Progressive Agreement for Trans-Pacific Partnership (CPTPP). The United States has managed to legislate rules on export restrictions through FTAs, but surprisingly, such rules are not as comprehensive as the USMCA or EU–Singapore or EU–Vietnam FTAs. This may be because most US FTAs were negotiated and concluded in the earlier 2000s. Most US FTAs, including the US–Korea FTA first concluded in 2007, regulate export taxes and export restrictions but do not touch on export licensing. Such a legal vacuum was only filled by the ill-fated TPP, which reflects greater complexity of regulation in export restrictions.

Several US FTAs, including the US–Chile, US–Australia, US–Singapore and US–Korea FTAs, regulate export taxes. Any duty, tax or other charge on the export of any good to the territory of the other party may not be imposed 'unless such duty, tax, or charge is adopted or maintained on any such good when destined for consumption in its territory'.[279] The main thrust of this provision is to level the competition advantage between domestic downstream producers and foreign producers relying on a good subject to export taxes. Therefore, when an export tax is levied, it has to be equally imposed against the same good meant for domestic consumption. Interestingly, the US–Singapore FTA prohibits the parties from imposing export taxes without any qualification,[280] which leads to interpretation ambiguity. According to the legal text, it appears that export taxes are strictly prohibited under any conditions.

With regards to export restrictions, the US FTAs regulate this issue in trifold fashion. First, it is restated that any prohibition or restriction on the importation or exportation or sale for export of any good is

[279] US–Australia FTA, Art. 2.11. See also US–Chile FTA, Art. 3.13 and US–Korea FTA, Art. 2.11.

[280] US–Singapore FTA, Art. 2.4.

prohibited, and for this purpose, Article XI of the GATT 1994 and relevant interpretative notes are incorporated into the FTAs.[281] Second, the US FTAs clarify the parties' understanding that rights and obligations under the GATT 1994 incorporated thereto prohibit certain forms of measure, including export price requirements,[282] and voluntary export restraints.[283] As the third step, the US FTAs regulate the consequential effects on parties, namely, re-exportation, in case of export restrictions imposed against non-parties. To be more precise, the US FTAs regulate this issue by clarifying that when a party imposes an export restriction against a non-party, it is to be construed that the rules in the FTAs do not prevent the party from 'requiring as a condition of export of such good of the Party to the territory of the other Party, that the good not be re-exported to the non-Party, directly or indirectly, without being consumed in the territory of the other Party'.[284] The objective of such provisions is to prevent the circumvention of export restrictions against a non-party through a party to the FTAs.

Finally, the ill-fated TPP contains more stringent disciplines on the transparency of export licensing procedures, which are brought into life through the CPTPP. Such rules are in fact predecessors of those in the USMCA. The TPP, in Article 2.13, first clarifies that it applies only to procedures for the application for an export license, namely, the condition for exporting a good, but not to customs documentation as required in ordinary administrative processes.[285] In the interest of transparency, a party maintaining or adopting export licensing procedures is required to notify other parties about relevant rules and publish them on the website.[286] The information notified by the party should include legal text, goods subject to export licensing procedure, contact points, the regulatory body concerned etc.[287] On the request of other parties, the imposing party should provide the aggregate number of licenses granted, and

[281] See e.g., US–Australia FTA, Art. 2.19.1; US–Chile FTA, Art. 3.11.1; US–Singapore FTA, Art. 3.7.1; US–Korea FTA, Art. 2.18.1.

[282] See e.g., US–Australia FTA, Art. 2.19.2; US–Chile FTA, Art. 3.11.2(a); US–Singapore FTA, Art. 3.7.2; US–Korea FTA, Art. 2.18.2(a).

[283] See e.g., US–Australia FTA, Art. 2.19.2; US–Chile FTA, Art. 3.11.2(c); US–Singapore FTA, Art. 3.7.2; US–Korea FTA, Art. 2.18.2(c).

[284] See e.g., US–Australia FTA, Art. 2.19.3; US–Chile FTA, Art. 3.11.3; US–Singapore FTA, Art. 3.7.3; US–Korea FTA, Art. 2.18.4(b).

[285] TPP, Art. 2.13.1.

[286] TPP, Art. 2.13.2.

[287] TPP, Art. 2.13.3.

'measures, if any, that the Party has taken in conjunction with the licensing procedure to restrict domestic production or consumption or to stabilise production, supply or prices for the relevant good'.[288] Finally, the TPP disconnects the obligations on export licensing thereunder from those under public international law, such as UN Security Council Resolutions and non-proliferation regimes,[289] just as does the USMCA.

2.5.6 *FTAs of Resource-Rich Countries*

Moving beyond the EU and the USMCA, it is worth a look at the practices of other trade nations in regulating export quantitative restrictions and export duties. Since China's accession protocol to the WTO dictates that China is to eliminate export duties, it is feasible to examine China's FTA practices. In addition, it would enhance our understanding about the regulation of export restrictions by investigating the practices of resource-rich countries. Therefore, this section examines some FTA practices of China, Australia and the Gulf Cooperation Council (GCC). Specifically, this section examines the regulation of export restrictions in the China–ASEAN (Association of the South East Asian Nations) Agreement on Trade in Goods, the China–Australia FTA and the GCC–EFTA (European Free Trade Association) FTA.

The China–ASEAN Agreement on Trade in Goods is a subsequent agreement under the Framework Agreement on Comprehensive Economic Co-Operation between ASEAN and the People's Republic of China (China–ASEAN Framework Agreement) concluded in 2004; represents an example of earlier FTA practices of both China and ASEAN; and constitutes a good case-study for the South–South FTA. The China–ASEAN Agreement on Trade in Goods only regulates export quantitative restrictions by incorporating the WTO disciplines, stating that '[e]ach Party undertakes not to maintain any quantitative restrictions at any time unless otherwise permitted under the WTO disciplines'[290] and does not touch on the issue of export duties. In fact, tariff reductions are categorised into normal track and sensitive track, which in turn should be carried out in accordance with their respective schedules. There is no across-the-board regulation on export duties in the legal text.

[288] TPP, Art. 2.13.4(b).
[289] TPP, Art. 2.13.5.
[290] China–ASEAN Agreement on Trade in Goods, Art. 8.1.

In the China–Australia FTA, the legal text mirrors that of NAFTA by dictating that parties do not adopt or maintain any prohibition or restriction or measure having equivalent effect, including quantitative restrictions on the 'exportation or sale for export of a good destined for the territory of the other Party, except in accordance with Article XI of GATT 1994'.[291] The China–Australia FTA then incorporates Article XI of the GATT 1994 and makes this provision part of the FTA *mutatis mutandis*. By contrast, the China–Australia FTA does not touch on export duties. Article 2.4 of the China–Australia FTA deals with the elimination and reduction of customs duties by dictating that parties eliminate or reduce customs duties in accordance with their respective schedules. Parties should also refrain from reintroducing or raising customs duties.[292] A 'Customs duty' is defined as 'any customs or import duty and a charge of any kind, including any form of surtax or surcharge, imposed in connection with the importation of a good'.[293] Therefore, under the China–Australia FTA, the elimination or reduction of customs duties does not extend to export duties.

Finally, the GCC–EFTA FTA addresses export restrictions slightly differently. With respect to export quantitative restrictions, Article 2.3 of the GCC–EFTA FTA incorporates Article XI of the GATT 1994 and makes it part of the GCC–EFTA FTA *mutatis mutandis*. Export duty is not covered by customs duties under the GCC–EFTA FTA, as customs duties relate only to a duty or a charge of any kind imposed in connection with the importation of a product.[294] Export duties therefore do not fall into the scope of customs duties, which are to be eliminated or reduced in accordance with the schedules and should not be reintroduced. However, the GCC–EFTA FTA in Article 2.4 does regulate the levy of export duties. The legal text reads as follows

> A Party may introduce or maintain duties on exports in conjunction with domestic measures, in so far as it considers that such duties are necessary. Such duties shall be applied irrespective of the destination of the product. The Parties shall inform the Joint Committee of all export duties applied.

This provision puts forward three conditions for the imposition of export duties: one procedural; two substantial. Procedurally, those export duties

[291] China–Australia FTA, Art. 2.7.1.
[292] China–Australia FTA, Art. 2.4.
[293] China–Australia FTA, Art. 1.3(a).
[294] GCC–EFTA FTA, Art. 2.4.

imposed should be notified to the Joint Committee for the purpose of transparency. Substantially, an export duty may be imposed insofar as the parties consider it necessary. Such criteria may turn out to be self-judging and lose force. However, the provisions add one additional element; namely, the export duty should be imposed in conjunction with domestic measures. This additional element aims to achieve even-handedness and set a level playing field between domestic and foreign downstream producers. However, due to the loosely defined character of 'domestic measures', it may have only limited bite. Finally, an export duty may only be imposed in accordance with Most-Favoured-Nation treatment, namely, irrespective of the destination of the product concerned. The contracting parties may not favour one country but discriminate against another.

With a short survey of the China–ASEAN Agreement on Trade in Goods, the China–Australia FTA and the GCC–EFTA FTA, some observations can be made. With regards to export quantitative restrictions, given that the WTO rules have regulated this subject matter, it can be simply incorporated into the FTAs and be made applicable to the parties. With respect to export duties, the regulation will differ corresponding to the political and economic situations of the parties. To begin with, conventional practices are not to bring export duties into the scope of customs duties, which only deal with the importation of a product. Second, the China–ASEAN Agreement on Trade in Goods, an agreement between ten South East Asian developing countries and China, a country plagued with WTO disputes due to its obligation on export duties under its accession protocol, chose to leave the regulation of export duties aside by focusing only on the elimination and reduction of customs duties. Similarly, the China–Australia FTA follows conventional practice by not extending the scope of customs duties to export duties and leaving export duties unregulated. This is understandable given that Australia is a country rich in natural resources and might opt to impose export duties for various policy objectives. Australia might thus not want to bind itself on export duties, while China is more than happy to accept such an arrangement. Third, regarding the GCC–EFTA FTA, an FTA between resource-exporting and importing countries, the arrangement is more interesting. Whereas the parties added some procedural and substantive conditions for the imposition of export duties, such conditions have fewer limiting effects given the self-judging nature of the necessity to impose export duties and the vague definition of conjunctive domestic measures.

2.6 Short Conclusion

This chapter examined relevant rules regulating export restrictions under the WTO framework, covering a set of WTO provisions having a bearing on export restrictions, WTO-plus obligations and commitments arising from accession protocols and Working Party Reports, relevant proposals in the DDA and regulations in the context of RTAs.

Under current WTO rules, the most comprehensive provision setting out the obligation on export restrictions stems from Article XI of the GATT 1994, which, in a comprehensive manner, obliges WTO members to eliminate prohibitions or restrictions other than duties, taxes or other charges. This obligation correlates with the Uruguay Round's efforts in tariffing quantitative restrictions, as they are believed to be more trade distortive than tariffs. This obligation is nonetheless subject to three exceptions, of which two are relevant here: temporary export restrictions preventing or relieving critical shortage of foodstuffs or other essential products, and export restrictions necessary to the application of standards or regulations for the classification, grading or marketing of commodities in international trade. These two provisions have been addressed in *Canada – Measure Affecting Exports of Unprocessed Herring and Salmon* in the GATT era and *China – Raw Materials* and *China – Rare Earths* in the WTO age. In addition, the AoA further elaborates the conditions to impose export restrictions on foodstuffs by obligating members to give due consideration to the impact of such export restrictions on the food security of importing countries and laying down the notification and consultation requirements.

Moreover, export restrictions, arguably, may constitute domestic subsidies to domestic downstream producers. The critical point is whether such criteria for a subsidy necessitate 'a charge on the public account'. Given the GATT rules did not contain a definition of the subsidy, the EEC and United States arrived at different conclusions in *FEDIO* and *Argentina – Leather*. In the WTO era, the same issue lingers but the point of contention shifts to whether the government may entrust or direct a private entity to carry out the functions normally vested in the government in subsidising domestic downstream producers in the form of export restrictions. The Panel in *US – Export Restraint* found in the negative. That said, whether export restrictions, in the form of double-pricing as generally maintained by resource-endowed countries, can be qualified as subsidy is a question to be explored.

Another issue running through the GATT era into the WTO age is the regulation of grey-area measures, notably, VERs. The wide spread of VERs during the 1980s had finally prompted negotiators to bring them into the discipline of WTO law. The ASG, in Article 11(b), thus lays down the following rule, 'a Member shall not seek, take or maintain any voluntary export restraints, orderly marketing arrangements or any other similar measures on the export or the import side', which include 'actions taken by a single Member as well as actions under agreements, arrangements and understandings entered into by two or more Members'. Nonetheless, the breadth of this provision has not been tested in the WTO dispute settlement mechanism. Whether this provision can capture export cartels in New Zealand's Zespri, or even production cartels, as maintained by OPEC, remains untested.

The deficiency of rules on export restrictions in the WTO agreements results in different attempts at legislating stronger discipline on this subject matter. Such efforts are seen in the accession negotiations processes, the DDA and RTA context.

Seizing the opportunity in accession negotiation processes, existent WTO members take the advantage of the vague concept of 'terms to be agreed' in demanding WTO-plus obligations and commitments in export restrictions, in particular with regard to resource-rich countries. Such examples can be best seen in China's Accession Protocols and Russia's Working Party Report. The format in legislating these obligations and commitments, in accession protocols or in Working Party Reports, has impact on their legal effects under WTO law, in particular with regards to the relationship between the accession protocol and WTO Agreement. Such issues have been recurring in *China – Raw Materials* and *China – Rare Earths* and attracted tremendous academic debates. The critical point is the role of the 'integration clause', which integrates the accession protocols into WTO law and thus constitutes an integral part of the WTO Agreement. This issue is concretized in the question of whether a general exception, as contained in Article XX of the GATT 1994, can be applicable to China's obligation to eliminate export duties as set out in Paragraph 11.3. The WTO judiciary's technical and textual interpretation prompted Russia to include its commitments in the Working Party Report with a view to avoiding similar controversies.

In the context of the DDA, negotiations are conducted on two fronts, agriculture and NAMA, but no significant progress has been reported. On the agriculture front, the ambition is to tariffy export prohibitions or restrictions or to bind and reduce export taxes but at the same time provide special and differential treatment to developing countries. However, most developing countries remain suspicious about various proposals tabled and fear that their food security may be threatened. On the NAMA front, procedural and substantive approaches are advanced. Procedurally, the United States and Japan aim to enhance the transparency of law and practice on export restrictions. Substantially, the EU aims to impose more stringent disciplines on export restrictions by reducing or eliminating export duties. Unsurprisingly, developing countries remain lukewarm to the EU's proposal and reiterate that export duties constitute legitimate tools for development and fall outside the scope of NAMA.

Finally, different RTAs display different characteristics. The EU imposes the most stringent disciplines on export restrictions by eliminating export duties, export quantitative restrictions and all measures having equivalent effect. The CJEU has laid down a rich jurisprudence on the term of 'all measures having equivalent effect', though whether these case-laws relate mainly to importation and their validity in exportation is subject to dispute. The USMCA (and its predecessor, NAFTA), a free trade area rather than a customs union as in the case of the EU, obliges contracting parties to eliminate export quantitative restrictions but permits the imposition of export duties with some conditions to be fulfilled. The USMCA, given its free trade area nature, also addresses the imposition of export restrictions against non-parties and its legal effects to parties to USMCA. Those FTAs concluded by resource-rich countries reflect a mixed picture. Whereas the China–ASEAN Agreement on Trade in Goods and the China–Australia FTA do not regulate export duties, the GCC–EFTA FTA does impose light obligations on their imposition.

3

Governing Export Restrictions

National Security and International Political Economy

3.1 Introduction

Export restrictions, controls and embargoes returned to the forefront of public international law in the wake of the Ukraine Crisis in 2014 and were intensified by the decision of the Trump Administration in the United States to add Huawei and its affiliates to the entity list. An important sanctions tool, export restrictions were frequently used by the United States and, to a lesser degree, European countries and Japan during the Cold War, either to prevent the technological advancement of the Soviet Union or to retaliate following such incidents as the Soviet invasion of Afghanistan in 1979 and involvement in the Polish imposition of martial law in 1981. The lifting of export restrictions is similarly significant. Under the Obama Administration, the United States started to reconcile with Cuba and lifted elements of its long-standing travel ban and export restrictions. Economic and technological developments are also reflected in export controls, as seen in the 2015 abolition of a 40-year-old US export ban on crude oil in response to the increasing volume of domestic shale gas production, which eroded the strategic importance of the resource.

The architects of post–World War II global economic architecture entrusted the General Agreement on Tariffs and Trade (GATT) and its successor the World Trade Organization (WTO) with the task of trade liberalisation, with a view to establishing a liberal international economic order. At the same time, following the lead of the United States, the countries of the North Atlantic Treaty Organization (NATO), with the exception of Iceland, in conjunction with Australia and Japan established an export control regime, the Coordinating Committee for Multilateral Export Controls (COCOM), to regulate or control East–West trade. These two regimes, with different rationales and philosophies, seemed to sit conformably with one another until China joined the WTO in 2001, and Russia in 2012.

With the dissolution of the Soviet Union, the COCOM lost its relevance. Competition between the United States and Soviet Union was gradually replaced by the new reality of the Sino–US race for global hegemony, and the COCOM was replaced by a loose regime underpinned by the Wassenaar Arrangement on Export Controls for Conventional Arms and Dual-Use Goods and Technologies (Wassenaar Arrangement). Concomitantly, the Convention on the Prohibition of the Development, Production and Stockpiling of Bacteriological (Biological) and Toxin Weapons and on their Destruction (Biological Weapon Convention), the Convention on the Prohibition of the Development, Production, Stockpiling and Use of Chemical Weapons and on their Destruction (Chemical Weapons Convention), the Treaty on the Non-Proliferation of Nuclear Weapons (NPT) and the Arms Trade Treaty (ATT) play a key role in regulating nuclear, biological and chemical weapons and arms trade. Moreover, entities subject to sanctions, in the form of export restrictions, extend from sovereign states to non-state actors and partial sovereigns.

Against this background, this chapter aims to trace the evolutional history of export controls, a major instrument for the imposition of sanctions, since the end of World War II. This chapter examines the rationale and political economy considerations related to the formation and dissolution of the COCOM, against the general trend of GATT-led trade liberalisation. The chapter then examines whether the newly established legal regimes on export controls contribute to arms trade flows or effective arms/weapons control. After exploring the broad context of the evolving international political economy, this chapter examines the development of law and policy on export restrictions in the United States, and the harmonisation of export restrictions policy in the EU. The chapter further explores legal issues arising from the interconnection of these two sets of legal regimes: trade liberalisation and controlled trade. Emphasis will be placed on whether Article XXI of the GATT 1994 provides sufficient policy space for trade nations or effective legal safeguards to prevent national security from being abused for protectionist purposes. Finally, this chapter focuses on recent cases of export restrictions, the EU's sanction measures against Russia; China's tourism embargo against South Korea; the Qatar diplomatic crisis; the United States' addition of Huawei to the entity list and Japan's removal of South Korea from the whitelist of trusted trading partners, to illustrate the complexity of international law and the international political economy surrounding export restrictions. A short conclusion summarising the main findings and key arguments will be provided at the end of this chapter.

3.2 The East–West Divide and Proliferation of Export Control Regimes

Following the traumatic experience of World War II, in part a consequence of the tariffs war resulting from the Smoot–Hawley Act of 1930, the United States and its alliance were determined to pursue liberal international trade relations, which underpinned the post-war GATT system. However, liberal international trade relations were subject to two qualifications. First, the GATT regime placed greater emphasis on the reduction of import barriers and paid less attention to export restrictions. Second, liberal international trade relations were limited to the United States and its allies and did not extend to Communist countries.[1] As is correctly articulated by the late John Jackson, '[t]he post–World War II international trading system is obviously based on rules and principles that more or less assume free market-oriented economies. The rules of GATT certainly were constructed with that in mind.'[2] Similarly, Alexander Polouektov argues that the GATT system 'was designed by the market economies and for market economies'.[3] Whereas some socialist countries, such as Hungary and Poland, joined the GATT in the 1960s and 1970s,[4] liberal international trade relations remained limited to the United States, its Western European allies and Japan. Trade between the US and Soviet camps was largely dominated by the rationales of national security concerns and foreign policy objectives, which gave rise to such economic strategies and policy instruments as economic warfare and strategic embargoes. To these ends, efficient coordination and effective enforcement were indispensable and a multilateral institution, the COCOM, was established. Threats and rewards could be dangled by the United States, with the leading countries imposing export restrictions when appropriate.[5]

[1] Michael Mastanduno, *Economic Containment: CoCom and the Politics of East–West Trade* (Cornell University Press 1992) 34.

[2] John H. Jackson, *The World Trading System: Law and Policy of International Economic Relations* (2nd ed., The MIT Press 1997) 325.

[3] Alexander Polouektov, 'Non-Market Economy Issues in the WTO Anti-Dumping Law and Accession Negotiations: Revival of a Two-tier Membership?' (2002) 36 *Journal of World Trade* 1, 5.

[4] M. M. Kostecki, *East–West Trade and the GATT System* (MacMillan Press 1979) 7–16.

[5] See generally, David A. Baldwin, *Economic Statecraft* (Princeton University Press 1985).

3.2.1 *From COCOM to Wassenaar Agreement*

3.2.1.1 Coordinating Committee for Multilateral Export Controls

'COCOM played an obvious role in the military sphere, complementing and reinforcing US and NATO deterrence strategies vis-à-vis the Soviet Union and Warsaw Pact'[6] and paradoxically helped to maintain a liberal international economic order among non-Communist states. To be more precise, the COCOM had been a key instrument for the United States to pursue liberal trade policies nationally, and to shape a liberal international legal order, as it served as a firebreak insulating the liberal orientation of US trade policy between the United States and its Western alliance from the economic nationalism inherent in US export control law and policy.[7]

A tension existed, therefore, between the belief in minimal government intervention and the primacy of market forces, which drove US domestic liberal trade policies (as well as liberal international trade relations), and the desire to intervene systematically in the market with the aim of regulating and restricting transactions in the interests of national security. Such tension might be minimalised if the intervention were limited to trade with adversary states (namely, during the Cold War, the Soviet Union and its allies); nonetheless, such tensions would be exacerbated if the restrictive measures extended to trade among the United States, the countries of Western Europe and Japan. Such tensions became acute when Western countries refused to participate, or were judged to do so insufficiently, in the efforts to control trade with adversaries and thus invited countermeasures, or secondary sanctions, from the United States.[8] When secondary sanctions arose, the alliance between the United States and Western countries was called into question.

The different attitudes taken by the United States and its Western alliance had economic foundations. Economic relations between Western European and Eastern European countries and the Soviet Union differed from those between the United States and the Soviet camp in that the former were much closer than the latter. The United States dominated international trade and technological innovations in the immediate post-war era but during the Cold War era, such lead became less apparent.

6 Mastanduno, *Economic Containment: CoCom and the Politics of East–West Trade* (n. 1) 5.
7 Ibid. 4.
8 Ibid. 14.

Therefore, Western European countries' reliance on East–West trade grew gradually. Further, the composition of the trade structure between the United States, Western European countries (and Japan) and the Soviet camp also played a role in making decisions on export restrictive measures. While US–Soviet trade related mainly to agriculture products, East–West European trade related mainly to mechanics, equipment and, possibly, energy. Therefore, when the United States imposed export restrictions on strategic products or dual-use products, such export restrictions, if extended to its Western alliance, economically impacted allies but not the United States.[9]

Unfortunately, export restrictions with a view to preventing the Soviet Union and its camp from obtaining strategic products or technologies would be doomed to failure if imposed or maintained only by the United States, as targeted products and technologies could be obtained from other countries. Moreover, unilateral export restrictions adopted by the United States, unlike import barriers, harmed US domestic producers while not impacting foreign enterprises, which were more than happy to take advantage of the trade opportunities created by US export restrictions. Whereas the United States might have to coerce its allies, by threat or compensation for lost trade, to act collectively, the ability of the United States to exercise this foreign policy tool faded gradually. Therefore, effective coordination with a view to overcoming the collective action problem was necessary; the COCOM was created to meet this regulatory end.

The COCOM was an informal institution without solid legal basis and possessing no legal personality.[10] It was created in the aftermath of World War II when the threat to national security of the United States and Western European countries was imminent. Therefore, the COCOM was a product of a bipolar international system[11] and served to maintain the technological lead of the United States; it did so with varying degrees of success during the Cold War era.

As former Senator (R-PA) John Heinz recalled, a question plaguing US policy-makers in the post-war era was where to sell American products,

[9] Lisa L. Martin, *Coercive Cooperation: Explaining Multilateral Economic Sanctions* (Princeton University Press 1992) 234–239.

[10] Cecil Hunt, 'Multilateral Cooperation in Export Controls – the Role of COCOM' (1982–1983) 14 *Toledo Law Review* 1285, 1287.

[11] Robert van den Hoven van Generen, 'Cooperation on Export Control between the United States and Europe: A Cradle of Conflict in Technology Transfer' (1989) 14 *North Carolina Journal of International & Commercial Regulation* 391, 393.

extend trade and safeguard American prosperity. The original hope was to revive east–west trade, a hope soon dampened by the growing Soviet sphere of influence in Eastern Europe, which led to the adoption of the Truman Doctrine and Marshall Plan. In the wake of the coup in Czechoslovakia and Soviet blockade of Berlin, the United States and recipient countries of the Marshall Plan soon agreed on the need for a multilateral control system, initially tucked secretly into the folds of the Marshall Plan. After intense bilateral negotiations in 1948–1949, multilateral negotiations were held in November 1949 in Paris with the United States, United Kingdom, France, Italy, the Netherlands, Belgium and Luxemburg participating, which resulted in an informal Consultative Group.[12] In January 1950, the Consultative Group convened its first meeting and agreed to establish an informal and voluntary organisation. Governed by secretive decision-making based on consensus, the group established the COCOM to oversee day-to-day coordinating tasks relating to export controls targeting the Soviet bloc, implementing control measures and recommending improvements.[13]

One of the major tasks of the COCOM was to develop the International List and approve exceptions. The International List comprised three parts: the International Munitions List; International Atomic Energy List and Industrial List. The former two focused on strategically significant technologies while the latter referred to so-called dual-use commodities and technologies, which had potential civilian and military applications. The Industrial List was greatly controversial due to its broad scope and ambiguity.[14] The Industrial List was separated into three subcategories in accordance with the sophistication and sensitivity of the controlled commodity or technologies: administration exceptions, favourable considerations and embargos. 'Administrative Exception' applied to commodities and technologies that might be freely exported to most destinations on prior notice of member countries; those commodities and technologies subject to 'favourable considerations' might be exported if there was no objection raised by any member country; and

[12] John Heinz, *U.S. Strategic Trade: An Export Control System for the 1990s* (Westview Press 1991) 44–46.

[13] Ibid. 46.

[14] Ibid. 124; Keneth A. Dursht, 'Notes: From Containment to Cooperation: Collective Action and the Wassenaar Arrangement' (1997) 19 *Cardozo Law Review* 1079, 1099–1100; Christopher F. Corr, 'The Wall Still Stands! Complying with Export Controls on Technology Transfers in the Post-Cold War, Post-9/11 Era' (2003) 25 *Houston Journal of International Law* 441, 451.

the 'embargo' category necessitated general consensus or unanimous approval from all member countries. The decision-making process of the COCOM effectively gave individual member countries veto power when the commodity or technology in question fell into the latter two categories of the Industrial List.

As generally shared, the United States enforced the COCOM control lists most strictly and, in addition to the COCOM list, the United States unilaterally subjected more items to export restrictions. With a view to inducing or forcing other COCOM member countries to enforce the COCOM control list with greater effort and diligence, the United States, from time to time, threatened to punish, and did punish, countries and enterprises that breached COCOM control measures. The incongruence between the United States and its alliance was most visible when secondary sanctioning measures were imposed against enterprises and countries that failed to comply with COCOM rules, as in the Toshiba–Kongsberg case.

In 1987, it was revealed that a Japanese company, Toshiba Machine Company (Toshiba), and a Norwegian company, Kongsberg Trading Company (Kongsberg), transferred sophisticated milling machines and technologies to the Soviet Navy for making submarine propellers, which were allegedly more difficult to detect. This transfer was believed to be in violation of COCOM rules. While the action did not involve US technology, Congress nonetheless passed §2443 of the Omnibus Trade and Competitiveness Act of 1988, which included sanctions against Toshiba and Kongsberg.[15] Another illustrative case is the Pipeline dispute during the Reagan Administration; interestingly, the controversies of Pipeline linger, as the Trump Administration threatened to impose sanctions against German companies if they continued to participate in the Nord Stream project.[16]

3.2.1.2 Wassenaar Arrangement on Export Controls for Conventional Arms and Dual-Use Goods and Technologies

With the fall of the Berlin Wall and the dissolution of the Soviet Union, the need and justification for maintaining an export control regime and,

[15] Corr, 'The Wall Still Stands! Complying with Export Controls on Technology Transfers in the Post-Cold War, Post-9/11 Era', ibid., 453; Trevor Hiestand, 'Swords into Plowshares: Considerations for 21st Century Export Controls in the United States' (1995) 9 *Emory International Law Review* 679, 702–703.

[16] Darko Janjevic, 'US Ambassador Richard Crenell Threatens German Firms over Russian Pipeline', *Deutsche Welle*, 13 January 2019, available at www.dw.com/en/us-ambassador-richard-grenell-threatens-german-firms-over-russian-pipeline/a-47062540.

consequently, the *raison d'être* of the COCOM came to be seriously questioned. The COCOM was finally terminated in 1994; nonetheless, the United States tried hard to persuade its allies of the need for maintaining a similar regime, if in a much looser or weaker form, to oversee exports of embargoed or restrictive commodities and technologies. Following intense negotiations, the Wassenaar Arrangement was agreed by the participating countries in a suburb of The Hague, Wassenaar, in 1996. However, the Wassenaar Arrangement is not an international legally binding instrument, and thus entails no international rights or obligations. According to the participating countries of the Wassenaar Arrangement,

> The [Wassenaar Arrangement] was designed to promote transparency, exchange of views and information and greater responsibility in transfers of conventional arms and dual-use goods and technologies, thus preventing destabilising accumulations. It complements and reinforces, without duplication, the existing regimes for non-proliferation of weapons of mass destruction and their delivery systems, by focusing on the threats to international and regional peace and security which may arise from transfers of armaments and sensitive dual-use goods and technologies where the risks are judged greatest. This arrangement is also intended to enhance co-operation to prevent the acquisition of armaments and sensitive dual-use items for military end-uses, if the situation in a region or the behaviour of a state is, or becomes, a cause for serious concern to the Participating States.[17]

The Wassenaar Arrangement sets out two Control Lists: Munitions List and Dual-Use Goods and Technologies List, which is subsequently separated into two categories, the Sensitive List and Very Sensitive List. The criteria for the selection of Dual-Use Goods and Technologies are defined as 'key elements directly related to the indigenous development, production, use or enhancement of advanced conventional military capabilities'.[18] The selection of Dual-Use Goods and Technologies is assessed against the following criteria: foreign availability outside participating states; the ability to control effectively the export of the goods; the ability to make a clear and objective specification of the item and whether controlled by another regime.[19] In accordance with the given definition

[17] Wassenaar Arrangement, *Agreed at the WA Plenary* (1998 Wassenaar Arrangement Decision), in Wassenaar Arrangement Secretariat, *Wassenaar Arrangement on Export Controls for Conventional Arms and Dual-Use Goods and Technologies: Basic Documents* (Wassenaar Arrangement Secretariat, 2016) 1.

[18] Agreed in 1998 and amended at the 2000 and 2004 Plenaries, in ibid. 77.

[19] Ibid.

and relevant criteria, those items subject to the Sensitive List of Dual-Use Goods and Technologies are 'key elements *directly related to* the indigenous development, production, use or enhancement of advanced conventional military capabilities whose proliferation would significantly undermine the objectives of the Wassenaar Arrangement'.[20] This is, in fact, the basic definition of dual-use goods and technologies. The items subject to the Very Sensitive List in turn refer to 'key elements *essential for* the indigenous development, production, use or enhancement of the most advanced conventional military capabilities whose proliferation would significantly undermine the objectives of the Wassenaar Arrangement'.[21]

Unlike the COCOM, the Wassenaar Arrangement does not empower any member country with a veto over the exports of another country; nor does it agree on a list of embargoed or restricted countries; nor does it require prior notification or approval for exports; the Wassenaar Arrangement only obliges member countries to submit an aggregated summary of exported goods after such transfer, as well as a notice of the denial of a license;[22] its decision-making is based on consensus. 'All measures undertaken with respect to the Arrangement are in accordance with member countries' national legislation and policies and are implemented on the basis of national discretion.'[23]

The transition from the COCOM to the Wassenaar Arrangement is marked by the expanded composition of participating countries, notably, the inclusion of Russia and Eastern European countries. Therefore, the rationale for the Wassenaar Arrangement differs significantly from that of the COCOM in that the Wassenaar Arrangement does not target Russia or any particular country. A delicate shift from the Cold War between the United States and its Western European alliance and the Soviet camp to US–China competition or rivalry may be foreshadowed in

[20] Agreed in 1998 and amended at the 2000 and 2004 Plenaries, in Wassenaar Arrangement Secretariat, *Wassenaar Arrangement on Export Controls for Conventional Arms and Dual-Use Goods and Technologies: Basic Documents* 78 (emphasis added).

[21] Agreed in 2000 and amended at the 2004 Plenary, in ibid. 79 (emphasis added).

[22] Corr, 'The Wall Still Stands! Complying with Export Controls on Technology Transfers in the Post-Cold War, Post-9/11 Era' (n. 14) 455.

[23] 1998 Wassenaar Arrangement Decision. This denial notice obligation is weakly enforced and a mandatory denial consultation, namely, an obligation to consult the member which has denied the export prior to granting the export license, was proposed and received inadequate support. Jamil Jaffer, 'Strengthening the Wassenaar Export Control Regime' (2002) 3 *Chicago Journal of International Law* 519, 523.

view of the exclusion of China from the Wassenaar Arrangement. Indeed, US export control policy in the twenty-first century relates more to China than to Russia.

3.2.1.3 Other Export Control Regimes and UN Sanctions

In addition to the Wassenaar Arrangement, three additional export control groupings exist, composed by political grouping of supplier's states and based on soft-law instruments, which are generally referred to as regimes: the Nuclear Supplier's Group (NSG) for nuclear weapons and materials; the Australia Group for biological and chemical weapon non-proliferation; and the Missile Technology Control Regime (MTCR) for missile and related delivery technologies. These regimes share some similarities. All are informal arrangements without hard legally binding obligations or commitments either in their constituent documents or in their secondary laws. These regimes are 'arrangements between states wherein members share identities, values, meanings concerning issues related to their survival, and have an expectation of peaceful co-operation among themselves'.

Apart from political grouping or soft-law instruments[24] governing export control policy, there are some international regimes for setting out a legal framework regulating this subject matter. Such international legal instruments relate mainly to non-proliferation agreements and the ATT. In addition, whereas member countries of the COCOM and Wassenaar Arrangement control their exports based largely on national security concerns and foreign policy objectives, a country may be under an international obligation to impose export restrictions against particular countries, entities or individuals on certain items. These legal obligations arise mainly from non-proliferation agreements and UN-related sanctions, while countries may also impose sanctions unilaterally. I will examine these two sets of instruments next.

Non-Proliferation Agreements and the Arms Trade Treaty Currently, four international legal instruments (Biological Weapons Convention, Chemical Weapons Convention, NPT and ATT) are set out for the major frameworks governing the export control and trade activities of (biological, chemical and nuclear) weapons and arms. They share some similarities in objectives and purposes but also demonstrate some distinct

[24] Daniel H. Joyner, 'Restructuring the Multilateral Export Control Regime System' (2004) 9 *Journal of Conflict and Security Law* 181, 183.

characteristics, in particular in terms of their attitude to the transfer or trade of weapons and arms. The Biological and Chemical Weapons Conventions and ATT sit at the two extremes, while NPT stands in the middle of the spectrum.

To be more specific, the Biological Weapons Convention and Chemical Weapons Convention prohibit the development, production, acquisition, stockpiling and retaining of biological and chemical weapons, and aim at their destruction. In line with this logic, these two conventions prohibit the trade or transfer of biological and chemical weapons and their precursors.[25] In WTO terms, these two conventions set out export prohibitions for biological and chemical weapons and their precursors.

By contrast, the objective of the ATT is rather mixed. On the one hand, the ATT '[u]nderlines the need to prevent and eradicate the illicit trade in conventional arms and to prevent their diversion to the illicit market, or for unauthorized end use and end users, including in the commission of terrorist acts';[26] on the other hand, it '[r]ecognizes the legitimate political, security, economic and commercial interests of States in the international trade in conventional arms'[27] and '[r]eaffirms the sovereign right of any State to regulate and control conventional arms exclusively within its territory, pursuant to its own legal or constitutional system'.[28] Therefore, international trade in conventional arms is not completely prohibited; on the contrary, the political, security, economic and commercial interests of states in the international trade are explicitly recognised in the ATT. The main thrust of the ATT is to establish a national control regime to monitor and assess the danger of diversion of arms transfer.[29] From the outset, the ATT prohibits three types of transfer of conventional arms, namely, transfers which would violate obligations under the UN Security Council measures adopted under

[25] Biological Weapons Convention, Art. 3 [Each State Party to this Convention undertakes not to transfer to any recipient whatsoever, directly or indirectly, and not in any way to assist, encourage, or induce any State, group of States or international organisations to manufacture or otherwise acquire any of the agents, toxins, weapons, equipment or means of delivery specified in Article I of the Convention.] Chemical Weapons Convention, Art. 1.1(a) [Each State Party to this Convention undertakes never under any circumstances: 1. (a) To develop, produce, otherwise acquire, stockpile or retain chemical weapons, or transfer, directly or indirectly, chemical weapons to anyone.]

[26] ATT, Recital 3.

[27] ATT, Recital 4.

[28] ATT, Recital 5.

[29] ATT, Art. 5.2 and 11.1.

Chapter VII of the UN Charter; those which would violate relevant international agreements; and those which would be used in the commission of international crime such as genocide, crimes against humanity, grave breaches of the Geneva Conventions of 1949 or war crimes.[30] In case such transfer is not prohibited, the state party is obliged to assess the potential that the conventional arms or items would contribute to or undermine peace and security or could be used to commit or facilitate a serious violation of international humanitarian law, international human rights law, terrorism or transnational organised crime.[31]

The NPT stands between these two extremes of the spectrum of non-proliferation regimes by establishing three pillars for the regulation of nuclear applications: non-proliferation, nuclear energy for peaceful purposes and disarmament.[32] By way of this three-pillar regime and the separation between nuclear weapons and nuclear energy for peaceful purposes,[33] the NPT thus creates a tradable market for the latter while prohibiting the transfer of the former.

Collective Sanctions under the United Nations and Autonomous Sanctions The UN Charter entrusts the Security Council with responsibility for the maintenance of international peace and security, to be carried out in accordance with principles and objectives of the Charter.[34] In particular, Chapter VII lays out the procedures, and sources of power, for the Security Council to exercise in discharging its responsibilities. The Charter first instructs the Security Council to 'determine the existence of any threat to the peace, breach of the peace, or act of aggression'[35] and to 'make recommendations, or decide what measures

30 ATT, Art. 6.

31 ATT, Art. 7.1.

32 The interrelated and mutually reinforcing relationship of these three pillars is best described by the US delegation to the NPT during the 2010 Treaty Review Conference. 'An effective nonproliferation regime whose members comply with their obligations provides an essential foundation for progress on disarmament and makes possible greater cooperation on the peaceful use of nuclear energy. With the right to access the benefits of peaceful nuclear technology comes the responsibility of nonproliferation. Progress on disarmament reinforces efforts to strengthen the nonproliferation regime and to enforce compliance with obligations, thereby also facilitating peaceful nuclear cooperation.' 2010 NPT Nuclear Nonproliferation US Delegation to the Treaty Review Conference, available at https://2009-2017.state.gov/documents/organization/141503.pdf, p. 5.

33 NPT, Art. 1, 2 and 4.

34 UN Charter, Art. 24(1).

35 UN Charter, Art. 39.

shall be taken in accordance with Articles 41 and 42, to maintain or restore international peace and security'.[36] Decisions of the Security Council are to be accepted and carried out by UN members in accordance with the Charter.[37] Among those adopted measures, generally referred to as sanctions, the most relevant to this book are those undertaken under Article 41 of the Charter. Article 41 of the Charter reads

> The Security Council may decide what measures not involving the use of armed force are to be employed to give effect to its decisions, and it may call upon the Members of the United Nations to apply such measures. These may include complete or partial interruption of economic relations and of rail, sea, air, postal, telegraphic, radio, and other means of communication, and the severance of diplomatic relations.

Those sanction measures aim to isolate the target (state) legally and politically from the rest of the international community and deprive it of the benefit of international intercourse.[38] The sanctions most frequently adopted cover prohibition of import and export of goods, services, movement of funds and of air, sea, and land communication; severance or reduction of diplomatic relations; and restrictions on the movement of persons.[39] Among these sanctions, the 'interruption of economic relations' in the form of import/export prohibition or restrictions, or embargo in sanctions terms, is most relevant to this book. As dictated by Article 25 of the Charter, UN members are bound by the sanctions resolutions of the Security Council and should carry out decisions in accordance with the Charter.

Moreover, autonomous sanctions taking the form of export restrictions or prohibitions may be imposed unilaterally in the absence of resolutions of the UN Security Council. Both the EU and the United States have domestic legislation to regulate the imposition of autonomous sanctions. The legality of such sanctions both under public international law and WTO law may be called into question. A detailed examination of domestic laws on autonomous sanctions will be provided in subsequent sections of this chapter.[40]

[36] UN Charter, Art. 39.

[37] UN Charter, Art. 25.

[38] Christopher C. Joyner, 'Collective Sanctions as Peaceful Coercion: Lessons from the United Nations Experience' (1995) 16 *Australian Yearbook of International Law* 241, 245.

[39] Vera Gowlland-Debbas, 'Sanctions Regimes under Article 41 of the UN Charter' in Vera Gowlland-Debbas (ed), *National Implementation of the United Nations Sanctions: A Comparative Study* (Martinus Nijhoff Publishers 2004) 6.

[40] See Section 3.3.

3.2.2 *From Soviet Union to China and Back to Russia*

The transition from the COCOM to the Wassenaar Arrangement marks a critical turning point in the export control regime not only because of the institutional features of these two regimes but also because of the composition of its membership. Interestingly, Russia, the country which the COCOM was established to target, became a member of the Wassenaar Arrangement. At the same time, it should also be noted that China, which has been subject to an arms embargo since 1989 following the Tiananmen Massacre, is still excluded from the Wassenaar Arrangement. This transition reflects the changing international political economy in the eras of the end of World War II, the Cold War, Détente and the dissolution of the Soviet Union.

Efforts to control exports to the People's Republic of China were initially motivated by the outbreak of the Korean War in June 1950. After Chinese forces crossed the Yalu River and entered the conflict in October of that year, the United States proposed an international embargo against China and tried to persuade its COCOM allies to cooperate on export controls targeting China. The United Nations Security Council adopted Resolution 500(V) on 18 May 1951, recommending every state '[a]pply an embargo on the shipment to areas under the control of the Central People's Government of the People's Republic of China and of the North Korean authorities of arms, ammunition and implementations of war, atomic energy materials, petroleum, transportation materials of strategic value, and items useful in the production of arms, ammunition and implements of war'.[41] In accordance with this resolution, in July 1952, the Truman administration persuaded its allies to establish a China Committee (CHINCOM) within the Consultative Group of the COCOM to coordinate export controls targeting China. Two years later, COCOM members decided to reduce the number of controlled items with respect to the Soviet Union and Eastern Europe by nearly 50 per cent while maintaining the same levels of control against China. The less favourable treatment China received, with the difference comprising around 200 items, was thus known as the 'China Differential'. With the relaxation of security concerns, the 'China Differential' gradually lost justification and COCOM members expressed a wish to liberalise export controls. The United Kingdom, in 1957, in line with its foreign policy objectives and its economic interests given its control of

[41] United Nation Security Council Resolution, 500(V), adopted 18 May 1951, para. 1(a).

Hong Kong, announced unilaterally its intention to eliminate the 'China Differential', and was followed in doing so by other European countries. By the end of 1957, CHINCOM was abolished, though the United States continued to maintain a unilateral 'China Differential' until the advent of Sino-American rapprochement in the 1970s.[42]

Sino-American rapprochement was conducted in the context of a US–China–Soviet trilateral diplomatic game featuring Sino-American rapprochement, Sino-Soviet hostility and Soviet-American Détente. Indeed, the tacit alliance between the United States and China was forged in response to the same threat presented by the Soviet Union. With the signing of the Shanghai Communiqué in 1972, the United States relaxed its trade restrictions with China – trade policy being part and parcel of the broader context of the normalisation of US–PRC relations. In accordance with the normalisation process, the level of exports to China gradually rose to the same level as those to the Soviet Union. A key milestone was the decision of the Nixon Administration to end the trade embargo against China on 10 June 1970, one month before Kissinger's secret trip to China, and subsequently to move China from Country Group Z (countries subject to total trade embargo) to Country Group X (countries including the USSR and other Eastern European countries). In the words of Hugo Meijer, this decision transformed the US export control policy against China from 'China Differential' to 'even-handedness'.[43] With the normalisation of US–PRC relations, trade between the United States and China intensified and exports to China surpassed those to the Soviet Union. The United States thus adopted a new policy, setting the ceiling for exports to China at twice the level of exports to the Soviet Union. The 'China Differential' thus turned from unfavourable to favourable towards China.

With the change of US domestic trade policy towards China, international export controls against China under the multilateral COCOM framework were adjusted correspondently, particularly in view of the heavy load of applications for exceptions submitted to the COCOM. With the proposal of the United States advanced in early 1985, COCOM members, after ten months of negotiations, finally agreed to liberalise the control of certain exports falling under the scope of the International Industrial List to China. The reworked control guidelines

[42] Hugo Meijer, *Trading with the Enemy: The Making of US Export Control Policy toward the People's Republic of China* (Oxford University Press 2016) 35–36.

[43] Ibid. 36–38.

for exports to China were categorised in accordance with technical parameters and resembled those of US domestic regulations of Green, Yellow and Red zones. The COCOM's new Green Line, which comprised twenty-seven categories of products, covering computers, software, instrumentation, telecommunication equipment and semiconductor manufacturing, was implemented at national discretion and not subject to prior approval of an export license under the auspices of the COCOM. The Yellow Line related mainly to intermediate level technologies and required monthly statistical reports to the COCOM. Items under the Red Line were to be referred to the COCOM with a presumption of denial. The division into different levels of export control to China was driven by the rationale that COCOM members, in particular the United States, aimed to balance the desire to support China's economic modernisation with minimising potential adverse effects to the security interests of the United States and its allies.[44] As trade exchanges between China and Western countries grew significantly, the trend of liberalising export controls with respect to China continued, only coming to a halt in response to the Tiananmen Square massacre in 1989.

Export restrictions imposed on China display different characteristics from those imposed on the Soviet Union. Since 1978, China has pursued a 'reform and open' policy that entails engaging with the international trading system. The forging of an implicit alliance between the United States and China was established in the context of the 1968 Soviet invasion of Czechoslovakia and Sino-Soviet military conflicts in 1969. Thus, the United States and China approached each other with an aim of containing or counteracting the Soviet Union.[45] At that time, China's technological development in civilian sectors lagged far behind that of Western countries, and was badly in need of high-technology machinery and equipment, whereas China' military and defence technology, in some areas, enjoyed strategic leverage that raised concerns in Western countries. The uneven development of China's civilian and military technologies complicated the export control policy-making of Western countries. The United States, given that China was far behind it in the civilian sector, felt relatively assured in its view that technological transactions could usually be carried out in this sector. By contrast, in the military and security sectors, the United States had to ensure that it maintained its

[44] Ibid. 77–79.

[45] Jong-Tsong Chiang, 'Dilemmas of US Control of Technology to China' (1987) 12 *Journal of Technology Transfer* 9, 11.

technological lead over China to safeguard its hegemony in Asia. However, this ambition to maintain a technological lead and ensure hegemony in Asia was not shared by European countries, which appeared to prefer to take full advantage of business opportunities arising from China's opening.[46] Therefore, collective action dilemmas arose with respect to coordination and implementation from time to time between the United States and its European allies, and to a certain degree, Japan.

With the fast moving of China's economy and close integration into the global economy, export restrictions against China became even more complicated. In the COCOM era, since the United States and, arguably, Western countries were not reliant on the Soviet Union, they had greater leverage to impose an export embargo against the Soviet Union or otherwise engage in economic warfare. In contrast, China became the biggest trading partner, and a lucrative investment destination, of many countries, making it difficult to sever economic ties with a view to preventing civilian or dual-use products or technologies from being transferred for military or security use.[47] Also, the US economy has been transformed from a domestic-consumption driven economy to one closely integrated into the global economy and heavily reliant on international trade activities since World War II. Such phenomenon did not, in fact, arise only in the twenty-first century. As early as the 1980s, during 1984–1985, US requests for COCOM exceptions accounted for as much as 90 per cent of China-related exceptions, which attracted resentment from European allies in the COCOM.[48] In theory, the United States wished to maintain stringent export controls targeting China, at least in the military and security sectors; in practice, the United States requested a large number of exceptions and gained economic benefits from circumventing those controls.

In parallel, the economic structure of the United States has significantly changed. Within the United States the dominant driver behind technological progress and innovation has shifted from governmental funding to private enterprises. In the years following World War II, the Department of Defense (USDOD) contributed much to technological innovation. In contrast, nowadays, this innovation is largely driven by

[46] Ibid.

[47] Tai Ming Cheung and Bates Gill, 'Trade Versus Security: How Countries Balance Technology Transfers with China' (2013) 13 *Journal of East Asian Studies* 443, 444–445.

[48] Mastanduno, *Economic containment: CoCom and the Politics of East–West Trade* (n. 1) 278–281.

enterprises. In fact, this development has been detailed in the Panel Report on the Impact of National Security Controls on International Technology Transfer, released in 1987: *Balancing National Interests.* According to *Balancing National Interests*, the disparity in technological innovation sponsored by private commercial funding and that sponsored by the USDOD has increased the difficulties associated with US imposition of export control policies. In the early post-war era, the United States and its allies recognised the importance of research and development to strategically critical technologies. Some critical sectors, such as aeronautics, propulsion and electronics, were first developed by the USDOD and then channelled into private and commercial uses. Therefore, the task of the USDOD was to develop and hold on to technologies, and then decide which, and whether, to channel into the private sector. As long as the USDOD maintained a technological lead, and as long as the United States and its allies could ensure the operationalisation of derived weapons before their commercialisation, the commercialisation of such technology would not introduce new threats to the United States. However, given cut-backs in budgets for the defence and military sectors, and the comparative strengths of the private and commercial sectors, some critical technologies, such as advanced microelectronics, were initially introduced in commercial sectors before being applied to defence and military ends. Therefore, the United States had to face the challenge of controlling technologies available in global markets.[49] In view of this new reality, it was necessary that the regulatory philosophy underpinning export control be adjusted. According to Hugo Meijer, two camps have been competing to shape and influence US export control policy: Control Hawks and Technological Hares (Run Faster camp in Meijer's words). Control Hawks demand more comprehensive and stringent export control policy against China with a view to preventing China from catching up, and thus maintaining the lead of the United States in science and technology development. In contrast, Technological Hares emphasise the pivotal importance of US research and development to maintaining the technological lead of the United States over China. As long as the United States runs fast enough, a strict export control policy will not be essential, and by doing so, US enterprises may benefit from trade opportunities with China. Therefore, for

[49] National Academy of Engineering and Institute of Medicine National Academy of Sciences, *Balancing the National Interest: U.S. National Security Export Controls and Global Economic Competition* (National Academy Press 1987) 55–56.

Technological Hares, the underlying issue is how to maintain a technological lead by running faster.[50]

3.2.3 From Sovereign States to Non-State Actors

In the COCOM era, the main focus of export control was sovereign states: the Soviet Union and countries of the Warsaw Pact. However, the emergence of non-state actors in non-proliferation activities, and their roles in commissioning terrorist attacks and international crimes, especially in the wake of the 9/11 attack, reminds academics and policy-makers of the critical roles of non-state actors in non-proliferation regimes. Here, non-state actors may include individuals associated with known terrorist groups, such as the Taliban, Al-Qaeda or Islamic State of Iraq and the Levant (ISIL, also known as Islamic State of Iraq and Syria, ISIS), and unrecognised violent entities. In referring to the National Security Strategy adopted by the Bush Administration in 2002, James Russell observes that the 'international environment is now dotted with unconventional adversaries which may have access to a wide array of new capacities',[51] and the supply network is 'dominated by transnational corporations, quasi-governmental entities, and individuals operating on the fringes of government control in weak or failing states that lack the will and the resources to implement effective export control regimes'.[52] Compared to state actions, non-state proliferation tends to operate within illicit networks, which reflects a shift from the public state regulatory ambit to the private realm in the proliferation of nuclear, chemical and biological weapons and related materials.[53] Whereas it is true that economic sanctions have already been used to fight terrorism for some time, as in the cases of Iran and Libya, these were cases of state-sponsored or supported terrorism, where the relevant states bore international legal responsibility and were targeted for economic sanctions.[54] Non-state actors surfaced as a new phenomenon and challenge in the

[50] Meijer, *Trading with the Enemy: The Making of US Export Control Policy toward the People's Republic of China* (n. 42)145–165.

[51] James A. Russell, 'Peering into the Abyss: Non-State Actors and the 2016 Proliferation Environment' (2006) 13 *Nonproliferation Review* 645, 646.

[52] Ibid. 646.

[53] Mike Bourne, 'Controlling the Shadow Trade' (2011) 32 *Contemporary Security Policy* 215, 219.

[54] See e.g., Kenneth W. Abbott, 'Economic Sanctions and International Terrorism' (1987) 20 *Vanderbilt Journal of Transnational Law* 289.

regulation of exports, and efforts to account for them under current regulatory regimes have intensified.

The most important initiative to regulate non-state actors via export controls is United Nations Security Council Resolution 1540 (UNSC Resolution 1540).[55] The Security Council first expressed a concern that 'the threat of illicit trafficking in nuclear, chemical, or biological weapons and their means of delivery, and related materials, which adds a new dimension to the issue of proliferation of such weapons and also poses a threat to international peace and security',[56] and decided to act in accordance with Chapter VII of the UN Charter. UNSC Resolution 1540 sets out three main obligations for UN members: to 'refrain from providing any form of support to non-State actors that attempt to develop, acquire, manufacture, possess, transport, transfer or use nuclear, chemical or biological weapons and their means of delivery';[57] to 'adopt and enforce appropriate effective laws which prohibit any non-State actor to engage in the aforementioned activities';[58] and to 'take and enforce effective measures to establish domestic controls to prevent the proliferation of nuclear, chemical, or biological weapons and their means of delivery'.[59] With a view to effectively preventing the proliferation of these items, Article 3 of UNSC Resolution 1540 puts forward four categories of measures,

> (a) Develop and maintain appropriate effective measures to account for and secure such items in production, use, storage or transport;
> (b) Develop and maintain appropriate effective physical protection measures;
> (c) Develop and maintain appropriate effective border controls and law enforcement efforts to detect, deter, prevent and combat, including through international cooperation when necessary, the illicit trafficking and brokering in such items in accordance with their national legal authorities and legislation and consistent with international law;
> (d) Establish, develop, review and maintain appropriate effective national export and trans-shipment controls over such items, including appropriate laws and regulations to control export, transit, trans-shipment and re-export and controls on providing funds and services related to

[55] United Nations Security Council Resolution 1540 (2004), Adopted by the Security Council at its 4956th meeting on 28 April 2004.
[56] UNSC Resolution 1540, 9th recital.
[57] UNSC Resolution 1540, Art. 1.
[58] UNSC Resolution 1540, Art. 2.
[59] UNSC Resolution 1540, Art. 3.

> such export and trans-shipment such as financing, and transporting that would contribute to proliferation, as well as establishing end-user controls; and establishing and enforcing appropriate criminal or civil penalties for violations of such export control laws and regulations.

In lit(d), export and trans-shipment controls are explicitly referred to as measures to be developed and maintained in the pursuit of the non-proliferation of nuclear, chemical and biological weapons and related materials, specifically to non-state actors. Following UNSC Resolution 1540, the UN Security Council adopted a series of resolutions addressing specific targeted groups, including the Taliban, Al-Qaeda and ISIL. Under the heading of arms embargo, UN members are obliged to

> [p]revent the direct or indirect supply, sale, or transfer to these individuals, groups, undertakings and entities from their territories or by their nationals outside their territories, or using their flag vessels or aircraft, of arms and related materiel of all types including weapons and ammunition, military vehicles and equipment, paramilitary equipment, and spare parts for the aforementioned, and technical advice, assistance or training related to military activities.[60]

The swift change in the international environment that arose as a consequence of the threat non-state actors posed to international peace and security prompted the UN to subject non-State actors to export controls. The targeted entities here are ISIL, Al-Qaida, the Taliban and associated individuals, groups, undertakings and entities. With a view to determining the scope of such associated individuals, groups, undertakings and entities, sanctioning committees are established under the UN Security Council to discharge this task.[61]

3.3 National Law and Policy on Export Control

Since the creation of the COCOM and the establishment of the Wassenaar Arrangement, the United States and its European allies have

[60] UN Security Council Resolution 2253 (2015), adopted by the Security Council at its 7587th meeting, on 17 December 2015, Art. 2(c); UN Security Council Resolution 1988 (2011) adopted by the Security Council at its 6557th meeting on 17 June 2011, Art. 1(c).

[61] On the critique of the role of the UN Security Council in the aspect of counter-terrorism, see e.g., Ian Johnstone, 'Legislation and Adjudication in the UN Security Council: Bringing Down the Deliberative Deficit' (2008) 102 *American Journal of International Law* 275.

been the key actors in putting forward disciplines on export control and ensuring their effectiveness. As noted previously, international relations have seen a sea change, as illustrated in the dissolution of the Soviet Union, the fall of the Berlin Wall, the opening up of China and its integration into the global economy, and the enlargement of the European Union to include Central and Eastern European countries. It is thus feasible to investigate the evolution of national law and policy on export control. This section examines domestic law and policy on the export controls of the United States and the EU and explores how the evolutionary process reflects changes in international relations. An introduction of relevant US and EU law and policy will provide good background knowledge on the discussion of US and EU export restrictions and their WTO-compatibility.

3.3.1 The Evolution of US Export Control Law and Policy

The US export control system is rooted in the World War II era. Congress granted the President the authority to control and curtail exports of munitions and related materials, with penalties for violations. The list of controlled items expanded to cover any articles, technical data, materials and supplies.[62] This wartime export control system was later transformed for peacetime application through the adoption of the 1949 Export Administration Act (EAA) with a view to preventing domestic economic shortages, protecting national security and promoting US foreign policy.[63]

Three factors contributed to the adoption of this act: prevailing ideology, the US position in international political and economic hierarchies and the alignment of domestic industries. The export control regime imposed unilateral, artificial and politically motivated barriers to free trade, which stood in stark contrast to liberal international economic orthodoxy that the United States propagated. The ideological basis for such illiberal components in a fundamentally liberal economic system is found in the powerful anticommunism of the era. Second, the unchallenged authority of the United States in the Western post-war international political and economic system, coupled with the insignificance of foreign trade to US gross economic

[62] William J. Long, *U.S. Export Control Policy: Executive Autonomy VS. Congressional Reform* (Columbia University Press 1989) 15.

[63] Ibid. 16.

product relative to other Western countries, lent tremendous strength to US efforts to exercise export control. Third, as a superpower emerging from the post-war era, the United States sought to maintain its strategic, technological and military superiority and domestic stability. Export controls to provide and safeguard collective security were costs the United States was willing to pay to maintain the liberal international economic order due to US–Soviet rivalry. Export controls on strategic goods were the result of a compromise between competing motives: the fear of Soviet expansion and the wish to enlarge trade volume.[64] That being said, it has been highly debated whether the contribution to 'economic potential' should be listed as a legitimate objective of export controls imposed on a given item, and whether export control measures should '*significantly* contribute to' the realisation of its objective, or whether passing a threshold of 'contributing to' is sufficient to establish their legitimacy.

The 1949 Export Administration Act was superseded by the 1969 Export Control Act (ECA), which was again amended by the 1985 Export Administration Amendment Act[65] and 1988 Export Enhanced Act. The main instrument implementing these acts is the Export Administration Regulation (EAR), the legal basis for which was provided by virtue of Executive Orders and a Presidential declaration of emergency under the authority of the International Emergency Economic Powers Act (IEEPA) when the 1979 Export Administration Act expired in 2001.[66] With the adoption of the Export Control Reform Act in 2018, in the midst of US–China trade conflict, the Export Control Act of 2018 (2018 ECA)[67] again provides a statutory basis for the implementation of the EAR.

The list of controlled items falling under the scope of the EAA and subsequently the ECA, as administered through the EAR by the Bureau of Industrial Security (BIS) under the Department of Commerce (DoC), are dual-use goods subject to the Commerce Control List (CCL), which

[64] Ibid. 13–14.

[65] See generally, John R. Liberman, 'The Export Administration Amendments Act of 1985' (1986) 20 *International Lawyer* 367.

[66] Ian F. Fergusson and Paul K. Kerr, 'The U.S. Export Control System and the Export Control Reform Initiative' (2018) CRS Report for Congress, R41916, 30 October 2018, p. 2; Eric L. Hirschhorn, *The Export Control and Embargo Handbook* (3rd ed., Oxford University Press 2010) 5–6.

[67] P.L.115-232, Subtitle B, Part I; 50 USC Chapter 58, Subchapter I.

comprises ten categories numbered through 0 to 9.[68] Export licensing and exemptions are the main policy tools for the BIS to enforce the export control system. As export is not a right enjoyed by US citizens and enterprises, but a privilege granted by US authorities, the BIS can prohibit or restrict the exportation of US-origin goods to designated entities through a 'denial order', violations of which are punishable under law. Items subject to the EAR are not limited to tangible goods but also include technology and software. Thus, the terms 'export' and 're-export' are carefully defined to suit such purposes. Export is not limited to actual shipment or transmission of items crossing US borders, but extends to 'the release of technology or software subject to the EAR to a foreign national in the United States', known as 'deemed export'.[69] Further, the EAR extends its reach to cover re-export, which refers to an actual shipment or transmission of items 'from one foreign country to another foreign country' or release of technology or software to 'a foreign national outside the United States'.[70]

As the EAR regulates re-exports of US-origin goods and technology from one foreign country to another, it is implicated in the sensitive issue of extraterritorial jurisdiction. Moreover, extraterritorial jurisdiction is not limited to re-exports of US-origin goods and technologies, but extends to foreign made items incorporating US components and technology.[71] According to the latest 2018 ECA, the President is authorised to control, inter alia, 'the export, reexport and in-country transfer of items subject to jurisdiction of the United States whether by United States persons or by foreign persons and specific activities of United States persons, wherever located'.[72] Two elements define the jurisdiction of the United States: items subject to US jurisdiction, and US persons engaging in specific activities. As noted previously, items subject to US jurisdiction extend to those incorporating US-origin components and technologies,

[68] These ten categories are: 0. Nuclear materials, facilities and equipment, miscellaneous; 1. Materials, chemicals, microorganisms and toxins; 2. Materials processing; 3. Electronics 4. Computers; 5. Telecommunications and information security; 6. Laser and sensors; 7. Navigation and avionics; 8. Marine; 9. Propulsion systems, space vehicles and related equipment. See further Hirschhorn, *The Export Control and Embargo Handbook* (n. 66) 25–26.

[69] 15 C.F.R. 734.2(b)(1) (2016).

[70] 15 C.F.R. 734.2(b)(4) (2016).

[71] Hirschhorn, *The Export Control and Embargo Handbook* (n. 66) 12; Editors, 'Comments: Extraterritorial Application of United States Law: The Case of Export Controls' (1984) 132 *University of Pennsylvania Law Review* 355, 360–361.

[72] 2018 ECA, Section 4812(a).

wherever they are manufactured. US persons also cover subsidiaries of US companies,[73] which is established in the 1982 pipeline case, where the US maintained that it had jurisdiction to entirely control foreign goods if those goods were to be exported by a European subsidiary of a US company.[74]

The reason why extraterritorial jurisdiction of export control has been a recurring source of conflict between the United States and its trade partners is the heavy reliance of the United States on it in pursuit of its foreign policy ends. Moreover, the internationalisation of economic activities characterised by a multiplicity of well-established business networks linking firms in different countries further complicates US exercise of extraterritorial jurisdiction of its export control law. This internationalisation of economic activities is shaped and strengthened through different channels and types of networks: international trade, technology transfer and investment.[75] However, the United States' exercise of extraterritorial jurisdiction of its export control law generally comes with political and economic costs. Third countries regard US extraterritorial jurisdiction as interfering in their territorial jurisdiction, especially when the re-exported items are subject to US claims that they contain US-origin components or technologies, though those goods are considered by the third countries as being locally manufactured. In addition, enterprises located in third countries may be hesitating in conducting business with US companies in view of the threat that a link with US companies through international trade, technology transfer and investment network may introduce the threat of sanctions.[76]

In addition to dual-use goods which are subject to CCL under the ECA and EAR and administered by the DoC, the United States also maintains the Munition List (USML) controlling exports of arms under the Arms Export Control Act of 1976,[77] as implemented by the International Traffic in Arms Regulation (ITAR) and administered by the

[73] Stanley J. Marcuss and D. Stephen Mathias, 'U.S. Foregin Policy Export Controls: Do they Pass Muister under International Law' (1984) 2 *Internatinal Tax & Business Lawyer* 1, 11.

[74] Hirschhorn, *The Export Control and Embargo Handbook* (n. 66) 12; Harold H. Tittmann, 'Extra-territorial Application to U.S. Export Control Laws on Foreign Subsidiaries of U.S. Corporations: An American Lawyer's View from Europe' (1982) 16 *The International Lawyer* 730, 732.

[75] Kenneth W. Abbott 'Defining the Extraterritorial Reach of American Export Control: Congress as Catalyst' (1984) 17 *Cornell Journal of International Law* 79, 92–98.

[76] Ibid. 100–102.

[77] P. L. 94-329, 22 USC ch.39.

Directorate of Defense Trade Control (DDTC) under the Department of State (DoS).[78] The USML now comprises twenty-one categories. An item may be designated as a defence article and thus fall under the jurisdiction of the ITAR if it either meets the criteria of a defence article or service under the USML, or provides the equivalent performance capacities of a defence article on the list.[79] Moreover, with a view to implementing international obligations and multilateral sanctions or unilateral sanctions, embargoes and other relevant sanctions may be imposed, which generally have two dimensions: a financial dimension implemented by the Office of Foreign Assets Control (OFAC) of the Department of the Treasury (DoT), and an export control dimension implemented either by the DoC or DoS. Finally, the aforementioned IEEPA provides the legal basis for the President to impose export control for exceptional purposes. Under this act, the President has broad discretionary power.

3.3.2 The Harmonisation of EU Export Control Regulation

The EU's export control regime evolves along two lines: one aiming to harmonise export control laws and regulations of Member States with a view to facilitating free movement of dual-use goods within an internal market and effectively controlling their exports; one aiming to adopt restrictive measures under the Common Foreign and Security Policy (CFSP) in implementing the EU's international obligations arising from, inter alia, a resolution of the United States Security Council, the Wassenaar Arrangement, or non-proliferation agreements. Of course, the EU may adopt autonomous restrictive measures without referring to international instruments.

Autonomous restrictive measures relate mainly to the Community regime for the control of exports, transfer, brokering and transit of dual-use items, currently governed by Council Regulation (EC) 428/2009 (hereinafter, Export Control Regulation),[80] as amended in 2011, 2012 and 2014. International instruments concern mainly the EU's actions through Council Decisions under the CFSP, in particular under

[78] Aubin and Idiart, *Export Control Law and Regulations Handbook: a Practical Guide to Military and Dual-Use Goods Trade Restrictions and Compliance* (2nd ed. Kluwer Law International 2011) 605.

[79] Ibid. 620–621.

[80] Council Regulation (EC) No 428/2009 of 5 May 2009 setting up a Community regime for the control of exports, transfer, brokering and transit of dual-use items, OJ L 134/1, 29 May 2009.

Articles 28 and 31 of the Treaty on the European Union (the TEU), to impose restrictive measures on targeted countries, groups or persons. In turn, these Council Decisions will be implemented by Council Regulations with the legal basis being Article 215 of the Treaty on the Functioning of the European Union (the TFEU). The EU's recent sanction measures against Russia over its annexation of Crimea have such legal bases.[81]

The Export Control Regulation was first written into law as Council Regulation (EC) 3381/94[82] on the proposal of the European Commission in 1994,[83] and was substantially revised and replaced by Council Regulation (EC) No 1334/2000[84] and again by the aforementioned 2009 Export Control Regulation. As the Commission stated in its proposal, the objectives of the Export Control Regulation are to eliminate controls on intra-Community trade in such goods and technologies, and to apply effective controls on their export to third countries.[85] As the differences in the Member States' export control laws and policies may divert trade and distort competitive conditions of the internal market,[86] the elimination of intra-Community trade in dual-use goods has to go hand-in-hand with the effective control of the export of dual-use goods to third countries. 'The existence of a common control system and harmonised policies for enforcement and monitoring in all Member States is a prerequisite for establishing the free movement of dual-use items inside the Community'.[87] Therefore, whereas the Export Control Regulation refers to Common Commercial Policy (Article 133 of the TEC, now Article 207 of the TFEU) for its legal basis, it has great internal market implications.

Given the parallel objectives of the Export Control Regulation, internally, to facilitate intra-Union trade of dual-use items and, externally, to control their export from the customs territory of the EU, the Council of the EU is to establish a list of dual-use items subject to control while

[81] Council Regulation (EU) No 833/2014 of 31 July 2014 concerning restrictive measures in view of Russia's actions destabilising the situation in Ukraine, OJ L 229/1, 31 July 2014.

[82] Council Regulation (EC) No 3381/94 of 19 December 1994 setting up a Community regime for the control of exports of dual-use goods, OJ L 367/1, 31 December 1994.

[83] Proposal for a Council Regulation (EEC) on the control of exports of certain dual-use goods and technologies and of certain nuclear products and technologies, COM (92) 317 final Brussels, 31 August 1992.

[84] Council Regulation (EC) No 1334/2000 of 22 June 2000 setting up a Community regime for the control of exports of dual-use items and technology, OJ L 159/1, 30 June 2000.

[85] COM (92) 317, para. 4.2.

[86] Ibid. para. 3.2.

[87] Export Control Regulation, 4th preambular.

authorisation of such goods is to be granted by national authorities of Member States. Dual-use items are defined as 'items, including software and technology, which can be used for both civil and military purposes, and shall include all goods which can be used for both non-explosive uses and assisting in any way in the manufacture of nuclear weapons or other nuclear explosive devices'.[88] The Export Control Regulation sets out a Commodity Control List in Annex I, which also comprises ten categories, numbered from 0 to 9.[89] The Export Control Regulation regulates both exports and re-exports of such dual-use items; nonetheless, the term re-export refers to the re-export of non-Community goods from the customs territory of the Community, and thus differs from re-export under the US ECA and EAR.

3.4 Legality of Export Restrictions under WTO Law: Trade and National Security Nexus

The GATT/WTO regime was established with the aim of pursuing a liberal international economic order, but did not neglect the necessity of sovereign states safeguarding their essential security interests. Therefore, the GATT/WTO regime is equipped with some rules for trade nations to preserve their policy space in ensuring essential security interests, the most pertinent being the national security exception as set forth in Article XXI of the GATT 1994, Article XIV bis of the GATS and Article 73 of the TRIPS Agreement. Since the GATT 1994, GATS and TRIPS Agreement all contain similar provisions regulating the security exception, I will now focus mainly on Article XXI of the GATT 1994, as it has been a subject of debate in some GATT/WTO case-law, and the discussion in the context of GATT 1994 can be translated into the GATS and TRIPS Agreement context. Article XXI of the GATT 1994 reads as follows

> Nothing in this Agreement shall be construed
>
> (a) to require any contracting party to furnish any information the disclosure of which it considers contrary to its essential security interests; or

[88] Export Control Regulation, Art. 2.1.

[89] These ten categories of items are: 0. Nuclear materials, facilities and equipment; 1. Special materials and related equipment; 2. Materials Processing; 3. Electronics; 4. Computers; 5. Telecommunications and information security; 6. Sensors and lasers; 7. Navigation and avionics; 8. Marine; 9. Aerospace and Propulsion.

(b) to prevent any contracting party from taking any action which it considers necessary for the protection of its essential security interests
  (i) relating to fissionable materials or the materials from which they are derived;
  (ii) relating to the traffic in arms, war and other emergencies of international relations and to such traffic in other goods and materials as is carried on directly or indirectly for the purpose of supplying a military establishment;
  (iii) taken in time of war or other emergency in international relations; or

(c) to prevent any contracting party from taking any action in pursuance of its obligations under the United Nations Charter for the maintenance of international peace and security.

Article XXI puts forward three key elements of the national security exception under which a member can legitimately act, or not act, without infringing WTO laws: disclosing information; protecting essential security interests and acting in accordance with the UN Charter.[90] These three elements can be sorted into two categories: one related to the essential security interests of a member; the other related to its obligations under the UN Charter. In the name of essential security interests, a member cannot be required either to positively furnish particular information, or to negatively be prevented from taking certain actions. A member may refuse to disclose any information that it considers contrary to its essential security interests; a member is also not prevented from taking necessary actions relating to the following three subsets: fissionable materials; traffic in arms, munitions and implements of war, and materials supplying a military establishment and actions taken in time of war or other emergency in international relations. The first two are objects of which the physical characteristics are easier to identity and are without doubt subject to the review of WTO adjudicators. By contrast, war or other emergency in international relations are situational scenarios, and whether tensions

[90] On the interpretation of Article XXI, see e.g., Alan S. Alexandroff and Rajeev Sharma, 'The National Exception Provision – GATT Article XXI' in Patrick F. J. Macrory, Arthur E. Appleton and Michael G. Plummer (eds), *The World Trade Organization: Legal, Economic and Political Analysis* (Springer 2005) 1571–1579; Andrew D. Mitchell and Glyn Ayres, 'General and Security Exceptions Under the GATT and the GATS' in Indira Carr, Jahid Bhuiyan and Shawkat Alam (eds), *International Trade Law and WTO* (Federation Press 2011) 226–268; Rüdiger Wolfrum, Peter-Tobias Stoll and Holger P. Hestermeyer (eds), *WTO-Trade in Goods* (Martinus Nijhoff 2011) 569–593.

between countries amount to an emergency in international relations may not be easy to tell. In contrast to paragraphs (a) and (b), Article XXI:(c) of the GATT 1994 regulates the relationship between the obligations under GATT/WTO law and those under the UN Charter. The designation of this paragraph enables a member to fulfil its obligations under the United Nations Charter for the maintenance of international peace and security without infringing GATT/WTO rules. I will first address the jurisdiction of the WTO Panel/ Appellate Body over justification based on the national security exception and then examine the common element in the first category for the protection of essential security interests, followed by obligations under the UN Charter for the maintenance of international peace and security.

3.4.1 The Jurisdiction of Panel/Appellate Body and the Justiciability of Article XXI: Institutional Design from GATT to the WTO

In assessing the legality of a measure invoking a security exception, the first question to ask is whether it falls within the ambit of the WTO dispute settlement mechanism and is thus subject to the jurisdiction of the Panel and Appellate Body. If the answer is affirmative, the following question is how this dispute is to be reviewed by the Panel and Appellate Body, and what is the appropriate standard of review.[91] The answers to these questions differ with time and context. The perception of international trade relations constantly evolves, and there is a strong trend calling for the constitutionalisation of international economic relations,[92] driven partly by the judicialisation of the GATT/WTO regime.[93]

[91] Hannes L. Schloemann and Stefan Ohlhoff, '"Constitutionalization" and Dispute Settlement in the WTO: National Security as an Issue of Competence' (1999) 93 *American Journal of International Law* 424, 426.

[92] See generally, Jan Klabbers, Ann Peters and Geir Ulfstein, *The Constitutionalization of International Law* (Oxford University Press 2009); Ernst Ulrich Petersmann, *Constitutional Functions and Constitutional Problems of International Economic Law* (University Press 1991).

[93] See generally, Deborah Z. Cass, 'The "Constitutionalization" of International Trade Law: Judicial Norm-Generation as the Engine of Constitutional Development in International Trade' (2001) 12 *European Journal of International Law* 39; Richard H. Steinberg, 'Judicial Lawmaking at the WTO: Discursive, Constitutional, and Political Constraints' (2004) 98 *The American Journal of International Law* 247.

Moreover, the constitutional change from the GATT positive consensus to WTO negative consensus decision-making processes,[94] will also play a critical role in answering these questions.

The first time the GATT contracting parties were called on to examine the GATT-consistency of an export licensing system imposed by the United States for security purposes dates back to 1949, one year after communists seized power in Czechoslovakia, subsequently bringing the country into the Warsaw Pact in 1955. Czechoslovakia alleged that the export licensing system did not apply equally to other countries looking to purchase goods from the United States, and that the United States' interpretation of 'war materials' was all too broad.[95] During the discussion, Pakistan maintained that as the measure was adopted in the interests of peace and security, disputes should be resolved through diplomatic channels and should not be delegated to a Working Party. The United Kingdom was of the opinion that 'since the question clearly concerned Article XXI, the United States action would seem to be justified because every country must have the last resort on questions relating to its own security. On the other hand, the CONTRACTING PARTIES should be cautious not to take any step which might have the effect of undermining the General Agreement.'[96] In the end, a vote was taken in response to Czechoslovakia's request for the establishment of a Working Party (the predecessor of a panel) with one affirmative (Czechoslovakia), three abstentions (India, Lebanon, Syria) and seventeen negatives.[97] Two observations can be made here. The prevailing view in *US – Export Restrictions*[98] is that a country invoking a security exception is entitled to determine its essential security interests, meaning that it is a question which the GATT contracting parties are not in a position to review. Second, this decision was made in the GATT context, wherein decision-making is based on consensus. Therefore, the United States and its allies were able to block the establishment of a panel; thus,

94 Ernst Ulrich Petersmann, 'From "Member-Driven Governance" to Constitutionally Limited "Multi-Level Trade Governance" in the WTO' in Giorgio Sacerdoti, Alan Yanovich and Jan Bohanes (eds), *The WTO at Ten: The Contribution of the Dispute Settlement System* (Cambridge University Press 2006) 86–110.

95 Summary Record of the Twenty-Second Meeting, CP.3/SR22 – II/28, Held at Hotel Verdun, Annecy on Wednesday, 8 June 1949, pp. 2–3.

96 Ibid. p. 3.

97 Ibid. p. 4.

98 II/28, Decision of 8 June 1949.

if a similar dispute arises in the WTO context, the result would differ, as *US – Steel and Aluminium*[99] reveals.

The GATT signatories' invocation of the Article XXI exception gradually evolved. Some cases had reached the panel stage while some had not; some countries explicitly invoked Article XXI of the GATT 1947 whereas others did not.[100] In 1962, the United States imposed an export embargo on all trade in goods against Cuba, only recently relaxed by the Obama Administration. Cuba notified the GATT of this export embargo but did not request that a panel be established. Interestingly, with the intensification of sanction measures against Cuba by the adoption of the Cuban Liberty and Democratic Solidarity (LIBERTAD) Act of 1996 under the Clinton Administration, the EU requested consultation with the United States, and a panel was subsequently established on 20 November 1996.[101] According to the EU, the LIBERTAD contains a number of provisions which 'have the intent and effect to restrain the liberty of the EC to export to Cuba or to trade in Cuban origin goods, as well as to restrict the freedom of EC registered vessels and their cargo to transit through US ports'.[102] At the request of the EU, dated 21 April 1997, the Panel suspended its work and its authority lapsed on 22 April 1998, pursuant to Article 12.12 of the DSU, with the suspension time exceeding 12 months. The LIBERTAD case makes clear that an export embargo may impact third countries, especially where secondary sanctioning measures are in place. In addition, the institutional design of the WTO dispute settlement mechanism makes it impossible for the United States to block the establishment of a panel in response to the EU's request. Nonetheless, the disputing parties are free to resolve their differences in a mutually satisfactory way.

With regards to the choice whether to refer explicitly to Article XXI of the GATT or not, the EU's positions in *EEC – Trade Restrictions Affecting Argentina applied for Non-Economic Reasons* and *EEC – Trade Measure against the Socialist Federal Republic of Yugoslavia* mark an interesting contrast. On 29 April 1982, Argentina circulated a

[99] *United States – Certain Measures on Steel and Aluminum Product*, WT/DS548, panel established, report not yet released.

[100] For a summary of measures relating to Article XXI of the GATT, see *WTO, Guide to GATT Law and Practice: Analytical Index* (6th ed., WTO 1995) 599–610; see also Miachel J. Hahn, 'Vital Interests and the Law of GATT: An Analysis of GATT's Security Exception' (1991) 12 *Michigan Journal of International Law* 558, 565–578.

[101] Request for Consultations by the European Communities, WT/DS38/1, 13 May 1996.

[102] Ibid. 1.

communication alleging that trade restrictions adopted by the EEC, Australia and Canada violated the GATT rules. Argentina also emphasised that Security Council Resolution 502 was limited to recognising that 'there was a breach of the peace in the region of the [Falkland/Malvinas] Islands … but it has not requested nor authorized, explicitly or implicitly, and accordingly did not consider appropriate, any action on the part of third parties, as would be the case for economic measures of international coercion, nor have any such measures been requested in that forum by any country'.[103] Argentina also argued that the measures taken by the United Kingdom could not be justified by Article XXI:(b) of the GATT, as Resolution 502 only addressed the situation of the Falkland/Malvinas Islands and did not touch on the metropolitan territory. In response, the EEC maintained that '(a) they have taken certain measures in the light of the situation addressed in the Security Council Resolution 502; (b) they have taken these measures on the basis of their inherent rights of which Article XXI of the General Agreement is a reflection'.[104] The EEC further stated that it wished to resolve the dispute satisfactorily through negotiations elsewhere. With a close look at the communications of Argentina and the EEC, it is clear that Argentina tried to make its case in GATT terms and assess the applicability of Article XXI:(b) of the GATT; by contrast, the EEC did not explicitly invoke Article XXI of the GATT by using the wording of 'their inherent rights of which Article XXI of the General Agreement is a reflection'.[105] The EEC also considered the GATT was not an appropriate forum to resolve the dispute, which should be resolved through negotiation in another setting.

In 1991, in attempting to halt the bloodshed in the Socialist Federal Republic of Yugoslavia (SFRY), the EEC adopted a number of Council Regulations and Decisions in suspending preferential trade preferences to Yugoslavia or restricting access of Yugoslavian products to the EEC market.[106] These measures included suspension of the EEC–Yugoslavia Cooperation Agreement, import restrictions on textile products and

[103] GATT Document, L/5317, 30 April 1982, para. 3.

[104] GATT Document, L/5319, 5 May 1982, para. 1(b).

[105] Ibid.

[106] These Council Regulations and Decisions include EEC Council Regulations 3300, 3301 and 3302/91, as well as in Decisions 91/586/ECSC, EEC and 91/587, 588 and 589/ECSC of 11 November 1991. In these Regulations and Decisions, UN Security Council Resolution 713 (1991), which referred to the situation in Yugoslavia as constituting a threat to international peace and security, was underlined.

suspension of trade preference under the Generalised System of Preferences. According to the EEC, these measures were taken 'upon consideration of its essential security interests and based on GATT Article XXI'.[107] In response, the SFRY requested consultation with the EEC and did not receive any response. With the lapse of the consultation period, the SFRY requested the establishment of a panel.[108] According to the SFRY, '[t]he situation in Yugoslavia is a specific one and does not correspond to the notion and meaning of Article XXI(b) and (c). There is no decision or resolution of the relevant UN body to impose economic sanctions against Yugoslavia based on the reasoning embodied in the United Nations Charter.'[109]

Some observations can be made here. We see a change of attitude in the EEC from the Falkland/Malvinas dispute to Yugoslavia. In its dispute with Argentina, the EEC merely stated that its measures were adopted in accordance with its inherent rights, of which Article XXI of the General Agreement is a reflection. In the case of the SFRY, the EEC explicitly referred to Article XXI as the legal basis for its actions. Regarding the response of the SFRY, it should be noted that its arguments were not entirely flawless, in legal terms. Whereas it is true that Resolution 713 (1991) did not oblige UN members to impose an export embargo, nor import restrictions, on civilian or dual-use materials or products, it expressed its concern that the situation in the SFRY constituted a threat to international security and peace,[110] imposed an arms embargo[111] and called on UN members to refrain from any action that would contribute to increasing tensions or impeding or delaying the peace.[112] Therefore, the question here is the scope of measures taken by WTO members in pursuance of their obligations under the UN Charter for the maintenance of international peace and security. In this present case, are the measures envisaged by UN Resolution 713 limited to arms embargo or do they extend to other trade restrictions?[113] Finally, in response to the request of the SFRY, a panel was established at the General Council meeting of 18 March 1992 'with the standard terms of reference unless, as provided

107 GATT Document, L/6948, 2 December 1991, p. 1.

108 *EEC – Trade Measures Taken for Non-Economic Reasons, Recourse to Article XXIII:2 by Yugoslavia*, DS27/2, 10 February 1992.

109 Ibid. p. 2.

110 UN Security Council Resolution 715 (1991), 4th preambular.

111 UN Security Council Resolution 715 (1991), para. 6.

112 UN Security Council Resolution 715 (1991), para. 7.

113 This issue will be further addressed later. See n.99 and accompanying text.

for in the Decision of 12 April 1989 (BISD 36S/61), the parties agreed on other terms within the following twenty days'.[114] The situation quickly evolved. The SFRY transformed into the Federal Republic of Yugoslavia (FRY), consisting of Serbia and Montenegro (dissolved in June 2006). As the UN General Assembly Resolution A/RES/47/1 decided that the FRY could not automatically inherit membership of the UN,[115] the General Council of the GATT also decided that the FRY should re-apply for its status as a contracting party to the GATT.[116] The work of the panel thus came to an end without a panel report.

Interestingly, the United States' positions in the GATT dispute settlement mechanism displayed a similar pattern: the United States did not invoke Article XXI in *United States – Imports of Sugar from Nicaragua* (*Nicaragua I*)[117] but did invoke this provision in *United States – Trade Measures affecting Nicaragua* (*Nicaragua II*).[118]

When the Sandinista National Liberation Front (FSLN) came to power in 1979, US–Nicaragua relations gradually deteriorated, particularly during the Reagan Administration, which was believed to be helping train rebel groups collectively known as the Contras. As part of efforts to weaken the FSLN and delegitimise it, the Reagan Administration imposed trade restrictive measures against Nicaragua. In an announcement dated 10 May 1983,[119] which amended Presidential Proclamation 4941 – Modification of Quotas on Certain Sugars, Sirups and Molasses, the Reagan Administration reduced the import quota for Nicaraguan sugar to 6,000 short tons. According to this announcement, it is claimed

> By denying to Nicaragua a foreign exchange benefit resulting from the high U.S. sugar price, we hope to reduce the resources available to that country for financing its military buildup and its support for subversion and extremist violence in the region. This is a signal of the United States seriousness with regard to the economic and political stability of its

[114] GATT Document, C/M/255, 10 April 1992, Minutes of Meeting Held in the Centre William Rappard, on 18 March 1992, p. 18.

[115] UN General Assembly Resolution, A/RES/47/1, 22 September 1992.

[116] GATT Document, C/M/264, 14 June 1993, on Minutes of Meeting Held in the Centre William Rappard, on 16–17 June 1993, p. 3.

[117] GATT Document, L/5607, *United States – Imports of Sugar from Nicaragua* (*Nicaragua I*) 2 March 1984.

[118] GATT Document, L/6503, *United States – Trade Measures affecting Nicaragua* (*Nicaragua II*) 13 October 1986, unadopted.

[119] Announcement of Revised United States Sugar Import Quotas for Nicaragua, Honduras, Costa Rica, and El Salvador, May 10, available at www.reaganlibrary.gov/research/speeches/51083c.

> neighbors in the hemisphere which is integrally related to the security of the region and the United States. The United States will continue to respond to developments in that region.[120]

In response to this reduction of its import quota, Nicaragua sought redress through the GATT dispute settlement mechanism as set forth in Article XXIII thereof. Nicaragua alleged that the import restrictions violated provisions of Articles II, XI and XIII and Part IV of the General Agreement. A panel was subsequently established with a view to addressing Nicaragua's complaint. The terms of reference of the panel are rather standardised, and read as follows

> To examine, in the light of the relevant GATT provisions, the matter referred to the CONTRACTING PARTIES by Nicaragua, relating to the measures taken by the United States concerning imports of sugar from Nicaragua (L/5492 and L/5513), and to make such findings as will assist the CONTRACTING PARTIES in making recommendations or rulings, as provided in Article XXIII.[121]

During the proceedings, the United States contended that the GATT was not the appropriate forum to address this subject matter. According to the United States,

> it was neither invoking any exceptions under the provisions of the General Agreement nor intending to defend its actions in GATT terms. The reduction in Nicaragua's sugar imports was not solely motivated by trade considerations, nor did this action secure any economic or trade benefit for the United States or for the sugar producers or any other industry of the United States. The action of the United States did of course affect trade, but was not taken for trade policy reasons … its action in reducing the Nicaraguan quota was fully justified in the context in which it was taken. The United States was of the view that attempting to discuss this issue in purely trade terms within the GATT, divorced from the broader context of the dispute, would be disingenuous. The resolution of that dispute was certainly desirable, and would also result in the lifting of the action which Nicaragua had challenged before the Panel, but the United States did not believe that the review and resolution of that broader dispute was within the ambit of the GATT.[122]

With the passive participation of the United States, the Panel in *Nicaragua (I)* eventually found against the United States and

[120] Ibid.
[121] *Nicaragua (I)*, para. 1.4
[122] *Nicaragua (I)*, paras. 3.10 and 11.

recommended that it bring the measure into conformity with the General Agreement.[123] However, *Nicaragua (I)* was only part of the litigation between the United States and Nicaragua; another of the critical battlefields was the International Court of Justice (ICJ)[124] and there is yet a *Nicaragua (II)* to come.

In Executive Order 12513,[125] President Reagan found that the policies and actions of Nicaragua constituted an unusual and extraordinary threat to the national security and foreign policy of the United States, and thereby declared a national emergency to deal with that threat.[126] In the context of this national emergency, the Reagan Administration adopted a series of trade restrictions against Nicaragua, including a prohibition on all imports of goods and services of Nicaraguan origin into the United States; of all exports from the United States of goods to, or destined for, Nicaragua with the exception of organised democratic resistance; and of sea and air transportation.[127] The GATT Secretariat was notified of this decision on 7 May 1985.[128] Nicaragua first requested consultation under Article XXII:1 of the General Agreement, but the United States did not respond. Nicaragua then requested the establishment of a panel to address the issue, but again, the United States objected. According to the United States, as the measures in question were adopted under Article XXI:(b)(iii) of the General Agreement, which leaves each contracting party to 'judge what actions it considered necessary for the protection of its essential security interests, [a] Panel could therefore not address the validity of, nor the motivation for, the United States' invocation of Article XXI:(b)(iii)'.[129] In practical terms, the GATT contracting parties could help in this case by authorising Nicaragua to suspend the application of the General Agreement, but such a move would be meaningless since the measures in question also prohibited all exports from the United States to Nicaragua.[130] Given the initial objection of the United States, a compromise was reached to establish a panel with specially designated terms of reference. In effect,

[123] *Nicaragua (I)*, para. 4.7.
[124] See text to n.109 and accompanying text.
[125] Executive Order 12513 – Prohibiting Trade and Certain Other Transactions Involving Nicaragua, 50 FR 18629, 3 CFR, 1985 Comp., p. 342.
[126] Ibid.
[127] Ibid.
[128] GATT Document, L/5803, 9 May 1985.
[129] *Nicaragua (II)*, para. 1.2.
[130] Ibid.

with these terms of reference, the Panel was barred from examining or judging the validity of or motivation for the invocation of Article XXI:(b)(iii) by the United States, the backbone of this dispute. The terms of reference read as follows

> To examine, in the light of the relevant GATT provisions, of the understanding reached at the Council on 10 October 1985 that the Panel cannot examine or judge the validity of or motivation for the invocation of Article XXI:(b)(iii) by the United States, of the relevant provisions of the Understanding Regarding Notification, Consultation, Dispute Settlement and Surveillance (BISD 26S/211-218), and of the agreed Dispute Settlement Procedures contained in the 1982 Ministerial Declaration (BISD 29S/13-16), the measures taken by the United States on 7 May 1985 and their trade effects in order to establish to what extent benefits accruing to Nicaragua under the General Agreement have been nullified or impaired, and to make such findings as will assist the CONTRACTING PARTIES in further action in this matter.[131]

Before the Panel proceedings, Nicaragua contended that Article XXI serves to offer the right of self-defence to a contracting party subject to aggression. The measures adopted by the United States had been held inconsistent with international law before the International Court of Justice in *Military and Paramilitary Activities in and against Nicaragua* (*Nicaragua* v. *United States of America*). UN Security Council Resolution 562 (1985)[132] and General Assembly Resolution A/RES/40/188[133] had also condemned the embargo for infringing the principles of free trade and had explicitly demanded that it be rescinded. Nicaragua emphasised that 'GATT did not exist in a vacuum but was an integral part of the wider structure of international law, and that the General Agreement must not be interpreted in a way inconsistent with international law'.[134] The United States could not be allowed to 'base itself on the existence of an "emergency" which it had itself created'.[135] Nicaragua further alleged that even if the Panel was excluded by its terms of reference to review the validity based on Article XXI:(b)(iii), the Panel might nonetheless carry

[131] *US–Nicaragua (II)*, para. 1.4.

[132] UN Security Council Resolution 562 (1985), 10 May 1985.

[133] UN General Assembly Resolution, A/RES/40/188, 17 December 1985.

[134] *US–Nicaragua (II)*, para. 1.4. In response to this argument, the Panel replied that [w]hile not refuting such argumentation, the Panel nevertheless considered it to be outside its mandate to take up these questions because the Panel's task was to examine the case before it 'in the light of the relevant GATT provisions, although they might be inadequate and incomplete for the purpose'. *US–Nicaragua (II)*, para. 5.15.

[135] *US–Nicaragua (II)*, para. 1.4.

out its task by finding Nicaragua's rights and benefits nullified or impaired in accordance with Article XXIII:2 of the General Agreement.

In addressing the subject matter before it, the Panel was handicapped, as it would not be able to examine the core of this dispute: the validity of Article XXI:(b)(iii) justification. Regardless of this constraint, the Panel examined Nicaragua's non-violation complaint independently of the GATT-consistency of the trade embargo. According to the Panel, the trade embargo robbed Nicaragua of trade opportunities and as a consequence US–Nicaragua trade sharply decreased. Nicaragua's rights and benefits under the General Agreement had been nullified and impaired. While the Panel might offer two options (the withdrawal of trade embargo by the United States; and authorisation of suspension of application of the General Agreement), these two option were neither feasible nor practicable, as the United States had made it clear that it would not withdraw the embargo unless the underlying political issue had been resolved, and suspension of the application of the General Agreement was meaningless to Nicaragua given its limited trade with the United States. The Panel thus made no substantial recommendation to the GATT contracting parties. However, the Panel underlined the importance of striking a balance between achieving the aim and objective of the General Agreement and safeguarding essential security interests of a contracting party. As the Panel noted, it 'recognized that the General Agreement protected each contracting party's essential security interests through Article XXI and that the General Agreement's purpose was therefore not to make contracting parties forego their essential security interests for the sake of these aims. However, the Panel considered that the GATT could not achieve its basic aims unless each contracting party, whenever it made use of its rights under Article XXI, carefully weighed its security needs against the need to maintain stable trade relations.'[136] The Panel then posed the following challenging question

> If it were accepted that the interpretation of Article XXI was reserved entirely to the contracting party invoking it, how could the CONTRACTING PARTIES ensure that this general exception to all obligations under the General Agreement is not invoked excessively or for purposes other than those set out in this provision? If the CONTRACTING PARTIES give a panel the task of examining a case involving an Article XXI invocation without authorizing it to examine the justification of that invocation, do they limit the adversely affected

[136] *US–Nicaragua (II)*, para. 5.16.

> contracting party's right to have its complaint investigated in accordance with Article XXIII:2? Are the powers of the CONTRACTING PARTIES under Article XXIII:2 sufficient to provide redress to contracting parties subjected to a two-way embargo?[137]

However, these questions were left largely unanswered by the GATT contracting parties. In particular, *Nicaragua (II)* was not adopted due to the opposition of the United States, even though the Panel's arguments remain valid. Importantly, in view of the shift towards legalism from the GATT to WTO in the regulation of trade relations with the aim of securing greater security and predictability of the world trade order, to argue that the permission of jurisdictional defence entirely or largely at the discretion of a country invoking the security exception would signal the end of the WTO as a rules-based system.[138] It is also to be remembered that the change of decision-making process from the GATT to the WTO dispute settlement body has rendered the responding party unable to block the establishment of a panel or to revise the terms of reference to suit the needs of a particular dispute, and the losing party is unable to block the adoption of the Panel or Appellate Body reports. Therefore, it is likely that these questions would be eventually brought before the WTO judiciary. Finally, *Russia – Traffic in Transit*[139] came before the Panel.

In the wake of the Ukraine crisis, Russia adopted a number of measures the main thrust of which is to prevent and prohibit goods from Ukraine from passing through its territory. Ukraine thus lodged a complaint in the WTO dispute settlement mechanism alleging that such measures are incompatible with WTO law, in particular freedom of transit as set out in Article V of the GATT 1994. Russia did not contend the WTO-inconsistency of its measures but invoked Article XXI:(b)(iii) as a justification. According to Russia, the WTO Panel/Appellate Body has no jurisdiction on a measure which is adopted in safeguarding its essential security interests.[140] A real national security case thus came before the WTO dispute settlement mechanism. Since Russia argued that the Panel has no jurisdiction in assessing the legality of a measure based on Article XXI, the Panel organised its order of analysis by investigating

137 *US–Nicaragua (II)*, para. 5.17.

138 Schloemann and Ohlhoff, '"Constitutionalization" and Dispute Settlement in the WTO: National Security as an Issue of Competence' (n. 91) 425–426.

139 Panel Report on *Russia – Measures Concerning Traffic in Transit (Traffic in Transit)*, WT/DS512/R, adopted on 26 April 2019.

140 Panel Report on *Traffic in Transit*, para. 7.4.

its jurisdiction first and then appreciating the legality of Russian measures based on Article XXI justification. To begin with, it is worthy of a closer look at the terms of reference of the Panel on *Russia – Traffic in Transit*, contrasted with those for the Panel on *Nicaragua (II)*. The terms of reference read as follows,

> To examine, in the light of the relevant provisions of the covered agreements cited by the parties to the dispute, the matter referred to the DSB by Ukraine in document WT/DS512/3 and to make such findings as will assist the DSB in making the recommendations or in giving the rulings provided for in those agreements.[141]

Compared to the terms of reference for the Panel on *Nicaragua (II)*, those for *Russia – Traffic in Transit* are rather standardised and do not prevent the panel from assessing the justification based on the national security exception. The differences in the departure point may predetermine the conclusions they reached. That said, whether the Panel has jurisdiction over a case invoking an Article XXI exception is heatedly debated not only between the complainant and respondent but also among third-party countries.

During the Panel proceedings, Russia maintained that an emergency in international relations arose in 2014, and evolved from 2014 to 2018. Such emergency continued to exist and constituted a threat to Russia's essential security interests. Whereas the Panel was established with standard terms of reference, it still lacked the jurisdiction to assess the legality of a measure adopted in accordance with Article XXI of the GATT 1994. In Russia's view, Article XXI confers sole discretion on the member invoking this exception to determine the 'necessity, form, design and structure' of the measures adopted under this provision. Russia read Article XXI:(b)(iii) as a right conferred by the GATT/WTO regime on a sovereign state to react to wars and other emergencies of international relations in a way it finds necessary. Any other interpretation of Article XXI:(b)(iii) would amount to interference in the external and internal affairs of a sovereign state.[142] Russia emphasised that 'a Member's subjective assessment cannot be doubted or re-evaluated by any other party or judicial bodies as the measures in question are not ordinary trade measures regularly assessed by WTO panels'.[143]

[141] Panel Report on *Russia – Traffic in Transit*, para. 1.4.
[142] Panel Report on *Russia –Traffic in Transit*, paras. 7.27–7.29.
[143] Panel Report on *Russia – Traffic in Transit*, para. 7.29.

Ukraine interpreted Article XXI as an affirmative defence that justifies an otherwise WTO-inconsistent measure. The Panel has the jurisdiction to review the provisions of covered agreements cited by the parties in this dispute in accordance with the standard terms of reference under Article 7 of the DSU and in line with the general standard of review under Article 11 of the DSU. According to Ukraine, 'if Article XXI of the GATT 1994 were non-justiciable, it would imply that in a dispute involving a measure that is WTO-inconsistent, the invoking Member, rather a panel, would decide the outcome of the dispute by determining that the WTO-inconsistent measure is nonetheless justified'.[144] Such unilateral determination of an invoking member is contrary to the spirit and letter of Article 23.1 of the DSU. Ukraine further argued that Article XXI does not grant *carte blanche* to WTO members. Had the drafters of the GATT intended to grant GATT contracting parties 'total discretion', there would have been no need to include different clauses and identify different types of security interests to justify a country's measures.[145]

The positions of third-party countries are also divided, though the vast majority, with the glaring exception of the United States, agreed that the Panel has jurisdiction over a case where the respondent invokes an Article XXI exception. The United States first submitted a letter to the Panel stating that 'the Panel lacks the authority to review the invocation of Article XXI and make findings on the claims raised in this dispute'.[146] This position is in line with its previous stances in *Nicaragua (I)* and *Nicaragua (II)*. Subsequently, the United States clarified its position by maintaining that the Panel has jurisdiction over this dispute 'in the sense that the DSB established it, placed the matter raised in Ukraine's complaint within the Panel's terms of reference under Article 7.1 of the DSU'.[147] Nonetheless, the United States interpreted Article XXI as non-justiciable since it does not set out objective legal criteria for adjudicators to follow. The chapeau of Article XXI:(b), by employing the language of 'which it considers necessary' pre-defines the 'self-judging' nature of this clause and thus prevents it from being reviewed by a WTO panel.[148]

Other third-party participants, including Australia, Brazil, Canada, China, the EU, Japan, Moldova, Singapore and Turkey, were of the view

144 Panel Report on *Russia – Traffic in Transit*, para. 7.31.
145 Panel Report on *Russia – Traffic in Transit*, para. 7.33.
146 Panel Report on *Russia – Traffic in Transit*, para. 7.52.
147 Panel Report on *Russia – Traffic in Transit*, para. 7.52.
148 Panel Report on *Russia – Traffic in Transit*, para. 7.52.

that the Panel has jurisdiction over Russia's invocation of the national security exception, but differed in the standard of review with which the Panel should assess Russia's justification for its measures. Largely, most third countries maintained that a deferential standard of review should be employed in view of the language 'which it considers necessary', which again relates to the 'self-judging' nature of Article XX:(b).

As for the question whether the WTO adjudicators have jurisdiction over a case invoking the Article XXI exception, the Panel answered in the affirmative. The Panel, citing the decision of the International Court of Justice on *Nuclear Test Case (Australia* v. *France)*, noted that international tribunal adjudicators, including the WTO dispute settlement panels, 'possessed inherent jurisdiction which derives from the exercise of their adjudicative function. One aspect of this inherent jurisdiction is the power to determine all matters arising in relation to the exercise of their own substantive jurisdiction.'[149] The Panel then turned to the standard terms of reference for its own establishment and observed that there were no special or additional rules of procedure applicable to disputes arising from Article XXI of the GATT 1994.[150] The Panel further emphasised that in order to respond to Russia's jurisdictional plea, it is obliged to look into the substance of Article XX:(b)(iii) so as to determine whether the power to decide the fulfilment of the criteria of that provision is vested solely in the member invoking this exception, or whether the Panel retains the power to review a member's decision.[151] In the view of the Panel, the jurisdictional issue is closely linked to the 'self-judging' nature of Article XXI:(b)(iii). If the member invoking such exception has total discretion, the Panel is precluded from assessing its justification and legality and thus have no jurisdiction over it.

In *Saudi Arabia – Protection of IPR*,[152] the Panel was called on again to address the national security exception, albeit in the context of the TRIPS Agreement. This case arose from the broad context of the Qatar diplomatic crisis. In June 2017, Saudi Arabia, joined by the United Arab Emirates and Bahrain, launched a series of measures aiming to isolate Qatar economically through blockade, accompanied by a number of political and diplomatic measures, such as the severance of diplomatic

[149] Panel Report on *Russia – Traffic in Transit*, para. 7.53.

[150] Panel Report on *Russia – Traffic in Transit*, paras. 7.55–7.56.

[151] Panel Report on *Russia –Traffic in Transit*, para. 7.58.

[152] Panel Report on *Saudi Arabia – Measures Concerning the Protection of Intellectual Property Rights*, WT/DS567/R, 16 June 2020.

relations. The immediate cause of this disagreement was that Qatar's Emir Tamim was alleged to have described Hamas as the legitimate representative of the Palestinian people and to call Iran a big power in the stabilization of the region on the occasion of a military graduation ceremony on 23 May 2017.[153] The blockage comprises a series of comprehensive measures, including trade in goods, trade in services and trade-related intellectual property rights, aiming to economically isolate Qatar. Not only was trade between Qatar and Saudi Arabia halted, but Saudi Arabia was joined by the United Arab Emirates and Bahrain in completely preventing Qatar from accessing the ports and airports of these three countries. Qatar's Minister of Defence, Khalid Al Attiyah, referred to this blockade as a 'bloodless declaration of war'.[154]

On 31 July 2017, Qatar, citing a long list of measures violating WTO rules, including Article XI of the GATT 1994, requested consultation with Saudi Arabia,[155] the United Arab Emirates[156] and Bahrain[157] under the WTO dispute settlement mechanism. The three countries, nevertheless, citing the national security exception as a justification, chose not to enter into consultation. Instead of advancing this fully fledged consultation request further on to the panel stage, Qatar, on 9 November 2018, submitted another consultation request targeting only Saudi Arabia and focusing on intellectual property rights. Saudi Arabia again refused to enter into consultation but this time Qatar decided to pursue this case further and requested the establishment of a panel.[158]

In *Saudi Arabia – Measures Concerning the Protection of Intellectual Property Rights (Saudi Arabia – Protection of IPR)*, Qatar alleged that Qatar's companies were not offered adequate intellectual property rights protection in Saudi Arabia as obliged under WTO law. Notably, beIN Media Group LLC and affiliates (beIN) were prevented from

[153] Kristian Coates Ulrichsen, 'What's Going on with Qatar?' in POMEPS (ed), *The Qatar Crisis* (The Project on Middle East Political Science 2017) 6.

[154] Shabina S. Khatri, 'Defense Minister: Blockade of Qatar a "Declaration of War"', *Doha News*, 1 July 2017, available at https://dohanews.co/defense-minister-blockade-of-qatar-a-declaration-of-war/.

[155] *Saudi Arabia – Measures Relating to Trade in Goods and Services, and Trade-Related Aspects of Intellectual Property Rights*, WT/DS528/1, 4 August 2017.

[156] *United Arab Emirates – Measures Relating to Trade in Goods and Services, and Trade-Related Aspects of Intellectual Property Rights*, WT/DS528/1, 4 August 2017.

[157] *Bahrain – Measures Relating to Trade in Goods and Services, and Trade-Related Aspects of Intellectual Property Rights*, WT/DS528/1, 4 August 2017.

[158] *Saudi Arabia – Measures Concerning the Protection of Intellectual Property Rights*, WT/DS567/3, 19 November 2018.

broadcasting content in Saudi Arabia and a broadcast pirate named beoutQ, with state involvement of Saudi Arabia, transmitted unauthorised content of beIN to its subscribers. Qatar alleged that Qatari nationals were treated less favourably than Saudi nationals and nationals of other WTO members and this violated the principles of MFN treatment and National Treatment. Moreover, effective judicial protection was not provided, as Qatari nationals were prevented from resorting to Saudi courts to enforce their intellectual property rights against the infringers.[159] Saudi Arabia invoked the national security exception as provided in Article 73 of the TRIPS Agreement in this complaint as well.

Article 73 uses similar language to Article XXI of the GATT 1994. In the interests of precision and clarity, the legal text of Article 73 is provided here

> Nothing in this Agreement shall be construed:
>
> (a) to require a Member to furnish any information the disclosure of which it considers contrary to its essential security interests; or
>
> (b) to prevent a Member from taking any action which it considers necessary for the protection of its essential security interests;
>
> (i) relating to fissionable materials or the materials from which they are derived;
>
> (ii) relating to the traffic in arms, ammunition and implements of war and to such traffic in other goods and materials as is carried on directly or indirectly for the purpose of supplying a military establishment;
>
> (iii) taken in time of war or other emergency in international relations; or
>
> (c) to prevent a Member from taking any action in pursuance of its obligations under the United Nations Charter for the maintenance of international peace and security.

In *Saudi Arabia – Protection of IPR*, neither Saudi Arabia nor third parties argued against the jurisdiction of the Panel over national security exceptions.[160] However, Saudi Arabia advances a novel argument that the Panel should decline to make any findings or recommendation based on Articles 3.4, 3.7 and 11 of the DSU, as the dispute is not of a legal, but

[159] *Saudi Arabia – Measures Concerning the Protection of Intellectual Property Rights*, WT/DS567/3, 19 November 2018, pp. 1–4.

[160] Panel Report on *Saudi Arabia – Protection of IPR*, footnote 215.

a political, geopolitical and essential security nature.[161] Since the recommendations by the Panel would not resolve satisfactorily the matter between Saudi Arabia and Qatar given the nature of broader disputes surrounding this WTO complaint, the Panel should decline to do so.[162] These arguments did not persuade the Panel.

The Panel first referred to *Mexico – Taxes on Soft Drinks*, where the subject matter relates to a broad dispute in the context of North America Free Trade Agreement (NAFTA) and the respondent suggested the Panel decline to exercise jurisdiction. The Panel in *Mexico – Taxes on Soft Drinks* held, supported by the Appellate Body, that a panel is not in a position to freely decide whether or not to exercise its jurisdiction, as it would not be able to fulfil its duty under Article 11 of the DSU to 'make such other findings as will assist the DSB in making the recommendations or in giving the rulings provided for in the covered agreements'.[163] Such a declination would also amount to impairment of the right of a member to seek redress of a violation of obligations within the meaning of Article 23 of the DSU.[164] The Panel further recalled the observations of the Panel in *Russia – Traffic in Transit*, noting that '[t]he ICJ has rejected the "political question" argument, concluding that, as long as the case before it or the request for an advisory opinion turns on a legal question capable of a legal answer, it is duty-bound to take jurisdiction over it, regardless of the political background or the other political facets of the issue'.[165] As the Panel opined, the subject matter before it is a complaint based on WTO covered agreements cited by Qatar, a trade dispute rather than the broader disputes as Saudi Arabia contended. The Panel further distinguished this dispute from *Nicaragua (II)*, as *Nicaragua (II)* concerns a non-violation complaint. What the GATT contracting parties could do is 'make a non-binding recommendation that the United States withdraw its embargo, or authorise Nicaragua to suspend the application of obligations toward the United States',[166] which was of no help to Nicaragua since the United States explicitly declared that it would not withdraw its embargo, and the authorisation for Nicaragua would not restore the balance of advantages accruing to the two parties by virtue of

[161] Panel Report on *Saudi Arabia – Protection of IPR*, para. 7.8.
[162] Panel Report on *Saudi Arabia – Protection of IPR*, para. 7.8.
[163] Panel Report on *Saudi Arabia – Protection of IPR*, para. 7.11.
[164] Panel Report on *Saudi Arabia – Protection of IPR*, para. 7.12.
[165] Panel Report on *Saudi Arabia – Protection of IPR*, para. 7.12.
[166] Panel Report on *Saudi Arabia – Protection of IPR*, para. 7.21.

the existent two-way embargo. This was not the case in this present complaint. The Panel thus reached the conclusion that it is under the obligation to objectively assess the subject matter and make appropriate recommendations.

From *Russia – Traffic in Transit* to *Saudi Arabia – Protection of IPR*, it seems that most, if not all, WTO members accept the view that the Panel/ Appellate Body has the jurisdiction to examine a complaint where national security is invoked. Nonetheless, it is still divided, even in *Saudi Arabia – Protection of IPR*, whether national security is 'self-judging' and thus not justiciable.

3.4.2 Self-Judging Nature of 'Which It Considers Contrary/Necessary'

The 'self-judging' nature of the security exception is circled around the legal text of 'any information the disclosure of which it considers contrary to its essential security interests' and 'any action which it considers necessary', as set out in Articles XXI:(a) and XXI:(b) of the GATT 1994. The wording of 'which it considers' invites the question as to whether the justification of these two clauses are self-judging. Interestingly, the thesis for this 'self-judging' nature comes from jurisprudence from the ICJ rather than the GATT panel. The ICJ, in *Case Concerning Military and Paramilitary Activities in and against Nicaragua*,[167] reached the conclusion that it is competent to examine the justification of the United States under Article XXI (Security Exception) of the 1956 Treaty of Friendship, Commerce and Navigation between the United States and Nicaragua (1956 FCN)[168] by comparing the legal texts providing in the treaty and Article XXI of the GATT. As the ICJ noted,

> This article [Article XXI of the 1956 FCN] cannot be interpreted as removing the present dispute as to the scope of the Treaty from the Court's jurisdiction. Being itself an article of the Treaty, it is covered by

[167] *Case Concerning Military and Paramilitary Activities in and against Nicaragua* (*Nicaragua* v. *United States of America*), Judgment. I.C.J. Reports 1986, p. 14.

[168] The relevant part of the 1956 Treaty of Friendship, Commerce and Navigation between the United States and Nicaragua provides, 'the present Treaty shall not preclude the application of measures (c) regulating the production of or traffic in arms, ammunition and implements of war, or traffic in other materials carried on directly or indirectly for the purpose of supplying a military establishment (d) necessary to fulfill the obligations of a Party for the maintenance or restoration of international peace and security, or necessary to protect its essential security interests'.

> the provision in Article XXIV that any dispute about the 'interpretation or application' of the Treaty lies within the Court's jurisdiction. Article XXI defines the instances in which the Treaty itself provides for exceptions to the generality of its other provisions, but it by no means removes the interpretation and application of that article from the jurisdiction of the Court as contemplated in Article XXIV. That the Court has jurisdiction to determine whether measures taken by one of the Parties fall within such an exception, is also clear *a contrario* from the fact that the text of Article XXI of the Treaty does not employ the wording which was already to be found in Article XXI of the General Agreement on Tariffs and Trade. This provision of GATT, contemplating exceptions to the normal implementation of the General Agreement, stipulates that the Agreement is not to be construed to prevent any contracting party from taking any action which it 'considers necessary for the protection of its essential security interests', in such fields as nuclear fission, arms, etc. The 1956 treaty, on the contrary, speaks simply of 'necessary' measures, not of those considered by a party to be such.[169]

The arguments of the ICJ are two-fold. From the outset, it held that Article XXI of the 1956 FCN constitutes part of the treaty of which the 'interpretation or application' falls within the jurisdiction of the ICJ. In particular, the ICJ compared the wording of the legal text in Article XXI of the 1956 FCN and Article XXI of the GATT and found that there is no such wording as 'it considers necessary' in the 1956 FCN. The ICJ thus arrived at the decision that it was competent to examine the United States' justification under Article XXI of the 1956 FCN. This ruling has, nonetheless, repercussions for GATT/WTO law. By implication, according to the ICJ, given that Article XXI of the GATT embodies such language as 'it considers necessary', the justification of the security exception under GATT/WTO law may not be subject to the jurisdiction of the Panel and Appellate Body.[170] The 'self-judging' thesis has its proponents and opponents, which continuously shuffle as international

169 *Nicaragua* v. *United States of America*, para. 222.

170 Such textual approach, by comparing whether the legal text contains a clause of 'it considers necessary', is followed by the *CMS* v. *Argentina* case. The arbitral tribunal followed the ruling of the ICJ and compared the legal text of the GATT, US–Russia BIT and accompanying protocol, on the one hand and the US–Argentina BIT on the other and finally reached the conclusion that the security exception as set out in the US–Argentina BIT is not self-judging in nature. The arbitral tribunal had the jurisdiction to examine the justification pursuant to the security exception. *CMS Gas Transmission Company* v. *The Argentine Republic (CMS* v. *Argentina)*, (ICSID Case No. ARB 01/8), paras. 339–340, 370.

law evolves, in particular under the influence of the constitutionalisation discourse.[171]

On the one side, Raj Bhala, emphasising the subject of the clause 'which it considers necessary', argues that this clause provides a member invoking a security exception sole discretion to determine whether the measures comply with the requirements of Article XXI of the GATT 1994. The implication of 'it' indicates that no other WTO member or even WTO Panel/Appellate Body has a right to determine whether such sanctioning measures fulfil these requirements.[172] Bhala maintains that, while the target member is entitled and may be free to refer to the WTO dispute settlement mechanism, such resort will inevitably turn out to be fruitless. Textual analysis of Article XXI:(b) leads to the conclusion that the invocation of the national security exception is a matter left to national discretion, and the *realpolitik* demands WTO members retain the sovereign prerogative. Therefore, he predicts that a WTO Panel would choose to defer to national discretion and avoid a substantive ruling on the security exception.[173]

Roger Alford concurs with Bhala's position. In examining state practice through the GATT era to the WTO age, he confirms the 'self-judging' nature of the security exception while acknowledging that a minority of states object to this view out of fear for the danger of its abuse by economically powerful countries.[174]

Susan Rose-Ackerman and Benjamin Billa, after reviewing the GATT disputes relating to the security exception, conclude that no panel had ever declared any part of a security exception to be at the sole discretion of a contracting party. They maintain that the arguments for reviewability of the security exception have grown stronger in view of the more judicialised character of the WTO dispute settlement mechanism and argue that trade restrictive measures based on the security exception are to be reviewed in accordance

[171] See e.g., Ernst Ulrich Petersmann, 'How to Constitutionalize International Law and Foreign Policy for the Benefit of Civil Society?' (1998b) 20 *Michigan Journal of International Law* 1; Deborah Z. Cass, *The Constitutionalization of the World Trade Organization* (Oxford University Press 2005).

[172] Raj Bhala, 'National Security and International Trade Law: What the GATT Says and What the United States Does' (1998) 19 *University of Pennsylvania Journal of International Law* 263, 268–269.

[173] Ibid. 279.

[174] Rogert P. Alford, 'The Self-Judging WTO Security Exception' (2011) 3 *Utah Law Review* 697, 708.

with 'customary rules of interpretation of public international law', which includes good faith.[175]

Hannes Schloemann and Stefan Ohlhoff also offer two arguments in rejecting the 'self-judgment claim'. According to them, 'the act of considering whether an interest is threatened and which means are necessary to protect it is a technical in nature. Once the interest (or political/military goal) is specified, the determination of appropriate means for security it is a matter of correctly assessing risks and possibilities.'[176] While the clause 'which it considers necessary' offers some margin of appreciation for a trade nation, this margin is not exclusively reserved for sovereign nations and precludes judicial review. Second, the different approaches adopted in paragraphs (a) and (b) of Article XXI indicate that 'consideration' does not equate to 'total discretion'; otherwise, differentiation between these two paragraphs in different contexts would be unnecessary. Thus, the critical question here is 'whether, and to what extent, these requirements embody objective concepts open to *legal* interpretation (as opposed to *political* definition) and are therefore susceptible to judicial review within the WTO'[177] For example, the thorny term of 'essential security interests' should be interpreted in good faith by the state invoking it. Moreover, at least a minimum degree of proportionality between the threat to the essential security interests and functioning of the multilateral system should be ensured. The proportionality test advanced here is the reasonableness of the measure in the given context.[178]

Similarly, Dapo Akande and Sope Williams, in dissecting the elements of Article XXI of the GATT 1994, argue that this provision does set out some objective criteria, which are subject to judicial review by the WTO Panel/Appellate Body. They further refer to the jurisprudence of some international courts and tribunals, in particular the Court of Justice of the European Union (the CJEU) and European Court of Human Rights (the ECtHR), to substantiate their claim that national security is a term susceptible to judicial review. According to these two authors, the assertion that security exception is self-judging

[175] Susan Rose-Ackermann and Benjamin Billa, 'Treaties and National Security' (2008) 40 *New York University Journal of International Law and Politics* 437, 468.

[176] Schloemann and Ohlhoff, '"Constitutionalization" and Dispute Settlement in the WTO: National Security as an Issue of Competence' (n. 91) 443.

[177] Ibid.

[178] Ibid. 444–445.

removes the legal nature of Article XXI, which is intended to produce legal obligations.[179]

The dividing line between the two camps lies in their perceptions of the world trade order and the role of international adjudicators,[180] which are embedded in divergent views of international relations. Depending on the various stages of international trade relations, different international theories offer different explanations on the role of security and its appropriate role in the WTO dispute settlement mechanism.

Realism, a dominant international relations theory, holds that international politics is basically a struggle for power, and endorses giving greater weight to power over law. Given that the existence and survival of a state is dependent on its national security, which in turn closely relates to the security exception, Realists thus view essential security interests as a reflection of a state's sovereignty subject to its own definition. The security exception is therefore an indispensable escape mechanism, or safety valve, when its very existence is under threat. With a view to exchanging concessions, and through exercising free will in the form of state consent, states enter into international obligations, which bind states and constrain their policy space. At the negotiation stage, with the security exception, states aim to retain a certain degree of autonomy, or sovereignty, on sensitive issues, which reflects Realists' perceptions of international economic relations.[181] The security exception serves as dual political exceptions. On the one hand, sovereign states, in view of the threat the WTO poses to their sovereignty, seek confirmation that their security interests supersede trade obligations. In consenting to WTO agreements, states are consenting to the norms they agreed, including a security exception which is subject only to their own determination. On the other hand, the security exception enables the WTO to preserve its institutional integrity without compromising the sovereignty of states. According to Andrew Emmerson, '[b]y including security exception,

[179] Dapo Akande and Sope Williams, 'International Adjudication on National Security Issues: What Role for the WTO' (2003) 43 *Virginia Journal of International Law* 366, 382–386.

[180] See e.g., Thomas Cottier and Matthias Oesch, 'The Paradox of Judicial Review in International Trade Regulation: Towards a Comprehensive Framework' in Thomas Cottier and Petros C. Mavroidis (eds), *The Role of the Judge in International Trade Regulation* (The University of Michigan Press 2003) 283–306 and other contributions to this edited volume.

[181] Andrew Emmerson, 'Conceptualizing Security Exceptions: Legal Doctrine or Political Excuse' (2008) 11 *Journal of International Economic Law* 135, 138–139.

states are encouraged to consent to WTO membership, underpinning the WTO's negotiated legitimacy'.[182] Pragmatism at the negotiation stage assumes that sovereign states' political power remains intact while the WTO circumscribes its decision-making authority.

At the invocation stage, the norms negotiated by sovereign states slip out of their control once interpretative authority is delegated to a third party,[183] in this case, the WTO Panel/Appellate Body. Legal formalism and institutionalism thus bring additional explanatory power to the role and function of the security exception. As Andrew Emmerson notes, legal formalism, as an institutional culture of resistance to power, is inherent in the security exception. The potential judicial refinement of the security exception by the WTO Panel/Appellate Body, through doctrinal constraint, led the United States and the EU to settle their divergence on the Helms–Burton Act. 'The doctrinal security exceptions therefore operate as ordering mechanisms, allowing for limited derogation from trade obligations with some autonomous power used to shape state behaviour.'[184] While Realists view international legal institutions as a sham, asserting that they unjustifiably encroach on the core interests of national security and state survival, Institutionalists point to the failure of Realists to appreciate the value of legal institutions in creating new norms, rules and decision-making procedures that shape the patterns of state expectation and behaviour.[185]

Moreover, in response to Realists' assertion that security exception is self-judging and operates as political excuses rather than legally limited carve-outs, Constructivists argue that Realists neglect the values inherent in the legalised exceptions. In entering into the WTO, members, through the exercise of free will, have ceded some aspect of their sovereignty and elevated the security exception to a self-constraining norm. In contrast to Realists' view of anarchy in international relations and absence of authoritative power, Institutionalists and Constructivists see the security exception as an instrument to mitigate the anarchic consequences of

[182] Ibid. 140.

[183] Indeed, delegation has been a core element of legalisation, as proposed by Kenneth Abbott, Robert Keohane, Andrew Moravcsik, Anne-Marie Slaughter and Duncan Snidal, who conceptualize legalisation as 'a particular form of institutionalization characterized by three components: obligations, precision and delegation'. See Kenneth Abbott and others, 'The Concept of Legalization' (200) 54 *International Organization* 401, 401.

[184] Emmerson, 'Conceptualizing Security Exceptions: Legal Doctrine or Political Excuse' (n. 181) 149–150.

[185] Ibid. 150.

Realists' premise. International institutions serve as sites for cooperative enterprises for relations between states and states, and states and institutions, thereby transforming international relations from chaos to order. The legalised WTO substitutes distrust and insecurity with values and norms that induce compliance and cooperation, as is manifested by the inclusion of the security exception at the negotiation stage. From the perspective of Institutionalists and Constructivists, the WTO is a forum of international society through which it organises its members through norms, rules, procedures, and rights and obligations, and gradually increases its constitutional authority and legitimacy. In this view, the security exception reinforces the cooperative identity of interdependence within the WTO.[186]

The WTO adjudicators in *Russia – Traffic in Transit* finally had an opportunity to address this long-debated issue and reached the conclusion that Article XXI:(b) is not of 'self-judging' nature. The question before the Panel is whether the clause in the chapeau of Article XXI:(b) qualified the determination of the matters in the enumerated subparagraphs of that provision, or put differently, the qualifying scope of the adjectival term 'necessary'. According to the Panel, the three sets of circumstances identified in Article XXI:(b) operate as limiting and qualifying clauses, which are to 'qualify and limit the exercise of the discretion accorded to Members under the chapeaux to these circumstances'.[187] If the clause 'which it considers necessary' extends to the three enumerated subparagraphs and is left to the sole discretion of a member invoking this exception, it will run counter to the principle of *effet utile*, since the identification and distinction of three types of circumstances become meaningless. Moreover, a closer look at the language of the three subparagraphs will find that they are substantially different and establish alternative (rather cumulative) requirements for an action to meet with a view to be justified under the national security exception. Not only 'fissionable materials' and 'traffic in arms' but also 'war' and 'other emergencies of international relations' are subjective to objective determination.[188]

The Panel then looked into the object and purpose of the WTO Agreement as well as the GATT 1994, which are to 'promote security and predictability of reciprocal and mutual advantageous arrangements

[186] Ibid. 149–150.

[187] Panel Report on *Russia – Traffic in Transit*, para. 7.65.

[188] Panel Report on *Russia – Traffic in Transit*, paras. 7.65–7.77.

and substantial reduction of tariffs and other barriers to trade'.[189] At the same time, the WTO agreements set out conditions for members to depart from WTO rules and provide them some latitude of autonomy with a view to pursuing non-trade interests. General exception, national security exception and escape clause are some of the built-in flexibilities in the WTO agreements. Therefore, to grant a WTO member total and unchecked discretion will compromise such balance and undermine the security and predictability of the world trading system that the GATT/ WTO aims to establish.

The Panel finally referred to the negotiating history to seek support for its view that Article XXI:(b) is not 'self-judging' but capable of being objective assessment. It pointed to the two opposing views presented during the negotiating processes. Some delegates, in particular the United States, argued for freedom of action in safeguarding their security interest and independent power to interpret the language of such exception, whereas some cautioned about the risk of abuse of such exception. In the end, the cautious view prevailed and it was favoured that some elements of the security exception should be subject to review.[190]

Based on these analyses, the Panel thus arrived at the conclusion that the clause 'which it considers necessary' does not extend to the determination of the circumstances identified in the three subparagraphs of Article XXI:(b). Rather, the existence of such circumstances should be objectively assessed.[191] Therefore, after confirming its jurisdiction over a case relating to the national security exception and finding the three subparagraphs of Article XXI:(b) capable of being objectively reviewed, the task before the Panel was thus who should and how to determine the necessity for the protection of essential security interests as contained in the chapeau of XXI:(b).

After looking into the language, object, purpose and negotiating history of Article XXI, the Panel concluded that it has jurisdiction over a complaint relating to the national security exception and held that the clause 'which it considers' does not qualify maximally the whole provision of Article XXI:(b), including its three subparagraphs. In the context of the 'self-judging nature' of 'which it considers', the Panel had to examine whether this clause qualifies only 'necessary' or also qualifies 'essential security interests'. The Panel reached the conclusion that this

[189] Panel Report on *Russia – Traffic in Transit*, para. 7.79.
[190] Panel Report on *Russia – Traffic in Transit*, paras. 7.89–7.91.
[191] Panel Report on *Russia – Traffic in Transit*, paras. 7.101.

clause qualifies both terms and it is thus for the member invoking the exception to decide what constitutes essential security interests and to what extent it is necessary.

As the Panel held, 'essential security interests' is clearly a narrower concept than 'security interests' and may be understood to refer to 'those interests relating to the quintessential functions of the state, namely, the protection of its territory and its population from external threat, and the maintenance of law and public order internally'.[192] The interests to be protected from internal and external threat depend on the particular situation and perceptions of the state, vary from country to country and change correspondingly with circumstances. It is thus, in principle, for the member to define what it considers to be its essential security interests. That said, it does not entail that a member can freely elevate an immaterial matter to an essential security interest. The exercise of discretion in defining essential security interests should be constrained by the application of Article XXI in good faith, a widely recognised general principle of law.[193] In line with this reasoning, the Panel further noted that the member invoking this exception is obliged to articulate its essential security interests sufficiently to demonstrate their veracity. In turn, 'what qualifies as a sufficient level of articulation will depend on the emergency in international relations at issue'.[194]

As for the necessity, the Panel, by comparing the language used in Article XXI:(b) of the GATT 1994 and Article 22.3 of the DSU, concluded that it is for the member invoking the exception to determine the necessity for the protection of its essential security interests. As the Panel explained, the arbitrators in *EC – Banana (III)* interpreted the phrase 'if the party considers' as contained in Article 22.3 of the DSU as 'providing a margin of appreciation to the party which was nevertheless subject to review by the arbitrators'.[195] The rationale for arbitrators to reach this conclusion is that discretion according to the complaining party in the retaliation process under the DSU is conditional on the introductory words of Article 22.3, which provides that '[i]n considering what concessions or other obligations to suspend, the complaining party shall apply the following principles and procedures'.[196] In light of this textual

[192] Panel Report on *Russia – Traffic in Transit*, para. 7.130.
[193] Panel Report on *Russia – Traffic in Transit*, paras. 7.131–132.
[194] Panel Report on *Russia – Traffic in Transit*, para. 7.135.
[195] Panel Report on *Russia – Traffic in Transit*, para. 7.147.
[196] DSU, Art. 22.3.

difference, the Panel concluded that '[t]here is no equivalent obligation anywhere in the text of Article XXI that expressly conditions the discretion according to an invoking Member under the chapeau of Article XXI(b)'.[197] It is thus solely for the invoking member to determine the necessity of a measure in safeguarding its essential security interests.

In *Saudi Arabia – Protection of IPR*, the Panel was again called on to rule on the 'self-judging' nature of the national security exception, albeit in the TRIPS context. Both the respondent and third parties touched on the justifiability of the national security exception. Norway, in its third-party submission, presented a well-reasoned argument in support of its justiciability. According to Norway, the non-justiciability of national security as set forth in Article 73 of the TRIPS Agreement finds no support in the rules of jurisdiction in the covered agreements and the DSU. The TRIPS Agreement, as part of the covered agreement listed in Appendix 1 to the DSU, falls within the scope of the DSU, over which the Panel/Appellate Body shall have jurisdiction since neither the DSU nor the TRIPS Agreement carves out their compulsory jurisdiction on the national security exception. If the mere invocation of Article 73 would render a claim non-justiciable, it would provide countries with easy means of circumventing their WTO obligations. This would amount to issuing a *carte blanche* excuse to WTO members for unilaterally bypassing the agreements that the legitimacy of the rules-based system rests on.[198]

The third-party submission of the United States, by contrast, constitutes a good example of arguments against the justifiability of the national security exception, by virtue of the 'self-judging' nature of the clause 'which it considers necessary'. The United States argued that the invocation of national security under Article 73(b)(iii) is non-justiciable and the Panel should thus limit its findings to 'a recognition that Saudi Arabia has invoked its essential security provisions at Article 73(b)'.[199] According to the United States, the clause 'which it considers necessary' appears only in the legal text of Article 73(a) and 73(b) but not in 73(c), which suggests that under the former two paragraphs, it is the judgement of the member

[197] Panel Report on *Russia – Traffic in Transit*, para. 7.147.

[198] Third Party Submission by Norway in the World Trade Organization, *Saudi Arabia – Measures Concerning the Protection of Intellectual Property Rights*, 15 June 2019, paras. 6–9.

[199] Ibid. para. 8.

that makes the determination. The Panel must give meaning to such a deliberate choice of textual usage.[200] Second, a comparison between the legal text of Article XX of the GATT (general exception) on the one hand and Article XXI of the GATT 1994 and Article 73 of the TRIPS Agreement on the other leads to the conclusion that, while these two categories of exception use the term 'necessary', only the necessity in the general exception is subject to the review of the Panel and Appellate Body, as it is not qualified by the clause 'which it considers'.[201] Third, the United States further compared the language used in Article 73(b) and Article 22.3 of the DSU, where the clause 'that party considers' is preceded by mandatory language in the chapeau and followed by permissive language in the subsections. Whereas Article 22.3 limits the discretion of the party suspending the concessions, Article 73(b) does not.[202]

Following the reasoning of *Russia – Traffic in Transit*, the Panel in *Saudi Arabia – Protection of IPR* ruled that 73(b)(iii) is not 'self-judging' and the clause 'which it considers necessary' does not qualify 'war or other emergencies of international relations', which is an objective fact amenable to objective assessment of the Panel. While the clause 'which it considers necessary' confers on the member invoking such exception broad discretion, such discretion is not unfettered and must be exercised in good faith with 'minimum requirement of plausibility'.[203] According to the Panel, a proper appreciation of the national security exception must be conducted based on a four-step analysis,

> a. whether the existence of a 'war or other emergency in international relations' has been established in the sense of subparagraph (iii) to Article 73(b);
> b. whether the relevant actions were 'taken in time of' that war or other emergency in international relations;
> c. whether the invoking Member has articulated its relevant 'essential security interests' sufficiently to enable an assessment of whether there is any link between those actions and the protection of its essential security interests and
> d. whether the relevant actions are so remote from, or unrelated to, the 'emergency in international relations' as to make it implausible that the

200 Ibid. para. 9.

201 Third Party Submission of the United States of America before *Saudi Arabia – Measures Concerning the Protection of Intellectual Property Rights*, 5 June 2019, para. 3.

202 Third Party Submission of the United States of America before *Saudi Arabia – Measures Concerning the Protection of Intellectual Property Rights*, 5 June 2019, para. 3.

203 Panel Report on *Saudi Arabia – Protection of IPR*, para. 7.255.

> invoking Member considers those actions to be necessary for the protection of its essential security interests arising out of the emergency.[204]

The Panel first examined the first two elements, i.e., whether the actions adopted by Saudi Arabia were taken *in time of* war or other emergency in international relations. The Panel observed that the severance of diplomatic and consulate relations are exceptional acts, usually adopted only as a last resort in case of a severe crisis between two countries.[205] The severance of diplomatic relations, as the UN Charter provides in Article 41, is used as an instrument for the UN Security Council to address threats to and breaches of the peace and acts of aggression.[206] The Panel further considered Saudi Arabia's allegations against Qatar's repudiation of the Riyadh Agreement aiming for regional security and stability; support for terrorism and extremism and interference into internal affairs of other countries, on which the Panel took no position. In view of these factors, the Panel concluded that the crisis between Saudi Arabia and Qatar constituted 'other emergency of international relations'.[207] As the crisis began on at least 5 June 2017 and the measures adopted by Saudi Arabia commenced no earlier than August 2017, these measures were adopted in time of other emergencies in international relations.[208]

The Panel then addressed whether Saudi Arabia articulated its essential security interests 'sufficiently to enable an assessment of whether the challenged measures are related to those [onerous] interests is . . . and is appropriately subject to limited review by a panel'.[209] Such an articulation is intended for the panel to assess whether the challenged measures are *implausibly* related to the protection of such essential security interests. As the Panel observed, Saudi Arabia claimed to protect its country from terrorism and extremism 'that clearly relates to the quintessential functions of the state',[210] namely, the protection of its territory and its population from external threats, and the maintenance of law and public order internally.

[204] Panel Report on *Saudi Arabia – Protection of IPR*, para. 7.242.
[205] Panel Report on *Saudi Arabia – Protection of IPR*, para. 7.260.
[206] Panel Report on *Saudi Arabia – Protection of IPR*, para. 7.261.
[207] Panel Report on *Saudi Arabia – Protection of IPR*, para. 7.263.
[208] Panel Report on *Saudi Arabia – Protection of IPR*, para. 7.269.
[209] Panel Report on *Saudi Arabia – Protection of IPR*, para. 7.281.
[210] Panel Report on *Saudi Arabia – Protection of IPR*, para. 7.280.

The Panel finally evaluated whether the two measures challenged by Qatar, namely, a comprehensive web of anti-sympathy measures, in particular the denial of beIN access to legal counsel to enforce its IP rights in Saudi courts and tribunals, and non-application of criminal procedures and penalties to beoutQ, 'meet a minimum requirement of plausibility in relation to the proffered essential security interests'.[211] According to the Panel, the anti-sympathy measures are aimed at severing contact or communication with Saudi and Qatari entities, with the latter precluded from access to Saudi Arabia. Saudi Arabia's instruction to Saudi lawyers to refrain from representing beIN constituted part of the anti-sympathy measures, and such denial was further strengthened with the ban on Qataris entering Saudi Arabia. The Panel thus concluded that the denial of beIN's access to legal counsel is 'not implausible as measures protective of these interests'.[212]

However, the same could not be said to the non-application of criminal procedures and penalties to beoutQ. The Panel first recalled Brazil's third party submission, questioning 'how the respondent's proffered essential security interests, or any country's essential security interests for that matter, could be protected by allowing the operation of a copyright pirate whose broadcasts have spread beyond the respondent's borders and encompass not only the copyrights held by the claimant's nationals but by other countries' nationals as well'.[213] The Panel then noted that there is neither a direct link nor temporal connection between the comprehensive anti-sympathy measures adopted in June 2017 and the non-application of criminal procedures and penalties to beoutQ. The Panel thus arrived at the conclusion that such non-application was not related to Saudi Arabia's ending nor preventing any form of contact between Saudis and Qataris, and it was so remote from, or unrelated to, the 'emergency in international relations' as to make it implausible that Saudi Arabia implemented these measures for the protection of its 'essential security interests'.[214]

From *Russia – Traffic in Transit* to *Saudi Arabia – Protection of IPR*, it appears settled that the Panel rejects the 'self-judging' thesis of the national security exception but develops a nuanced step-by-step analysis for this justification: the existence of 'war and other emergencies of

[211] Panel Report on *Saudi Arabia – Protection of IPR*, para. 7.288.
[212] Panel Report on *Saudi Arabia – Protection of IPR*, para. 7.288.
[213] Panel Report on *Saudi Arabia – Protection of IPR*, para. 7.291.
[214] Panel Report on *Saudi Arabia – Protection of IPR*, para. 7.293.

international relations'; timing of the adopted measures; the articulation of 'essential security interests' and the plausibility of such measures for the protection of these interests. The Panel in *Saudi Arabia – Protection of IPR* built on the ruling of *Russia – Traffic in Transit* and went a step further in ruling against the respondent on the grounds that the contested measure is remote or unrelated to the emergency of international relations, which makes it implausible for the protection of essential security interests. The Panel's decision pronounces that justification based on the national security exception may eventually fail.

3.4.3 Any Action in pursuance of Its Obligations under the United Nations Charter for the Maintenance of International Peace and Security

In contrast to paragraphs (a) and (b) of Article XXI of the GATT 1994, paragraph (c) of the same article does not include the language of 'which it considers'. The difference in the language in paragraphs (a) and (b) on the one hand, and paragraph (c) on the other, poses some challenges to treaty interpretation. It may be argued that such a difference reflects the intention of the drafters to embed the 'self-judging' nature into paragraphs (a) and (b) while maintaining the objective and reviewable nature in paragraph (c). However, it may also be contended that the clause of 'which it considers' is unnecessary, as paragraph (c) is meant for the implementation of obligations arising from the UN Charter. Therefore, there is no need for a member to consider whether it is necessary to adopt measures for the maintenance of international peace and security as the UN and relevant bodies, the Security Council in particular, have already spelled out such a necessity.

In addition, paragraph (c) speaks of actions in pursuance of obligations under the UN Charter for the maintenance of international peace and security; a question thus surfaces: in the absence of UN Security Council Resolutions, can a member impose measures for the maintenance of international peace and security when it considers necessary? Such a question is not fictional, as trade restrictive measures may not always fall into the scope of paragraphs (a) and (b) for the protection of essential security interests. A member may adopt or impose trade restrictive measures for the purpose of the maintenance of international peace and security. In fact, this controversy surfaced in the dispute between the EEC and Argentina arising from the Falkland/Malvinas tension. Argentina alleged that UN Security Council Resolution 502 did not authorise sanctioning actions by third parties and thus contested the GATT-consistency of the trade restrictive measures adopted by the EEC. A similar controversy may also be seen in the sanction measures against Russia that resulted from the Ukraine crisis, which will be further elaborated later.

3.4.4 *Economic Security and Vital Industry*

At the General Council Meeting on 31 October 1975, Sweden informed the GATT contracting parties of its intention to introduce a global import quota on certain footwear products. According to Sweden,

> [t]he continued decrease in domestic production [of leather shoes, plastic shoes and rubber boots] has become a critical threat to the emergency planning of Sweden's economic defence as an integral part of the country's security policy. This policy necessitates the maintenance of a minimum domestic production capacity in vital industries. Such a capacity is indispensable in order to secure the provision of essential products necessary to meet basic needs in case of war or other emergency in international relations.[215]

The critical issue here is whether the connotation of national security extends to economic security, which asserts that the protection of vital industry safeguards economic security and thus falls within the scope of Article XXI. During the Council Meeting, many representatives of the GATT contracting parties expressed their concerns about the GATT-consistency of such a measure and maintained that it could not be justified under the General Agreement. Sweden referred to Article XXI as the legal basis for its import quota, but this argument was not convincing and failed to persuade other GATT contracting parties.[216] In the end, Sweden notified the Secretariat that the import quota, as far as leather shoes and plastic shoes were concerned, was terminated as of 1 July 1977.[217] The case of Sweden has two major weaknesses. First, it is highly doubtful whether the footwear industry constitutes a vital industry to Sweden's economy. Second, how to avoid the protection of vital industry being used as a form of protectionism is another difficult task if Article XXI extends to economic security.

The protection of vital industry based on national security resurfaced in 2017 when the Trump Administration revived the dormant Section

[215] GATT Document, L 4250, 17 November 1975, para. 4.

[216] C/M/109, 10 November 1975, Minutes of Meeting, Held in the Palais des Nations, Geneva, on 31 October 1975, pp. 8–9.

[217] GATT Document, L/4250/Add.1, 15 March 1977.

232 and initiated an investigation on steel and aluminium products. On 17 and 26 April 2017, the Department of Commerce of the US (the USDOC), under Section 232 of the Trade Expansion Act of 1962, as amended (19 U.S.C. 1862), initiated an investigation to determine the effect of imports of these two products on national security. The relevant provision of Section 232 reads

> the Secretary shall submit to the President a report on the findings of such investigation with respect to the effect of the importation of such article in such quantities or under such circumstances upon the national security and, based on such findings, the recommendations of the Secretary for action or inaction under this section. If the Secretary finds that such article is being imported into the United States in such quantities or under such circumstances as to threaten to impair the national security, the Secretary shall so advise the President in such report.[218]

The critical point here is whether imports of the investigated article are in such quantities, or under such circumstances, as to threaten to impair national security. The USDOC released its investigation reports on two products and found affirmatively based on similar analysis. From the outset, the USDOC defines 'national security' broadly; for the purposes of Section 232, it is 'general security and welfare of certain industries, beyond those necessary to satisfy national defense requirements, which are critical to minimum operations of the economy and government'.[219] Based on this understanding of national security, the USDOC found that both steel and aluminium products are important to US national security; imports of these two products are in such quantities as to adversely impact the economic welfare of the US steel and aluminium industry; excessive quantities of imports of these products have displaced domestic steel and aluminium products and have seriously weakened the internal US economy; finally, global excess steel and aluminium capacity contributes to weakening the domestic US economy.[220] With Proclamation

[218] 19 U.S.C. 1862(b)(3)(A).

[219] U.S. Department of Commerce Bureau of Industry and Security Office of Technology Evaluation, The Effects of Imports of Steel on the National Security: An Investigation Conducted under Section 232 of the Trade Expansion Act of 1962, as Amended, 11 January 2018 (hereinafter The USDOC Steel 232 Report), p. 1.

[220] The USDOC Steel 232 Report, pp. 1–5; U.S. Department of Commerce Bureau of Industry and Security Office of Technology Evaluation, The Effects of Imports of Aluminium on the National Security: An Investigation Conducted under Section 232 of the Trade Expansion Act of 1962, as Amended, 17 January 2018 (hereinafter The USDOC Aluminium 232 Report), pp. 1–5.

9705 of March 8, 2018, US President Donald Trump concluded that 'under current circumstances, this tariff is necessary and appropriate to address the threat that imports of steel articles pose to the national security'[221] and decided to impose additional 25 and 10 per cent tariffs on steel and aluminium products. This decision nonetheless invited tremendous critiques from other trade nations.

The EU contends that such measures are safeguard measures in nature and represent protectionism instead of national security concerns and will refer to the WTO at the earliest opportunity.[222] In commenting on the United States' recourse to Section 232, the Canadian Ambassador to the WTO is reported to have commented that 'we fear that the United States may be opening a Pandora's Box that we would not be able to close'.[223] Indeed, if a trade nation can refer to national security to protect its internal economy, it would undermine the value of the binding concessions and commitments it has made and seriously undermine the effectiveness of the multilateral WTO framework and its dispute settlement mechanism. Several WTO members, including the EU, China, Mexico, Canada and Norway, launched a complaint against the United States in the WTO dispute settlement mechanism. In this complaint, the United States invokes the national security exception and argues that such measures do not constitute safeguard measures. At the time of writing, the panel proceedings are ongoing.

3.4.5 Security Exception and Countermeasures under Public International Law

The security exception may also be linked to countermeasures under public international law, with the security exception being explicitly or implicitly referred to. In the history of the GATT, rules of countermeasures under public international law were relied on by Germany during its

[221] Proclamation 9705 of March 8, 2018, Adjusting Imports of Steel into the United States, 83 FR 11625, para. 8.

[222] European Commission, *European Commission Responds to the US Restrictions on Steel and Aluminium Affecting the EU*, Press Release, 1 March 2018, available at http://trade.ec.europa.eu/doclib/press/index.cfm?id=1805.

[223] 'China Leads Charges against US Tariffs at the WTO Meeting', *Reuters*, 7 March 2018, available at https://uk.reuters.com/article/us-usa-trade-wto/china-leads-charge-against-u-s-tariffs-at-wto-meeting-idUKKCN1GJ1SC.

coastal dispute with Iceland in 1974;[224] today, it may be used as a justification for autonomous sanction measures.

On 29 November 1974, the Federal Republic of Germany and its four coastal Länder imposed a ban prohibiting the landing of Icelandic fish in German harbours. After unsuccessful consultations held in Geneva and other bilateral channels, Iceland formally requested consultation with Germany under Article XXIII of the General Agreement, alleging that the landing ban was inconsistent with Articles XI and XIII thereof. Germany declined to respond to this consultation request, as it maintained that the measure in question was a countermeasure in accordance with public international law and had nothing to do with GATT obligations. The root cause of this dispute lay in Iceland's unilateral decision to extend its fishery zone from 12 to 50 nautical miles in 1972, which was held to be inconsistent with international law on 15 July 1974 by the International Court of Justice.[225] The immediate cause derived from the incident in which a German trawler, Arcturus, was fired on and seized by Iceland about 35 nautical miles off the Icelandic coast.[226] In view of this train of events, Germany thus claimed that its landing ban constituted a countermeasure in accordance with rules of public international law, while Iceland focused on the GATT-compatibility of this landing ban.

Iceland alleged that the landing ban was a simple prohibition of Icelandic exports which were made directly to Iceland. By this prohibition, it changed the balance of concessions between Iceland and Germany under the General Agreement, and impaired access of Icelandic fishery products to the German market, which infringed the rules under Article XI and XIII thereof. According to Iceland, Germany's argument for countermeasures was irrelevant, 'as the GATT could only be concerned with the application or functioning of the General Agreement and not with any other international principles'.[227] By contrast, Germany argued that its landing ban was a temporary measure in response to Iceland's unilateral extension of its fishery zone, its disregard of an ICJ judgment and its firing at and seizure of a German trawler, Arcturus. The measure was to be cancelled as soon as conditions existed

[224] *Germany – Icelandic Fishery Dispute – Ban on Icelandic Fish Landings*, C/M/103, 18 February 1975, Minutes of Meeting, held in the Palais des Nations, Geneva, on 3 and 17 February 1975, p. 13.

[225] *Germany* v. *Iceland*, Merits, Judgment, 25 July 1974, International Court of Justice, ICJ Rep 175 (1974).

[226] Ibid. 13–14.

[227] Ibid. 15.

for the resumption of talks between the two governments. According to Germany, the landing ban was a countermeasure justified under rules of public international law and thus violated no obligations under the General Agreement; a justified ban under public international law could not be held GATT-inconsistent. 'The General Agreement did not represent an isolated legal system. Rather, it was embedded in the general rules of international law. Otherwise, any State could constantly violate the economic interests of its neighbouring State which would be forced to renounce any counter-measure it wanted to take.'[228]

In view of the arguments between Iceland and Germany, some observations can be made. It is intriguing to see that Germany did not refer to Article XXI of the General Agreement to justify its landing ban against Iceland, though it is understandable in view of the fact that such ban was imposed in 1974, when trade nations were still not in the habit of invoking security exceptions as a justification for their actions. Besides, it is important to note that the relationship between GATT/WTO law and public international law has a long troubling history throughout the GATT and WTO eras, which is subject to academic and jurisprudential debates.[229] Finally, how to assess the legality of trade restrictive measures for sanction purposes under GATT/WTO law still plagues international trade and public international lawyers. Such a controversy is particularly acute when the sanctions are not supported by UN Security Council Resolutions.

In summarising different positions of scholarly works, Matthew Happold notes that providing sanctions through trade restrictive measures does not breach any applicable treaty (such as GATT/WTO law, regional trade agreements and treaty on friendship, commerce and navigation) or customary rules (such as the treatment of foreign nationals) – a country is free to adopt such restrictive measures, as a sovereign nation has freedom to revise its trade relations with other countries.[230] Such a position can also

[228] Ibid. 16.

[229] See e.g., Pieter Jan Kuyper, 'The Law of GATT as a Special Field of International Law' (1994) 25 *Netherlands Yearbook of International Law* 227; Joost Pauwelyn, *Conflicts of Norms in Public International Law: How WTO Relates to other Rules of International Law* (Cambridge University Press 2003); Joost Pauwelyn, 'Bridging Fragmentation and Unity: International Law as a Universe of Inter-Connected Islands' (2004) 25 *Michigan Journal of International Law* 903.

[230] Matthew Happold, 'Economic Sanctions and International Law: An Introduction' in Matthew Happold and Paul Eden (eds), *Economic Sanctions and International Law* (Bloomsbury 2016) 2–3.

find support from *Nicaragua* laid down by the ICJ, where the Court held that '[a] State is not bound to continue particular trade relations longer than it sees fit to do so, in the absence of a treaty commitment or other specific legal obligation';[231] however, this argument is not particularly helpful, as the Court continued to note that 'where there exists such a commitment, of the kind implied in a treaty of friendship and commerce, such an abrupt act of termination of commercial intercourse as the general trade embargo . . . will normally constitute a violation of the obligation not to defeat the object and purpose of the treaty'.[232] Therefore, where an obligation or commitment on a particular trade relation exists, the freedom enjoyed by a sovereign nation is to be constrained. Happold thus maintains that if an international obligation regulating trade relations exists, the adoption of unilateral or autonomous sanctions (in the form of export embargo) can only be lawful when they fulfil the criteria of countermeasures codified in the Articles on the State Responsibility and Draft Articles on the Responsibility of International Organisations adopted by the International Law Commission (the ILC).[233] This argument is not very impressive, as the applicability of the rules of countermeasures within the GATT/WTO system is also subject to debate. A trade nation adopting autonomous sanction measures through export embargo may always be free to invoke the security exception as a justification; nonetheless, two difficult questions persist. First, the assessment of the WTO-compatibility of an export restrictive measure based on the security exception involves challenging legal issues, as evidenced in the aforementioned discussion. Second, if the trade nation imposing such a measure chooses not to invoke the security exception, but rather to rely on rules of countermeasures under public international law, the question of in which forum and based on what applicable laws can the legality of an export restrictive measure be examined complicates the thorny issue of competition of jurisdiction between international tribunals and begs the fundamental question whether the GATT/WTO system is a 'self-contained' regime.[234]

[231] *Nicaragua* v. *USA*, merits, ICJ Rep. 14(1986), para. 276.

[232] *Nicaragua* v. *USA*, merits, para. 276.

[233] Happold, 'Economic Sanctions and International Law: An Introduction' (n. 230) 2.

[234] See e.g., Bruno Simma, 'Self-Contained Regimes' (1985) 16 *Netherlands Yearbook of International Law* 111; Bruno Simma and Dirk Pulkowski, 'Of Planets and the Universe: Self-Contained Regimes in International Law' (2006) 17 *European Journal of International Law* 483.

3.5 Case Studies

As the landscape of international political economy changes swiftly, in the past decade, we evidence a strong temptation and growing inclination to impose export restrictions for political purposes. Some countries invoke the national security exception and some do not. Therefore, in this section, I will use several case studies to illustrate the complexity of the international political economy in adopting export control/embargoes and explore possible policy space, which finds its legal basis from, and can thus be justified by, GATT/WTO law or public international law. This section focuses on the EU's sanction measures against Russia in response to the Ukraine crisis; China's tourism embargo against South Korea in response to the installation of the Terminal High Altitude Area Defence (THAAD) anti-ballistic missile system; Qatar's diplomatic crisis; United States' export control against Huawei and finally Japan's removal of South Korea from the whitelist of trusted trade partners. These cases represent key issues surrounding export restrictions under GATT/WTO law and public international law and reflect the evolution of the international public economy. While the Cold War has ended, Russia continues to be the main target for sanctions measures, taking the form of export restrictions. Supported by its economic strength, China, which was, and still is, subject to export control, is now using export restrictive measures as an instrument for its coercive diplomacy.

3.5.1 EU's Sanctions against Russia

On 21 November 2013, Ukrainian President Viktor Yanukovych announced his decision not to sign the EU–Ukraine Association Agreement, which angered proponents of the agreement and resulted in mass protests and demonstrations. The protests and demonstrations eventually led to the ousting of Yanukovych and culminated in the February 2014 Revolution. The ousting of Yanukovych nevertheless triggered unrest in southern and eastern regions of Ukraine where the majority of the population are Russophone and supporters of Yanukovych. The unrest and political crisis in Ukraine led to Russian military intervention in February 2014 and the installation of a pro-Russia government in Crimea. The Crimean government declared independence on 16 March 2014, and two days later Russia annexed Crimea.

In response to Russia's intervention in the Ukrainian crisis, the EU, United States, Australia and other states imposed sanctions against

Russia, targeting Russian officials and assets, and banning exports on dual-use goods and key strategic technologies. Given that Russia is a permanent member of the UN Security Council, authorisation from the Security Council for the sanctions was not possible, though the General Assembly adopted Resolution 68/262, calling on UN members to refrain from actions disrupting the national security and territorial integrity of Ukraine.[235] Russia claimed that such sanctioning measures are incompatible with WTO law and raised its concerns in the meeting of the Councils of Trade in Goods, and of Trade in Services. Among the measures imposed by the EU, export embargoes on dual-use goods and strategic technologies are more relevant to this book.

In accordance with Article 215 of the TFEU and Council Regulation (EC) No 428/2009, the Council adopted Council Regulation (EU) No 833/2014 imposing restrictive measures against Russia with a view to increasing the economic costs of Russia's actions in undermining Ukraine's territorial integrity, sovereignty and independence, and with a view to promoting peaceful settlement of the Ukrainian crisis. These restrictive measures mainly target two categories of products: dual-use goods and technologies; and technologies closely linked to the Russian economy.

Article 2.1 of Council Regulation (EU) No 833/2014 prohibits the sale, supply, transfer or export of dual-use goods or technology to any natural or legal person, entity or body in Russia or for use in Russia, if such items are or may be intended for military use or for a military end-user.[236] Council Regulation (EC) No 428/2009 should be applied to the authorisation of dual-use goods and technologies exported to Russia. Article 3.1 imposes an export authorisation procedure for equipment and technologies listed in Annex II to Council Regulation (EU) No 833/2014, which mainly concerns products, equipment and technologies related to the oil and gas industries, the core area of the Russian economy. Article 3.5 of the Regulation further prohibits the grant of export authorisation if the competent authorities have reasonable grounds to believe that such technologies are intended for projects relating to deep water oil exploration and production, Arctic oil exploration and production or shale oil projects in Russia. These measures are export restrictive in nature and

235 UN General Assembly Resolution 68/262, Territorial Integrity of Ukraine, adopted on 27 March 2014.

236 Council Regulation (EU) No 833/2014, Art. 2.1.

may be incompatible with WTO rules, in particular Article XI of the GATT 1994.

The sanctions against Russia in response to the Ukraine crisis differ from those imposed in the Cold War era or under the auspices of the COCOM in that Russia joined the WTO in 2012 and relations between Russia and Western countries are thus governed by WTO rules, and the WTO dispute settlement mechanism may have a say on the WTO-compatibility of such sanctioning measures. Indeed, Russia raised this issue in the Council Meetings of Trade in Goods and Trade in Services. Interestingly, Russia named the United States, Canada and Australia, but left aside the EU. According to Russia, the WTO 'constituted a unique forum whose agenda, to the maximum extent possible, was free from political issues – an approach to be safeguarded by Members. This required Members not to sacrifice their WTO obligations for non-economic objectives that were not covered by the WTO Agreement.'[237] Specifically, the sanctioning measures, including the restrictive measures adopted by the EU, violate the MFN principle and constituted quantitative restrictions as prohibited by Article XI of the GATT 1994.[238] In response, the United States, Canada and Australia saw their sanctions as legal and consistent with their WTO obligations. Russia, despite its discontent with the sanctioning measures, did not bring the case before the WTO dispute settlement mechanism. Instead, Russia retaliated by imposing an import ban on live pigs and pork products in the name of health concerns connected with African fever.[239]

Since the dispute has not reached the WTO dispute settlement mechanism, it is not clear whether the EU (or the United States, Canada and Australia) will invoke the security exception. Some scholarly work has attempted to assess the WTO-consistency of the EU's restrictive measures based on the security exception and reaches the conclusion that these measures can be justified by such exception. According to Lukasz Gruszczynski and Marcin Menkes, in assessing the justifiability of the security exception, the EU would predominantly rely on XXI:2(b)(iii): necessary actions taken for the protection of its essential security interests

[237] Council for Trade in Goods, Minutes of the Meeting of the Council for Trade in Goods 19 June 2014, G/C/M/119, 31 October 2014, para. 9.4

[238] Ibid. para. 9.2.

[239] Appellate Body Report on *Russian Federation – Measures on the Importation of Live Pigs, Pork and other Pig Products from the European Union*, WT/DS475/AB/R and Add.1, adopted 21 March 2017.

in the emergence of international relations. In substantiating that the EU's essential security interests are threatened, Gruszczynski and Menkes first point to the threat presented by Russia to the EU Member States neighbouring it. Incidents involving Russian troops along the borders with Baltic countries proved that such a threat is neither theoretical nor fictional. They further refer to the historic experiences of Central and Eastern European countries being locked behind the Iron Curtain. Moreover, the eruption of the Ukraine crisis has led a number of international organisations to adopt resolutions or statements referring to the situation in Ukraine as an international emergency. Notably, the UN General Assembly, with 100 votes in favour, 11 against and 58 abstentions, adopted Resolution 68/262, maintaining that any attempt at partial or total disruption of the unity or territorial integrity of a State is incompatible with the purpose and principles of the UN Charter and calling for States to refrain from any action recognising the alteration of status of Crimea and Sevastopol. In relying on these proofs, Gruszczynski and Menkes conclude that the EU's economic sanctions against Russia can pass the scrutiny of the WTO dispute settlement mechanism.[240]

3.5.2 China Tourism Embargo

The swift change of international economic relations has seen the transformation of China from the victim of sanctions to an aggressive country using trade as an instrument in pursuit of its political and diplomatic aims. As James Reilly observes, compared to the United States, the leading country for adopting unilateral sanctions through formalized domestic laws or presidential orders, China rarely declares its economic sanctions and prefers to employ informal acts, such as vague threats, variations of leadership visits and selective purchases and non-purchases.[241] China's sanctioning measures against South Korea in response to the installation of THAAD in 2016 best demonstrate these characteristics. Angered by South Korea's decision to accept the installation of THAAD on its territory, China retaliated by imposing a number of trade

[240] Lukasz Gruszczynski and Marcin Menkes, 'The Legality of the EU's Trade Sanctions Imposed on the Russia Federation under WTO Law' in Władysław Czapliński and others (eds), *The Case of Crimea's Annexation under International Law* (Scholarly Publishing House 2017) 243–255.

[241] James Reilly, 'China's Unilateral Sanctions' (2012) 35 *The Washington Quarterly* 121, 123–124.

restrictive measures against South Korea, including a ban on group travel to South Korea and South Korean distribution services in China, Lotte Mart. The former measure, the travel ban, is of more interest to this author as it falls within the scope of export restrictions, the main theme of this book.

At the 16–17 March 2017 GATS Council Meeting, South Korea presented this issue under the title of other business of the agenda. South Korea first expressed its deep concern with the situation and then underlined China's obligation to comply with WTO rules and implement its commitments, in particular in tourism.[242] In response, the Chinese representative stated that 'the latest developments in the Korean peninsula had triggered strong feelings in the general public in China'.[243] The Chinese representative nonetheless turned to elaborating on the close economic relationship and good neighbourliness between Korea and China without commenting on the trade restrictive measures.

At the 16 June GATS Council Meeting, South Korea brought up this issue under the rubric of another agenda item. South Korea claimed it believed that the trade restrictive measures still existed and such restrictive measures on tourism and distribution services were inconsistent with the MFN, National Treatment and Market Access disciplines of the GATS.[244] The Chinese representative nonetheless responded by saying that his country was not aware of such restrictive measures as mentioned by Korea.[245] The United States commented on the restriction of the sale of travel packages. If such a restriction did exist, it would fall under Mode 1 (consumption abroad) and Mode 2 (cross-border services) of China's commitment on that sector. This restriction impacted negatively not only South Korea but also other countries whose suppliers were invested in South Korea or provided cross-border services that benefited from travel and tourism between the two countries. Moreover, such restriction was of systemic significance, as other countries may be subject to the same measure and it was of critical importance to see how China justify itself.[246]

As can be seen in the debates in the GATS Council Meeting, China has kept denying the existence of a travel ban against South Korea, let alone

[242] S/C/M/130, 6 June 2017, para. 8.1
[243] S/C/M/130, 6 June 2017, para. 8.2.
[244] S/C/M/132, 28 August 2017, paras. 9.1–9.2.
[245] S/C/M/132, 28 August 2017, para. 9.4.
[246] S/C/M/132, 28 August 2017, para. 9.4.

invoking the security exception. The reason why China chooses not to officially declare its sanctions is due to its assertion in adhering to the principle of non-interference. In line with this principle, China endorses the thesis that 'no country or group of countries, has the right to impose its will on others, to interfere, under whatever pretext, in other countries' internal affairs, or to impose unilateral coercive economic measures on others'.[247] In admitting imposing of sanctioning measures, China will violate its self-upholding principles of mutual respect and sovereign equality. On the other hand, South Korea also has no incentive to escalate the tension by bringing the case before the WTO dispute settlement mechanism, as it has to hedge between the United States and China, in particular on the North Korea issue. Moreover, South Korea is economically dependent on China, as China has long been its largest trading partner. Therefore, China's travel ban on tourism remains unsettled, with China's denial of its existence and South Korea's reluctance to bring it into the WTO dispute settlement mechanism.

Given that Chinese tourism has become an important vehicle for boosting national economic growth for many countries, in particular for those countries highly dependent on tourism, China has frequently used its restriction on tourism as an instrument to pursue its political and diplomatic aims. Such examples can also be seen in China's travel ban against Taiwan's diplomatic allies, such as Palau and the Vatican.[248] Similarly, with the election of the pro-independence President Tsai Ing-Wen in 2016, who refuses to recognize the so-called 1992 consensus,[249] China reduced the level of its group travel to Taiwan in order to step up its pressure against the regime. Unsurprisingly, China denies the existence of such travel bans.

[247] Beijing Declaration of the Forum on China–Africa Cooperation, adopted on 10–12 October 2000, para. 1.

[248] See Keoni Everington, 'China Bans China Bans Tour Groups to Vatican, Palau to Isolate Taiwan', *Taipei News*, 23 November 2017, available at www.taiwannews.com.tw/en/news/3304777.

[249] The 1992 consensus is a highly contentious concept. Even its existence is subject to debate, letting alone its substance. According to the former ruling party, Kuomintang, the 1992 consensus means that both Taiwan and China agree that there is only one China in the world and such China is subject to different interpretations, be it the People's Republic of China or Republic of China (the official tile of Taiwan). Nevertheless, China (the PRC) seems not to accept the possibility of different interpretations. China's new rhetoric on the one China policy is that both sides of the Taiwan Strait (namely, Taiwan and the Chinese mainland) belong to one China. Here, the only China undoubtedly refers to the PRC.

3.5.3 *US Export Controls on Huawei*

In the midst of the US–China trade war, on 16 April 2018, the Bureau of Industry and Security (BIS) of the DOC imposed a denial of export privileges against Zhongxing Telecommunications Equipment Corporation (ZTE) and its subsidiary on the grounds that ZTE made a false statement to BIS during the settlement negotiations and during the probationary period.[250] The denial of export privileges has the effect of prohibiting any person from participating in any way in any transaction subject to the EAR. By virtue of this denial, Qualcomm, the key supplier of ZTE, was prevented from supplying ZTE chips. While the denial against ZTE was subsequently lifted, another blow was struck against China's telecommunication giant Huawei. On 16 May 2019, the BIS of the DOC announced its decision to add Huawei and its sixty-eight non-US affiliates to the Entity List of the EAR, as the BIS found that there was 'reasonable cause to believe that Huawei has been involved in the activities contrary to national security or foreign policy interests of the United States'.[251] Huawei's transactions with Iran with the effect of causing the export, reexport, sale and supply, directly and indirectly, of goods, technology and services without obtaining a license from the Department of Treasury's Office of Foreign Assets Control (OFAC), as required by OFAC's Iranian Transactions and Sanctions Regulations, is cited as evidence for such threat to US national security or foreign policy interests. The decision to add Huawei to the Entity List nonetheless came with a temporary general licence for 90 days ending on 19 August 2019,[252] which was renewed for an additional 90 days.

The legal consequence of such addition is the imposition of licensing requirements and limitation of license exceptions for exports, re-export and in-country transfer, and the licensing review policy to these entities is presumption of denial. Such export licensing requirement is not

[250] Bureau of Industry and Security, Commerce. In the Matter of: Zhongxing Telecommunications Equipment Corporation ZTE Plaza, Keji Road South Hi-Tech Industrial Park Nanshan District, Shenzhen China; ZTE Kangxun Telecommunications Ltd. 2/3 Floor, Suite A, Zte Communication Mansion Keji (S) Road Hi-New Shenzhen, 518057 China Respondent; Order Activating Suspended Denial Order Relating to Zhongxing Telecommunications Equipment Corporation and Zte Kangxun Telecommunications Ltd., 15 April 2018, 83 Federal Register 17644.

[251] Bureau of Industry and Security, Commerce. Addition of Entities to the Entity List, 16 May 2019, 84 Federal Register 22961.

[252] Bureau of Industry and Security, Commerce. Temporary General License, 20 May 2019, 84 FR 23468.

limited to tangible goods but also extends to non-tangible goods and services. Google's decision to prevent Huawei from using its Android operating system is a case in point. Moreover, US export control regulations catch not only US enterprises and citizens but also items of US origin subject to EAR. The control of US origin items subject to EAR may be enforced through the licensing requirement of re-exports; it may also be implemented through the *de minimis* rule imposed against foreign products that contain components of US origin subject to EAR. This *de minimis* rule sets out two thresholds for US content, 10 per cent and 25 per cent, respectively, and may take three different forms: a foreign-made commodity incorporating controlled US-origin commodities or 'bundled' with US-origin software, foreign-made software incorporating controlled US-origin software.[253]

The decisions to impose export restrictions against ZTE and Huawei are to be appreciated by the United States' sense of threat to its information and communication technologies and services and its efforts in containing Huawei in the fifth generation (5G) telecommunication technological race. On 15 May 2019, President Trump, in accordance with the International Economic Emergency Powers Act of 1977 (IEEPA) and the National Emergencies Act, issued an Executive Order to safeguard the supply chain of information and communication.[254] President Trump found that foreign adversaries are increasingly creating and exploiting the vulnerabilities of information and communication technologies and services, which is augmented by unrestricted acquisition or use of information and communication technologies or services by foreign adversaries. Based on this finding, President Trump thus declared a national emergency based on this threat and ordered that any transaction regarding information and communication technologies or services that involves foreign adversaries and poses an undue risk to US information and communication, critical infrastructure, the digital economy, US national security or the security and safety of US persons is to be prohibited.[255] While this Executive Order has not explicitly identified the foreign adversaries, it is beyond doubt that it refers to Chinese communication giants Huawei and ZTE.

[253] EAR, Art. 734.4(c).

[254] U.S. Department of Commerce. Securing the Information and Communications Technology and Services Supply Chain, 23 December 2019, 84 Federal Register 70445.

[255] Ibid. Section 1.

As Huawei was added to the entity list, the immediate legal consequence is that US citizens and enterprises are prohibited from exporting to Huawei and its affiliates without a prior export licence. The application of export licensing will be reviewed with a presumption of denial. Such addition to the entity list may have extraterritorial reach and impact third-country nationals and enterprises with its re-exports regulation and *de minimis* rule. Therefore, not only China but also third countries have a standing to challenge the legality of the United States' decision to add Huawei to the entity list, but so far, no country has chosen to do so, and how the United States will respond once a complaint does arise is unclear. Nonetheless, judging from the United States' defence of its safeguard measures on steel and aluminium, where it contends that 'the tariffs imposed pursuant to Section 232 are issues of national security not susceptible to review or capable of resolution by WTO dispute settlement, and that the consultations provision in the *Agreement on Safeguards* is not applicable',[256] it is highly likely that the United States would invoke the national security exception. Since the addition of Huawei to the entity list is not adopted in pursuance of the United States' obligations under the UN Charter for the maintenance of international peace and security, the provision relied on by the United States will be Article XXI:(b)iii: any action which it considers necessary for the protection of its essential security interests in time of war or other emergency in international relations. For a measure to be legally justified by this clause, three criteria have to be fulfilled: necessity, 'essential security interests' and 'in time of war or other emergency in international relations'.[257]

The Panel in *Russia – Traffic in Transit* held that the clause 'which it considers' qualifies 'necessary' and 'essential security interests' but does not extend to 'in time war or other emergency in international relation'. War or other emergency of international relations is an objective fact subject to judicial review of the Panel. According to the Panel, while it is left for a member invoking an Article XXI exception to define what it considers to be its essential security interests, the invoking member is not free to 're-label' trade interests as 'essential security interests' and thus exclude what has been agreed through reciprocal and mutually

[256] WT/DS547/7 6 July 2018.

[257] Andrew D. Mitchell, 'Sanctions and the World Trade Organization' in Larissa van den Herik (ed), *Research Handbook on UN Sanctions and International Law* (Edward Elgar 2017) 292–303.

advantageous arrangements from judicial scrutiny. The general principle of good faith requires an invoking member not to use an Article XXI exception as a means to circumvent its obligations under the WTO agreements. Moreover, this good faith principle dictates a clear articulation of 'essential security interests' which corresponds to the extent of emergency of international relations. War, or armed conflicts, are one extreme of emergency of international relations. When an invoking member moves from this extreme to other non-hardcore and less characteristic types, it bears more obligation to articulate and demonstrate what it considers essential security interests.

As is generally understood, the addition of Huawei to the entity list is situated in a broader context of the United States' sense of threat in information and telecommunication technology and its diplomatic containment against Huawei in the 5G technological race. President Trump, in his Executive Order, declared a state of emergency on the grounds that 'foreign adversaries are increasingly creating and exploiting vulnerabilities in information and communications technology and services . . . in order to commit malicious cyber-enabled actions, including economic and industrial espionage against the United States and its people'[258] and that 'unrestricted acquisition or use in the United States of information and communications technology or services designed, developed, manufactured, or supplied by persons owned by, controlled by, or subject to the jurisdiction or direction of foreign adversaries augments the ability of foreign adversaries to create and exploit vulnerabilities in information and communications technology or services . . . constitutes an unusual and extraordinary threat to the national security, foreign policy, and economy of the United States'.[259] It is doubtful such characterisation of threat posed to the national security, foreign policy and economy of the United States is sufficiently clearly articulated. Moreover, it is not entirely clear whether the addition of Huawei to the entities list is based on national security purposes or is a protectionist measure in disguise. The BIS reference to Huawei's breach of sanctions against Iran, in conjunction with US diplomatic efforts in dissuading its allies from using telecommunication equipment from Huawei, may serve the United States' purpose in securitising export restrictions against Huawei. Nonetheless, Huawei has always argued such assertion of economic espionage is

[258] U.S. Department of Commerce. Securing the Information and Communications Technology and Services Supply Chain, 23 December 2019, 84 Federal Register 70445.

[259] Ibid.

fictional and China alleges the United States' export restrictions against Huawei are protectionist measures born of economic considerations.

This issue can be framed in two ways: interpretative and metaphysical. Interpretatively, one may ask whether the term 'war and emergency in international relations' can be interpreted as covering 'trade war'. Metaphysically, if the United States aims to launch a fully blown trade war against China, one may wonder whether and how the trade rules underpinned by the GATT/WTO regime can have a role to play. The Panel in *Russia – Traffic in Transit* sees war as a fully fledged armed conflict, manifested in military combat or similar physical force. The term 'war' is difficult to be interpreted as covering 'trade war'. Neither can trade war fall into the scope of 'emergency of international relations', as economic engagements and diplomatic negotiations between these two countries are maintained while tariffs, normal or punitive, are continuously levied.

However, if the purpose of the trade war is to reshape the economic order and remake the trade rules underpinned by the GATT/WTO regime, as manifested by President Trump's continuous complaint about the WTO's bias against the United States and the US boycott of the nomination of Appellate Body members, it is doubtful whether Article XXI has a role here, either to constrain or justify measures adopted in the name of a trade war. On the one hand, this question relates to how much autonomy a sovereign nation retains after entering reciprocal and mutually advantageous arrangements in safeguarding its essential security interests or pursuing its foreign policy objectives. On the other hand, it also touches on the delicate institutional balance between sovereigns as rule-makers in international law through negotiations and adjudicators as rule-enforcers and implementors.

3.5.4 Japan's Export Licensing Requirements on Semi-conductor Materials against South Korea

On 11 September 2019, the Republic of Korea circulated a request for consultation with Japan under the DSU concerning Japan's removal of South Korea from the whitelist of trusted trading partners. Such decision subjects exports to South Korea, notably, fluorinated polyimide, resist polymers and hydrogen fluoride, to stringent licensing requirements. With its decision, effectuated on 4 July 2019, Japan removed South Korea from the category of Region *I* ① and put it into a newly established category of Region *Ri*. Such decision has prevented Korean enterprises from having the benefit of 'bulk license'. Whereas Japan asserted such decision was made in response to the inadequate management of certain exporting companies, South Korea considers it a politically motivated disguised restriction to trade. According to South Korea, Japan's decision infringes several provisions of WTO agreements, in particular, Article XI of the GATT 1994, and thus requested consultation in accordance with the DSU.[260]

Japan has agreed to this consultation request but the two sides failed to resolve their differences. South Korea thus requested establishment of a panel,[261] which was established on 29 July 2020. In its communication on the request for the establishment of a panel, South Korea alleges that '[a]pplications for individual export licenses are subject to a significant number of requirements and are placed under increased scrutiny, giving rise to unnecessary delays, uncertainties, costs, and other serious restrictions to the exportation of the subject products and technologies to Korea'.[262] As the export licensing requirements disallow 'bulk license' for exports to Korea, Korea is less favourably treated, which violates the fundamental principle of Most-Favoured-Nations treatment. Moreover, the licensing procedures constitute a restriction other than a duty, tax or other charge, and thus violate Article XI of the GATT 1994.[263]

Japan's removal of South Korea from the whitelist of trusted trade partners is slightly different from the United States' addition of Huawei to the entity list in that under the new regulatory regime, exports to South Korea have to go through ordinary export licensing procedures just as exports to other non-whitelist countries do. The WTO rules do not guarantee South Korea benefits as a trusted trading partner under the whitelist countries. Moreover, whereas export to the entity list under US law is under presumption of denial, export to non-trusted trade partners under Japanese law does not suffer from more stringent licensing requirements. Therefore, it is not self-evident that South Korea can make a *prima-facie* case in establishing the WTO-inconsistency of Japan's regulatory change in removing South Korea from the whitelist.

[260] *Japan – Measures Related to the Exportation of Products and Technology to Korea*, WT/DS590/1, 16 September 2019, pp. 1–5.

[261] *Japan – Measures Related to the Exportation of Products and Technology to Korea*, Request for the Establishment of a Panel by the Republic of Korea, WT/DS590/4, 19 July 2020.

[262] Ibid. para. 9.

[263] Ibid. para. 16.

That said, it is also unlikely that Japan can make its case on the national security exception. South Korea alleged but Japan denied that the removal of South Korea from the whitelist was politically motivated. Regardless of the divergence between the dispute parties, it is generally held by the outside world that the feud between Japan and South Korea since World War II and the recent judgement on forced labour during the war period constitute the broad context prompting Japan to deny South Korea the privilege of trusted trade partners. Regardless of these historical feuds and diplomatic incongruence, it is doubtful the tension between these two countries has escalated and amounted to 'emergency of international relations'. As the Panel in *Russia – Traffic in Transit* held, Japan is obliged to articulate the 'essential security interests' it intended to protect through the export licensing procedures in a clearer manner. As it stands, justification under Article XXI of the GATT is likely to fail.

3.6 Short Conclusion

The architects of the post-war international economic order set out the legal framework for liberal international trade underpinned by the GATT regime. Nonetheless, the East–West division between the United States and its allies on the one hand and the Soviet Union and the Warsaw Pact on the other necessitated a regime regulating trade between these two camps with the main objective of preventing strategic and technological articles from being transferred to the Soviet Bloc. The United States, along with its Western allies, Japan and Australia, established the COCOM so as to control trade with the Soviet Bloc. By setting up a firewall between the East and West, liberal international trade could be maintained and reserved among Western countries. With the collapse of the Soviet Union and the fall of the Berlin Wall, the COCOM lost its relevance and was transformed into an even looser form, the Wassenaar Arrangement. At the same time, some other regimes were established to regulate biological and chemical weapons, nuclear materials and the arms trade. With technological advancement and increasing complexity, the regulation of dual-use products and technology presents a tremendous challenge to the GATT/WTO regime, and the WTO-compatibility of sanctioning measures in the form of export control has been gradually called into question.

The landscape of the international political economy since World War II has significantly changed. Russia joined the Wassenaar Arrangement while China is still out. The market economy-oriented GATT/WTO widens its membership and importantly accepted China in 2001 and

Russia in 2012. The diversity of WTO membership makes the organisation a real 'world trade organisation' but at the same time introduces huge challenges for its governance, as manifested in the proliferation of national security exceptions. Article XXI:(c) establishes the link between GATT/WTO law and UN law by providing the legal basis for WTO members to adopt measures in accordance with its obligation under the UN Charter. Moreover, Articles XXI:(a) and XXI:(c) provide legal bases for a WTO member to adopt measures which it considers necessary to protect its essential security interest or refuse to furnish information which it considers contrary to those interests.

Whether these two provisions are 'self-judging' has been debated since the GATT era, but has intensified in the past decade owing to the transformation of 'negative consensus' to 'positive consensus'. More and more members refer to national security as a justification for their measures in pursuit of political objectives. The Panel in *Russia – Traffic in Transit* finally had an opportunity to address this thorny issue and held that national security exception is not 'self-judging'. What constitutes 'emergency of international relations' is subject to the review of the Panel and Appellate Body. Nonetheless, the Panel in *Russia – Traffic in Transit* also held that the phrase 'which it considers necessary' qualifies both 'necessary' and 'essential security interests', and a member invoking this exception has sole discretion to determine, but is obliged to articulate, the necessity and essential security interests in a sufficient manner. This is in line with the obligation of good faith, a general principle of law. The Panel Report on *Russia – Traffic in Transit* has not been appealed and has been adopted by the Dispute Settlement Body. Two cases relating to the justification of national security are still at the Panel proceedings stage and the 'self-judging' nature of the national security exception is far from settled.

The 'self-judging' debate of national security points to the underlying tension between sovereign nations as masters of treaties and adjudicators as treaty-interpreters. Sovereign states at the negotiation stage include a national security clause as a way to facilitate the conclusion of negotiating text on which they agree; at the enforcement stage, they also wish to retain full and complete interpretative power on national security issues so as to escape obligations in the name of national security. How one sees the dialectic nature of treaty-making and treaty-interpretation is reflective of one's view of the dynamics between law and politics, which is in turn embedded with one's perception of international relations.

4

Export Restrictions in the Global Supply Chain

Investment and Competition

4.1 Introduction

The integrated globalised economy is paradoxically characterised by the fragmentation of production processes and the multiplication of jurisdictions involved in this production chain, and the blurring of the distinction between 'us' and 'them' that previously drove trade policy. Producers who previously guarded their domestic market jealously against foreign industries have come to worry about market access conditions and trade costs in a wide range of foreign markets.[1] Moreover, in the wake of the Trump Administration's denial order of export privileges for Zhongxing Telecommunications Equipment Corporation (ZTE) and its subsidiaries, which effectively prohibited any person from participating in any way in any transaction subject to the Export Administration Regulation (EAR),[2] the security of the global supply chain surfaces as a critical issue in supply chain risk management (SCRM). The Trump Administration's decision to add Huawei and its affiliates to the entity list of the EAR has the effect that US enterprises and citizens are prohibited from suppling goods, services or technologies subject to the jurisdiction of EAR without export licensing, which is reviewed with presumption of denial. The denial order against ZTE and the addition of Huawei to the entity list resulted in serious disruption of the production chain of these two companies, the most notable being the prevention of Qualcomm from supplying ZTE with chips and Google's decision not to authorise Huawei to use its Android system. ZTE even temporarily suspended its trading on the

1 Patrick Low and Richard Baldwin, 'Introduction' in Patrick Low and Richard Baldwin (eds), *Multilateralizing Regionalism: Challenges for the Global Trading System* (Cambridge University Press 2009) 2.

2 Order Activating Suspended Denial Order Relating to Zhongxing Telecommunication Equipment Corporation and ZTE Kangxun Telecommunications LTD, 15 April 2018, available at www.iranwatch.org/sites/default/files/180415-zte_denial_order.pdf.

Hong Kong Stock Exchange. These two decisions made China painfully realise how fragile its supply chain can be and strengthened its determination to ensure supply chain security.

The term 'security' refers to multiple dimensions and SCRM should be observed from various perspectives. Obviously, ZTE and Huawei are obliged to reflect on its strategy in SCRM, as Qualcomm was prevented from supplying ZTE with chips and Huawei is denied the access to the Android system. From the perspective of the United States, the Trump administration has asserted that over-reliance on Chinese enterprises, such as ZTE and Huawei, over telecommunication equipment and devices has undermined the security of federal information and communication technology of the United States.[3] But SCRM with a view to preventing the interruption of supplies of key components or raw materials is not limited to governments' prohibitive measures, such as the aforementioned denial order and additions to the entity list, as well as export restrictions on Chinese raw materials and rare earths, but extends to private (illicit) commercial practices, such as export cartels. Practices between private actors may well undermine the security of the supply chain.

With a view to securing supply, economic actors may seek access to raw materials and critical technologies and components through investment policies. They may also enter into agreements, anti-competitive or not, with upstream or downstream producers to ensure the smooth functioning of the supply chain. In view of these, this chapter aims to explore how to ensure security in the era of the global supply chain and remedy the interruption thereof through investment and competition law and policy. This chapter will first introduce the global supply chain and the role of security in SCRM, and then examine how investment and competition law and policy help to redress the threat posed by export restrictions in the context of global supply chains. The chapter concludes with a short conclusion summarising the key arguments and main findings.

4.2 Risk Management and the Governance of the Global Supply Chain

Economic globalisation driven by multinational enterprises has resulted in ever faster trade and investment flows; dispersion of international

[3] See generally, Interos Solutions, 'Supply Chain Vulnerabilities from China U.S. Federal Information and Communications Technology', Prepared for the U.S.-China Economic and Security Review Commission, April 2018.

production networks; international division of labour through specialisation; fragmentation of production and ownership; international outsourcing and growing intra-firm trade and almost simultaneous transition of information.[4] Supply chains are as old as industry and are nothing new: automobiles need tyres that require rubber; steel requires iron that necessitates iron ore extraction. The supply chain is understood as the sequence of plants that provide these inputs. As early as 1997, scholars pointed to the difficulties in locating the exact origin of Swiss drugs, Japanese televisions and French videos, and proposed the concept of 'made in the world'.[5] Writing in 2002, Snyder used the example of Barbie dolls to illustrate the complexity of components originating from different parts of the world and being assembled in China with the logo 'Made in China'.[6] Today, the best example may be Apple's iPhone with 'Designed in US' in place of 'Made in China'.

The recent rapid development of connective technologies, namely, transportation and transmission, has significantly contributed to the forces of globalisation. In characterising the phenomena accompanying economic globalisation, trade economists use the term 'fragmentation' to describe the physical separation of different parts of the production process.[7] According to Gary Gereffi et al., 'fragmentation allows production in different countries to be formed into cross-border production networks that can be within or between firms'.[8] The fragmentation (or disintegration) of production processes is paradoxically closely linked with the integration of global trade.[9] As the global economy integrates through trade liberalisation, enterprises disintegrate their productions processes through outsourcing non-core manufacturing and services at home and abroad and thus establishing production networks, generally referred to as global supply chains or global value chains.

[4] Francis Snyder, 'Governing Economic Globalisation: Global Legal Pluralism and European Law' (1999) 5 *European Law Journal* 334, 335–336.

[5] Kasra Ferdows, 'Made in the World: The Global Spread of Production' (1997) 6 *Production and Operation Management* 102, 102–109.

[6] Snyder, 'Governing Economic Globalisation: Global Legal Pluralism and European Law' (n. 4), 336–337.

[7] Sven W. Arndt and Henryk Kierzkowski, 'Introduction' in Sven W. Arndt and Henryk Kierzkowski (eds), *Fragmentation: New Production Patterns in the World Economy* (Oxford University Press 2001) 1–16.

[8] Gary Gereffi, John Humphrey and Timothy Sturgeon, 'The Governance of Global Supply Chains' (2005) 12 *Review of International Political Economy* 78, 79–80.

[9] See Robert C. Feenstra, 'Integration of Trade and Disintegration of Production in the Global Economy' (1998) 12 *Journal of Economic Perspectives* 31.

4.2.1 Globalisation and Its Two Unbundling Processes

In examining economic activities in the past three centuries, Richard Baldwin argues that globalisation has led to two unbundling processes. In the pre-globalisation world, production was closely linked with consumption due to the limitation of transportation. Therefore, the first unbundling surfaced as a consequence of the steam revolution, steamships and railroads in particular, which dramatically reduced trade costs and thus made it possible to separate production from consumption, starting from the 1830s and accelerating from the 1870s. Once possible, scale economies and comparative advantage made separation profitable, which subsequently led to the industrial revolution and transformed the world. During this first unbundling, whereas international trade in goods and migration boomed, freer trade led production to cluster locally in factories and industrial districts, which Baldwin refers to as globalisation's first paradox.[10] As Baldwin elaborates, this paradox is resolved by the following explanation: cheap transport favours large-scale production, which is complex and thus necessitates extreme proximity to lower the coordination costs. Geographic proximity of clusters constitutes the key characteristic of globalisation's first unbundling.[11]

The development of information and communication technologies (ICT) in the 1980s contributed to reducing or minimising coordination costs and has thus brought about globalisation's second unbundling. During this second unbundling, ICT makes it possible to coordinate complexity at distance, while the vast differences in wages between developed and developing countries make it profitable to separate production processes.[12] The internationalisation of supply chains introduces a unique phenomenon: a trade nation may export and import products in some sectors, such as electronic machinery and electronics, at an extraordinary volume. Such a phenomenon was unimaginable during the first unbundling, as a nation may not have comparative advantage (that leads it to export large volumes) but comparative disadvantage

[10] Richard Baldwin, 'Global Supply Chains: Why They Emerged, Why They Matter, and Where They Are Going?' (2012) The Graduate Institue Centre for Trade and Economic Integration, CETI Papers, CETI 2012–2013, pp. 2–3; see also Richard Baldwin, 'Globalisation: The Great Unbundling(s)' (2006) contribution to the Project *Globalisation Challenges for Europe and Finland*, organised by Secretariat of the Economic Council of Finland, 20 September 2006.

[11] Baldwin, 'Global Supply Chains: Why They Emerged, Why They Matter, and Where They Are Going?' 3–4.

[12] Ibid. 4.

(that leads it to import large volumes) at the same time. But under the second unbundling, the overlapping of such comparative advantage and disadvantage is one of the key features of supply chain trade.[13]

The immediate impact of supply chain trade is that developing countries can benefit from economic globalisation by participating in the global supply chain without having to build up their own.[14] By so doing, they are able to reap the benefit of economic growth and thus narrow the wealth gap between developed countries and themselves. Supply chain trade in this context is largely North–South trade and, importantly, it is not exactly global but rather regional in that it is centred on major developed manufacturing countries, namely, the United States, Germany and Japan.[15]

Globalisation's second unbundling works in two ways: functionally and geographically. Functional unbundling refers to the fact that, in line with Adam Smith's conventional wisdom of specialisation, a finer division of labour contributes to productivity. Nonetheless, it introduces the difficulty of coordination and risk of supply chain management. Therefore, the advancement of ICT helps to resolve this coordination problem but, paradoxically, it impacts functional unbundling in both directions. On the one hand, better ICT reduces the cost of specialisation, as complex information can be exchanged quickly and thus fosters functional unbundling; on the other hand, the advancement of ICT reduces the benefit of specialisation, as one single worker can operate different tasks, through computer-aided manufacturing, numerically controlled machines, computerised tasks, etc., and thus disfavours unbundling.[16]

Geographic unbundling is based on the rule of thumb assigning each production stage to its lowest cost location, which relates to direct costs (such as wages, capital cost and subsidies) and separation costs (including transportation costs, increased risk and managerial time).

[13] Ibid. 5.

[14] Gary Gereffi, 'Global Value Chains in a Post-Washington Consensus World' (2014) 21 *Review of International Political Economy* 9, 18; Jennifer Bair, 'Global Capitalism and Commodity Chains: Looking Back, Going Forward' (2005) 9 *Competition & Change* 153, 161–162.

[15] Baldwin, 'Global Supply Chains: Why They Emerged, Why They Matter, and Where They Are Going?' (n. 10) 7–10; Gereffi, 'Global Value Chains in a Post-Washington Consensus World' (n. 14) 18–23.

[16] Baldwin, 'Global Supply Chains: Why They Emerged, Why They Matter, and Where They Are Going?' (n. 10) 12–13.

The location of geographic unbundling is a balance of dispersion forces and agglomeration forces. In the supply chain context, there are two key dispersion forces. The difference between skilled and unskilled labour determines 'vertical specialisation', which results in North–South outsourcing between headquarter economies in developed countries and factory economies in developing countries. By contrast, firm-level specialisation and excellence may lead to 'horizontal specialisation', a key characteristic of internationalisation of the supply chain among high-wage nations.[17] Agglomeration forces, which encourage spatial concentration and geographic clustering, operate in opposition to dispersion forces. Agglomeration forces in the global supply chain context can be categorised into supply-side (cost of inputs) and demand-side linkage (market size). Largely, supply-side linkage operates on a sectoral basis, while demand-side linkage operates on an economy-wide basis.[18]

Based on these findings, Baldwin offers two insightful messages in the context of the global supply chain. First, supply-chain trade often involves producing either directly or via long-term relationships with independent suppliers. Thus, barriers to doing business abroad, including prohibition of outbound investments and technology transfer, are now trade barriers. Second, supply-chain trade necessitates coordination between different production sites, which in turn relies heavily on the safe and smooth two-way flow of goods, services, people, capital and know-how. Barriers to these flows, such as export restrictions and deemed export under the EAR, are also barriers to trade.[19]

4.2.3 Supply Chain Trade and Its Three Conceptual Types

In analysing the patterns of supply-chain trade, three conceptual types may be identified: import to produce (I2P), import to export (I2E), and re-importing and re-exporting. I2P, which refers to anything produced with foreign inputs and thus constitutes part of the international production network, is the broadest concept of supply-chain trade. I2P covers not only foreign intermediate inputs but also capital equipment, as it contains foreign factors in the production of domestic goods. I2E focuses on intermediates related to exports, which

[17] Ibid. 13–14.
[18] Ibid. 14–15.
[19] Ibid. 21.

corresponds to the popular conception of the global supply chain. The importing country in this context constitutes a node of the international production network, formal or informal, coordinated or uncoordinated. The key feature of I2E is that foreign intermediates are used to produce goods and services that are subsequently exported. Re-importing and re-exporting is a complex form based on I2E. Re-importing and re-exporting is a trade 'symptom' arising from outsourcing abroad, which results in the phenomenon that a nation imports intermediate items which contain goods it previously exported. This type of global supply trade is seen in closely integrated economies, such as the United States and Canada.[20]

Global supply chains have brought about a phenomenon that exports of final products are composed of imports of intermediate inputs traded across borders.[21] As a nation's imported intermediates often contain intermediates from third nations or from the nation itself, trade volume is often inflated due to double-counting. An evolved concept is thus advanced with a view to capturing the clear value a nation contributes to the production of a given product in the international production network. This is normally referred to as 'value-added trade'. The value added to a product in a given nation can be calculated through two approaches based on the sale value of that product, which are: the cost of intermediate inputs (domestic or abroad) and the value added in that nation; and the sum of value added accreted domestically and abroad in the product's sector and all sectors that provide it with intermediate goods.[22] The concept of value-added trade brings us a clearer understanding of a nation's position in the global supply chain and its contribution to the international production process.

4.2.4 *The Governance of the Global Supply Chain and the Management of Its Risks*

The fragmentation of production processes and internationalisation of supply chains complicate coordination and risk management, which necessitates a fresh look at the governance mechanism. Different

[20] Richard Baldwin and Javier Lopez-Gonzalez, 'Supply-Chain Trade: A Portrait of Global Patterns and Several Testable Hypotheses' (2013) National Bureau of Economic Research, Working Paper 18957, pp. 7–8.

[21] Gereffi, 'Global Value Chains in a Post-Washington Consensus World' (n. 14) 19.

[22] Baldwin and Lopez-Gonzalez, 'Supply-Chain Trade: A Portrait of Global Patterns and Several Testable Hypotheses' (n. 20) 8.

approaches are advanced to design and explain the functioning of the global supply chain.

Based on the power structure and depending on the role of leading firms in supply chains, the production networks can be distinguished as producer-driven chains and buyer-driven chains. Producer-driven chains are characterised by the producers' position in designating and allocating the locations of productions sites and the tasks such sites assume. Such producer-driven chains are vertically integrated and closely linked with investment policies or outsourcing decisions. Buyer-driven chains are centred on the role of global buyers in coordinating global supply chains without direct ownership.[23] Given their tremendous buying and bargaining power, global buyers are able to coordinate and build up competent supply chains without controlling them directly. In this context, competition law and policy, in particular the abuse of dominant power, may be of great relevance here.

Looking from the perspective of suppliers and judging from the standardisation and substitutability of their products, global supply chains can further be categorised into commodity suppliers, captive suppliers and turn-key suppliers. Commodity suppliers produce those products with the highest substitutability and little specialisation, supply their products at arms-length and thus have no fixed relations with buyers. Buyers can switch suppliers easily and suppliers are also free to sell their products to other buyers. Captive suppliers supply non-standardised products and have close collaborative relationships with the buyer through exchange of information. As these non-standardised products are often designed and produced for the needs of particular buyers, which often necessitate certification processes, captive suppliers cannot switch from one supplier to another and are thus 'captive'. Competition laws and policies thus play a critical role in this kind of vertical agreement between captive suppliers and buyers. Alternatively, buyers may attempt to control captive suppliers through investment policy, such as joint-venture or shareholding. Turn-key suppliers lie in between, equipped with complex but flexible machinery and competent in sophisticated production processes, and are capable of providing customised products but meeting the needs of different buyers. This categorisation contributes to our understanding of the complexity in

[23] See Gary Gereffi, 'The Organization of Buyer-Driven Global Commodity Chains: How U.S Retailers Shape Overseas Production Networks' in Gary Gereffi and Miguel Korzeniewicz (eds), *Commodity Chains and Global Capitalism* (Praeger 1995) 95–122.

the exchange of information and asset speciality, which determines the position of a supplier in global supply chains.[24]

Network governance researchers conceptualise the networks into three categories: modular, relational and captive. Suppliers in modular supply chains are able to provide products meeting the demands of buyers with various requirements; nonetheless, given that they are normally turn-key suppliers with generic machinery and technology that can satisfy the needs of other buyers without being constrained by transactional-specific investments, they are able to switch among multiple buyers. Production networks under relational value chains involve complex interactions between suppliers and buyers that bring about mutual dependence and a high degree of asset specificity. Relational value chains are normally managed through reputation, family and ethnic ties. Suppliers under captive supply chains are dependent on larger buyers and are faced with significant costs when switching to other buyers. Suppliers under captive supply chains are under the monitoring or control of the buyers, and thus captive.[25]

Building on research on network governance and their previous work, Gary Gereffi et al., in their seminal work, introduce a typology of global supply chain governance comprising five categories based on three criteria: complexity of information and technology transfer; the extent to which such information and technology are codified so as to be transmitted efficiently; and the capacities of actual and potential suppliers in meeting the demand of buyers. Gereffi et al. added two extremes to network governance, market and hierarchy, into these three categories. 'Market' refers to supply chains when products are highly substitutable. Therefore, suppliers and buyers can easily switch from one to another under such supply chain networks with market mechanism being the underlying functional rationale. 'Hierarchy' refers to the scenario of vertical integration, with the dominant form of governance being managerial control, ranging from managers to subordinates and from headquarters to subsidiaries and affiliates.[26] These five modes of global supply chain governance display a spectrum, running from the lowest degree of explicit coordination and power asymmetry between suppliers and buyers (market) to the highest one (hierarchy). Nonetheless, they all

[24] See Timothy Sturgeon, 'Modular Production Networks: A New American Model of Industrial Organization' (2002) 11 *Industrial and Corporate Change* 451.

[25] Gereffi, 'Global Value Chains in a Post-Washington Consensus World' (n. 14) 83–84.

[26] Ibid. 83–84.

share the same feature of trade-off between risks and benefits of outsourcing.[27] How to manage the smooth and secure two-way flows of inputs and outputs constitutes the key challenge facing global supply chain governance. Moreover, the governance model introduced by Gereffi focuses on the power asymmetry between buyers and suppliers with the presupposition that buyers have an upper hand. Such a model seems to fail to appreciate the role of critical component/input suppliers in the governance of the global supply chain.

With the prolongation of production processes and multiplication of jurisdictions involved in these processes, global supply chains can be easily interrupted at their weakest links. Managing risks in global supply chains constitutes a key challenge for MNCs moving towards internationalisation and globalisation. Risk is generally conceived of as comprising three elements: likelihood of occurrence of a particular event or outcome; consequences of the particular event or outcome occurring and casual pathway leading to the event.[28] Risk management, in turn, is conceived of as covering multiple dimensions: risk identification, estimation and evaluation.[29] In the context of global supply chains, risk can be internal or external, arising from endogenous uncertainty or exogenous uncertainty.[30] In turn, supply chain disruption arising from uncertainties can be defined as the combination of '(1) an unintended, anomalous event that materializes somewhere in the supply chain or the supply chain environment and (2) a consequential situation which significantly threatens the normal course of business operations of the affected firms in the supply chain'.[31]

[27] Ibid. 87–88.

[28] Bob Ritchie and Clare Brindley, 'Supply Chain Risk Management and Performance: A Guilding Framework for Future Development' (2007) 27 *International Journal of Operations and Production Management* 303, 305; see also Omera Khan and Bernard Burnes, 'Risk and Supply Chain Management: Creating a Research Agenda' (2007) 18 *The International Journal of Logistics Management* 197, 198–199. Khan and Burnes define risk as covering the first two elements but do not touch on the causal pathway.

[29] Khan and Burnes, 'Risk and Supply Chain Management: Creating a Research Agenda' 202.

[30] Peter Trkman and Kevin McCormack, 'Supply Chain Risk in Turbulent Environment – A Conceptual Model for Managing Supply Chain Risk' (2009) 119 *International Journal of Production Economics* 247, 249; Stephan M. Wagner and Christoph Bode, 'Dominant Risks and Risk Management Practices in Supply Chains' in George A. Zsidisin and Bob Ritchie (eds), *Supply Chain Risk: A Handbook of Assessment, Management, and Performance* (Springer US 2009) 275.

[31] Wagner and Bode, 'Dominant Risks and Risk Management Practices in Supply Chains' 274.

Stephan Wagner and Christoph Bode categorise risks leading to supply chain disruption into five genres: demand side; supply side; regulatory, legal and bureaucratic; infrastructural and catastrophic. Demand side risks result from disruptions arising from downstream supply chain operations and may take different forms, covering physical disruptions in distributing products to end-customers due to transportation and distribution network reasons, or a mismatch in projection and actual demand.[32] Supply side risks relate to purchasing, supplier activities and supplier relationships and cover supplier business risks, production capacity constraints on the supply market, quality problems, technological changes and product design changes.[33] Regulatory, legal and bureaucratic risks refer to 'the legal enforceability and execution of supply chain-relevant laws and policies (e.g., trade and transportation laws) as well as the degree and frequency of changes in these laws and policies'.[34] The common feature of regulatory, legal and bureaucratic risks is that the sources of such risks are external to the supply chain and arise from exogenous uncertainty. Infrastructural risks relate to disruptions arising from the infrastructure a firm maintains for its operations, covering facilities within its business operations, equipment malfunctions, breakdowns and IT failures, and general electricity and water supply.[35] Catastrophic risks refer to natural hazards (force majeure), disease, social-political instability, civil unrest, economic disruptions and terrorist attacks, and have a severe impact on global supply chains. Due to the globalisation of markets and the global span of supply chain operations, even a local catastrophe could have global repercussions.[36] Among these five risks, supply side risks may emerge if upstream producers adopt private forms of export restrictions; and regulatory, legal and bureaucratic risks surface when the government adopts export restrictions. Above all, catastrophic risks, as the COVID-19 pandemic demonstrates, will heavily impact global supply chains as governments prohibit or restrict exports, enterprises hold inventory or raw materials awaiting better prices and individuals engage in panic buying.

[32] Ibid. 275.
[33] Ibid. 276.
[34] Ibid. 277.
[35] Ibid. 277.
[36] Ibid.

4.2.5 *Export Restriction and the Disruption of the Global Supply Chain*

As export restrictions, imposed by governments or private actors, can cause serious damage to economic actors and their home countries, how to circumvent export restrictions and ensure the security of global supply chains constitutes a challenging task facing multinational enterprises and trade nations. If we look at Gereffi et al.'s typology of global supply chains from their focus on explicit coordination and power asymmetry between suppliers and buyers from the lowest degree (market) to the highest (hierarchy), it seems clear that two key factors determine the governance of global supply chains in preventing disruption: *control* and *market*. Control over global supply chains can be maintained through investment with ownership or a captive global supply chain via exclusive supply agreements. With regards to market logic, competition law plays a critical role in ensuring that supply is not disrupted through anti-competitive practices, such as export cartels and abuse of dominant power in horizontal and vertical agreements.

Therefore, in thinking of export restrictions in the context of global supply chain governance, investment and competition that correspond to the logic of control and market come into play. Potential export restrictive measures relate not only to the vertical relationship between buyers and suppliers but also the horizontal relationship between suppliers and suppliers. I will now examine the role of investment and competition in regulating export restrictions.

4.3 Linkage between Trade and Investment: Investors as Traders

Export restrictions provide illustrative examples of the linkage between trade and investment policies. Countries rich in natural resources may be tempted to impose export restrictions with a view to attracting foreign direct investment, or to promoting industrial restructuring, and thus fostering high valued added industries. On the other hand, enterprises or countries in need of natural resources may use investment strategies as a means to circumvent trade export restrictions and secure the supply of raw materials. However, it must be noted that not all countries imposing trade export restrictions welcome foreign direct investment. Export restrictions may be used as a strategy to protect domestic downstream processors. These countries may also be concerned with the potential threat to national security due to the control of strategic assets by foreign investors. Finally, in examining export restrictions in the context of trade and investment linkage, it should also be remembered that in this global integrated economy, investors are normally also traders. Therefore, a country that imposes export restrictions with a view to attracting foreign direct investment may find that the tactic backfires, as investors may be worried about the potential for trade interests being undermined by similarly restrictive trade measures.

In this section, I will introduce policy considerations and legal frameworks relating to export restrictions in the context of trade and investment linkages. Regarding policy considerations, I will present different attitudes embraced by producer countries and consumer countries when it comes to raw materials or critical components or technologies. The different regulatory approaches relating to outbound and inbound investments will also be examined. I will then examine the legal framework governing trade and investment. In this connection, the Agreement on Trade-Related Investment Measures in the WTO framework and the failed initiative of Multilateral Agreement on Investments (MAI) in the framework of OECD will be presented. Finally, I will address legal issues arising from export restrictions in the context of international investment law through two case studies: *Pope & Talbot* v. *Canada*[37] and *SD Myers* v. *Canada*.[38]

4.3.1 Policy Considerations Relating to Export Restrictions in the Context of Trade and Investment Linkage

4.3.1.1 Four Types of Investment

In appreciating the rationales why multi-national enterprises pursue foreign investments, John Dunning categorises foreign direct investments into four types based on the objectives investors aim to achieve through investments: market access; resources; efficiency and strategic assets.[39] Market-seeking, or demand-oriented, investments aim to access a particular market; investors, lured by this particular market, achieve their objectives in penetrating a given market through

[37] *Pope & Talbot, Inc.* v. *The Government of Canada*, UNCITRAL (1976).

[38] *S. D. Myers, Inc.* v. *The Government of Canada*, UNCITRAL (1976).

[39] See John H. Dunning, 'The Eclectic Paradigm as an Envelope for Economic and Business Theories of MNE Activity' (2000) 9 *International Business Review* 163, 164–165; John H. Dunning and Sarianna M. Lundan, *Multinational Enterprises and the Global Economy* (2nd ed., Edward Elgar 2008).

investments. Resource-seeking, or supply-oriented, investments aim to gain access to natural resources, e.g. minerals, agricultural products or unskilled labour. It is these factors of production that attract investors to a host country. Efficiency-seeking investments aim to achieve more efficient division of labour or specialisation of an existing portfolio of foreign and domestic assets. MNEs rationalise their resource distribution and production processes through efficiency-seeking investment. Finally, strategic asset-seeking investment aims to protect or strengthen the existing specific advantages of investors and/or to weaken those of their competitors. Resource-seeking and strategic asset-seeking investments are most relevant to this book, as investors aim to secure access to natural resources and strategic assets through investment policies, while a host country may use investment screening mechanisms, complementary to export restrictive measures, to prevent this. However, efficiency-seeking investment is also of great relevance to export restrictions given that in a globalised world economy characterised by the global supply chain, the production of the various components of a complex end product will be carried out in different countries for efficiency purposes. The imposition of export restrictive measures by a particular country will seriously hamper the proper functioning of this global supply chain, as is evidenced by the ZTE and Huawei cases. Based on these four typologies, countries may determine their trade and investment policies in accordance with their positions in the global supply chain. Are they producers or consumers of a given resource? Is the proposed policy related to inbound or outbound investment? Should export restrictive measures be put in place to complement investment screening mechanisms? I will address these questions next.

4.3.1.2 Producer Countries' and Consumer Countries' Approaches towards Investments

Given the strategic importance of raw materials, states, most notably those with formerly state-controlled or transitional economies, may intervene through investment policies to help their domestic enterprises secure reserves abroad. Producer countries and consumer countries may have different approaches towards foreign direct investments with respect to raw materials overseas. Consumer countries pursue aggressive foreign direct investment policies towards raw materials with a view to securing inputs for their domestic producers and to enhance supply security. Producer countries may attempt to gain control over reserves overseas and expand foreign markets. In these respects, China and Russia are the most illustrative examples.

Due to its remarkable economic progress as the world's factory during the past few decades, China demands significant raw materials as inputs for producing industrial goods, as well as energy to fuel its economic growth. As observed, China's efforts to secure access to raw materials abroad are channelled through governmental assistance to domestic and state-owned enterprises. Chinese governments may grant subsidies to domestic enterprises to acquire foreign assets; such practices are most visible in the steel industry. State-owned enterprises may serve as major agents for governmental policies rather than commercial gains. Sovereign wealth funds, such as the China Investment Corporation, have also played a key role. China is establishing closer relationships with private equity firms, such as Morgan Stanley and Blackstone, which are believed to advise China on foreign asset acquisition. Further, state-owned banks, including China Development Bank, Industrial and Commercial Bank of China (ICBC) and China Export and Import Bank (China EXIM Bank), also play key roles in facilitating China's foreign direct investments with the provision of preferential loans to Chinese enterprises. Some examples are the funding of China Development Bank to Aluminium Corporation of China's (Chinalco) purchase of Rio Tinto shares; financial support extended by China EXIM Bank and China Development Bank to Sinosteel in obtaining raw materials overseas; the investment of ICBC in South Africa's largest lender, Standard Bank. Finally, China may exercise governmental influence in private commercial negotiations between Chinese enterprises and foreign companies to help Chinese enterprises gain better negotiation positions.[40]

In terms of the destinations of China's foreign direct investments, Australia and Africa are most important. China has concluded a free trade agreement with Australia; in Africa, China has concluded bilateral investment agreements with a number of countries, including Ghana, Tunisia, Egypt, Kenya, South Africa, Mozambique and Mali. China's engagements with African countries are characterised by development

[40] Alan H. Price and others, 'Raw Deal: How Government Trade Barriers and Subsidies Are Distorting Global Trade in Raw Materials' prepared by Wiley Rein LLP for American Scrap Coalition, November 2008, pp. 13–14; Gordon Peeling and others, 'Export Restrictions on Strategic Raw Materials and Their Impact on Trade and Global Supply' in OECD (ed), *The Economic Impact of Export Restrictions on Raw Materials* (OECD Publishing 2010) 166–168.

aid linked to access to natural resources.[41] Sometimes, there is little distinction between aid and investment when it comes to China's engagements in African countries, as they are so intermingled.[42]

There are reasons for China to use its state power as leverage to secure supply. Andreas Goldthau argues there are three specific reasons for this. First, economic growth is the cornerstone of Chinese social stability and the political legitimacy of its ruling party, the Chinese Communist Party. Thus, the Chinese government has strong political motivation to help its enterprises secure access to raw materials abroad so as to sustain its economic growth. Second, China, being a latecomer to international resource markets with the rules of the game set by dominant Western countries and enterprises, is forced to venture into countries with great political and commercial risks. With a view to helping its enterprises compete with existent Western multinational companies, the Chinese government has to aid its domestic enterprises by lessening risks and enhancing profitability. Third, even Chinese enterprises, eyeing investment opportunities and commercial interests, may wish to extend their outreach. These three factors combined explain the aggressive acquisition of foreign assets by Chinese enterprises.[43]

As regards Russia, it accounts for the lion's share of oil and gas exports. Regardless its leading role as an exporter, it strives to secure reserves and markets abroad through energy diplomacy. Given its heavy reliance on Gazprom for revenue, Russia has strong incentives to support Gazprom's overseas expansion. As regards Gazprom, it is also economically motivated to explore new reserves, boost its gas products and acquire new markets with political backing. It also aims to regain control of the pipeline infrastructure by cancelling outstanding debts in exchange for ownership over pipelines and transportation infrastructure in the Commonwealth of Independent States countries.[44] In contrast to China's development-centred approach, Russia relies more on subsidies, price incentives and preferential treatment of the states of the former Soviet Union with a view to securing access and transit rights. Russian energy diplomacy coincides with Gazprom's ambition to maximise its

[41] Andreas Goldthau, 'Energy Diplomacy in Trade and Investment of Oil and Gas' in Andreas Goldthau and Jan Martin Witte (eds), *Global Energy Governance: The New Rules of the Game* (Brookings Institution Press 2010) 34.

[42] Price and others, 'Raw Deal: How Government Trade Barriers and Subsidies Are Distorting Global Trade in Raw Materials' (n. 40), at 22–23.

[43] Goldthau, 'Energy Diplomacy in Trade and Investment of Oil and Gas', (n. 41), at 26–30.

[44] Ibid. at 31–34.

monopoly power. Fourth, the absence of multilateral disciplines in foreign acquisitions also complicates the picture. Finally, with heavy reliance on bilateral investment treaties, the regulatory regime may suffer from inefficiency and inefficacy.[45]

4.3.1.3 Outbound and Inbound Investment with a view to Securing Access to Raw Materials or Maintaining Sufficiency for Domestic Usage

The impact of export restrictions on investment policies can be further analysed by ascertaining whether the investments are inbound or outbound. With the imposition of export restrictions, domestic prices of the relevant materials will decrease relative to global prices. This price differential constitutes a comparative advantage to domestic downstream processers. By means of this price differential and the resultant comparative advantage, a trading nation imposing export restrictions may attract foreign direct investments to establish processing industries in that country. Therefore, export restrictions may have investment diversion effects.

However, not all countries imposing export restrictions may wish to attract foreign direct investments in that particular sector or its downstream industries. Instead, they may choose to restrict or prohibit foreign direct investments in relevant sectors, which will exacerbate adverse effects arising from export restrictions. There are some reasons for such prohibitions, or restrictions, on foreign direct investments. First, a country may want to ensure the value chain, anchored by the pertinent raw materials, is built in its territory so as to reap the economic fruits itself; there is some suspicion that foreign enterprises may relocate the processing sectors after they own and control the raw materials concerned. Second, in a period of high commodity prices, some sectors are considered to enjoy above-normal profits, which countries may wish not to share with distant foreign enterprises.[46]

As observed by Alan H. Price and D. Scott Nance, China has erected a number of barriers to foreign investments in, and ownership of, raw materials. These barriers include prohibitions on surveying and mapping activities: prerequisites for the exploration and exploitation of natural

[45] Agata Antkiewicz and John Whalley, 'Recent Chinese Buyout Activity and the Implications for Global Architecture' (2006) NBER Working Paper Series 12072, 21–37.

[46] Peeling and others, 'Export Restrictions on Strategic Raw Materials and Their Impact on Trade and Global Supply', (n. 40) 167.

resources. The regulatory procedures are opaque and the lack of transparency prevents foreign enterprises from competing effectively. Weak legal protection further worsens the treatment of foreign enterprises; in some cases, foreign enterprises are deprived of the right to exploit their discoveries even though they are formally granted a license to explore for minerals.[47]

In contrast to cautious attitudes towards inbound investments, Chinese enterprises, as directed by the 'Go Global' policy in 2001, are encouraged to go global as a means of obtaining access to natural resources, stimulating exports and expanding sales in foreign markets. Within the past decade, China's foreign direct investments have significantly increased. From an economic point of view, by virtue of vertical integration, the competitiveness of Chinese enterprises may have been greatly strengthened. However, economic interests are normally intermingled with strategic considerations. This explains why a large proportion of these foreign direct investments have gone to resource-rich countries.[48] Various initiatives are adopted with a view to intensifying trade and investment relationships between China and African countries. In 2006, China published its first African Policy Paper and established the Forum on China–Africa Cooperation (FOCAC) as a platform for collaboration between China and African countries. The closer political cooperation has yielded various economic, trade and investment projects. State-owned enterprises are at the forefront of China's venture into Africa, the most prominent of these being the China National Petroleum Corporation, China Petroleum and Chemical Corporation (Sinopec) and China National Offshore Oil Corporation (CNOOC). Operating under the aegis of the State Economic and Trade Commission, these three state-owned enterprises have been aggressively establishing overseas oil exploration and buying operating rights abroad.[49] In addition to African countries, there have been attempts to

[47] Alan H. Price and D. Scott Nance, 'Export Barriers and the Steel Industry' in OECD (ed), *The Economic Impact of Export Restrictions on Raw Materials* (OECD Publishing 2010) 88–89. See also Price and others, 'Raw Deal: How Government Trade Barriers and Subsidies Are Distorting Global Trade in Raw Materials', (n. 40) at 13–14.

[48] Price and Scott Nance, 'Export Barriers and the Steel Industry' 88–89. See also Price and others, 'Raw Deal: How Government Trade Barriers and Subsidies Are Distorting Global Trade in Raw Materials', (n. 40) at 13–14.

[49] Uche Ewelukwa Ofodile, 'Trade, Empires, and Subjects – China-African Trade: A New Fair Trade Arrangement, or the Third Scramble for Africa' (2008) 41 *Vanderbilt Journal of Transnational Law* 505, 524–529.

expand to other countries through buyouts, including the CNPC's involvement with the Russian oil company Yukos; the failed attempt of China's MinMetals Corporation to purchase Canada's largest mining company, Noranda; and the withdrawn bid of CNOCC to buy American oil firm Unocal.[50]

China's aggressive attempts to acquire foreign assets give rise to great controversies. First, it is widely believed that these buyout efforts are subsidised by the Chinese government. Second, such worries are worsened in view of the lack of transparency under the Chinese regulatory regime and decision-making processes within the pertinent state-owned enterprises. Third, China's attempted buyouts have given rise to national security concerns in host states.[51]

4.3.1.4 Export Control of Critical Technology and Investment Screening Mechanism on Sensitive Sectors

While investors may aim to circumvent export restrictive measures and thereby gain access to raw materials or strategic assets, host states may adopt investment review mechanisms and block proposed investments. Such dynamics in export control and investment review are most vividly seen in the recent revision of the Foreign Investment Risk Review Modernization Act of 2018 (FIRRMA) and Export Control Reform Act of 2018 (ECRA) under the Trump Administration. These two pieces of legislation have effectively strengthened the US investment review mechanism, under the Committee on Foreign Investment in the United States (CFIUS), in screening inbound investment and preventing emergent or foundational technologies from being exported.

The CFIUS was established by Executive Order 11858 in 1975 by President Ford[52] and finds its legal basis in section 721 of the Defense Production Act (DPA) of 1950, which was subsequently amended by the Exon-Florio amendment in 1988[53] and by the Foreign Investment and National Security Act (FINSA) in 2007.[54] The CFIUS is an interagency committee that serves the President to oversee foreign investment that may result in the control of a US business by a foreign corporation or

[50] Antkiewicz and Whalley, 'Recent Chinese Buyout Activity and the Implications for Global Architecture', available at www.nber.org/papers/w12072, pp. 10–15.

[51] Ibid. 21–37.

[52] Executive Order 11858, 5 May 1975, 40 FR 20263.

[53] P. L. 100-418, Title V, Section 5021, 23 August, 1988; 50 USC Appendix §2170.

[54] See generally, James K. Jackson, 'The Commitee on Foreign Investment in the United States (CFIUS)' CRS Report for Congress, RL33388, 11 October 2017.

government and pose threats to US national security.[55] Three key transactions play a critical role in the evolution of the CFIUS review: Fujitsu's failed acquisition of Fairchild semiconductor in 1983; the attempt of Chinese National Offshore Oil Corp (CNOOC) to acquire the Union oil company of California (Unocol) in 2005; and Dubai Port World's bid to purchase shares of the Peninsular and Oriental Steam Navigation Company (P&O) in 2006. Recently, incidents of blocks on foreign investment in the United States predominantly concern Chinese investment. These three transactions reflect a change in the perception of the United States about the key threat to its national security: Japan in the 1980s; the Arabian world after the September 11 attack, and China recently.[56]

As directed by Executive Order 11858, the CFIUS is responsible for the monitoring of the impact of foreign investment on the United States, both direct and portfolio, and the coordination of US policy on such investment. In discharging its responsibilities, the CFIUS shall, inter alia, 'review investments in the United States which, in the judgment of the Committee, might have major implications for United States national interests'.[57] On completion or termination of any investigation, the Committee shall report to the President and present a recommendation.[58]

Prompted by various merger and acquisition bids by Japanese enterprises, Congress in 1998 passed the Exon-Florio amendment to the DPA, which grants the President the authority to review any merger, acquisition or takeover (covered transaction as defined) and to determine the effects of the transaction on the national security of the United States.[59] The President may suspend or prohibit any covered transaction that threatens to impair the national security of the United States.[60] The FINSA formally grants the CFIUS statutory status and widens factors to be taken into consideration during the national security review process

[55] Theodore H. Moran, *Three Threats: An Analytical Framework for the CFIUS Process* (Peterson Institute for Internatioanl Economics 2009) 2–3.

[56] Weitseng Chen, ' Screening the "Dragon's Gift"? National Security Review of China's Foreign Direct Investment' in John Garrick and Yan Chang Bennett (eds), *China's Socialist Rule of Law Reforms under Xi Jinping* (Routledge 2016) 198–199; Joanna Rubin Travalini, 'Foreign Directive Investment in the United States: Achieving a Balance between National Economy Benefits and National Security Interests' (2009) 29 *Northwestern Journal of International Law and Business* 779, 787–791

[57] Executive Order 11858, Section 1(b)(3).

[58] Executive Order 11858, Section 7(2).

[59] 50 USC Appendix, Art. 2170(b)(1)(A).

[60] 50 USC Appendix, Art. 2170(d)(1).

with the inclusion of critical infrastructure, critical technology and the ownership of foreign enterprises being state-controlled or not. Finally, the FINSA sets out broad and vague legal criteria to satisfy in order for the President to take action

(A) there is credible evidence that leads the President to believe that the foreign interest exercising control might take action that threatens to impair the national security; and
(B) provisions of law, other than this section and the International Emergency Economic Powers Act, do not, in the judgment of the President, provide adequate and appropriate authority for the President to protect the national security in the matter before the President.[61]

In assessing the risk to national security, the CFIUS engages a three-step analysis. The CFIUS first looks at the threat by assessing the intent and capacity of the acquirer; the CFIUS then examines the vulnerability of US enterprises, which may impact national security; finally, the CFIUS assesses the potential national security consequences if the vulnerability is to be exploited.[62] Theodore Moran, a professor at Georgetown University, further clarifies the meaning of threat and categorizes the potential threat into three types. The first type of threat relates to any acquisition that would make the United States dependent on a foreign-controlled supplier for certain critical goods and services, which might deny, delay or condition such supply. The second type relates to an acquisition that may lead to transfer of technology or expertise to a foreign-controlled entity or its government that may undermine US security interests. The third type of threat relates to an acquisition that would lead to infiltration, surveillance or sabotage in goods and services crucial to the fuctioning of the US economy.[63]

The investment screening mechanism is further strengthened by the ECRA and FIRRMA, part of the John S. McCain National Defense Authorisation Act for Fiscal 2019 (NAAA).[64] The main objective of these two pieces of legislation is to strengthen export and investment controls to address national security concerns arising from the release of critical and foundational technologies to end uses, end users and destinations

[61] 50 USC Appendix, Art. 2170(d)(4).
[62] Jackson, 'The Commitee on Foreign Investment in the United States (CFIUS)' (n. 54) 9.
[63] Moran, *Three Threats: An Analytical Framework for the CFIUS Process* (n. 55) 1.
[64] Public Law No: 115-232.

of concern.[65] Therefore, the FIRRMA expands the jurisdiction of the CFIUS by creating four new types of 'covered transactions' subject to CFIUS review. Moreover, those investments subject to CFIUS review are not limited to inbound investment but extend to outbound investments, an additional element strengthening the CFIUS. The regulation of outbound investment concerns critical and foundational technologies, which corresponds to the strengthening of efforts to control the export of critical products and technologies.

Section 1758 of the ECRA instructs the President, in coordination with relevant agencies, to establish an interagency process to identify emergent and foundational technologies essential to the national security of the United States. The list of emergent and foundational technologies subject to Section 1758 of the ECRA excludes those critical technologies described under the scope of clauses (i) through (v) of section 721(a)(6)(A) of the DPA, as amended by section 1703 of the ECRA. Those critical technologies identified in the aforementioned five clauses of the DPA cover Munitions List under the International Traffic in Arms Regulations (ITAR), Commerce Control List under the Export Administration Regulations (EAR), nuclear and toxin items. As the mandatory exception of the Section 1758 explicitly excludes those technologies subject to the jurisdiction of the International Emergency Economic Powers Act (IEEPA), EAR or any other regulation, Section 1758 creates another category of emergent and foundational technologies subject to export control. Once identified as an emergent or foundational technology, the Secretary of Commerce, taking into consideration the countries to which the specific technology is exported and potential end uses and end users of that technology, has to decide the level of control, with the minimum requirement being an export licensing system. In reviewing the export licensing application, the threat posed to the national security of the United States by exportation of such technology should be taken into account. Moreover, with a view to ensuring the effectiveness of such control, Section 1758 instructs the Secretary of State, in consultation with the Secretary of the DOC and Department of Defense, to propose adding such technologies to the control list of multilateral control regimes.

[65] Akin Gump Strauss Hauer and Feld LLP, 'The Export Control Reform Act of 2018 and Possible New Controls on Emergent and Foundational Technologies', *International Trade Alert*, 12 September 2018, p. 1. While the acts do not contain any blacklist or whitelist, China and Russia are the main targeted countries.

The attempt to prevent critical infrastructure and critical technologies from being accessed or acquired by foreign countries through an investment review mechanism is not limited to the United States. In 2017, the European Commission proposed a draft Regulation of the European Parliament and of the Council establishing a framework for screening of foreign direct investments into the European Union (FDI Screening Regulation),[66] which was subsequently adopted on 19 March 2019.[67] As foreign direct investment becomes part of common commercial policy and falls under the exclusive competence of the EU, by virtue of this regulation, the Member States are authorised to establish or maintain an investment review mechanism on the grounds of threat to security or public order.[68] In addition to reviews at the level of Member States, the Commission itself may initiate review on the grounds of a security or public order when the investments are likely to affect Union interest, such as those projects and programmes involving a substantial amount, or a significant share of EU funding, or regarding critical infrastructure, critical technologies or inputs.[69] With a view to fostering coordination, the Regulation establishes a cooperation mechanism, under which the reviewing Member State is obliged to report and the Commission or other affected Member States may comment on the proposed investment.[70]

In determining the potential adverse impacts of the proposed investment on security and public order, five factors are of deciding importance: critical infrastructure and land and real estate crucial for the use of such infrastructure; critical technologies and dual-use items; supply of critical inputs; access to sensitive information and freedom and pluralism of the media.[71] In addition, the relationship between the foreign investor and the government of the third country as well as its past track record or potential risks in undermining security and public order in a Member State or engaging in illegal and criminal activities are also to be considered.[72]

[66] COM (2017) 487 final, Brussels 19 September 2017.

[67] Regulation (EU) 2019/452 of the European Parliament and of the Council of 19 March 2019 establishing a framework for the screening of foreign direct investments into the Union, OJ L 79/1, 21 March 2019.

[68] FDI Screening Regulation, Art. 3.1.

[69] FDI Screening Regulation, Art. 3.2 and 3.3.

[70] FDI Screening Regulation, Art. 8.

[71] FDI Screening Regulation, Art. 4(1).

[72] FDI Screening Regulation, Art. 4(2).

Section 1758 of the ECRA evidences the increasing national security concerns of the United States with respect to Chinese inbound investment in sensitive sectors and critical infrastructure, and reflects its effort in controlling outbound investments in critical and foundational technologies, which is to be complemented by export controls in the trade context. Following the practices of the United States' CFIUS screening mechanism, the EU enacted the FDI Screening Regulation to prevent foreign, and Chinese in particular, investments in critical infrastructure, technologies or inputs. Again, such legislation demonstrates the close link between trade and investment regimes.

4.3.2 Legal Framework Governing Trade and Investment: Multilateral Initiatives and Bilateral Practices

In response to export restrictions, a country may strive to circumvent imposed restrictions through investment policies with a view to securing access to raw materials. As noted previously, such investment may or may not be welcomed by host states. Regardless of the different attitudes of host states, the exploration and exploitation of natural resources necessitates a long period of time and a huge amount of capital, and the protection of investments thus constitutes the main concern of foreign investors. In the context of the WTO, the commercial presence (mode 3) of service providers may be deemed a form of investment by service industries; of relevance to access to natural resources are such services as mining services. In addition to GATS, trade-related investment measures (TRIMs) may also be subject to the scrutiny of the WTO. Notwithstanding these provisions, the WTO touches on investment policies only slightly and further negotiations have not brought about noticeable progress.[73]

In view of the limited regulation of investments under the WTO framework and perhaps in recognition of the WTO's inability to move forward to set out a multilateral framework governing investment policies, countries of the OECD decided to go it alone and launch ambitious negotiations on a Multilateral Agreement on Investments (MAI). Unfortunately, negotiations over the MAI have been fruitless as well,

[73] The so-called Singapore issues (investments, competition, government procurement and trade facilitation) are mostly dropped from the Doha negotiations with the exception of trade facilitation.

and were suspended in 1998. The failure of the MAI was a result of a combination of a lack of ambition and inability or unwillingness to compromise.[74]

In the context of energy materials and products, modest progress has been achieved with the conclusion of the Energy Charter Treaty (ECT) by mostly European countries and non-European OECD countries. In contrast to the comprehensive approach embraced by the MAI, the ECT has limited coverage, addressing only energy materials and products. The Energy Charter Conference found its roots in the proposal advanced by the former Premier of the Netherlands Ruud Lubbers in the 1990 Dublin European Council in the wake of the fall of the Berlin Wall.[75] The creation of the Energy Charter Conference and subsequent adoption of the ECT is an initiative of the EU (then: EC) to bolster its energy security by exchanging its technology and capital with Central and Eastern European countries, as well as former Soviet states, rich in energy resources.[76] Due to disagreements on transit issues, Russia decided not to ratify the ECT in 2009[77] and terminated its provisional application after giving 60 days' notice to the ECT secretariat. While some scholars argue that China may benefit from the ECT,[78] so far, China has only participated in the ECT as an observer.

Apart from the failure of the MAI and the limited success of the ECT, the vast majority of investment activities are governed by a network of bilateral agreements. Therefore, the application of an investment regime to natural resource or strategic sectors remains fragmented. Disciplines before the establishment of investment are even more limited, and host states tend to adopt an investment screening mechanism, such as the CFIUS and FDI Screen Regulation, to exclude foreign investors from accessing these sensitive areas.

[74] Stefan D. Amarasinha and Juliane Kokott, 'Multilateral Investment Rules Revisited' in Peter Muchlinski, Federico Ortino and Christoph Schreuer (eds), *The Oxford Handbook of International Investment Law* (Oxford University Press 2008) 127.

[75] Andrey Konoplyanik, 'Lubbers Plan: Soviet Energy as Standpoint for Improving Economic Reforms in USSR' (1992) 12 *Energy Journal* 281, 281–294.

[76] Jean Touscoz, 'The Role of the European Union in the Framework of the Energy Charter Treaty' (1997) 2 *European Foreign Affairs Review* 23, 23–24.

[77] www.encharter.org/index.php?id=414&L=0%3B#c1338.

[78] See e.g., Noriko Yodogawa and Alexander M. Peterson, 'An Opportunity for Progress: China, Central Asia, and the Energy Charter Treaty' (2012–2013) 8 *Texas Journal of Oil, Gas and Energy Law* 111, 111–142.

4.3.3 *Legal Issues of Export Restrictions in the Context of International Investment Law*

In the post-establishment phase, investors facing export restrictions imposed by host states may rely on international investment treaties and challenge the legality of these export restrictive measures. Those claims may be based on National Treatment, Fair and Equitable Treatment and performance requirements. In the jurisprudence of international investment law, two cases are of great pertinence to the theme of this book: *Pope & Talbot* v. *Canada*, and *SD Myers* v. *Canada*. Both cases are handed down in the context of NAFTA Chapter 11 arbitration and are good examples of trade and investment linkage.

4.3.3.1 Pope & Talbot v. Canada

Pope & Talbot v. *Canada* relates to the well-known softwood lumber dispute between the United States and Canada[79] and presents a vivid example of the interaction between trade measures and investment policies. With a view to ending a series of notorious litigation, the United States and Canada concluded a Softwood Lumber Agreement (SLA) on 29 May 1996. Pursuant to the SLA, the United States undertook not to take trade defence measures against Canadian softwood lumber products; in exchange, Canada would place softwood lumber on the export control list under the Export and Import Permit Act and the exportation of Canadian softwood lumber to the United States thus became subject to federal export permit.[80] However, this SLA only covered some Canadian provinces (named as the covered provinces; one of which was British Columbia). Therefore, in its implementation measures, Canada only required softwood lumber industries located in the covered provinces to comply with its export control regulations. The claimant, a US investor that has a wholly owned subsidiary in British Columbia, relying on Chapter 11 of the NAFTA, brought this case before the arbitral tribunal. The investor claimed that the export restrictions

[79] On the US–Canada soft lumber dispute, see *e.g.*, Joost Pauwelyn, 'Editorial Comment: Adding Sweeteners to Softwood Lumber: the WTO–NAFTA "Spaghetti Bowl" is Cooking' (2006) 9 *Journal of International Economic Law* 197; Daowei Zhang, *The Softwood Lumber War: Politics, Economics, and the Long U.S.-Canadian Trade Dispute* (Reource for the Future Press 2007); Gugiya, 'The Interplay of International Dispute Resolution Mechanisms: The Softwood Lumber Controversy'.

[80] *Pope & Talbot, Inc.* v. *The Government of Canada*, UNCITRAL (1976), award on the merits of phase 2 by Arbitral Tribunal, 10 April 2001, para. 18.

imposed by Canada infringed Canada's obligations under the NAFTA relating to National Treatment, the prohibition of performance requirements and expropriation. The Arbitral Tribunal agreed with the claimant on some claims, but rejected others.

National Treatment The claimant, Pope & Talbot, Inc., first referred to Article 1102, in particular the second paragraph, and argued that its investment in Canada, Pope & Talbot, Ltd., was treated less favourably than those of Canadian investors. Article 1102(2) of the NAFTA provides as follows

> Each Party shall accord to investments of investors of another Party treatment no less favorable than that it accords, in like circumstances, to investments of its own investors with respect to the establishment, acquisition, expansion, management, conduct, operation, and sale or other disposition of investments.[81]

The claimant and Canada did not dispute that Canada's SLA implementing measures, notably, the export control regulation, related to the 'expansion, management, conduct [and] operation' of the claimant's investments in Canada. The bone of contention nonetheless concerned the standard of 'no less favourable' treatment and the comparison of 'like circumstances'.

Regarding the standard of 'no less favourable' treatment, both the claimant and Canada agreed that there was no *de jure* violation of National Treatment obligation since Canada's implementation measures did not facially discriminate between foreign investors and other NAFTA parties. However, in the case of *de facto* discrimination, Canada argued, and the claimant did not agree, that the infringement of National Treatment obligation out of *de facto* discrimination can only be found to exist when the foreign investors or investments are disproportionately disadvantaged.[82] In support of its argument, Canada referred to some GATT/WTO jurisprudence, such as the *EC – Bananas*, *EC– Asbestos*, *US – Beers* and one NAFTA Chapter 11 arbitral award, *SD Myers* v. *Canada*. Nonetheless, this argument was not accepted by the Arbitral Tribunal.

According to the Arbitral Tribunal, there was no reason to set out different thresholds for *de jure* and *de facto* discriminations, which were,

[81] NAFTA, Art. 1102(2).

[82] *Pope & Talbot, Inc.* v. *The Government of Canada*, award on the merits of phase 2, para. 43.

in the first place, very difficult to distinguish. The Arbitral Tribunal then referred to *US – Section 337* to justify its analysis. As the Panel in *US – Section 337* held, in ascertaining whether imported products were accorded treatment less favourable than that of domestic products, the decision should be based on the distinction made by laws, regulations or requirements themselves and their potential impact, rather than on the actual consequences on the imported products. The requirement of 'no less favourable' should be understood to be applicable to each individual case. The notion of balancing between some more favourable imported and other less favourable imported products cannot be accepted.[83] The Arbitral Tribunal further referred to the Panel Report on *US – Beer*, an authority relied on by Canada. The Panel in *US – Beer* emphasised that the fact that only a small portion of US domestic beer was eligible for a lower tax rate, a treatment more favourable than imported products, did not shield the United States from the infringement of National Treatment obligation.[84] The Arbitral Tribunal further added that the 'disproportionate advantage' theory as advanced by Canada would in effect force the claimant to ascertain whether there were other US investors suffering from the same prejudices and to compare the treatment of US investors with the predominant treatment of Canadian investors. Such position would seriously constrain foreign investors seeking to vindicate their rights under Article 1102.[85] Therefore, the Arbitral Tribunal rejected the concept of 'disproportionate advantage' as advanced by Canada.

Regarding the comparison of 'like circumstances', the key issue before the Arbitral Tribunal was to identify domestic entities whose treatment should be compared with that accorded to the claimant and its investments. Given that the export control regime applied only to the covered provinces, the question was thus whether Canadian entities located in the uncovered provinces were situated in like circumstances and thus eligible for such comparison exercise. In answering this question, the Arbitral Tribunal looked at the legal context of 'like circumstances' and found that both the trade and investment liberalising objectives of NAFTA and

[83] Panel Report on *US – Section 337*, paras. 5.13–5.14, citing from *Pope & Talbot, Inc.* v. *The Government of Canada*, award on the merits of phase 2, para. 68.

[84] *Pope & Talbot, Inc.* v. *The Government of Canada*, award on the merits of phase 2, para. 69.

[85] *Pope & Talbot, Inc.* v. *The Government of Canada*, award on the merits of phase 2, paras. 71–72.

the aim of bringing an end to the US–Canada softwood lumber dispute constituted the legal context for the 'like circumstances'.

In exploring the implications of this legal context, the Arbitral Tribunal held that the comparison of 'like circumstances' should be based on investments of the same business or economic sector. In cases where different treatments were found to exist, the measures in question would presumably violate the National Treatment obligation unless they 'have a reasonable nexus to rational government policies that (1) do not distinguish on face or *de facto*, between foreign-owned and domestic companies, and (2) do not otherwise unduly undermine liberalizing objectives of NAFTA'.[86] As the Arbitral Tribunal further explained, such an approach corresponded with the nationality test advanced by Canada and other NAFTA parties. However, relying solely on whether different treatments are accorded based on nationality may excuse discrimination facially not based on nationality. Therefore, the Arbitral Tribunal thus stressed that the inquiry of 'like circumstances' would require 'addressing *any* difference in treatment, demanding that it be justified by showing that it bears a reasonable relationship to rational policies not motivated by preference of domestic over foreign owned investments'.[87]

In applying these legal standards to the case before it, the Arbitral Tribunal addressed three scenarios in which a comparison of 'like circumstances' was to be made: covered provinces and uncovered provinces; British Columbia and other covered provinces; interior and coastal areas of British Columbia.

As the export control regime applied only to covered provinces, the claimant argued that it suffered from less favourable treatment than those Canadian investors located in the uncovered provinces. In response to this contention, the Arbitral Tribunal observed that the export of softwood lumber in the covered provinces constituted 95 per cent of Canadian total export volume to the United States and that softwood lumber industries in the uncovered provinces had never been subject to countervailing duties by the US government. The Arbitral Tribunal thus concluded that the investor and other Canadian softwood lumber

[86] *Pope & Talbot, Inc.* v. *The Government of Canada*, award on the merits of phase 2, para. 78.

[87] *Pope & Talbot, Inc.* v. *The Government of Canada*, award on the merits of phase 2, para. 79 (emphasis original).

enterprises in the uncovered provinces are not in 'like circumstances'. The obligation of National Treatment was not infringed.[88]

The claimant further argued that the export control regime favoured other covered provinces, in particular Quebec, than British Columbia by offering new entrants quotas. This resulted in the trend that the market share of Quebec's softwood lumber steadily increased while that of British Columbia steadily declined. In response to this argument, the Arbitral Tribunal observed that prior to the SLA, there were more investments in new mills and improvement of the capacity of existent mills in Quebec than British Columbia. Therefore, these new entrants into the softwood lumber industries necessitated additional quota allocation. Given that these new entrants were not evenly located in the covered provinces, it would be illogical to assign additional quotas in accordance with the tiny percentage of distribution in the covered provinces. In conclusion, the Arbitral Tribunal found that 'it was the underlying economics of softwood lumber industry in Canada that placed the Investment and other producers in B. C. in unlike circumstances to those in other covered provinces'.[89] Based on this finding, the Arbitral Tribunal thus ruled that Canada's allocation of quotas to new entrants had a reasonable nexus with rational policy objectives and contained no elements of discrimination against foreign investors.

The third contention made by the claimant related to the difference in stumpage fee reduction between interior and coastal areas of British Columbia. On 1 June 1998, B. C. government decided to reduce the stumpage fee for softwood lumber industries on Crown land. On the recommendation of industries, the B. C. government decided to allocate the budget evenly between interior and coastal areas. Given that there were more softwood lumber industries in the interior areas, the percentage for the reduction of stumpage fee was less. In this pertinent case, the investments of the claimant happened to be located in the interior. This reduction in stumpage fee nonetheless resulted in a dispute between the United States and Canada where the United States contended that such a reduction constituted a subsidy and thus infringed the SLA. This dispute was finally settled by an agreement to amend the SLA and impose a Super Fee on B.C. softwood lumber. Under this circumstance, the

[88] *Pope & Talbot, Inc.* v. *The Government of Canada*, award on the merits of phase 2, paras. 84–88.

[89] *Pope & Talbot, Inc.* v. *The Government of Canada*, award on the merits of phase 2, para. 93.

investor arguably suffered from dual adverse effects with less stumpage fee reduction but at the same time higher export charge from the Super Fee. In response to this argument, the Arbitral Tribunal began with the recognition that there might be different treatments in the reduction of stumpage fee. However, this reduction did not fall into the jurisdiction of the Arbitral Tribunal. Second, the Super Fee did not distinguish between interior and coastal areas of B.C. and thus failed to rectify the imbalance arising from the difference in the reduction of stumpage fee. This failure did not discriminate against the claimant as it was the difference in the reduction of stumpage fee that placed the investor and other B.C. coastal softwood lumber industries in unlike circumstances.[90] Therefore, the Arbitral Tribunal held that the unlike circumstances between the investor and other B.C. coastal softwood lumber industries did not result from the challenged export control regime. Further, while the settlement regarding the Super Fee had a greater adverse effect on some B.C. softwood lumber enterprises, including the investor, than others, such settlement nonetheless aimed to avoid potential threat arising from the SLA. The Arbitral Tribunal thus considered Canada's implementation measures a rational choice of remedies and found no National Treatment violation.

In assessing the claim of National Treatment, the Arbitral Tribunal reached the conclusion that there was no violation of this obligation. It is interesting to note that both Canada and the Arbitral Tribunal relied heavily on GATT/WTO jurisprudence. This provides some evidence for the linkage between trade and investment regimes. On the one hand, an export control regime may be subject to the scrutiny of both international trade and investment regimes. On the other hand, the substantive rules embraced by these two regimes may be similar or identical. International adjudicators may refer to the jurisprudence of the counterpart regime for guidance in interpreting a pertinent obligation in question. National Treatment is a case in point.

Export Control Regime as Performance Requirements The second legal claim asserted by the claimant related to a performance requirement as set out for in Article 1106 of NAFTA. As provided, in connection with an investment in its territory of an investor of a Party or of a non-Party in its territory, no Party may impose or enforce the requirement 'to export a

[90] *Pope & Talbot, Inc.* v. *The Government of Canada*, award on the merits of phase 2, paras. 96–101.

given level or percentage of goods or services'[91] or enforce any commitment or undertaking to export a given level or percentage of goods or services; nor may any Party condition the receipt or continued receipt of an advantage on compliance with the requirement to 'restrict sales of goods or services in its territory that such investment produces or provides by relating such sales in any way to the volume or value of its exports or foreign exchange earnings'.[92] The argument advanced by the claimant was two-fold. On the one hand, with an export control regime gradually escalating export charges, the investor was required to export less than it would have if the export fee was not in place. On the other hand, due to the 'use it or lose it' designation of the fee-free quota regime, the investor was required to export to the amount set out by the quota or lose its fee-free quota.[93]

In response to this argument, Canada first pointed to Article 1106(5) of NAFTA and stressed that the enumerated performance requirements should be narrowly interpreted. Canada then relied on the ordinary meaning of Article 1106 and argued that performance requirements entailed compelling the observance of a mandatory condition. A *de facto* performance requirement did not exist. Canada further referred to the object and purpose of NAFTA and stressed that the provisions relied on by the claimant aimed to prohibit requirements to increase export or foreign exchange earnings. The measures in question did not fall within that scope. Finally, Canada submitted that the claimant's interpretation would effectively transform a prohibition on performance requirements into an export restriction.[94]

In assessing the arguments advanced by the disputing parties, the Arbitral Tribunal first referred to the Vienna Convention on Law of Treaties (VCLT) for guidance on the interpretation of the provision in question. From the outset, the Arbitral Tribunal agreed with Canada's position that, as informed by Article 1106(5), the performance requirements had to be interpreted strictly. Nonetheless, based on the ordinary meaning of the legal text as contained in Articles 1105(1)(a) and 1105(3)(d), the Arbitral Tribunal did not rule out the possibility that

[91] Art. 1106(1)(a), NAFTA.

[92] Art. 1106(3)(d), NAFTA.

[93] *Pope & Talbot, Inc.* v. *The Government of Canada*, UNCITRAL (1976), interim award by Arbitral Tribunal, 26 June 2000, paras. 47–49.

[94] *Pope & Talbot, Inc.* v. *The Government of Canada*, interim award by Arbitral Tribunal, paras. 50–57.

performance requirements may oblige the investors to export only up to a certain level. As the Arbitral Tribunal noted, '[t]he language of that Article is not expressly limited to the imposition or enforcement of a *higher* level or percentage of exports of goods and services but could admit equally the imposition or enforcement at *any* given level or percentage of those exports'.[95] In other words, if a country imposes a requirement obliging the investor to export the goods it produced only to a certain level, such requirement may be considered a performance requirement, and thus breach Article 1106 of NAFTA. Nonetheless, the Arbitral Tribunal went on to note that the export control regime functioned as a tariff-rate export restraint regime imposing different tariff-rates in accordance with the export level. While this export restraint regime did deter the investor from increasing its exports to the United States, such deterrence did not constitute a requirement for expanding, managing, conducting or operating a foreign-owned business in Canada.[96] In view of the Arbitral Tribunal, a requirement to oblige the investor to export only up to a certain level can be deemed as a performance requirement, and thus to violate Article 1115 of NAFTA. However, in this present dispute, the claimant did not make a valid case that Canada's export control regime constituted a requirement. Although the investor might be discouraged from exporting more to the United States due to the increased export fee, the investor was not prevented or prohibited from doing so. Therefore, such an export control regime did not constitute a requirement. This reasoning has significant legal implications. Once a trade export restriction has the capacity of 'requiring' an investor to export its products only up to a certain level, this trade export restriction may also constitute a performance requirement in the context of international investment law.

Export Control Regime as Expropriation The third legal claim asserted by the claimant was related to expropriation. According to the claimant, the export control regime had deprived the claimant's investment's ordinary capacity to sell its product to a traditional or natural market. The claimant further argued that the wording 'tantamount to expropriation' as contained in 1110(1) of NAFTA effectively expanded

[95] *Pope & Talbot, Inc.* v. *The Government of Canada*, interim award by Arbitral Tribunal, para. 74 (emphasis original).

[96] *Pope & Talbot, Inc.* v. *The Government of Canada*, interim award by Arbitral Tribunal, para. 75.

the scope of regulatory measures subject to compensation. Therefore, expropriation under the ambit of this provision was broader than that commonly understood in customary international law.[97] In response, Canada argued that the potential to access US markets was not a property right eligible for protection under Article 1110. While expropriation is not defined under NAFTA, under international law, it necessitated actual interference with fundamental ownership rights. 'Mere interference is not expropriation; rather a significant degree of deprivation of fundamental rights of ownership is required.'[98] Moreover, 'tantamount' simply meant 'equivalent', and was not intended to broaden the concept of expropriation. Further, a state was not required under international law to compensate an investor for losses suffered from non-discriminatory regulatory measures.

In conclusion, the Arbitral Tribunal agreed partly with the claimant and partly with Canada. The Arbitral Tribunal first pointed out that the true interests at stake were the claimant's investment's asset base, which was largely dependent on its being exported to the US market. Therefore, the investment's ability to sell its product to the US market was a property interest subject to the protection of Article 1110 of NAFTA. Besides, the Arbitral Tribunal did not agree with Canada on the contention that non-discriminatory exercise of policy power may completely escape the scrutiny of this provision. However, the Arbitral Tribunal held that in the pertinent case, the interference to the claimant's investment was not substantial enough to be characterised as expropriation under international law. As the Arbitral Tribunal explained, 'tantamount' meant 'equivalent'. Therefore, 'tantamount to expropriation' aimed to catch what was generally understood as 'creeping expropriation' and did not intend to broaden its scope. In the pertinent case, the only interference with the claimant's investment related to its capability to export to the US market. While this interference might reduce the export volume of the investment and diminish the investor's profit, the investment continued to export a significant volume to the United States and profited therefrom. Relying on *Harvard Draft* and *Third Restatement of the Foreign Relations Law of the US*, the Arbitral Tribunal held that in determining whether a particular form of interference constituted

[97] *Pope & Talbot, Inc.* v. *The Government of Canada*, interim award by Arbitral Tribunal, paras. 83–86.

[98] *Pope & Talbot, Inc.* v. *The Government of Canada*, interim award by Arbitral Tribunal, para. 88.

expropriation, 'the test is whether that inference is sufficiently restrictive to support a conclusion that the property has been taken from the owner'.[99] With the property being taken, the owner is no longer able to use, enjoy or dispose of it. Based on this criterion, the Arbitral Tribunal held that the interference introduced by the export control regime had not reached such extent that substantially deprived the investor's property and thus prevented the investor from using, enjoying or disposing of its property. Therefore, the Arbitral Tribunal rejected the claimant's claim based on expropriation.

4.3.3.2 SD Myers v. Canada

SD Myers v. *Canada* is also a dispute arising from the context of Chapter 11 of NAFTA, which relates to an export ban imposed by Canada on a toxic chemical compound known as PCB (Polychlorinated biphenyl). The claimant, SD Myers, Inc., a privately held company incorporated in Ohio, United States, is a company whose businesses cover original transformer oil testing, oil reclaiming, and rewinding, rebuilding and manufacturing transformers, and subsequently PCB remediation activities. Remediation of PCB consists of such activities as analysing equipment and oil with a view to assessing the level of contamination, and transporting the pertinent equipment and oil to a facility where the PCBs are extracted. After such extraction, the decontaminated equipment and oil are to be recycled.

In the 1990s, SD Myers became increasingly interested in the Canadian market given that PCB remediation activities in the United States had been constrained. A shareholder in SD Myers, a Myers family member, established Myers Canada in accordance with the Canada Business Corporation Act, with each member holding equal shares. Since 1980, the cross-border transportation of PCB between the United States and Canada had not been possible as the United States, under the Toxic Controlled Substances Act (the TSCA), imposed restrictions on the manufacture, sale, use, import, export and disposal of PCBs and PCB-contaminated waste. Exemptions could only be granted when the US Environment Protection Agency (US EPA) was satisfied that no unreasonable risk would arise from the activities. Similarly, Canada, in 1977, placed PCBs under the control of the Environmental Contaminants Act and prohibited the use of PCBs in new products manufactured or

[99] *Pope & Talbot, Inc.* v. *The Government of Canada*, interim award by Arbitral Tribunal, para. 102.

imported into Canada. This prohibition was also supplemented by PCB Waste Export Regulations 1990.[100] Therefore, when SD Myers sought to expand its business to Canada, it lobbied heavily to have the border opened. From early 1995, Canada was aware that the United States might open the border for the transportation of PCBs, though it was unsure about the exact timing and method. On 26 October 1995, SD Myers succeeded in obtaining enforcement discretion from the US EPA, valid from 15 November 1995 to 31 December 1997. This enforcement discretion, regardless of its lack of clear definition under US law, basically allowed SD Myers to import PCBs and PCB waste from Canada to the United States on the condition that SD Myers fulfilled detailed obligations attached to enforcement discretion. With the border on the US side opening, Canadian PCB disposing industries were worried about the potential adverse effects on their business and thus lobbied the Canadian government to impose an export ban on the Canadian side. An interim order and final order for an export ban on PCB waste were subsequently issued on 6 November and 28 November 1995.[101] SD Myers thus brought a claim under Chapter 11 of NAFTA, arguing that its investment was injured by the export ban imposed by Canada. The claimant's legal claims related mainly to National Treatment, prohibition of performance requirements and expropriation, which will be examined next.

National Treatment The first legal claim relied on by the claimant related to National Treatment obligation. According to the claimant, the export ban was not based on *bona fide* environmental or health concerns but aimed to protect the market share of Canadian domestic industries that undertook PCB remediation within Canada. In response, Canada argued that the export ban was a non-discriminatory regulatory instrument applicable to both domestic industries and foreign investors. Therefore, the obligation of National Treatment was not infringed.[102]

In assessing whether Canada's PCB export ban violated National Treatment obligation, the Arbitral Tribunal had to examine two

[100] *S. D. Myers, Inc.* v. *The Government of Canada*, UNCITRAL (1976), partial award by the Arbitral Tribunal, done on 13 November 2000, paras. 100–102.

[101] *S. D. Myers, Inc.* v. *The Government of Canada*, partial award by the Arbitral Tribunal, paras. 117–126.

[102] *S. D. Myers, Inc.* v. *The Government of Canada*, partial award by the Arbitral Tribunal, para. 241.

elements: like circumstances and different treatment. A finding of different treatments in like circumstances would then invite inquiry as to whether the different treatment of circumstances found to be 'like' is justified by legitimate public policy measures pursued in a reasonable manner.[103]

Regarding 'like circumstances', the Arbitral Tribunal referred to the WTO jurisprudence, which emphasised that great attention should be paid to the legal context in which the word 'like' appeared since the same word would have different meanings in different provisions of the GATT 1994. In translating this concept to the NAFTA context, the Arbitral Tribunal considered that various provisions in NAFTA and its companion agreement, the North American Agreement on Environmental Co-operation (NAAEC), constituted the legal context of Article 1102. The legal context put forward some important principles for the Arbitral Tribunal to take into account in determining the likeness of circumstances. These principles were the right of states to establish high levels of environmental protection without compromising their standards merely to satisfy political or economic interests of foreign states; the obligations of states to avoid trade distortion and the mutual supportiveness of environmental protection and economic development. The Arbitral Tribunal then referred to OECD practices in determining 'like situations', given that all NAFTA parties are members thereof. The Arbitral Tribunal thus concluded that the sameness of sectors (including economic sectors and business sectors) played a key role in defining the likeness of circumstances, and policy objectives should also be taken into account in this determination. After noting these considerations, the Arbitral Tribunal concluded that as SD Myers, Myers Canada and Canadian operators engaged in the same PCB remediation activities and may compete with each other, SD Myers and Myers Canada, from a business perspective, were in like circumstances with Canadian operators.[104]

Regarding 'different treatment', the Arbitral Tribunal pointed to two sets of factors to be considered: first whether the measure, on its face, appeared to favour nationals over non-nationals; second, whether the practical effects of the measure created disproportionate benefits for nationals over non-nationals. The Arbitral Tribunal then noted that

[103] *S. D. Myers, Inc.* v. *The Government of Canada*, partial award by the Arbitral Tribunal, para. 246.

[104] *S. D. Myers, Inc.* v. *The Government of Canada*, partial award by the Arbitral Tribunal, paras. 243–251.

while the export ban was imposed with intent to protect Canadian PCB remediation operators, such an intent did not necessarily result in a breach of National Treatment if the measure in question did not result in practical adverse effects on foreign investments. Based on this criterion, the Arbitral Tribunal then examined whether the export ban gave rise to a practical disadvantage for SD Myers. As the Arbitral Tribunal explained, to ensure the capacity for disposing of PCB waste and maintaining the economic strength of domestic operators were legitimate policy objectives; nonetheless, these objectives might be achieved by other means without infringing SD Myers' interests in exporting PCBs.[105] Based on this reasoning, the Arbitral Tribunal ruled that Canada, by imposing an export ban on PCBs, violated its National Treatment obligation under NAFTA.

The conclusion of the Arbitral Tribunal seems unproblematic. However, there are some interesting points to note. First, the Arbitral Tribunal identified different general principles and various considerations, such as the right of states to set higher levels of environmental protection and policy objectives in determining the likeness of circumstances; in reaching its conclusion, the Arbitral Tribunal seemed to rely solely on business considerations. Second, the Arbitral Tribunal used the term 'disproportionate benefit'. It is not entirely clear whether the Arbitral Tribunal intended to set a higher threshold for *de facto* discrimination. Indeed, in the subsequent analysis, the Arbitral Tribunal did not specify whether Canada's export ban had presented a disproportionate benefit for its national PCB remediation enterprises. However, this usage had been relied on by Canada in *Pope & Talbot* v. *Canada*, though the Arbitral Tribunal there did not accept this argument and held that *de facto* discrimination did not necessitate a disproportionate test.[106] Third, the Arbitral Tribunal pointed to subsidies to Canadian PCB remediation operators as an alternative; however, subsidies may be subject to challenge in the WTO dispute settlement mechanism under the Agreement on Subsidies and Countervailing Measures (ASCM). Most importantly, it is doubtful whether the same measure, Canada's export ban, would violate the WTO obligation on National Treatment even if such measure is aimed at protecting domestic

[105] *S. D. Myers, Inc.* v. *The Government of Canada*, partial award by the Arbitral Tribunal, paras. 252–256.

[106] *Pope & Talbot, Inc.* v. *The Government of Canada*, award on the merits of phase 2, paras. 64–67.

producers. The answer seems negative. The main reason relates to the fact that in the trade law context, what is at stake is 'like products' instead of investors/investments in like circumstances. Therefore, the question for the Panel/Appellate Body to decide is whether Canadian PCB waste and US PCB waste are treated in a non-discriminatory manner under the export ban. It appears that the export ban does not favour Canadian over US PCB waste.

Export Ban as a Performance Requirement The second legal claim asserted by the claimant related to performance requirements. According to the claimant, with an export ban, Myers Canada was forced to dispose of PCB waste in Canada and consume goods and services in Canada. The opinion of the Arbitral Tribunal diverged. The majority found that this was not a performance requirement case given that there was no 'requirement' contained in the export ban; however, one member was of the opinion that the export infringed Article 1106(1)(b) by requiring Myers Canada to 'achieve a given level or percentage of domestic content' in conducting or operating its business.[107]

Some observations may be offered here. While the Arbitral Tribunal opined that one had to look into the substance of a measure, it nonetheless stressed that it could not take into account any restrictions or limitations that did not 'fall squarely within the "requirements" listed in Articles 1106(1) and (3)'.[108] This position is in fact a bit ambiguous. If the Arbitral Tribunal takes a substantive approach, its task is to assess whether the export ban has the effect of dictating the result caught by Articles 1106(1) and (3). Second, the majority seemed to recognise that the export ban was indeed a requirement, though the majority did not read it as a requirement as defined in Articles 1106(1) and (3). In line with this reasoning, assuming that the export ban is a requirement and looking into the substance of this requirement means ascertaining whether this requirement dictating the result is caught by Articles 1106 (1) and (3), the gravity of the analysis should thus be whether such result is inevitable with the export ban in place.

The answer seems affirmative. Two dimensions may be explored regarding Canada's export ban. First, the export ban effectively prohibits

[107] *S. D. Myers, Inc.* v. *The Government of Canada*, partial award by the Arbitral Tribunal, paras. 270–278.

[108] *S. D. Myers, Inc.* v. *The Government of Canada*, partial award by the Arbitral Tribunal, para. 275.

and prevents the export of PCB waste. One may wonder whether this complete prohibition can be qualified as 'a certain given level or percentage of goods'. As the Arbitral Tribunal in *Pope & Talbot* v. *Canada* noted, the language of this provision is not expressly limited to the imposition or enforcement of a higher level or percentage of exports of goods and services but applies equally to the imposition or enforcement at any given level or percentage of those exports. A zero-level of exports seems logically to fall within the scope of this provision. Besides, with this export ban in place, Canada Myers was faced with two options: disposing of PCB waste in Canada, or leaving Canada. In this way, Myers Canada was effectively forced either to achieve a given level or percentage of domestic content as the minority opinion suggested, or to purchase goods and services produced in Canada as the claimant argued. No matter whether Myers Canada was forced to export its goods at zero-level or to achieve a given level or percentage of domestic content or purchase goods and services, this export ban is incompatible with the prohibition of performance requirements as set out for in Article 1105 of NAFTA.

Export Ban as Expropriation The third legal claim asserted by the claimant related to expropriation, with heavy reliance on the word 'tantamount'. The Arbitral Tribunal referring to the interim award of *Pope & Talbot* v. *Canada*, held that 'tantamount' meant simply 'equivalent' and did not expand the scope of expropriation as generally understood in public international law.[109] In rejecting the claimant's argument, the Arbitral Tribunal held that 'the term "expropriation" carries with it the connotation of a "taking" by a governmental-type authority of a person's "property" with a view to transferring ownership of that property to another person, usually the authority that exercised its *de jure* or *de facto* power to do the "taking"'.[110] Expropriation entailed the deprivation of ownership rights while regulation involved lesser interference. The distinction between expropriation and regulation protected a host state from potential complaints in exercising its power in economic or industrial policies. Expropriation often amounted to a lasting removal of an owner's ability to make use of his/her economic rights, though in

[109] *S. D. Myers, Inc.* v. *The Government of Canada*, partial award by the Arbitral Tribunal, paras. 285–286.

[110] *S. D. Myers, Inc.* v. *The Government of Canada*, partial award by the Arbitral Tribunal, para. 280.

some contexts and circumstances, partial and temporary inability to make use of these rights may amount to expropriation.[111] In this pertinent case, the export ban lasted around 16 months and was thus temporary. The competitive advantage of the claimant was prejudiced and the possibility for profiting from the PCB remediation activities was delayed. Nonetheless, such delay did not amount to deprivation of ownership right or substantial interference of the exercise of such right. The Arbitral Tribunal thus ruled that the export ban did not constitute expropriation.

4.4 Export Restrictions and Competition Law and Policy

Export restrictions may be situated in the interface between trade and competition policy, with the most notable example being export cartels. The dividing line between international trade law and competition law is that the former addresses trade barriers imposed by governments while the latter deals with private trade barriers. In contrast with international trade law, which is underpinned by the WTO legal system, competition law has no international regulatory framework and tends to be diffuse and diverse. National competition authorities are thus major regulatory agencies for private trade barriers. This section will begin by drawing the distinction between government measures and private measures, and then look at export cartels – a private form of export restrictions – with a view to exploring the linkage between trade and competition policy. Further, between the two extremes of government and private measures lies export monopoly, voluntary export restraint with the encouragement or support of governments and state trading enterprises. Moreover, if we see export restrictions from the perspective of private measures, they can take the form of vertical agreements and horizontal agreements. These issues will be examined in this section.

4.4.1 The Distinction between Government Measures and Private Measures

4.4.1.1 The Definition of a 'Measure' in the WTO Agreements

The term 'measure' appears in various provisions of the WTO agreements and the Panel/Appellate Body has delivered a rich jurisprudence

[111] *S. D. Myers, Inc.* v. *The Government of Canada*, partial award by the Arbitral Tribunal, paras. 281–283.

on this point. In exploring this concept, the Appellate Body in *US – Corrosion-Resistant Steel Sunset Review* first refers to Article 3.3 of the DSU, which provides as follows

> The prompt settlement of situations in which a Member considers that any benefits accruing to it directly or indirectly under the covered agreements are being impaired by measures taken by another Member is essential to the effective functioning of the WTO and the maintenance of a proper balance between the rights and obligations of Members.

In referring to this provision, the Appellate Body emphasises that the measures under the purview of the WTO Agreement are measures taken by another member. According to the Appellate Body, for the purpose of dispute settlement proceedings, there must be a 'relevant nexus' between the measures and a member. The Appellate Body then continues, '[i]n principle, any act or omission attributable to a WTO Member can be a measure of that Member for purposes of dispute settlement proceedings. The acts or omissions that are so attributable are, in the usual case, the acts or omissions of the organs of the state, including those of the executive branch.'[112] The key point here is whether an act or an omission may be attributed to a WTO member, which makes it possible to be subject to the review of the WTO dispute settlement mechanism. If an act or an omission is not attributable to a member, then it constitutes a private measure and thus falls outside the scope of WTO dispute settlement proceedings.

The prevalence of trade barriers taking the form of private measures gradually gains its weight in international trade given that governmental measures are subject to scrutiny of WTO dispute settlement proceedings. In circumventing WTO disciplines, domestic industries seek to erect trade barriers through private measures and thus breach no international obligations. As Brendan Sweeney observes, trade barriers taking the form of private measures cover 'a whole range of exclusionary tactics that may be employed by private actors to impede entry to a market, including horizontal and vertical exclusionary agreements and monopolistic practices, such as predatory pricing, price discrimination and refusals to deal'.[113] Therefore, private trade barriers are composed of three elements: vertical exclusionary agreements; horizontal exclusionary agreements;

[112] Appellate Body Report on *United States – Sunset Review of Anti-Dumping Duties on Corrosion Resistant Carbon Steel Flat Products from Japan* (*US – Corrosion-Resistant Steel Sunset Review*), WT/DS244/AB/R, adopted 9 January 2004, DSR 2004:I, 3, para. 81.

[113] Brendan J. Sweeney, *The Internationalisation of Competition Rules* (Routledge 2010) 26.

and monopolistic practices. In the context of export restrictions, private trade barriers may take the form of export cartels, and vertical and horizontal exclusionary agreements.

4.4.1.2 The Continuum of Government Measure, Private Measure and Hybrid

In addition to governmental measures and private measures, a hybrid may exist in between. Such hybrid measures refer to 'private measures that are approved, encouraged or tolerated by the local government'.[114] The government's involvement in private measures may be overt, or subtler and less transparent. In the continuum of government measures, hybrid and private measures, a key task is to clarify the scope of government measures and to conduct attribution analysis. Whether a measure can be attributable to government determines whether it falls within the scope of government measures and is thus subject to scrutiny of the WTO dispute settlement mechanism. On this point, the WTO Panel/Appellate Body has handed down a rich jurisprudence, especially in the context of subsidies and countervailing measures, and Japan's heavy reliance on administrative guidance in achieving its policy goals. In the context of ASCM, two pertinent issues are at stake. The first point relates to the definition of 'government', namely, whether a public body constitutes part of government and, if yes, what a public body is. Second, if a government acts through private entities, whether and under what circumstances can such acts by private entities be attributed to the government of a member and thus be regarded as government measures. In the context of Japan's administrative guidance, the WTO judiciary has to decide whether the measures as set out in the WTO agreements may embrace the government's actions without legally binding force. In addition, the grey-area measures prevalent in the 1980s led to some GATT panel reports and prompted the negotiators of the Uruguay Round to bring these measures into the discipline of WTO law under the Agreement of Safeguards (ASG). These grey-area measures may cover voluntary export restraints, orderly market arrangements or any other similar measures, and a WTO member is prohibited from encouraging or supporting public or private enterprises to adopt or maintain them.[115] When a WTO member is found to encourage or support public or private enterprises to maintain or adopt these measures, the encouragement or support in question constitutes measures

[114] Ibid.

[115] Agreement on Safeguards, Art. 11.3.

as set out in the WTO agreements and is thus subject to the WTO dispute settlement mechanism. Finally, a WTO member may rely on state trading enterprises in achieving public policy objectives through import and export restrictions as well as purchase and sales decisions. Given that state trading enterprises are granted special or exclusive rights or privileges and may take the form of national marketing boards, private enterprises or cooperatives, it constitutes the fourth of the hybrids that have a bearing on export restrictions. Next, I will examine these four types of hybrid measures.

4.4.3 *Four Types of Hybrid Measures*

4.4.3.1 Hybrid in the Context of the ASCM

Regarding the first question on the definition of 'government', the legal text of the ASCM provides a clear answer. According to Article 1.1(a)(1), 'a subsidy shall be deemed to exist if there is a financial contribution by a government or any public body within the territory of a Member'.[116] In other words, for the purpose of the ASCM, a public body is considered to be part of the government. With regards to the definition of a public body, there has been a subtle evolution in WTO jurisprudence. The early view suggests that 'an entity will constitute a "public body" if it is controlled by the government (or other public bodies)'.[117] Such view is manifested in several panel reports. In *Korea – Commercial Vessels*, the Panel is requested to determine whether the Export-Import Bank of Korea (KEXIM) constitutes a public body. According to the complainant, the KEXIM is established by and operated in accordance with a public statute, by virtue of which the government of Korea retains control over its decision-making. The Panel agrees with the complainant and rules that '[i]f an entity is controlled by the government (or other public bodies), then any action by that entity is attributable to the government, and should therefore fall within the scope of Article 1.1(a)(1) of the SCM Agreement'.[118] Such a view is also followed by the Panel in *US – Anti-Dumping and Countervailing Duties (China)*,[119] which is nonetheless reversed by the Appellate Body, limiting a public body only to those possessing, exercising or being vested with governmental authority.

116 ASCM, Art. 1.1(a)(1).

117 Panel Report on *Korea – Commercial Vessels*, para. 7.50.

118 Panel Report on *Korea – Commercial Vessels*, para. 7.50.

119 Panel Report on *US – Anti-Dumping and Countervailing Duties (China)*, para. 8.79. According to the Panel, 'interpreting "any public body" to mean any entity that is controlled by the government best serves the object and purpose of the SCM Agreement'.

The Appellate Body in *US – Anti-Dumping and Countervailing Duties (China)* first refers to the dictionary definition of a public body and finds that the potential meanings of the term 'public body' may encompass a wide variety of entities, covering entities that are vested with or exercise government authority and entities that are owned by the nation or community. This broad definition nonetheless raises the question 'as to what kind of authority or responsibility an entity must exercise or be vested with to constitute a public body in the sense of the SCM Agreement'.[120] The Appellate Body then refers to subparagraph (iv) as a context for further guidance in interpreting the term 'public body'. When a private entity is entrusted or directed by the government of a member to carry out functions that are normally vested in the government, the acts of such private entity will be attributed to the government and considered the existence of a subsidy. The Appellate Body thus views functions normally being vested in the government as an essential element in defining the scope of a public body in the context of Article 1.1(a)(1) of the ASCM. In conclusion, the Appellate Body holds that 'the concept of "public body" shares certain attributes with the concept of "government"'.[121] A public body within the meaning of Article 1.1(a)(1) of the SCM Agreement must be an entity that possesses, exercises or is vested with governmental authority.

The second question then concerns the attribution of the acts of a private entity to the government of a member. As noted previously, this relates the entrustment or direction of a government to a private entity in carrying out functions that are normally vested in the government. The terms 'direction' and 'entrustment' have also been addressed by the WTO Panel/Appellate Body on a number of occasions. The Appellate Body in *US – Countervailing Duty Investigation on DRAMS* first refers to the objective of Article 1.1(a)(1)(iv) of the ASCM to prevent the government of a member from evading the obligations of the ASCM by relying on a private entity to 'take actions that would otherwise fall within Article 1.1(a)(1), were they to be taken by the government itself'.[122] In view of

[120] Appellate Body Report on *US – Anti-Dumping and Countervailing Duties (China)*, para. 295.

[121] Appellate Body Report on *US – Anti-Dumping and Countervailing Duties (China)*, para. 317.

[122] Appellate Body Report on *United States – Countervailing Duty Investigation on Dynamic Random Access Memory Semiconductors (DRAMS) from Korea*, WT/DS296/AB/R, adopted 20 July 2005, DSR 2005:XVI, 8131, para. 113.

this objective, the finding of such entrustment or direction preconditions that the government of a member gives responsibility to a private body or exercises its authority over a private body with the aim of conferring a financial contribution to its domestic industry. Based on this interpretation, the Appellate Body continues to note that not all government acts amount to direction or entrustment. It would be difficult to identify in the abstract whether or not those actions constitute direction or entrustment.[123] However, the Appellate Body makes it clear that entrustment and direction does not equal delegation and command.[124] Therefore, in deciding whether a private measure falls into the scope of Article 1.1(a)(1)(iv) of the ASCM, the decisive point is whether the objective of the ASCM has been circumvented by the government of a member with reliance of the private body in question as a proxy to take actions 'that would otherwise fall within Article 1.1(a)(1), were they to be taken by the government itself'.[125] A characterisation of delegation or command seems to be of little help.

4.4.3.2 Hybrid in the Context of Japan's Administrative Guidance

The difficulty in distinguishing between a government and private measure, and in disentangling them, is manifested in Japan's practice of using administrative guidance in achieving policy goals. Japan's reliance on administrative guidance in regulating trade has been subject to several challenges in the GATT and WTO dispute settlement proceedings. In *Japan – Agricultural Products I*, the Panel was called on to determine whether the practice of administrative guidance constitutes a restriction as set out in Article XI of the GATT 1947. In that case, the Panel observed that administrative guidance plays a key role in achieving government policies through peer pressure and based on consensus. Given this particularity, the Panel decided to ascertain the nature of the measures based on their *effectiveness*. In other words, whether the practice of administrative guidance constitutes a measure in terms of Article XI:2 of the GATT 1947 relies on the effectiveness of the

[123] Appellate Body Report on *US – Countervailing Duty Investigation on DRAMS*, paras. 114 and 116.

[124] Appellate Body Report on *US – Countervailing Duty Investigation on DRAMS*, paras. 118.

[125] Appellate Body Report on *United States – Countervailing Duty Investigation on Dynamic Random Access Memory Semiconductors (DRAMS) from Korea*, WT/DS296/AB/R, adopted 20 July 2005, DSR 2005:XVI, 8131, para. 113.

administrative guidance in restricting the importation or exportation of a given product.[126]

In *Japan – Semi-Conductors*,[127] the Panel was again faced with Japan's reliance on administrative guidance in achieving policy goals and the complexity arising therefrom. This dispute relates mainly to the enforcement of an arrangement on voluntary export restraint between Japan and the United States, one central element of which was to monitor costs and export prices to third countries with a view to avoiding dumping. Japan argued that there were no legally binding rules involving these monitoring processes and thus no governmental measures falling within the scope of Article XI:1 of the GATT 1947. The limitation on exports was initiated by private parties in their own interests to prevent dumping and was thus not subject to dispute settlement proceedings. This argument nonetheless did not persuade the Panel. The Panel first noted that Article XI:1, unlike other provisions of the GATT 1947, did not refer to laws and regulations but used the broader catch-all term 'other measures'. 'This wording indicated clearly that any measure instituted or maintained by a contracting party which restricted the exportation or sale for export of products was covered by this provision, irrespective of the legal status of the measure.'[128] In recognition of the different degrees of intensity of government involvement in private actions, the task of a panel was to carefully assess whether the measures in question fell into the purview of Article XI:1, bearing in mind that 'government-industry relations varied from country to country, from industry to industry, and from case to case'.[129] With this variance taken into consideration, the Panel then put forward two criteria to determine whether a measure falls into the scope of Article XI of the GATT 1947. 'First, there were reasonable grounds to believe that sufficient incentives or disincentives existed for non-mandatory measures to take effect. Second the operation of the measures to restrict export of semi-conductors at prices below company-specific costs was essentially dependent on Government action or intervention.'[130] As the Panel explained, if these criteria were met, the difference between the measures in question and mandatory requirements was only

[126] GATT Panel Report on *Japan – Restrictions on Imports of Certain Agricultural Products*, L/6253, adopted 2 March 1988, BISD 35S/163, 242.

[127] GATT Panel Report on *Japan – Trade in Semi-Conductors*, L/6309, adopted 4 May 1988, BISD 35S/116.

[128] GATT Panel Report on *Japan – Trade in Semi-Conductors*, para. 106.

[129] GATT Panel Report on *Japan – Trade in Semi-Conductors*, para. 108.

[130] GATT Panel Report on *Japan – Trade in Semi-Conductors*, para. 109.

one of form and not of substance; the disputed measures should thus be considered measures caught by Article XI:1 of the GATT 1947.

Regarding the first criterion, the Panel noted that one of the main elements of the 1986 US–Japan Agreement was to monitor exports and costs to third countries with a view to preventing dumping. Japan had assured the United States that certain below-cost transactions would not take place. Japanese producers and exporters were fully aware of this obligation and potential adverse effects arising from the failure to implement it. In view of these circumstances, the Panel considered that the measures taken by Japan did not need to be legally binding to take effect, as there were sufficient incentives and disincentives for Japanese producers and exporters to comply with the informal administrative guidance.[131]

Regarding the second criterion, the Panel first examined the purpose and effects of the measures in question. In referring to Japan's communication to the United States that it had imposed production cut-backs and imposed stringent export licensing rules, the Panel observed that these measures were aimed at preventing below-cost sales in third countries. The Panel then examined the structure and elements of the adopted measures and found that the Japanese government played a decisive role in the supply and demand forecasts, and that the disputed measures heavily relied on government action. In view of these factors, the Panel thus concluded that the difference between a legally binding measure and administrative guidance in this present complaint is only 'a difference in form rather than substance because the measures were operated in a manner equivalent to mandatory requirements'.[132] '[T]he complex of measures constituted a coherent system restricting the sale for export of monitored semi-conductors at prices below company-specific costs to markets other than the United States, inconsistent with Article XI.1.'[133]

In the WTO era, the close cooperative relationship between the Japanese government and private sectors, and the difficulties in ascertaining government measures and private measures resulting therefrom, were again subject to the scrutiny of the WTO dispute settlement mechanism. In *Japan – Film*, the complainant argued that, with a close cooperative relationship between the government and private sectors,

[131] GATT Panel Report on *Japan – Trade in Semi-Conductors*, paras. 110–111.
[132] GATT Panel Report on *Japan – Trade in Semi-Conductors*, para. 117.
[133] GATT Panel Report on *Japan – Trade in Semi-Conductors*, para. 117.

Japan was able to restructure its photo materials distribution system in such a way as to effectively exclude foreign competitors without referring to legally binding measures, but merely soft administrative guidance. In this cooperative relationship, a lot of quasi-governmental agencies were established to facilitate the implementation of government policies. These quasi-governmental agencies were not acting independently of government authority or discretion. The complaint thus argued that measures adopted by these quasi-governmental agencies also fell into the scope of non-violation complaints, as set out in Article XXIII:1(b) of the GATT 1994.[134] The case before the Panel is thus whether the challenged measures were measures falling within the scope of Article XXIII:1(b) of the GATT 1994[135] and Article 26.1 of the DSU,[136] and thus subject to the WTO dispute settlement mechanism

In response to the complainant's arguments, the Panel started with a general consideration stating that the term 'measures' as used in Article XXIII:1(b) of the GATT 1994 covers a wider range than laws and regulations, extending to governmental actions without legally enforceable enactments. In the context of Japan, the government sometimes resorts to administrative guidance in order to achieve its policy goals. Regardless of the lack of legal binding force, compliance with administrative guidance 'may be expected in light of the power of the government and a system of government incentives and disincentives arising from the wide array of government activities and involvement in the Japanese economy'.[137]

From this departure point, the Panel then referred to the GATT Panels on *Japan – Agricultural Products I* and *Japan – Semi-Conductors* and held

[134] Panel Report on *Japan – Measures Affecting Consumer Photographic Film and Paper*, WT/DS44/R, adopted 22 April 1998, DSR 1998:IV, p. 1179, paras. 6.107–108.

[135] Article XXIII:1(b) of the GATT 1994 reads, '[i]f any contracting party should consider that any benefit accruing to it directly or indirectly under this Agreement is being nullified or impaired or that the attainment of any objective of the Agreement is being impeded as the result of (*b*) the application by another contracting party of any *measure*, whether or not it conflicts with the provisions of this Agreement' (emphasis added).

[136] Article 26.1 of the DSU reads, '[w]here the provisions of paragraph 1(b) of Article XXIII of GATT 1994 are applicable to a covered agreement, a panel or the Appellate Body may only make rulings and recommendations where a party to the dispute considers that any benefit accruing to it directly or indirectly under the relevant covered agreement is being nullified or impaired or the attainment of any objective of that Agreement is being impeded as a result of the application by a Member of any *measure*, whether or not it conflicts with the provisions of that Agreement ... ' (emphasis added).

[137] Panel Report on *Japan – Film*, para. 10.44.

that in deciding whether the measures in question fell into the scope of Article XXIII:1(b) of the GATT 1994, due regard must be paid to the context of the measures being taken and their effect on private actors. The Panel further referred to criteria put forward in *Japan – Semi-Conductors* and added that the incentives/disincentives test was nonetheless not an exclusive one. The decisive point was whether the government's non-binding actions, including incentives and disincentives, had given rise to adverse effects on competitive conditions of market access.[138]

In conclusion, the Panel declared that the WTO Agreement is an international agreement with obligations to which only national governments are directly subject, and the measures as set out in Article XXIII:1 (b) of the GATT 1994 refer only to actions and policies of governments, not to private measures. Nonetheless, some ambiguity exists when a private measure is connected with, or endorsed by, governments and may be attributable to governments. In this case, a private measure, with sufficient government involvement, is not immune to the WTO dispute settlement mechanism.[139]

4.4.3.3 Hybrid in the Context of Voluntary Export Restraint or Orderly Marketing Arrangement

A third type of hybrid measure relates to voluntary export restraints (VERs) or orderly marketing arrangements (OMAs) that are encouraged or supported by the government. In the context of extensive Japanese use of administrative guidance, one of the objectives was to implement the VER between Japan and the United States by establishing export agreements between exporters and producers with a view to maintaining minimum export prices. This was exactly the issue before the Panel in *Japan – Semiconductors*, where the Japanese government intervened through administrative guidance with a view to implementing its obligations under the Japan–US Arrangement. Government involvement may come from a foreign government when a VER is reached between the importing government and the exporting industry. The agreement may be reached before or after the commencement of import controls or, sometimes, contingency measures.

The Agreement on Safeguards (the ASG) sets out some disciplines by stating that 'Members shall not encourage or support the adoption or maintenance by public and private enterprises of non-governmental

[138] Panel Report on *Japan – Film*, paras. 10.45 and 10.49.
[139] Panel Report on *Japan – Film*, paras. 10.52 and 10.56.

measures equivalent to those referred to'[140] in Article 11.1 of the ASG. The measures under the purview of this provision cover 'voluntary export restraints, orderly marketing arrangements or any other similar measures on the export or the import side'[141] and extend to 'actions under agreements, arrangements and understandings entered into by two or more Members'.[142] Article 11.1 is thus wider in coverage than the concept that a VER or OMA generally entails as it addresses measures both on the export and import side. If a measure is adopted by the exporting or importing country that has the effect of limiting exports, but is not consistent with Article XIX of the GATT 1994, it may be captured by this provision.

In addition to government measures, Article 11.4 of the ASG further strengthens the disciplines on grey-area measures by prohibiting WTO members from encouraging or supporting non-governmental measures with equivalent effect to grey-area measures adopted or maintained by public or private enterprises. In this context, even though private measures adopted by enterprises fall outside the ambit of the WTO dispute settlement mechanism, the encouragement or support of WTO members is nonetheless a government measure subject to its scrutiny. Support or encouragement may come from an importing or exporting country. An importing country may be held to breach its WTO obligations if it is found to encourage or support enterprises to impose the equivalent of grey-area measures.

In this connection, what constitutes an equivalent to grey-area measures as referred to in Article 11.1 of the ASG is pertinent. Given that the objectives of the VERs or OMAs are to limit the quantity of exports, and consequently to afford protection, non-governmental measures adopted by enterprises must share the same characteristics. Further, given that this provision is situated in the context of the ASG, these measures must bear similar characteristics to those falling within the purview of Article XIX of the GATT 1994 and the ASG. An intriguing question would then be how this provision impacts measures adopted under other provisions of the GATT 1994 or other Annex 1A agreements, the most relevant example being price-undertaking under the Anti-Dumping Agreement. In fact, in the 1980s, a large number of VERs were generated from

[140] Art. 11.4 of the ASG.
[141] Art. 11.1(b) of the ASG.
[142] Art. 11.1(b) of the ASG.

anti-dumping proceedings.[143] With the imminent threat of definite anti-dumping duties, exporting countries or enterprises would be more willing to enter into 'voluntary' restraint agreements with importing countries. With the entry into force of the WTO Agreement, these VERs induced by anti-dumping proceedings have been subject to the regulation of the ASG. What is interesting is that, if the importing country continues its anti-dumping investigations, it tends to find domestic industry is being materially injured, or that there is a threat of being injured by dumping. Nonetheless, the importing country chooses not to impose anti-dumping duties but reach a price undertaking with the exporting industry dictating that the exporting industry raises the export price to a certain level. A price undertaking and a VER do share similar characteristics. As Michael Moore illustrates, in a perfectly competitive small country model, a maximum level of imports arising from a VER and a minimum import price level dictated by a price undertaking lead to the same result of higher prices, lower imports, increased domestic profits and higher domestic production compared to free trade. Both policies 'allow foreign firms to obtain identical quota rents in the domestic market'.[144] Further, a price undertaking may hurt domestic consumers more severely than quantitative restrictions under a VER given that a price undertaking gives domestic industry the upper hand over its foreign competitors.[145] Moore thus proposes that the ADA should be amended in order not to preclude foreign competitors from underselling domestic industry. Foreign competitors should be required to raise the export price only to the original free trade price; otherwise, it would allow domestic industry to reap excessive rent through the cartelisation of the national market.[146]

4.4.3.4 Hybrid in the Form of State Trading Enterprises

A fourth hybrid is state trading enterprises, which may take the form of national marketing boards, private cooperation or cooperatives. Economic scholarly works put forward different definitions focusing on state conduct of foreign trade, government monopolising of foreign trade

[143] On the interrelationship between anti-dumping proceedings and VERs, see, e.g., B. Peter Rosendorff, 'Voluntary Export Restraints, Antidumping Procedure, and Domestic Politics' (1996) 86 *American Economic Review* 544, 544–561.

[144] Moore, 'VERs and Price Undertakings under the WTO' (n 2) 308.

[145] Ibid. 308.

[146] Ibid. 308.

and government ownership of enterprises. Some scholarly work, from a functional approach, focuses on the determination of what constitutes a government agency or agency-backed entity on the essential conditions for exports and imports.[147] In the context of GATT/WTO law, Article XVII of the GATT 1944 lays down the definitional element of 'exclusive or special privileges' of state trading enterprises and dictates that such enterprises act in a manner consistent with the general principles of non-discriminatory treatment and solely in accordance with commercial considerations when making purchases or sales involving imports or exports. Given the lack of clarity in Article XVII of the GATT 1994 on the definition of state trading enterprises, the Understanding on the Interpretation of Article XVII of the General Agreement on Tariffs and Trade 1994 (hereinafter, Article XVII Understanding) puts forward a working definition

> Governmental and non-governmental enterprises, including marketing boards, which have been granted exclusive or special rights or privileges, including statutory or constitutional powers, in the exercise of which they influence through their purchases or sales the level or direction of imports or exports.

This working definition puts forward three elements. First, state enterprises may take the form of governmental or non-governmental and include marketing forms. Second, such state trading enterprises must be granted exclusive or special rights or privileges relating to purchases or sales. By virtue of these rights or privileges, state trading enterprises may be able to influence the level or direction of imports or exports. More elaboration is feasible.

Ownership is a key element in explaining the behaviour of state trading enterprises in influencing purchases or sales of imports and exports. Some are integrated into governments and some managed autonomously even though the governments are subscribed to their capital stock wholly or partially. A large number of state trading enterprises lie in between taking the form of parastatal organizations and institutions over which governments hold a minority of shares but exert influence. The nature and scope of exclusive and special rights and privileges differ. A state trading enterprise may be designated as the sole

[147] Karen Z. Ackerman and Praveen M. Dixit, 'An Introduction to State Trading in Agriculture' (1999) Market and Trade Economics Division, Economic Research Service, US Department of Agriculture, Agricultural Economic Report No 783, p. 2.

exporter/importer in a country or as the chief administrator of import/export licenses. They may also be authorised by the government to import for government inventories or export surpluses and empowered to set producer and consumer prices in the domestic market, or act as the exclusive exporter or distributor.[148]

Finally, regarding the influence on the level and direction of imports and exports, Karen Ackerman and Praveen Dixit categorise state trading enterprises into four types based on their ability to control the domestic market and foreign trade. Specifically, a state trading enterprise may control the domestic market, foreign trade, or both. A state trading enterprise which is able to control both the domestic market and foreign trade has the greatest potential to distort trade, followed by a state trading enterprise capable of controlling foreign trade but having to compete with private enterprises in the domestic market.[149] The restrictions on imports and/or exports by a state trading enterprise may be equivalent to tariff or export subsidy; other rules of WTO law may be applicable. The most relevant disciplines in the export dimension may be related to anti-dumping laws,[150] subsidies and countervailing duties.[151]

State trading enterprises are prevalent in agriculture sectors where the public policy objectives support domestic producers, price stabilisation for producers or consumers, and there is an assurance of reasonable price supplies.[152] In *Canada – Wheat*, it is disputed whether the requirement to act 'solely in accordance with commercial considerations' obliges state trading enterprises to act as commercial actors and thus excludes the possibility of public policy objectives of state trading objectives. The Panel, supported by the Appellate Body, held that state trading

[148] Ibid. 2–3; Bernard Hoekman and Joel P. Trachtman, 'Canada-Wheat: Discrimination, No-Commercial Considerations, and the Right to Regulate through State Trading Enterprises' (2008) 7 *World Trade Review* 45, 48–52; see also Ernst-Ulrich Petersmann, 'GATT Law on State Trading Enterprises: Critical Evaluation of Article XVII and Proposals for Reform' in Thomas Cottier and Petros C. Mavroidis (eds), *State Trading in the Twenty-First Century* (The University of Michigan Press 1998a) 87–88.

[149] Ackerman and Dixit, 'An Introduction to State Trading in Agriculture' (n. 147) 17–18.

[150] N. David Palmeter, 'The WTO Antidumping Agreement and the Economies in Transition' in Thomas Cottier and Petros C. Mavroidis (eds), *State Trading in the Twenty-First Century* (The University of Michigan Press 1998) 115–120.

[151] Gary N. Horlick and Kristin Heim Mowry, 'The Treatment of Activities of State Trading Enterprises under the WTO Subsidies Rules' in Thomas Cottier and Petros C. Mavroidis (eds), *State Trading in the Twenty-First Century* (The University of Michigan Press 1998) 97–114.

[152] Ackerman and Dixit, 'An Introduction to State Trading in Agriculture' (n. 147) 11.

enterprises are not necessarily used only for commercial purposes and may be established or maintained to carry out governmental policies or programmes.[153] In a broader challenge, it is disputed whether non-discrimination principles, as put forward in Article XVII:1(a) and commercial considerations in Article XVII:1(b), constitute independent obligations that entail a comprehensive competition law-like obligation. The Appellate Body answered in the negative and held that an inquiry of commercial considerations should look into discriminatory behaviour of a state trading enterprise in market practice. The task of a panel is not to make a general inquiry into whether a state trading enterprise is acting commercially, but to examine whether non-discriminatory principles are violated. Therefore, a comprehensive competition-law-type obligation does not exist under Article XVII for state trading enterprises.[154]

An export-oriented state trading enterprise may attempt to improve its terms of trade by achieving a higher price on the world market. This is rare but can be done when a state trading enterprise enjoys a large share of exports on the world market and thus acts as a price maker. For this to happen, the state trading enterprise has to hold back its exports and prevent other domestic producers from exporting. In such a case, therefore, the state trading enterprise is normally a monopsony in the domestic market. With an export ban in place and monopsony power in purchasing domestic products, the state trading enterprise may maximise its profit.[155]

Moreover, an export-oriented state trading enterprise will be tempted to pursue economies of scale in trading operations, which may attract challenges under competition law. It will be frequently accused of colluding to raise prices and/or limit the quantity of products delivered to the importing country.[156] In practice, the New Zealand Dairy Board (NZDB, now transformed into a farmers cooperative, Fonterra) has faced challenges under US anti-trust law as a price-setting and export cartel. The NZDB was established through parliament with the authority, inter

[153] Panel Report on *Canada – Measures Relating to Exports of Wheat and Treatment of Imported Grain*, WT/DS276/R, adopted 27 September 2004, upheld by Appellate Body Report WT/DS276/AB/R, DSR 2004:VI, p. 2817, para. 6.96.

[154] Appellate Body Report on *Canada – Measures Relating to Exports of Wheat and Treatment of Imported Grain*, WT/DS276/AB/R, adopted 27 September 2004, DSR 2004:VI, p. 2739, para. 145.

[155] Ackerman and Dixit, 'An Introduction to State Trading in Agriculture' (n. 147) 14.

[156] Anna Kingsbury, 'Should United States Antitrust Law be Applied to State Trading Enterprises in Agricultural Trade' (2004) 9 *Drake Journal of Agricultural Law* 185, 190.

alia, 'to acquire, pay for, and market such export produce as the Board may from time to time determine'; and 'to control the export of dairy produce other than dairy produce acquired and marketed by the Board . . . '.[157] In general, the NZDB was the sole purchaser and exporter of the dairy products of fifteen cooperatives of Zealand farmers. The NZDB established, under Delaware law, Milk Products Holdings (North America) Inc. (MP Holdings) as its wholly owned subsidiary for the purpose of holding the stock of other United States corporations. The NZDB also created Western Dairy Products, a Delaware corporation and a wholly owned subsidiary of MP Holdings, to act as the Board's agent in the distribution and sale of New Zealand dairy products in the United States.[158] By virtue of this arrangement, cheese importers in the United States had to purchase from MP Holdings and Western Dairy Products at the set price, and direct purchases from New Zealand farmers were not possible. The plaintiffs, two US cheese importers, thus filed a claim against NZDB based on Article 1 of the Sherman Act.

> This claim is asserted against New Zealand Dairy Board for injuries to plaintiffs' business and property caused by the inflation of export prices on New Zealand cheese that has resulted from the unlawful combination and conspiracy among the New Zealand Dairy Board and New Zealand dairy manufacturers that have collectively refused to sell dairy produce, including cheese, to United States importers in a free and open competitive market but have instead combined and conspired to create an export cartel.[159]

The critical question here is whether the fifteen cooperatives, the NZDB, MP holdings and Western Dairy Products are a single entity or multiple entities, as the Sherman Act makes the fundamental distinction between concerted and independent action. The court first opined that the requisite plurality of § 1 [of the Sherman Act] conspirators does not exist in this case unless the fifteen New Zealand dairy cooperatives or the dairy farmers who make up those cooperatives pursued 'diverse interests'.[160] Nonetheless, the Court did not reach a final decision as it, in the subsequent memorandum opinion, found that there was actual and material conflict between US antitrust law and New Zealand law with regards to the marketing of dairy products. This conflict enabled the defendants to

157 Dairy Board Act of 1961, New Zealand, Art. 14.

158 *Trugman-Nash, Inc.* v. *New Zealand Dairy Bd.*, 942 F. Supp. 905, at 911 (S.D.N.Y. 1996).

159 Ibid. 916.

160 Ibid. 919.

invoke the doctrines of act of state, foreign sovereign compulsion and international comity.[161] While the Court did not look into the substance of the claim based on antitrust law, it pointed to the relevance of competition law in regulating export restrictions, especially such restrictions that may be imposed by private entities collectively or individually, where GATT/WTO law is of limited help. Next, I will examine the private form of export restrictions.

4.4.4 Private Form of Export Restrictions

Private export restrictions may take the form of horizontal agreements between exporters, or vertical agreements between upstream and downstream producers. Enterprises may restrict their sales on their own initiative, generally known as 'refusal to deal', but such initiatives rarely work unless the party is in a dominant position. Horizontal private export agreements are normally referred to as export cartels. According to the OECD, an export cartel is 'an agreement or arrangement between firms to charge a specified export price and/or to divide export markets'.[162] In addition to hard-core cartels, cooperation in export-related activities between producers may take a wide range of forms, including exclusive export arrangements for members; refusal of association for exports to non-members; fixing of resale prices of foreign distributors or sales quotas and price-fixing agreements.[163] Similarly, when a horizontal agreement is reached among producers, it constitutes a production cartel. An illustrative example of a production cartel is OPEC, though that agreement is formed among national governments. Vertical agreements between upstream and downstream producers do not address exports per se, but prevent suppliers from providing industrial inputs, such as raw materials or components, to other competitors. This is generally known as an exclusive supply agreement.

Given that export agreements, horizontal or vertical, involve no government measures and are permitted in many countries, they fall outside the ambit of the WTO Agreement and are thus not subject to the WTO dispute settlement mechanism. Although there are some efforts in the

[161] *Trugman-Nash, Inc.* v. *New Zealand Dairy Bd.*, 954 F. Supp. 733 at 736 (S.D.N.Y. 1997).

[162] R. S. Khemani and D. M. Shapiro (eds), *Glossary of Industrial Organisation Economics and Competition Law* (OECD 1993) 43.

[163] Florian Becker, 'The Case of Export Cartel Exemptions: Between Competition and Protectionism' (2007) 3 *Journal of Competition Law and Economics* 97, 100.

WTO to attempt to address competition issues, in particular in the Working Group on Trade and Competition Policy (the WGTCP), no significant progress has been made. Further, unlike trade regimes, there is no multilateral framework governing competition law, so competition issues are thus largely subject to the regulation of national frameworks.

4.4.4.1 Horizontal Agreement

Horizontal Agreements, explicit or implicit, between producers not to export, or to export only limited quantities, are generally known as export cartels, which sit between the interface of trade and competition policy. In a globalised economy, trade policy and competition policy deal with the same objective of the level of completion between producers, foreign or domestic, and are thus two sides of a coin.[164] An export cartel and its exemptions are particular manifestations of a competition policy for trade policy ends. Activities through which producers may seek to increase their collective profits, such as price fixing, limiting supply or other restrictive practices, are in principle prohibited by national competition laws, but export cartels are frequently exempted from similar restrictions.

While governments do not intervene directly in the market through trade policy instruments such as tariffs and non-tariff measures, the exemption of an export cartel on the grounds that it does not affect the domestic market but only impacts the targeted foreign country can occur, but such exemption harms its consumers and producers as much as barring its economy from exporting. State involvement in an export cartel varies from mere disregard through implicit exemption from competition law, or a lack of competition law, to active protection or encouragement, to state compulsion, or even the state itself being an economic actor. A strong form of state participation in an export cartel blurs the line between state and industry, and thus gives rise to the issue of state immunity. An attempt to challenge the practice of OPEC in US courts through anti-trust law eventually failed, as the court looked into the purpose of OPEC, which is to coordinate and unify the petroleum policies of the Member States.[165]

The effort to exempt an export cartel from the discipline of anti-trust law started with the Webb–Pomerene Export Trade Act (Webb–Pomerene Act) in 1918. The main motivation for this legislation was to

[164] Ibid. 99.
[165] Ibid. 99, 108–109.

encourage US industries to work together and advance their interests vis-à-vis powerful foreign cartels and to reduce the high cost of exporting, in particular on small and medium enterprises. This legislation nonetheless has domestic repercussions, as domestic prices may increase due to producers' coordination efforts. Regardless of this controversy, the position to exempt export cartels from the scrutiny of anti-trust law was reinstated and further expanded in the Export Trading Company Act of 1982 (ETC Act). As observed by Spencer Weber Waller, Congress expected the ETC Act to encourage the vertical integration of industries and formation of general trading companies; to contribute to the coordination and cooperation of competitors to exploit foreign markets by offsetting the power of the private cartel or foreign government; and to unleash the export potential of small and medium enterprises.[166]

EU competition law does not explicitly exempt export cartels. The foundational principles underpinning EU competition law are to prohibit 'all agreements between undertakings, decisions by associations of undertakings and concerted practices which may affect trade between Member States and which have as their object or effect the prevention, restriction or distortion of competition within the internal market'[167] and to prohibit the abuse of a dominant position within the internal market if such abuse 'may affect trade between Member States'.[168] Therefore, EU competition law only bites when competition within the internal market is restricted or distorted by anti-competitive agreements of undertakings affecting the internal market. In practice, export cartels obliging a participating enterprise to export a certain amount of products may prevent it from selling the goods where it is most advantageous, or prevent it from re-importing into the EU. The export cartel may restrict trade within the internal market and restrict its competition. Only then will EU competition law be applicable with the triggering of the 'effects doctrine'. To avoid being caught by EU competition law, enterprises may design their export cartel agreement in a way so as to have no effect on the internal market. Such a strict export agreement with no impact on the domestic market may introduce even more harm to targeted countries.

In view of this analysis, exemptions of export cartels from the discipline of competition law have come under challenge and a growing

[166] Spencer Weber Waller, 'The Failure of the Export Trading Company Program' (2005) 17 *North Carolina Journal of International Law and Commercial Regulation* 239, 240.
[167] TFEU, Art. 101(1).
[168] TFEUDPA, Art. 102.

number of policymakers are advocating the abandonment of such policies and their replacement with international cooperation on anti-trust enforcement. Four main arguments are advanced against the export cartel exemption. The first argument emphasises the information asymmetry between the exempting and targeted countries affected by export cartel activities, and argues for a positive comity by cancelling the exemption and thus enabling cooperation between those countries where export cartel activities are hosted and those harmed by them. The second argument challenges the policy rationale of export cartels, arguing that the major beneficiaries of export cartel exemptions are not small and medium enterprises but large multinational enterprises. Therefore, the pro-competitive and efficiency-enhancing argument for export cartel exemptions through coordination between small and medium enterprises is not sustained. The third argument relates to the North–South divide, as developing countries tend to be the targets of export cartels which worsen economic inequality between developed and developing countries. The fourth argument relates to free trade policies and argues that export cartels run counter to the objective of deeper market integration and freer international trade.[169]

The fundamental flaw of export cartel exemptions is the reversal of conventional jurisdictional doctrine in pursuit of 'beggar-thy-neighbour' policies. As long as the effects of export cartels are not felt in domestic markets, such anti-competitive measures will be exempted. As the territorial principle dictates, a state exercises its jurisdiction either in terms of its conduct or its result. In the context of competition law, an 'effects doctrine' is developed to overcome the jurisdictional constraint over anti-competitive measures adopted abroad but affecting the domestic market. An export cartel exemption is thus a jurisdictional renouncement of anti-competitive measures on the grounds of the absence of effect towards the domestic market. Only foreign targeted countries are harmed by export cartels. This brings about a 'race to the bottom' between countries, which eventually prevents competition in foreign markets, undermines market efficiency and harms consumers therein. Coordination between competition authorities at the international level to discipline export cartels is thus necessary. Unfortunately, as mentioned previously, limited progress has been produced so far.

[169] Margaret C. Levenstein and Valerie Y. Suslow, 'The Changing International Status of Export Cartel Exemptions' (2005) 20 *American University International Law Review* 785, 793–798.

4.4.4.2 Vertical Agreement

Vertical agreements between suppliers and distributors may contain various form of vertical restraints, including direct and indirect 'export bans', with competition law regulating such vertical agreements to different degrees. According to Article 1(1)(a) of the Block Exemption Regulation, Commission Regulation (EU) No 330/2010[170] defines a vertical agreement as 'an agreement or concerted practice entered into between two or more undertakings each of which operates, for the purposes of the agreement or the concerted practice, at a different level of the production or distribution chain, and relating to the conditions under which the parties may purchase, sell or resell certain goods or services'.[171] As for export bans referred to here, they are not related to those imposed by a trade nation, and thus constituting a government measure, but those imposed by private enterprises, and therefore subject to competition law. A typical example of such an export ban is a producer agreeing with a distributor that it will sell only to that distributor in a designated territory and that it will impose terms on other distributors prohibiting them from selling into that assigned territory. In effect, other distributors are banned by contract terms from exporting goods or services into the assigned territory.[172] Indirect export-ban may take different forms, including the use of monitoring clauses preventing or controlling parallel importing; price discrimination to prevent exports and withdrawal of discounts granted in case of reexportation to another Member State.[173]

Such an export ban is of critical importance to EU competition law, as its main objective is to ensure that the internal market is unaffected by anti-competitive measures of economic undertakings. In a nutshell, such an export ban is generally incompatible with 101(1) of the TFEU and will not be permitted under Article 101(3) except in exceptional circumstances. Accordingly, the Block Exemption Regulation, in Article 4(b) under the heading of territorial and customer restrictions, blacklists export bans and prevents such export bans from being exempted under Article 2 thereof. It should be made clear that Article 4(b) of the Block

[170] Commission Regulation (EU) No 330/2010 of 20 April 2010 on the application of Article 101(3) of the Treaty on the Functioning of the European Union to categories of vertical agreements and concerted practices, OJ L 102/1, 23 April 2010 (hereinafter Block Exemption Regulation).

[171] Block Exemption Regulation, Art. 1(1)(a).

[172] Richard Whish and David Bailey, *Competition Law* (8th ed., Oxford University Press 2015) 670.

[173] Ibid. 673.

Exemption Regulation deals with restrictions on the *buyer's* right to sell, but not the supplier's sales, which are not considered hard-core restrictions.[174]

The European Commission has launched investigations against a wide range of vertical agreements containing direct and indirect export bans, which subsequently have given rise to a number of cases before the Court of Justice in the European Union (the CJEU, formerly European Court of Justice). In *General Motors* v. *Commission*,[175] the Court was called on to rule on the legality of a Commission decision imposing a fine on General Motors BV on the grounds that General Motors BV adopted a general strategy aimed at restricting or preventing all export sales from the Netherlands, comprising a restrictive supply policy; a restrictive bonus policy excluding export sales to final consumers from retail bonus campaigns; and an indiscriminate direct export ban on sales to final consumers from other Opel dealers.[176] In challenging the legality of the Commission's decision, General Motors argued that 'the strategy was aimed solely at limiting irregular export sales to unauthorised resellers and not at restricting lawful export sales to final consumers or other dealers'.[177] In assessing the legality of the Commission decision, the Court of First Instance (CFI) held that the general strategy constituted an agreement with the object of restricting competition in view of 'the nature of the measure and the aims which it pursued, and in the light of the economic context in which it was to be applied'.[178] On appeal, the CJEU held that 'an agreement may be regarded as having a restrictive object even if it does not have the restriction of competition as its sole aim but also pursues other legitimate objectives'.[179] The CJEU continued to note that 'the case-law shows that an agreement concerning distribution has a restrictive object for the purposes of Article [101 TFEU] if it clearly manifests the will to treat export sales less favourably than national sales and thus leads to a partitioning of the market in question'.[180] Moreover, such an objective may be achieved not only by direct restrictions on exports but also through indirect measures.[181]

174 Ibid. 704.
175 Case C-551/03 P, *General Motors* v. *Commission* [2006] ECR I-3173.
176 *General Motors* v. *Commission*, paras. 17–18.
177 *General Motors* v. *Commission*, para. 24.
178 *General Motors* v. *Commission*, para. 39.
179 *General Motors* v. *Commission*, para. 64.
180 *General Motors* v. *Commission*, para. 67.
181 *General Motors* v. *Commission*, para. 68.

In *GlaxoSmithKline Services Unlimited* v. *Commission*, there was a challenge to a dual-pricing system and whether it had the effect of restricting parallel trade and infringed Article 101 of TEC, now Article 101 of TFEU. According to the Commission, GlaxoSmithKline Services Unlimited entered into an agreement with its Spanish wholesalers, charging the latter a lower price for domestic sales and a higher price for exports to other Member States.[182] The CJEU held that 'agreements aimed at prohibiting or limiting parallel trade have as their object the prevention of competition',[183] which is applicable to the pharmaceutical sector as well. The CJEU continued to note, 'an agreement between producer and distributor which might tend to restore the national divisions in trade between Member States might be such as to frustrate the Treaty's objective of achieving the integration of national markets through the establishment of a single market'.[184]

The formation and well-functioning of the internal market is one of the key objectives of the European integration project, and direct and indirect export bans have the effect of partitioning the national market and impeding the achievement of such an objective. It is not surprising that both the European Commission and the CJEU have held vertical agreements containing export bans illegal under EU law. However, from the perspective of the internal market, such an export ban to other EU Member States is in fact not an 'export' ban, but rather a barrier to the free circulation of goods and services within the internal market. Therefore, it may be a different story if the export ban is imposed against distributors *outside* instead of *within*. *Javico* v. *Yves St Laurent*[185] is a case in point.

In response to a request for a preliminary ruling from the Cour d'Appel de Versailles, France, the Court of Justice had to rule on the legality of a contract containing territorial restrictions for sales outside the EU, precisely, Ukraine, Russia and Slovenia (before accession). The question before the Court was whether Article 85 of the TEC, now 101 of the TFEU, should be interpreted 'as prohibiting provisions in that contract which preclude the distributor from effecting any sales in a territory other than the contractual territory, and hence any sale in the Union, either by direct marketing or by re-exportation from the contractual

[182] Case 501/06 P, *GlaxoSmithKline Services Unlimited* v. *Commission* [2009] ECR I-9291.
[183] *GlaxoSmithKline Services Unlimited* v. *Commission*, para. 59.
[184] *GlaxoSmithKline Services Unlimited* v. *Commission*, para. 61.
[185] Case 306/96, *Javico* v. *Yves St Laurent* [1998] ECR I-1983.

territory'.[186] While the Court recalled its case-law and reiterated considerations in assessing the legality of a contract containing territorial restrictions, the Court nonetheless ruled that, in the case of agreements intended to apply outside the EU, the contractual terms were to be 'construed not as being intended to exclude parallel imports and marketing of the contractual product within the Community but as being designed to enable the producer to penetrate a market outside the Community by supplying a sufficient quantity of contractual products to that market'.[187] As regards a clause obliging the distributor to sell the contractual product only in the designated third country, 'a market outside the Community cannot be regarded as having the object of appreciably restricting competition within the common market or as being capable of affecting, as such, trade between Member States'.[188] For the Court, the critical issue is whether competition within the common market is restricted and trade between Member States affected. As the agreement in question concerns only third countries and is not related to the internal market, Article 101 of the TFEU is not relevant. Moreover, the Court seems to imply that the agreement in question is justified by its contribution to the penetration of the market of third countries.

In addition to export bans imposed by suppliers on their distributors, a private form of export restrictions may be found in vertical agreements between suppliers and buyers, generally between producers and upstream industries, which oblige suppliers to sell only to one buyer, in general or for a particular use. Such vertical agreements between suppliers and buyers are widely referred to as exclusive supply agreements, or broadly exclusive agreements or exclusive contracts. Under EU competition law, the Guidelines on Vertical Restraint[189] published by the European Commission prescribe that such exclusive supply agreement may be exempted by the Block Exemption Regulation provided that neither market share of the buyer nor that of the supplier exceeds the 30 per cent cap.[190]

The main risk posed by an exclusive supply agreement to market competition is the anti-competitive foreclosure of other buyers. In

[186] *Javico* v. *Yves St Laurent*, para. 9.
[187] *Javico* v. *Yves St Laurent*, para. 19.
[188] *Javico* v. *Yves St Laurent*, para. 20.
[189] Commission Notice, Guidelines on Vertical Restraints, Brussels, SEC (2010) 411 (hereinafter Vertical Guidelines).
[190] Vertical Guidelines, para. 193.

appreciating the impact of an exclusive supply agreement on market competition, regard should be first paid to the market share of the buyer in the downstream market, which determines the capacity of the buyer to foreclose other buyers from accessing supply, and 30 per cent of market share is indicative of such capacity. Therefore, the market position of the buyer is critical. If other potential buyers are in a similar position, they are able to offer similar or better conditions to the upstream supplier and foreclosure of the market is unlikely. If the buyer possesses a dominant position in the market, an exclusive supply agreement is likely to have anti-competitive effects.[191] From the perspective of suppliers, the countervailing power of suppliers is also critical in assessing the potential foreclosure. A powerful supplier will not easily agree to be prevented from access to other potential buyers. Moreover, entry barriers at the supply level are also relevant in that, if other buyers are able to secure supply through upstream integration, then market foreclose is not an issue.[192]

Under US anti-trust law, exclusive supply agreements may fall under the purview of the Sherman Act, as such agreements are exclusionary in that 'they can exclude those competitors from the marketplace or materially handicap their ability to compete'[193] by denying competitors access to the goods or services (inputs) offered by suppliers. Exclusive supply agreements are not necessarily illegal, as they may introduce efficiency, ensure product quality and strengthen supplier loyalty, and are normally appraised by the court on a case-by-case basis in accordance with the rule of reason. Under conventional US anti-trust analysis, courts will not look critically at such exclusive supply agreements, which fall within the scope of vertical restraints in general, and exclusive dealings in particular, unless there is evidence of market power on the party benefiting from the restraint.[194]

That said, in cases where a dominant input buyer insists on its suppliers refusing to deal with other competing buyers, it may preclude or limit its competitors from accessing essential inputs.[195] *FTC v. Mylan*[196] is a case in point. Mylan is a drug manufacturer of both branded and generic drugs. Although the generic drugs are chemically

[191] Vertical Guidelines, paras. 194 and 196.
[192] Vertical Guidelines, paras. 197–198.
[193] A. Douglas Melamed (2006) 73 *Antitrust Law Journal* 375, 375.
[194] Peter C. Carstensen, *Competition Policy and the Control of Buyer Power: A Global Issue* (Edward Elgar 2017) 221.
[195] Ibid. 98.
[196] *FTC* v. *Mylan Labs Inc.*, 62 F. Supp. 2d 25 (D.D.C. 1999).

identical versions of branded drugs, they are sold at substantially reduced prices. The entry into market of a generic drug necessitates the approval of the Food and Drug Administration (FDA) to establish that it is therapeutically equivalent to the branded drug. A generic drugs manufacturer that purchases the Active Pharmaceutical Ingredient (API) from a specialty chemical manufacturer (API Supplier) with a view to selling the API in the United States has to file a Drug Master File (DMF) with the FDA explaining the processes that the API supplier uses to make the API and to test chemical equivalence and bioequivalence to the brand product. Profarmaco is an Italian company specialised in producing such API and has distributors in the United States, one being Gyma, from which Mylan purchases the API.

Mylan entered into a contract with Profarmaco and Gyma with an exclusive license for ten years. Under the terms of this contract, Mylan would control the supply of the API from Profarmaco into the United States and prevent other distributors from selling the API. In so doing, Mylan would deny its competitors access to the most important ingredient for producing the generic drugs in question. Subsequently, Mylan raised the price of the generic drugs by between 1,900 and over 3,200 per cent, which invited an investigation by the Federal Trade Commission (FTC). This complaint was finally settled and Mylan agreed to pay 100 million USD.[197]

With regards to the legality of exclusive dealing, it is observed that US case-law has experienced four periods of changes. Prior to the enactment of the Clayton Act in 1914, exclusive dealing was regarded as partial restraint and generally upheld except when it led to actual monopoly. From the Clayton Act through *Tempa Electric*[198] in 1961, the courts were largely concerned with market foreclosure. When competitors were foreclosed from a substantial portion of the relevant market, such exclusive agreements were normally struck down. Between *Tempa Electric* and the 1990s, the focus shifted to the potential benefits brought to consumers, with increasing doubts about the harm done to competition due to exclusive dealing agreements. Therefore, exclusive agreements were generally upheld except when the percentage of market foreclosure was very high. Since 1997, the Courts have come to realise the importance of

[197] See www.ftc.gov/enforcement/cases-proceedings/9810146/mylan-laboratories-inc-cambrex-corporation-profarmaco-sri-gyma.

[198] *Tempa Elec. Co.* v. *Nashville Coal Co.*, 365 US 320 (1961).

the effects of exclusive dealing agreements on the parties' market power, as reflected by the threat of increasing price and restriction on output.[199]

4.5 Short Conclusion

Integration of the globalised economy, with the advancement of ICT technologies, has led to fragmentation of production processes, which were allocated to their lowest-cost production sites. The internationalisation of production processes introduces a unique phenomenon that a trade nation may both export and import products in some sectors; the overlapping of such comparative advantage and disadvantage is one of the key features of supply chain trade. Global supply chains have brought about a phenomenon that exports of final products are composed of imports of intermediate inputs traded across borders, and make it possible for developing countries to benefit from economic globalisation without having to build their own production network.

With the internationalisation of production processes and multiplication of jurisdictions involving in these processes, global supply chains can be easily interrupted through weakest links. The fragmentation of production processes and internationalisation of supply chains complicate coordination and risk management, which necessitates a fresh look at the governance mechanism. Different approaches are advanced to design and explain the functioning of the global supply chain. An important way to examine the governance of global supply chains is to look into the coordination and power structure between buyers and suppliers with the extremes being hierarchy and market. Control over global supply chains can be achieved through investment with ownership or captive global supply chains via exclusive supply agreements. With regards to market logic, competition law plays a critical role in ensuring that supply is not disrupted through anti-competitive practices, such as export cartels and abuse of dominant power in horizontal and vertical agreements.

In linking export restrictions to investment law and policies, two types of investment, in terms of John Dunning's typology, are most relevant: resource-seeking and strategic asset-seeking investments. The interaction of export restrictions and investment law and policies can be observed from two perspectives: producers v. consumers; outbound

[199] Jonathan M. Jacobson, 'Exclusive Dealing, "Foreclosure," and Consumer Harm' (2002) 70 *Antitrust Law Journal* 311, 312.

v. inbound. Enterprises or countries (consumers) in need of natural resources may use investment strategies as a means to circumvent trade export restrictions and to secure the supply of raw materials. Countries rich in natural resources (producers) may be tempted to impose export restrictions with a view to attracting foreign direct investment, or to promoting industrial restructuring, and thus fostering high valued added industries. With the imposition of export restrictions, domestic prices of the relevant materials will decrease relative to global prices. This price differential constitutes a comparative advantage to domestic downstream processers. This price differential and the resultant comparative advantage may attract foreign direct investment to establish processing industries in that country. Therefore, export restrictions may have investment diversion effects.

However, not all countries imposing export restrictions welcome investments, as countries may not like their economic fruit reaped by foreign enterprises. A country imposing export restrictions on natural resources or strategic assets, such as critical components, may use trade (export restrictions) and investment measures (investment screen mechanism) simultaneously to prevent foreign countries or enterprises from accessing them. Such dynamics in export control and investment review are most vividly seen in the recent revision of the Foreign Investment Risk Review Modernization Act of 2018 (FIRRMA) and Export Control Reform Act of 2018 (ECRA) under the Trump Administration. These two pieces of legislation have effectively strengthened US investment review mechanisms in screening inbound investment and preventing emergent or foundational technologies from being exported. Similar legislative attempt can also be seen in the EU FDI Screening Regulation.

Export restrictions may be situated in the interface between trade and competition policy, with the most notable example being export cartels. The dividing line between international trade law and competition law is that the former addresses trade barriers imposed by governments while the latter deals with private trade barriers, even though it is sometimes difficult to distinguish the governmental and private nature of trade barriers. In the continuum between government measures and private measures there is a hybrid, where private measures are approved, encouraged or tolerated by the government. Such hybrids include where a government entrusts or directs a private body to carry out government functions; administrative guidance in the Japanese context; grey-area measures such as voluntary export restraints or orderly marketing arrangements; and state trading enterprises. These hybrids, in view of the involvement of government authorities may be subject to review of the WTO dispute settlement mechanism. Moreover, an export-oriented state trading enterprise will be tempted to pursue economies of scale in trading operations, which may attract challenges under competition law. It will be frequently accused of colluding to raise prices and/or limit the quantity of products delivered to the importing country. The lawsuit against the New Zealand Dairy Board under the Sherman Act is a case in point.

Moving beyond hybrids to private forms of export restrictions, which may take the form of horizontal and vertical restrictive agreements, competition law comes into play. As regards horizontal restrictive agreements, US anti-trust law has explicitly excluded its application if the export cartel does not produce adverse effects on the US domestic market. Although the EU does not exempt export cartels, if such cartel does not affect trade between Member States or restrict competition within the internal market, it remains outside the purview of EU competition law. As regards vertical restrictive agreements, the abuse of dominant market power is of critical importance. Nonetheless, as the fundamental objective is to ensure the free circulation of goods and services within the internal market, the outreach of EU competition law is different when it comes to trade within the internal market and trade with third countries. Thus, an 'export ban' to prevent distributors from re-exporting a product from one EU Member State to another is strictly prohibited; however, if a vertical agreement including such an export ban prevents distributors from exporting to third countries outside the EU, such vertical restrictive agreements may not be caught by EU competition law since they do not affect trade or competition in the internal market. Under US anti-trust law, vertical restrictive agreements, notably exclusionary ones, may be held illegal if they can exclude competitors from the marketplace or materially handicap their ability to compete.

5

Conclusion

Reconfiguring the Global Supply Chain in the Post–COVID-19 Era

The COVID-19 pandemic is broadly impacting global supply chains, with enterprises being prevented from producing and shipping raw inputs, semi-finished articles and end products, and governments adopting and maintaining exporting restrictions on ventilators, masks, gloves, personal protective equipment (PPE) and relevant inputs.[1] The pandemic has amplified and accelerated the decoupling of US–China economic relations, reflecting US President Trump's maxim 'economic security is national security'[2], manifested in a US–China trade war with numerous trade measures, including sanctions against Zhongxing Telecommunications Equipment Corporation (ZTE) and Huawei. The pandemic has strengthened the United States' determination to reconfigure its global supply chains with 'reliable partners', encouraging or forcing US enterprises to move out of China either back to the United States or to its allies, such as India. Thus President Trump has declared, '[t]his pandemic has underscored the crucial importance of building up America's economic independence, reshoring our critical supply chains and protecting America's scientific and technological advances'.[3] This statement reflects a reversal of economic globalisation, which used to posit economic interdependence as a safeguard of national security, but there is now a theory that overdependence is a threat to national security. In this context, there is a need for a fresh look at the law and politics on export restrictions and sombre thought on the restructure of the global supply chains. Three key elements will be of critical importance in the

[1] See WTO, Export Prohibition and Restrictions: Information and Note, 23 April 2020; Joost Pauwelyn, 'Export Restrictions in Times of Pandemic: Options and Limits under International Trade Agreements' (2020) 54 *Journal of World Trade* 727 Timothy Meyer, 'Trade Law and Supply Chain Regulation in a Post-COVID World' (2020) 114 *American Journal of International Law* (forthcoming).

[2] National Security Strategy of the United States of America (NSS), December 2017, p. 3.

[3] Remarks by President Trump on Actions against China, 30 May 2020, available at www.whitehouse.gov/briefings-statements/remarks-president-trump-actions-china/.

post–COVID-19 world: 'beggar-thy-neighbour', economic security and the decoupling of the US–China economy.

'Beggar-thy-neighbour' commercial policies, notably, the Hawley-Smoot Act and the spiralling escalation of tariffs leading to economic depression and the catastrophe of the second World War, are what the post-war international economic order, underpinned by the GATT/WTO, has attempted to address. The policy objectives and the gravity of the GATT/WTO rules and commitments focusing on the liberalisation of import tariffs and non-tariff barriers illustrate that trade nations were, and are still, largely concerned with access to foreign markets for their exports. Given this export bias, the GATT/WTO system touches only lightly on export restrictive measures, as most trading nations, and their domestic producers, are happy to see less competition from foreign countries. If a trading nation chooses not to export its products, such a restriction introduces little harm to other countries. Therefore, GATT/WTO law only addressed export restrictive measures exceptionally under Article XI of the GATT by prohibiting quantitative restrictions. The weaknesses of such an export-biased regulatory regime are exposed when resource-rich countries, from time to time, impose export restrictions or export tariffs, such as *China – Raw Materials* and *China – Rare Earths*, subsequently exemplified by the interruption of the global supply chain in a globalised world, the United States' export restrictions against Huawei being the prime example.

In attempting to redress the legal lacuna, trade nations, in the context of regional integration, impose more stringent rules on export restrictions, as can be seen in the laws of the EU and NAFTA, and its successor the USMCA. The weakness of this approach is that such rules are of only limited geographic application. Second, when resource-rich countries enter the WTO, country-specific obligations and commitments are demanded by existent WTO members. Such bilateral rule-making through accession negotiations has its pitfalls, as it undermines the spirit of multilateralism and such country-specific rules and obligations pose a thorny interpretative question as to the relationship between such obligations and multilateral WTO agreements. The application of the Article XX exception under the GATT 1994 to China's Accession Protocol and Russia Working Party Report is a case in point.

The controversies associated with export restrictions, generally known as export controls in the context of sanctions and public international law, are exacerbated by the dissolution of the COCOM and the limited regulatory force of the Wassenaar Arrangement. During the Cold War, when the world was divided between East and West, free trade only existed within the Western camp, and trade between the East and West was subject to strict regulation by the COCOM, if not prohibited. In this context, free trade in the context of the GATT, which was designed by market economies for market economies, was complemented by controlled trade under the COCOM. The fall of the Berlin Wall and dissolution of the Soviet Union introduced great challenges to the GATT/WTO system, as formerly controlled economies and transitional economies joined the WTO. East–West trade, originally subject to COCOM regulation, came under the purview of the WTO. Moreover, with the advance of technology and its sophistication and wider application, the line between civilian, dual-use and strategic products blurred. In combination with greater geographical coverage there was economic structural diversification of WTO membership and complexity of goods and services; thus the regulating or restricting of trade in the name of national security or considerations of international political economy surfaced as a challenge facing the WTO.

The multiplication of measures invoking national security exceptions in the past few years is an inevitable result of the combined effects of greater WTO geographical coverage, economic structural diversification and greater product complexity. Legally, the critical issue surrounding the debate over the national security exception is whether such an exception is 'self-judging' and thus to be exempted from judicial review. Politically, one has to be aware that the GATT/WTO regime was originally designed to regulate civilian trade and promote free trade within market economies. Considerations based on international political economy or national security concerns are not areas with which the GATT/WTO is familiar. Constitutionally, one has to bear in mind the shift in decision-making from 'positive consensus' to 'negative consensus'; by virtue of this power-shift, it is inevitable that there will be an endorsement of the WTO adjudicators' authority to rule on the justification of the national security exception. A single WTO member, unlike any GATT contracting party, is not in a position to carve out the terms of reference of a panel, or to block its decision if it finds it unsatisfactory.

Moving beyond the WTO, the spectre of 'beggar-thy-neighbour' commercial policies lingers. States impose export restrictions with a view to attracting investment, diversifying their economies or providing a comparative advantage to domestic producers. Other countries, and their enterprises, aim to circumvent these export restrictions through investment policies but may face obstacles under investment screening mechanisms. As the US–China trade war reveals, export restrictions on critical components under the EAR, in conjunction with investment screening under the

CFIUS, exemplify their effect in excluding an adversary or any third country from global supply chains or disrupting their supply security.

Moreover, state domestic competition law and policies share similar characteristics. The exemption of export cartels under US anti-trust law and EU competition law on the grounds that these do not adversely affect the domestic market is an illustrative example. The fact that an EU supplier, in the context of vertical restrictive agreements, is not prevented from prohibiting its distributor from re-exporting to third countries outside the Union is also a case in point. In a globalised economy where production processes are fragmented and distributed across jurisdictions, global supply chains may be severely disrupted and undermined through export restrictive measures, and such measures can be imposed both by governments and private entities – powerful multinational enterprises in particular. In export restrictions, the link between trade, investment and competition is evident.

In responding to, and regulating, export restrictions, redress can be sought at three levels. At the WTO level, new rules on export restrictions may be negotiated, though the prospect is not so promising in view of challenges facing the multilateral trading system. Moreover, as export restrictions are generally imposed for the purposes of food security and national security, the delicate institutional balance between WTO legislative function and judicial function and allocation of power between the WTO and members may give rise to great controversies. The potential erosion of national sovereignty or regulatory autonomy prevents negotiations in the WTO from moving to discipline export restrictions. At the national level, states consuming or producing natural resources and raw materials have different attitudes towards export restrictions, and subsequently adopt different strategies in attracting foreign direct investment and diversifying their economic structures. Similarly, at the firm level, upstream producers and downstream producers have different approaches to complying with, or circumventing, export restrictions, and relocation through investment is an important policy instrument in this connection. Moreover, as both buyers and suppliers in the global supply chain may impose vertical and horizontal exclusive agreements – a private form of export restrictions – a balance is to be struck between the security of supply chain management and the abuse of dominant power. In the context of global supply chain, trade, investment and competition all play a key role in disciplining export restrictions, while the shadow of international political economy and the ghost of 'beggar-thy-neighbour' policies linger.

Economic security is a reactionary response to economic interdependence arising from trade liberalisation and economic integration which aims for self-sufficiency, and export restrictions/control are a key instrument for achieving it.[4] The idea of economic security is embodied in the fear that a nation that is economically dependent on others, in particular its adversaries, is doomed to be weakened and dominated by them. Such is emphasised by geo-economics positing a state of economic 'warfare',[5] which presupposes that economic performance predetermines a country's military capacity, or projection of power.[6] Such strategic thinking is embraced by the Trump Administration, and the COVID-19 pandemic exposes and exacerbates such compelling need. As President Trump declared, '[t]his pandemic has underscored the crucial importance of building up America's *economic independence*, reshoring our critical supply chains and protecting America's scientific and technological advances' (emphasis added).[7] With a view to addressing the disruptions of the global supply chain and ensuring domestic sufficiency on health and medical resources, President Trump refers to the Defense Production Act (DPA) of 1950 and relevant laws to issue memoranda or Executive Orders to address *production*, *distribution* and *finance* issues. President Trump first noted his declaration of a national emergency, recognising the threat that the novel (new) coronavirus known as SARS-CoV-2 poses to US national security[8] and the WHO's announcement of the outbreak of COVID-19 as a pandemic.[9]

4 See Henry Farrell and Abraham L. Newman, 'Weaponized Interdependence: How Global Economic Networks Shape State Coercion' (2019) 44 *International Security* 42.

5 On geo-economics, see e.g., Edward N. Luttwak, 'From Geopolitics to Geo-Economics: Logic of Conflict, Grammar of Commerce' (1990) 20 *The National Interest* 17; Mikael Wigell, Sören Scholvin and Mika Aaltola (eds), *Geo-economics and Power Politics in the 21st Century: The Revival of Economic Statecraft* (Routledge 2019); Robert D. Blackwill and Jennifer M. Harris, *War by Other Means: Geoeconomics and Statecraft* (The Belknap Press of Harvard University Press 2016).

6 Vincent Cable, 'What is International Economic Security?' (1995) 71 *International Affairs* 305, 306–307.

7 Remarks by President Trump on Actions against China, 30 May 2020, available at www.whitehouse.gov/briefings-statements/remarks-president-trump-actions-china/.

8 Proclamation on Declaring a National Emergency Concerning the Novel Coronavirus Disease (COVID-19) Outbreak, 13 March 2020, www.whitehouse.gov/presidential-actions/proclamation-declaring-national-emergency-concerning-novel-coronavirus-disease-covid-19-outbreak/.

9 WHO Director-General's opening remarks at the media briefing on COVID-19 – 11 March 2020, available at www.who.int/dg/speeches/detail/who-director-general-s-opening-remarks-at-the-media-briefing-on-covid-19—11-march-2020.

As for the *production* dimension, President Trump determined that health and medical resources needed to respond to the spread of COVID-19, including ensuring the supply of PPE and ventilators, and meet the criteria specified in Section 101(b) of the DPA (50 U.S.C. 4511(b)),[10] and thus instructed the Secretary of Health and Human Services (Health Secretary) to

> use any and all authority available under the Act to require General Motors Company to accept, perform, and prioritize contracts or orders for the number of ventilators that the Secretary determines to be appropriate[11]

and the Secretary of Homeland Security, through the Administrator of the Federal Emergency Management Agency (Administrator), to

> use any and all authority available under the Act to acquire, from any appropriate subsidiary or affiliate of 3M Company, the number of N-95 respirators that the Administrator determines to be appropriate.[12]

As for the *distribution dimension*, President Trump instructed the Health Secretary to determine, in consultation with relevant agencies, 'the proper nationwide priorities and allocation of all health and medical resources, including controlling the distribution of such materials (including applicable services) in the civilian market, for responding to the spread of COVID-19 within the United States'.[13] The Health Secretary subsequently determined that fifteen categories of health and medical resources were scarce materials and that US domestic supplies will be threatened due to accumulation in excess of reasonable demands, or for the purpose of resale at prices in excess of prevailing market prices.

[10] The legal text reads, (b) Critical and strategic materials: The powers granted in this section shall not be used to control the general distribution of any material in the civilian market unless the President finds (1) that such material is a scarce and critical material essential to the national defense, and (2) that the requirements of the national defense for such material cannot otherwise be met without creating a significant dislocation of the normal distribution of such material in the civilian market to such a degree as to create appreciable hardship.

[11] Memorandum on Order under the Defense Production Act Regarding General Motors Company, 27 March 2020, available at www.whitehouse.gov/presidential-actions/memorandum-order-defense-production-act-regarding-general-motors-company/.

[12] Memorandum on Order under the Defense Production Act Regarding 3M Company, 2 April 2020, Sec 2, available at www.whitehouse.gov/presidential-actions/memorandum-order-defense-production-act-regarding-3m-company/.

[13] Executive Office of the President. Executive Order 13909 of March 18, 2020, Prioritizing and Allocating Health and Medical Resources to Respond to the Spread of COVID-19, 18 March 2020, 85 Federal Register 16227.

President Trump thus pronounced the United States' policy to prevent domestic brokers, distributors and other intermediaries from diverting such material overseas, and instructed the Department of Homeland Security, through the Administrator in consultation with the Health Secretary, to allocate the domestic use of scarce or threatened materials.[14] Naming the virus an *invisible enemy* with which the United States is at war, President Trump notes that the pandemic has led 'wartime profiteers to purchase domestic supplies of scarce and critical materials, hoard them while they engage in profiteering and speculation, and then export them can generate foreign demand, and lead to price gouging'.[15] Thus, it is essential to prevent critically needed PPE and other scarce or threatened materials from being exported and retain them in the United States to defeat the virus.

As for the *finance dimension*, as the overarching aim is to ensure the United States 'has the capacity, capability, and strong and resilient domestic industrial base necessary to respond to the COVID-19 outbreak',[16] it is thus the policy of the United States to 'further expand domestic production of strategic resources needed to respond to the COVID-19 outbreak, including strengthening relevant supply chains within the United States and its territories'.[17] With this aim, the US International Development Finance Corporation is authorised to offer 'loans that create, maintain, protect, expand, or restore domestic industrial base capabilities supporting: (i) the national response and recovery to the COVID-19 outbreak; or (ii) the resiliency of any relevant domestic supply chains'.[18] In addition, President Trump delegated authority under Title III of the DPA to 'guarantee loans by private institutions, make loans, make provision for purchases and commitments to purchase, and take additional actions to create, maintain, protect, expand, and restore domestic industrial base capabilities to produce such resources'.[19]

[14] Ibid.

[15] Statement from the President Regarding the Defense Production Act, 13 April 2020, available at www.whitehouse.gov/briefings-statements/statement-president-regarding-defense-production-act-3/.

[16] U.S. International Development Finance Corporation. Submission for OMB Review, 4 June 2020, 85 Federal Register 35418.

[17] Ibid.

[18] Ibid.

[19] Executive Office of the President. Executive Order 13911 of March 27, 2020, Delegating Additional Authority under the Defense Production Act with Respect to Health and Medical Resources to Respond to the Spread of COVID-19, 27 March 2020, 85 Federal Register 18403.

Finally, *decoupling of US–China relations* seems to be the trend for years to come, and a major aim and means under this trend is to establish a global supply chain with reliable partners, including Japan, India and Taiwan. Three key measures best represent this decoupling process: the investment of Taiwan Semiconductor Manufacturing Company (TSMC) in Arizona, enhanced efforts on export control against Huawei and the clean network initiative. Given the importance of chips in high technologies and the weight of TSMC in producing and supplying wafers, TSMC, and of course Taiwan, constitute key actors in the US–China economic competition and trade war. The undersecretary for Economic Growth, Energy, and the Environment, Keith Krach, termed TSMC's decision in Arizona 'a game changer for the U.S. semiconductor industry that will bolster American national security and our economic prosperity'.[20] Second, whereas Huawei has been added to the entity list and denied supplies from US enterprises without export licensing from the Bureau of Industry and Security (BIS), it still can obtain supplies from enterprises based in other countries taking advantage of US export control. Therefore, the United States decided to amend the Foreign Direct Product Rule such that foreign enterprises using US technologies to produce their own semiconductors are obliged to obtain approval from the BIS if they are to supply Huawei. Third, the United States intends to collaborate with its allies to form a coalition of trusted partners and establish a clean network, rooted in 'internationally accepted digital trust standards and is a reflection of [the US] commitment to an open, interoperable, and secure global internet based on shared democratic values and respect for human rights',[21] and covering clean carriers, stores, apps, cloud services and cables. Therefore, at least in the information and communication technology sector, the decoupling of US–China economic relations is foreseeable.

In the post-COVID-19 era, we will see further securitisation – a reaction against de-politicisation or constitutionalisation – of international economic relations and a heavy reliance on export restrictions. Two factors are driving this securitisation process. On the one hand, the

[20] Briefing on Taiwan Semiconductor Manufacturing Corporation's Intent to Invest $12 Billion in the U.S. and on the CCP's Ability to Undermine U.S. Export Controls, 15 May 2020, available at www.state.gov/briefing-with-under-secretary-for-growth-energy-and-the-environment-keith-krach-science-and-technology-adviser-to-the-secretary-mung-chiang-and-assistant-secretary-for-international-security-and-n/.

[21] The Clean Network Safeguards America's Assets (Fact Sheet), 11 August 2020, available at www.state.gov/the-clean-network-safeguards-americas-assets/.

accession of non-market economies, in particular China, to the WTO has intensified the economic exchanges between Western countries and former socialist countries. This form of *trading with enemies*[22] gives rise to the fear of economic domination by adversaries and constitutes a setback to global economic interdependence. On the other hand, technological advancement blurs the line between civilian trade and controlled trade (as well as dual-use goods); even civilian trade may pose a challenge to national security, especially in view of its broadened form covering economic security. With the aim of political mobilisation, identity distinction, and authority authorisation and justification, the Trump Administration has securitised US–China economic relations, and such securitisation process has spread to other countries/regions. As sovereign states aim to retain the final say on what their national security is by preventing the WTO judiciary from adjudicating on or interfering in this sensitive issue, the WTO Appellate Body is inevitably an immediate victim.

[22] See e.g., Meijer, *Trading with the Enemy: The Making of US Export Control Policy toward the People's Republic of China.*

BIBLIOGRAPHY

Abbott, K. W., 'Defining the Extraterritorial Reach of American Export Control: Congress as Catalyst' (1984) 17 *Cornell Journal of International Law* 79.

'Economic Sanctions and International Terrorism' (1987) 20 *Vanderbilt Journal of Transnational Law* 289.

Abbott, K. W. and others, 'The Concept of Legalization' (2000) 54 *International Organization* 401.

Ackerman, K. Z. and Dixit, P. M., 'An Introduction to State Trading in Agriculture' (1999) Market and Trade Economics Division, Economic Research Service, US Department of Agriculture, Agricultural Economic Report No 783.

Adamantopoulos, K. and Pereyra-Friedrichsen, M., *EU Anti-Subsidy Law and Practice* (2nd ed., Sweet & Maxwell 2007).

Akande, D. and Williams, S., 'International Adjudication on National Security Issues: What Role for the WTO' (2003) 43 *Virginia Journal of International Law* 366.

Alexandroff, A. S. and Sharma, R., 'The National Exception Provision: GATT Article XXI' in Macrory, P. F. J., Appleton, A. E. and Plummer, M. G. (eds), *The World Trade Organization: Legal, Economic and Political Analysis* (Springer 2005).

Alford, R. P., 'The Self-Judging WTO Security Exception' (2011) 3 *Utah Law Review* 697.

Amarasinha, S. D. and Kokott, J., 'Multilateral Investment Rules Revisited' in Muchlinski, P., Ortino, F. and Schreuer, C. (eds), *The Oxford Handbook of International Investment Law* (Oxford University Press 2008).

Anderson, A. D. M., 'An Analysis of the Proposed Subsidies Code Procedures in the "Dunkel Text" of the GATT Uruguay Round: The Canadian Exporters' Case' (1993) 27 *Journal of World Trade* 71.

Antkiewicz, A. and Whalley, J., 'Recent Chinese Buyout Activity and the Implications for Global Architecture' (2006) NBER Working Paper Series 12072.

Antoniadis, A., 'The European Union and WTO Law: A Nexus of Reactive, Coactive, and Proactive Approaches' (2007) 6 *World Trade Review* 45.

Arndt, S. W. and Kierzkowski, H., 'Introduction' in Arndt, S. W. and Kierzkowski, H. (eds), *Fragmentation: New Production Patterns in the World Economy* (Oxford University Press 2001).

Aubin, Y. and Idiart, A., *Export Control Law and Regulations Handbook: A Practical Guide to Military and Dual-Use Goods Trade Restrictions and Compliance* (3rd ed., Kluwer Law International 2016).

Bair, J., 'Global Capitalism and Commodity Chains: Looking Back, Going Forward' (2005) 9 *Competition & Change* 153.

Baldwin, D. A., *Economic Statecraft* (Princeton University Press 1985).

Baldwin, R., 'Globalisation: the Great Unbundling(s)' (2006) contribution to the Project *Globalisation Challenges for Europe and Finland*, organised by Secretariat of the Economic Council of Finland, 20 September 2006.

'Global Supply Chains: Why They Emerged, Why They Matter, and Where They Are Going?' (2012) The Graduate Institute Centre for Trade and Economic Integration, CETI Papers 2012–13.

Baldwin, R. and Lopez-Gonzalez, J., 'Supply-Chain Trade: A Portrait of Global Patterns and Several Testable Hypotheses' (2013) National Bureau of Economic Research, Working Paper 18957.

Basra, H., 'Increased Legalization or Politicalization? A Comparison of Accession under the GATT and WTO' (2012) 46 *Journal of World Trade* 937.

Becker, F., 'The Case of Export Cartel Exemptions: Between Competition and Protectionism' (2007) 3 *Journal of Competition Law and Economics* 97.

Benitah, M., *The Law of Subsidies under the GATT/WTO System* (Kluwer Law International 2001).

Bhala, R., 'National Security and International Trade Law: What the GATT Says and What the United States Does' (1998) 19 *University of Pennsylvania Journal of International Law* 263.

Bond, E. W. and Trachtman, J., 'China - Rare Earths: Export Restrictions and the Limits of Textual Interpretation' (2016) 15 *World Trade Review* 189.

Bourne, M., 'Controlling the Shadow Trade' (2011) 32 *Contemporary Security Policy* 215.

Carstensen, P. C., *Competition Policy and the Control of Buyer Power: A Global Issue* (Edward Elgar 2017).

Cass, D. Z., 'The "Constitutionalization" of International Trade Law: Judicial Norm-Generation as the Engine of Constitutional Development in International Trade' (2001) 12 *European Journal of International Law* 39.

The Constitutionalization of the World Trade Organization (Oxford University Press 2005).

Charnovitz, S., 'Mapping the Law of WTO Accession' in Janow, M. E., Donaldson, V. and Yanovich, A. (eds), *The WTO: Governance, Dispute Settlement & Developing Countries* (Juris Publishing 2008).

Chen, W., 'Screening the "Dragon's Gift"? National Security Review of China's Foreign Direct Investment' in Garrick, J. and Bennett, Y. C. (eds), *China's Socialist Rule of Law Reforms under Xi Jinping* (Routledge 2016).

Cheung, T. M. and Gill, B., 'Trade versus Security: How Countries Balance Technology Transfers with China' (2013) 13 *Journal of East Asian Studies* 443.

Cheyne, I., 'International Agreements and the European Community Legal System' (1994) 19 *European Law Review* 581.

Chiang, J.-T., 'Dilemmas of US Control of Technology to China' (1987) 12 *Journal of Technology Transfer* 9.

Cormley, L. W., *EU Law of Free Movement of Goods and Customs Union* (Oxford University Press 2009).

Corr, C. F., 'The Wall Still Stands! Complying with Export Controls on Technology Transfers in the Post-Cold War, Post-9/11 Era' (2003) 25 *Houston Journal of International Law* 441.

Cottier, T. and Oesch, M., 'The Paradox of Judicial Review in International Trade Regulation: Towards a Comprehensive Framework' in Cottier, T. and Mavroidis, P. C. (eds), *The Role of the Judge in International Trade Regulation* (The University of Michigan Press 2003).

Dashwood, A. and others, *Wyatt and Dashwood's European Union Law* (6th ed., Hart Publishing 2011).

de la Torre, F. C., 'The EEC New Instrument of Trade Policy: Some Comments in the Light of the Latest Developments' (1993) 30 *Common Market Law Review* 687.

de Melo, J. and Winters, L. A., 'Do Exporters Gain from VERs?' (1993) 37 *European Economic Review* 1331.

de Mestral, A. L. C. and Gruchalla-Wesierski, T., *Extraterritorial Application of Export Control Legislation:Canada and the U. S. A.* (Kluwer Academic Publishers 1990).

Desta, M. G., 'The Organization of Petroleum Exporting Countries, the World Trade Organization, and Regional Trade Agreements' (2003) 37 *Journal of World Trade* 523.

Dunning, J. H., 'The Eclectic Paradigm as an Envelope for Economic and Business Theories of MNE Activity' (2000) 9 *International Business Review* 163.

Dunning, J. H. and Lundan, S. M., *Multinational Enterprises and the Global Economy* (2nd ed., Edward Elgar 2008).

Dursht, K. A., 'Notes: From Containment to Cooperation: Collective Action and the Wassenaar Arrangement' (1997) 19 *Cardozo Law Review* 1079.

Editors, 'Comments: Extraterritorial Application of United States Law: the Case of Export Controls' (1984) 132 *University of Pennsylvania Law Review* 355.

Ehlermann, C.-D. and Ehrin, L., 'Decision-Making in the World Trade Organization: Is the Consensus Practice of the World Trade Organization Adequate for Making, Revising and Implementing Rules on International Trade?' (2005) 8 *Journal of International Economic Law* 51.

Emmerson, A., 'Conceptualizing Security Exceptions: Legal Doctrine or Political Excuse' (2008) 11 *Journal of International Economic Law* 135.

Espa, I., *Export Restrictions on Critical Minerals and Metals: Testing the Adequacy of WTO Disciplines* (Cambridge University Press 2015).

Feenstra, R. C., 'Integration of Trade and Disintegration of Production in the Global Economy' (1998) 12 *Journal of Economic Perspectives* 31.

Gereffi, G., 'The Organization of Buyer-Driven Global Commodity Chains: How U.S Retailers Shape Overseas Production Network' in Gereffi, G. and Korzeniewicz, M. (eds), *Commodity Chains and Global Capitalism* (Praeger 1995).

'Global Value Chains in a Post-Washington Consensus World' (2014) 21 *Review of International Political Economy* 9.

Gereffi, G., Humphrey, J. and Sturgeon, T., 'The Governance of Global Supply Chains' (2005) 12 *Review of International Political Economy* 78.

Goldthau, A., 'Energy Diplomacy in Trade and Investment of Oil and Gas' in Goldthau, A. and Witte, J. M. (eds), *Global Energy Governance: The New Rules of the Game* (Brookings Institution Press 2010).

Goode, W. (ed), *Dictionary of Trade Policy Terms* (3rd ed., Cambridge University Press 2003).

Gowlland-Debbas, V., 'Sanctions Regimes under Article 41 of the UN Charter' in Gowlland-Debbas, V. (ed), *National Implementation of the United Nations Sanctions: A Comparative Study* (Martinus Nijhoff Publishers 2004).

Gruszczynski, L. and Menkes, M., 'The Legality of the EU's Trade Sanctions Imposed on the Russia Federation under WTO Law' in Czapliński, W. and others (eds), *The Case of Crimea's Annexation under International Law* (Scholarly Publishing House 2017).

Grynberg, R. and Joy, R. M., 'The Accession of Vanuatu to the WTO: Lessons for the Multilateral Trading System' (2000) 34 *Journal of World Trade* 159.

Gugiya, L., 'The Interplay of International Dispute Resolution Mechanisms: the Softwood Lumber Controversy' (2011) 2 *Journal of International Dispute Settlement* 175.

Häberli, C., 'After Bali: WTO Rules Applying to Public Food Reserves' (2014) FAO Commodity and Trade Policy Research Working Paper No 46.

Hahn, M. J., 'Vital Interests and the Law of GATT: An Analysis of GATT's Security Exception' (1991) 12 *Michigan Journal of International Law* 558.

Happold, M., 'Economic Sanctions and International Law: An Introduction' in Happold, M. and Eden, P. (eds), *Economic Sanctions and International Law* (Bloomsbury 2016).

Heinz, J., *U.S. Strategic Trade: An Export Control System for the 1990s* (Westview Press 1991).

Hiestand, T., 'Swords into Plowshares: Considerations for 21st Century Export Controls in the United States' (1995) 9 *Emory International Law Review* 679.

Hirschhorn, E. L., *The Export Control and Embargo Handbook* (3rd ed., Oxford University Press 2010).

Hoekman, B. and Trachtman, J. P., 'Canada-Wheat: Discrimination, No-Commercial Considerations, and the Right to Regulate through State Trading Enterprises' (2008) 7 *World Trade Review* 45.

Horlick, G. N. and Mowry, K. H., 'The Treatment of Activities of State Trading Enterprises under the WTO Subsidies Rules' in Cottier, T. and Mavroidis, P. C. (eds), *State Trading in the Twenty-First Century* (The University of Michigan Press 1998).

Huang, D., 'Legal Interpretation of Paragraph 242 of the Report of the Working Party on the Accession of China under the World Trade Organization Legal Framework' (2006) 40 *Journal of World Trade* 137.

Huang, T. W., 'The Gathering Storm of Antidumping Enforcement in China' (2002) 36 *Journal of World Trade* 255.

Hunt, C., 'Multilateral Cooperation in Export Controls: The Role of COCOM' (1982–1983) 14 *Toledo Law Review* 1285.

Irwin, D. A., Mavroidis, P. C. and Sykes, A. O., *The Genesis of the GATT* (Cambridge University Press 2008).

Jackson, J. H., *World Trade and the Law of GATT* (The Michie Company Law Publishers 1969).

The World Trading System: Law and Policy of International Economic Relations (The MIT Press 1994).

The World Trading System: Law and Policy of International Economic Relations (2nd ed., The MIT Press 1997).

Jackson, J. H., Davey, W. J. and Sykes, A. O. J., *Legal Problems of International Economic Relation: Case, Materials and Texts on the National and International Regulation of Transnational Economic Regulations* (4th ed., West Group 2002).

Jackson, J. H., Louis, J.-V. and Matsushita, M. (eds), *Implementing the Tokyo Round: National Constitutions and International Economic Rules* (University of Michigan Press 1984).

Jacobson, J. M., 'Exclusive Dealing, "Foreclosure," and Consumer Harm' (2002) 70 *Antitrust Law Journal* 311.

Jaffer, J., 'Strengthening the Wassenaar Export Control Regime' (2002) 3 *Chicago Journal of International Law* 519.

Janow, M. E. and Staiger, R. W., 'The Treatment of Export Restraints as Subsidies under the Subsidies Agreement of the WTO' in Horn, H. and Mavroidis, P. C. (eds), *The WTO Case Law of 2001* (Cambridge University Press 2004).

'US – Export Restraints United States – Measures Treating Export Restraints as Subsidies' in Henrik, H. and Mavroidis, P. C. (eds), *The WTO Case Law of 2001* (Cambridge University Press 2011).

Johnstone, I., 'Legislation and Adjudication in the UN Security Council: Bringing Down the Deliberative Deficit' (2008) 102 *American Journal of International Law* 275.

Jones, K. A., *Export Restraint and the New Protectionism: The Political Economy of Discriminatory Trade Restrictions* (University of Michigan Press 1994).

Joyner, C. C., 'Collective Sanctions as Peaceful Coercion: Lessons from the United Nations Experience' (1995) 16 *Australian Yearbook of International Law* 241.

Joyner, D. H., 'Restructuring the Multilateral Export Control Regime System' (2004) 9 *Journal of Conflict and Security Law* 181.

Karapinar, B., 'Defining the Boundaries of Export Restrictions: A Case Law Analysis' (2012) 15 *Journal of International Economic Law* 443.

Khan, O. and Burnes, B., 'Risk and Supply Chain Management: Creating a Research Agenda' (2007) 18 *The International Journal of Logistics Management* 197.

Khemani, R. S. and Shapiro, D. M. (eds), *Glossary of Industrial Organisation Economics and Competition Law* (OECD 1993).

Kim, J., 'Recent Trends in Export Restrictions on Raw Materials' in OECD (ed), *The Economic Impact of Export Restrictions on Raw Materials* (OECD Publishing 2010).

Kingsbury, A., 'Should United States Antitrust Law Be Applied to State Trading Enterprises in Agricultural Trade' (2004) 9 *Drake Journal of Agricultural Law* 185.

Kitt, D., 'Note: What's Wrong with Volunteering? The Futility of the WTO's Ban on Voluntary Export Restraints' (2009) 47 *Columbia Journal of Transnational Law* 359.

Klabbers, J., Peters, A. and Ulfstein, G., *The Constitutionalization of International Law* (Oxford University Press 2009).

Konoplyanik, A., 'Lubbers Plan: Soviet Energy as Standpoint for Improving Economic Reforms in USSR' (1992) 12 *Energy Journal* 281.

Korinek, J. and Bartos, J., 'Multilateralising Regionalism: Disciplines on Export Restrictions in Regional Trade Agreements' (2012) OECD Trade Policy Papers No 139.

Kostecki, M. M., *East–West Trade and the GATT System* (MacMillan Press 1979).

Kuyper, P. J., 'The Law of GATT as a Special Field of International Law' (1994) 25 *Netherlands Yearbook of International Law* 227.

Lanoszka, A., 'The World Trade Organization Accession Process: Negotiating Participation in a Globalizing Economy' (2001) 35 *Journal of World Trade* 575.

Lenaerts, K. and van Nuffel, P., *European Union Law* (3rd ed., Sweet & Maxwell 2011).

Levenstein, M. C. and Suslow, V. Y., 'The Changing International Status of Export Cartel Exemptions' (2005) 20 *American University International Law Review* 785.

Liberman, J. R., 'The Export Administration Amendments Act of 1985' (1986) 20 *International Lawyer* 367.

Liu, H.-W. and Maughan, J., 'China's Rare Earths Export Quotas: Out of the China-Raw Materials Gate, but Past the WTO's Finish Line?' (2012) 15 *Journal of International Economic Law* 971.

Lochmann, M. W., 'The Japanese Voluntary Restraint on Automobile Exports: An Abandonment of the Free Trade Principles of the GATT and the Free Market Principles of United States Antitrust Laws' (1986) 27 *Harvard International Law Journal* 99.

Long, W. J., *U.S. Export Control Policy: Executive Autonomy VS. Congressional Reform* (Columbia University Press 1989).

Low, P. and Baldwin, R., 'Introduction' in Low, P. and Baldwin, R. (eds), *Multilateralizing Regionalism: Challenges for the Global Trading System* (Cambridge University Press 2009).

Lowenfeld, A. F., *International Economic Law* (Oxford University Press 2008).

Marceau, G., 'The WTO in the Emerging Energy Governance Debate' (2010) 5 *Global Trade and Customs Journal* 83.

'WTO and Export Restrictions' (2016) 50 *Journal of World Trade* 563.

Marcuss, S. J. and Mathias, D. S., 'U.S. Foregin Policy Export Controls: Do they Pass Muster under International Law' (1984) 2 *Internatinal Tax & Business Lawyer* 1.

Martin, L. L., *Coercive Cooperation: Explaining Multilateral Economic Sanctions* (Princeton University Press 1992).

Mastanduno, M., *Economic Containment: CoCom and the Politics of East–West Trade* (Cornell University Press 1992).

Matsushita, M., 'A Japanese View of United States Trade Laws' (1987) 8 *Northwestern Journal of International Law and Business* 29.

'Export Controls of Natural Resources and the WTO/GATT Disciplines' (2011) 6 *Asian Journal of WTO and International Health Law and Policy* 281.

Meijer, H., *Trading with the Enemy: The Making of US Export Control Policy toward the People's Republic of China* (Oxford University Press 2016).

Melamed, A. D. 'Exclusive Dealing Agreements and Other Exclusionary Conduct – Are There Unifying Principles?' (2006) 73 *Antitrust Law Journal* 375.

Meyer, T., 'Trade Law and Supply Chain Regulation in a Post-COVID World' (2020) 114 *American Journal of International Law* (forthcoming).

Mineiro, M., *Space Technology Export Controls and International Cooperation in Outer Space* (Springer 2012).

Mitchell, A. D., 'Sanctions and the World Trade Organization' in Van Den Herik, L. (ed), *Research Handbook on UN Sanctions and International Law* (Edward Elgar 2017).

Mitchell, A. D. and Ayres, G., 'General and Security Exceptions under the GATT and the GATS' in Carr, I., Bhuiyan, J. and Alam, S. (eds), *International Trade Law and WTO* (Federation Press 2011).

Moore, M. O., 'VERs and Price Undertakings under the WTO' (2005) 13 *Review of International Economics* 298.

Moran, T. H., *Three Threats: An Analytical Framework for the CFIUS Process* (Peterson Institute for Internatioanl Economics 2009).

National Academy of Sciences NAoEaIoM, *Balancing the National Interest: U.S. National Security Export Controls and Global Economic Competition* (National Academy Press 1987).

Ofodile, U. E., 'Trade, Empires, and Subjects – China–Africa Trade: A New Fair Trade Arrangement, or the Third Scramble for Africa' (2008) 41 *Vanderbilt Journal of Transnational Law* 505.

Oliver, P., *Free Movement of Goods in the European Community under Articles 30 to 36 of the Rome Treaty* (3rd ed., Sweet & Maxwell 1996).

Palmeter, N. D., 'The WTO Antidumping Agreement and the Economies in Transition' in Cottier, T. and Mavroidis, P. C. (eds), *State Trading in the Twenty-First Century* (The University of Michigan Press 1998).

Pauwelyn, J., *Conflicts of Norms in Public International Law: How WTO Relates to other Rules of International Law* (Cambridge University Press 2003).

'Bridging Fragmentation and Unity: International Law as a Universe of Inter-Connected Islands' (2004) 25 *Michigan Journal of International Law* 903.

'Editorial Comment: Adding Sweeteners to Softwood Lumber: The WTO–NAFTA 'Spaghetti Bowl' Is Cooking' (2006) 9 *Journal of International Economic Law* 197.

'Export Restrictions in Times of Pandemic: Options and Limits under International Trade Agreements' (2020) 54 *Journal of World Trade* 727.

Peeling, G. and others, 'Export Restrictions on Strategic Raw Materials and Their Impact on Trade and Global Supply' in OECD (ed), *The Economic Impact of Export Restrictions on Raw Materials* (OECD Publishing 2010).

Petersmann, E. U., *Constitutional Functions and constitutional Problems of International Economic Law* (Westview Press 1991).

'GATT Law on State Trading Enterprises: Critical Evaluation of Article XVII and Proposals for Reform' in Cottier, T. and Mavroidis, P. C. (eds), *State Trading in the Twenty-First Century* (The University of Michigan Press 1998a).

'How to Constitutionalize International Law and Foreign Policy for the Benefit of Civil Society?' (1998b) 20 *Michigan Journal of International Law* 1.

'From "Member-Driven Governance" to Constitutionally Limited "Multi-Level Trade Governance" in the WTO' in Sacerdoti, G., Yanovich, A. and Bohanes, J. (eds), *The WTO at Ten: The Contribution of the Dispute Settlement System* (Cambridge University Press 2006).

Polouektov, A., 'Non-Market Economy Issues in the WTO Anti-Dumping Law and Accession Negotiations: Revival of a Two-tier Membership' (2002) 36 *Journal of World Trade* 1.

Pomfret, R., 'The Economics of Voluntary Export Restraint Agreements' (1989) 3 *Journal of Economic Surveys* 199.

Price, A. H. and others, 'Raw Deal: How Government Trade Barriers and Subsidies Are Distorting Global Trade in Raw Materials' prepared by Wiley Rein LLP for American Scrap Coalition, November 2008.

Price, A. H. and Scott Nance, D., 'Export Barriers and the Steel Industry' in OECD (ed), *The Economic Impact of Export Restrictions on Raw Materials* (OECD Publishing 2010).

Qin, J. Y., '"WTO-plus" Obligations and Their Implications for the World Trade Organization Legal System – An Appraisal of the China Accession Protocol' (2003) 37 *Journal of World Trade* 483.

'The Challenge of Interpreting WTO-Plus Provisions' (2010) 44 *Journal of World Trade* 127.

Reilly, J., 'China's Unilateral Sanctions' (2012) 35 *The Washington Quarterly* 121.

Ritchie, B. and Brindley, C., 'Supply Chain Risk Management and Performance: A Guilding Framework for Future Development' (2007) 27 *International Journal of Operations and Production Management* 303.

Roessler, F., 'GATT and Access to Supplies' (1975) 9 *Journal of World Trade Law* 25.

Rose-Ackermann, S. and Billa, B., 'Treaties and National Security' (2008) 40 *New York University Journal of International Law and Politics* 437.

Rosendorff, B. P., 'Voluntary Export Restraints, Antidumping Procedure, and Domestic Politics' (1996) 86 *American Economic Review* 544.

Rubini, L., *The Definition of Subsidy and State Aid: WTO and EC Law in Comparative Perspective* (Oxford University Press 2009).

Russell, J. A., 'Peering into the Abyss: Non-State Actors and the 2016 Proliferation Environment' (2006) 13 *Nonproliferation Review* 645.

Ryngaert, C., 'Extraterritorial Export Controls (Secondary Boycotts)' (2008) 6 *Chinese Journal of International Law* 625.

Schloemann, H. L. and Ohlhoff, S., '"Constitutionalization" and Dispute Settlement in the WTO: National Security as an Issue of Competence' (1999) 93 *American Journal of International Law* 424.

Schoenbaum, T. J., 'The International Trade Laws and the New Protectionism: The Need for a Synthesis with Antitrust' (1994) 19 *North Carolina Journal of International Law and Commercial Regulation* 393.

Selivanova, Y., 'World Trade Organization Rules and Energy Pricing: Russia's Case' (2004) 38 *Journal of World Trade* 559.

Selivanova, Y. (ed), *Regulation of Energy in International Trade Law – WTO, NAFTA and Energy Charter* (Wolters Kluwer 2012).

Sharma, R. and Konandreas, P., 'WTO Provisions in the Context of Responding Soaring Food Prices' (2008) FAO Commodity and Trade Policy Research Working Paper No 25.

Simma, B., 'Self-contained Regimes' (1985) 16 *Netherlands Yearbook of International Law* 111.

Simma, B. and Pulkowski, D., 'Of Planets and the Universe: Self-contained Regimes in International Law' (2006) 17 *European Journal of International Law* 483.

Snyder, F., 'Governing Economic Globalisation: Global Legal Pluralism and European Law' (1999) 5 *European Law Journal* 334.

Steinberg, R. H., 'Judicial Lawmaking at the WTO: Discursive, Constitutional, and Political Constraints' (2004) 98 *The American Journal of International Law* 247.

Stoler, A. L., 'The Evolution of Subsidies Disciplines in GATT and the WTO' (2010) 44 *Journal of World Trade* 797.

Sturgeon, T., 'Modular Production Networks: A New American Model of Industrial Organization' (2002) 11 *Industrial and Corporate Change* 451.

Sweeney, B. J., *The Internationalisation of Competition Rules* (Routledge 2010).

Sykes, A., *The WTO Agreement on Safeguards: A Commentary* (Oxford University Press 2006).

Szydlo, M., 'Export Restrictions within the Structure of Free Movement of Goods. Reconsideration of an Old Paragigm' (2010) 47 *Common Market Law Review* 753.

Tittmann, H. H., 'Extra-territorial Application to U.S. Export Control Laws on Foreign Subsidiaries of U.S. Corporations: An American Lawyer's View from Europe' (1982) 16 *The International Lawyer* 730.

Touscoz, J., 'The Role of the European Union in the Framework of the Energy Charter Treaty' (1997) 2 *European Foreign Affairs Review* 23.

Travalini, J. R., 'Foreign Directive Investment in the United States: Achieving a Balance between National Economy Benefits and National Security Interests' (2009) 29 *Northwestern Journal of International Law and Business* 779.

Trkman, P. and McCormack, K., 'Supply Chain Risk in Turbulent Environment: A Conceptual Model for Managing Supply Chain Risk' (2009) 119 *International Journal of Production Economics* 247.

Tyagi, M., 'Flesh on a Legal Fiction: Early Practice in the WTO on Accesion Protocols' (2012) 15 *Journal of International Economic Law* 391.

Ulrichsen, K. C., 'What's Going on with Qatar?' in POMEPS (ed), *The Qatar Crisis* (The Project on Middle East Political Science 2017).

van Bael, I., *EU Anti-Dumping and Other Trade Defence Instruments* (5th ed., Wolters Kluwer Law & Business 2011).

van den Hoven van Generen, R., 'Cooperation on Export Control between the United States and Europe: A Cradle of Conflict in Technology Transfer' (1989) 14 *North Carolina Journal of International Law and Commercial Regulation* 391.

Wagner, S. M. and Bode, C., 'Dominant Risks and Risk Management Practices in Supply Chains' in Zsidisin, G. A. and Ritchie, B. (eds), *Supply Chain Risk: A Handbook of Assessment, Management, and Performance* (Springer US 2009).

Waller, S. W., 'The Failure of the Export Trading Company Program' (2005) 17 *North Carolina Journal of International Law and Commercial Regulation* 239.

Wassenaar Arrangement Secretariat, *Wassenaar Arrangement on Export Controls for Conventional Arms and Dual-Use Goods and Technologies: Basic Documents* (Wassenaar Arrangement Secretariat 2016).

Whish, R. and Bailey, D., *Competition Law* (8th ed., Oxford University Press 2015).

Wolfram, F., '*Agreeement on Safeguard, Article 11 SA*' in Wolfrum, R., Stoll, P.-T. and Koebele, M. (eds), *WTO-Trade Remedies* (Martinus Nijhoff 2008).

Wolfrum, R., 'Article XI GATT' in Wolfrum, R., Stoll, P.-T. and Hestermeyer, H. P. (eds), *WTO-Trade in Goods* (Martinus Nijhoff 2010).

Wolfrum, R., Stoll, P.-T. and Hestermeyer, H. P. (eds), *WTO-Trade in Goods* (Martinus Nijhoff 2011).

WTO, *Guide to GATT Law and Practice: Analytical Index* (6th ed., WTO 1995).

Export Prohibition and Restrictions: Information and Note (23 April 2020).

Wu, C.-H., 'From Fragmentation to Coherence: A Constitutionalist Take on the Trade and Public Health Debates' in Jakubowski, A. and Wierczyńska, K. (eds), *Constitutionalisation of International Law Re-Visited: Between Pluralism and Unity* (Routledge 2016).

Wu, M., 'China's Export Restrictions and the Limits of WTO Law' (2017) 16 *World Trade Review* 673.

Yodogawa, N. and Peterson, A. M., 'An Opportunity for Progress: China, Central Asia, and the Energy Charter Treaty' (2012–2013) 8 *Texas Journal of Oil, Gas and Energy Law* 111.

Zhang, D., *The Softwood Lumber War: Politics, Economics, and the Long U.S.-Canadian Trade Dispute* (Resource for the Future Press 2007).

INDEX

Lightning Source UK Ltd.
Milton Keynes UK
UKHW021940190622
404668UK00004B/38

9 781108 844789